Elementary Tagalog

Tara, Mag-Tagalog Tayo!
Come On, Let's Speak Tagalog!

Jiedson R. Domigpe
American Ethnic Studies, University of Washington

Nenita Pambid Domingo
Asian Languages and Cultures Department, UCLA

TUTTLE Publishing

Tokyo | Rutland, Vermont | Singapore

"Books to Span the East and West"

Tuttle Publishing was founded in 1832 in the small New England town of Rutland, Vermont [USA]. Our core values remain as strong today as they were then—to publish best-in-class books which bring people together one page at a time. In 1948, we established a publishing outpost in Japan—and Tuttle is now a leader in publishing English-language books about the arts, languages and cultures of Asia. The world has become a much smaller place today and Asia's economic and cultural influence has grown. Yet the need for meaningful dialogue and information about this diverse region has never been greater. Over the past seven decades, Tuttle has published thousands of books on subjects ranging from martial arts and paper crafts to language learning and literature—and our talented authors, illustrators, designers and photographers have won many prestigious awards. We welcome you to explore the wealth of information available on Asia at **www.tuttlepublishing.com**.

Published by Tuttle Publishing, an imprint of Periplus Editions (HK) Ltd.

www.tuttlepublishing.com

Copyright © 2012; 2015 by Jiedson Domigpe and Nenita Domingo

Library of Congress Cataloging-in-Publication 2011043963

ISBN: 978-0-8048-4117-7 (hardcover)
ISBN: 978-0-8048-4514-4 (paperback)

Distributed by

North America, Latin America & Europe
Tuttle Publishing
364 Innovation Drive
North Clarendon,
VT 05759-9436 U.S.A.
Tel: (802) 773-8930
Fax: (802) 773-6993
info@tuttlepublishing.com
www.tuttlepublishing.com

Asia-Pacific
Berkeley Books Pte. Ltd.
3 Kallang Sector #04-01
Singapore 349278
Tel: (65) 6741-2178
Fax: (65) 6741-2179
inquiries@periplus.com.sg
www.tuttlepublishing.com

First edition

28 27 26 25 24   11 10 9 8 7 6
2402CM

Printed in China

Contents

Acknowledgments

The authors gratefully acknowledge the following permission:

"Pers Lab" by Dennis Garcia, copyright © 1975 by Dennis Garcia, used by permission of the artist.

* * *

Jed Domigpe is grateful to the following people at the University of Washington's Southeast Asia Center and the American Ethnic Studies Department for their valuable assistance during the development of this project: Dr. Sara Van Fleet, Dr. Laurie Sears, Professor Enrique Bonus, Professor Francisco Benitez, and Professor Lauro Flores.

He is especially grateful to his graduate students Matthew Nicdao, Michael Viola, Russell Tanenbaum, and Joseph Bernardo for giving him feedback and helping him with the culture note sections, to Rica Ortiz and Hanna and Jennifer Nicdao for the illustrations, and to Joysha Fajardo for her work on the photographs.

And finally, profound thanks to my family and my friends Hiro, Theron, Dan, Sarah, Fred, and Eric for support and encouragement.

Tita Pambid gratefully acknowledges the unqualified support of Reuben Domingo and Jose Domingo for giving her space and time to work uninterrupted on the book; Dr. Gynam Mahajan of South and Southeast Asian Languages and Cultures Program, Asian Languages and Cultures Department at UCLA for her unwavering support for the Filipino program; all Tita's students who have greatly contributed to clarifying Tagalog grammar in their desire to acquire the Tagalog language; and Calvert Barksdale, our editor, without whose sharp perception the present shape of this book would not have been possible. To Jed Domigpe— Thank you! Higit sa lahat, kay Bathala.

Maraming Salamat po!

The authors also thank the following colleagues in the field of Tagalog language teaching: Dr. Teresita Ramos, Dr. Ruth Mabanglo, Dr. Joi Barrios, Dr. Thess Savella, Ms. Clemen Montero, Mr. Julius Soria, Ms. Imelda Gasmen, Ms. Sheila Zamar, Ms. Rhodalyne Crail, Mrs. Blesilda Eata, Ms. Irma Peña, Sally Idos, Tily Alicio, Priscilla Ruedas, Bernardo Bernardo, Linda Juliano, Edith Borbon, Julia Camagong, Vic Romero, Bing Magtoto, Alma Andersson, Carlos Cuyugan, Paul Shacter, J. Donald Bowen, Alfonso O. Santiago, Norma G. Tiangco, Luis Umali Stuart, Ms. Daisy Pee, and Mrs. Susana Felizardo.

Introduction

Tara, mag-Tagalog tayo! *Come on, let's speak Tagalog!*

Elementary Tagalog is an introductory textbook for learning Tagalog, the basis of the national language of the Philippines, Filipino. This book aims to teach students how to speak, write, and comprehend Tagalog, as it is used in real-life contexts. Tagalog is a vibrant language, spoken by millions of people, and this book seeks to enhance its relevance to students in various ways, from classroom activities that reinforce the student's ability to navigate the language in both its conversational and written forms to a series of culture notes that offer information about contemporary life in the Philippines.

Elementary Tagalog is a grammar-oriented textbook. In developing it, the authors have followed the order-of-acquisition principle, which holds that there is a natural order in which first- and second-language learners acquire and learn different grammatical structures. The sequencing of the grammar lessons is also based in practice on the authors' extensive experience teaching Tagalog. The lessons are organized around different themes that commonly appear in foreign-language curricula. To present the structures and themes in a fun and engaging way, this textbook employs current pedagogical language activities such as "information gap," "simulation," "personalization," and many more. These strategies cater to the diverse student populations that make up most foreign-language classrooms. This means that both heritage and non-heritage language learners will learn well from the clear and systematic progression of activities presented in the book.

The grammar is presented in a way intended to make sense to any type of language learner. Definitions of grammar concepts are provided as they are needed. Whether or not students have a strong grasp of the sentence structure of their first language, they should be able to understand the explanation for each Tagalog structure. The lessons, exercises, and activities in this book have been classroom-tested, and the authors have combined their backgrounds in linguistic theory with insights gained from daily encounters with students to develop techniques, such as the use of mnemonics, for making the grammar accessible to everyone.

Each lesson includes numerous activities, both written and spoken, to provide students with ample exposure to the forms being taught. The vocabulary, introduced at the beginning of each lesson, should allow students to express what they want to say regarding the lesson's theme and focus. In addition, the activities are organized in such a way that the level of difficulty increases as the lessons progress. For example, at the beginning of Unit 1, students are only expected to memorize phrases. In the next lesson, students respond to questions using single or multiple words, and in later lessons they acquire the ability to create sentences and string sentences into cohesive paragraphs.

The online audio recordings of *Elementary Tagalog* contains the vocabulary words and expressions and the listening practice exercises for each lesson, and it is provided to allow students to practice listening comprehension independently. These twenty-four exercises correspond to each lesson's theme and grammar presentation and progress from easy to more challenging.

A note on Filipino culture is provided at the beginning of every unit. These culture notes range from a discussion of key concepts in Filipino culture to travel and tourism in the Philippines and aspects of contemporary pop culture. The authors believe that culture and language go hand in hand, and that it is crucial for language learners to understand not just the language itself, but how native speakers of the language think and make sense of the world.

Finally, *Elementary Tagalog* is designed to be used over the course of an academic year. After completing the course, students are expected to have achieved intermediate low- to intermediate mid-level Tagalog proficiency. This means that students should be able to express their own thoughts in the language, initiate and maintain conversations, and successfully to accomplish a variety of fundamental communicative tasks that involve communicating about oneself and one's family, home, daily activities, and interests, as well as social activities centering around food, shopping, travel, and lodging.

Organization

Elementary Tagalog is composed of twenty-four lessons in eight units that follow the normal progression of most basic foreign-language curricula, starting with themes such as the self, the family, and social activities and culminating with Filipino culture. Each thematic lesson is presented in the following order:

1) **Cultural Notes**
   Culture notes at the beginning of each unit offer explanations of social, economic, and historical aspects of contemporary Filipino life that will help students understand Filipino behavior and beliefs. The notes contribute some of the cultural knowledge that is fundamental to effective communication.

2) **Vocabulary List**
   The vocabulary in each lesson ties in to the theme of the unit and both the reading text and the aural activities presented in the specific lesson. These are words that most native speakers use when conversing about the themes in the book, and they are meant to equip students with a natural, colloquial vocabulary. Students are expected to memorize these words in order to facilitate their language learning. It is best to begin to work on memorization before proceeding to the dialogue and other activities in the book, and listening to the vocabulary track on the online audio recordings that accompanies this book will assist in this.

3) **Reading and Reading Comprehension**
   The texts for reading, which are presented mostly in the form of dialogues, are designed to expose the students to real-life conversations as might be had by Filipino native speakers. One of the main goals of the dialogues is to present the vocabulary and the grammatical structures that are covered in the lesson. Presented here in context, the grammatical structures are then explained later in the lesson. As the lesson progresses, the length and complexity of the sentences incorporating the vocabulary words and grammatical forms increases.

4) **Active Learning Activities**
   Three activities follow the dialogue and dialogue comprehension in each lesson. The activities ask the student to employ the vocabulary presented at the beginning of the lesson and observe how the words are strung together. Often students are asked to work together with a partner, and sometimes to report to the class. The students' accuracy is not the purpose of these activities. Rather, students are encouraged to engage creatively with the language and formulate their own conclusions as to how Tagalog sentences are formed. This helps them become accustomed to the normal flow of the language.

5) **Grammar**

The grammar section is divided into four parts: definition of terms, examining form, grammar presentation, and grammar notes. The definition of terms provides a concise and straightforward explanation of linguistic terminologies that students can refer to at any stage. The examining form leads the students in analyzing the specific grammatical component of a Tagalog sentence that is being taught, comparing how it is similar to or the same as with their first language. The grammar presentation then explains the particular forms or elements that are being studied and shows how the words or components are strung together to make a meaningful sentence. The authors use charts and boxes to illustrate as simply as possible the different sentence patterns in Tagalog. Grammar notes following the presentation call out the important highlights to be remembered.

6) **Practice**

Following the grammar, four practice exercises or activities target students' speaking, reading, writing, and listening skills. This section serves to practice the language skills that the students acquire throughout the lesson. The online audio recordings that accompanies this book is to be used for the listening activity. The Workbook that accompanies *Elementary Tagalog—Elementary Tagalog Workbook*—has been designed to provide additional practice. Listening activities in the workbook are also intended for use with this online audio recordings.

To Download or Stream Audio Recordings:

1. You must have an internet connection.
2. Type the URL below into to your web browser.

https://www.tuttlepublishing.com/elementary-tagalog-audio

For support email us at info@tuttlepublishing.com.

Pronunciation Guide

Tagalog has its own set of phonological rules and principles. Acquiring a solid understanding of these rules and principles, coupled with the phonetic knowledge of how the sounds of Tagalog are articulated by actual native speakers, is the first step in making one's speech comprehensible to Philippine ears. Tagalog has a total inventory of 25 sounds, comprising 18 consonants, 5 vowels and 2 semi-vowels or glides. The present-day Tagalog alphabet, like the sixteenth-century Spanish alphabet on which it was based, is highly phonetic. For the English-speaking student of Tagalog, the nasals <m, n> and glides <y, w> are essentially identical in spelling and pronunciation to their English equivalents. However, Tagalog has a velar nasal, spelled **ng**, that will seem unfamiliar to English speakers. Its symbol, <ng>, represents a sound different from the <n> and <g> that make it up (namely, the last sound in the English word **bang**; and, unlike in English, it may appear at the beginning of a word, as in **ngayon** "now."

A few other letter combinations display the same behavior, in that their phonetic whole is different from the sum of their phonetic parts: in particular, <sy> (which is comparable to the first sound in the English word *shoe*), <dy> (like the first sound in *judge*), and <ts> (like the first sound in *chair*). The remaining sounds are fairly straightforward, but care must be taken not to import any foreign details into one's Tagalog pronunciation. The symbols <t> as in **tatlo** "three" and <d> as in **dingding** "wall" represent dental stops, produced with the tongue pressed against the back of the teeth, not at the alveolar ridge (behind the top front teeth) as in English. Furthermore, the voiceless stops in Tagalog, which are represented by the symbols <p>, <t>, and <k>, are not aspirated, as they are in English. That is to say, there is no puff of air accompanying the vowel in the word **pa** "still" as there is in the English word *paw*.

Tagalog makes frequent use of the glottal stop, which shouldn't be totally unfamiliar to English speakers, as it's the sound that appears in the middle of the exclamation *uh-oh* or right before the **m** in *nutmeg* in all but the most hyper-articulated of pronunciations. One final phonetic discrepancy worth mention is that the Tagalog <b> in a word like **baka** "cow" is often produced by native speakers as an implosive, with air being sucked into the mouth for a brief moment before being expelled again in the course of the vowel; the perceptual effect is that of a mild "twang." These are the basics of Tagalog phonetics, which any diligent student who has at her or his disposal a high quality recording and a sharp set of ears can acquire.

These basic phonetic characteristics are the quirks of Tagalog phonology. Take the vowels, for example. The five Tagalog vowels (a, e, i o, u) are by and large distinct from each other. Each can be uniquely mapped in terms of tongue height and backness, as the chart below shows:

	Front	**Central**	**Back**
HIGH	i		u
MID	e		o
LOW		a	

Starting with the front vowels, for example, **mesa** means "table," whereas **misa** means "Catholic mass." But that distinction relies on the fact that the vowels in question are stressed. When these two vowels are unstressed, the contrast is lost, so there need be no difference in vowel quality between the first syllable in **bili** "purchase" and the last syllable in **pare** "priest," each being optionally produced as either [i] or [e] or something in between the two in quality. The same logic applies to the back vowels, [u] and [o]: when in stressed position, they are contrastive; e.g., **Kora** "Cora" (a girl's name) vs. **kura** "parish priest'" But when unstressed, the distinction vanishes; thus, the pronunciation of the second syllable of **guro** "teacher" is no different from the second syllable of **puro** "pure." Finally, the Tagalog low vowel [a] is reduced to a more centralized [ə] in unstressed position, comparable to the difference in English <a> between *frat* and *fraternity*. Hence, a Tagalog word like **alam** "know," with the stress on the second syllable, is commonly pronounced [əlam].

The consonants of Tagalog also display interesting phonological behavior. Intervocalic effects are particularly common. [d], [k], and [g], when between vowels, sound differently than they do when not between vowels. [d] between vowels becomes a flapped [r]—this is the reason a verb like **dating** "to arrive" is reduplicated into the contemplative form **darating** "will arrive" instead of **da-dating**. The voiceless velar stop [k] between vowels has the tendency to become a velar fricative [x], like the final sound in the German name *Bach*; and even in word-initial position, it often comes out as [kx]. Meanwhile, [g] often undergoes lenition between vowels, changing from a voiced velar stop to a slightly softer sound, a so-called "approximant," which is conventionally marked in the International Phonetic Alphabet with the symbol <ɣ>. Hence the <g> in the Tagalog word **toga** "judicial robe" isn't nearly as acoustically prominent as its counterpart in the English cognate *toga*.

One final word is in order on the Tagalog glottal stop, which in IPA notation is marked with the symbol <ʔ>. While it may be easy enough for English speakers to pronounce on command, students must be careful not to *overproduce* it in the misguided hope of giving their Tagalog pronunciation a more authentic sound. Crucially, a large number of Tagalog words ending in a glottal stop sound very much like other words that end in open vowels, but give rise to totally different meanings. Consider the following minimal pair (both with stress on the first syllable): [bagə] "glowing ember" ~ [bagəʔ] "lung." This is unlike English, where a word like *momma* could be pronounced either as [mamə] or as [maməʔ] with no difference in meaning.

Mastering the above-mentioned rules and principles of Tagalog phonology is an indispensible step in learning to speak well. But it's a challenge that can easily be met.

Consonants and Vowels of Tagalog

Letter	How to Pronounce It	Example
a	Between the **a** in *father* and the **a** in *apple* In unstressed position (and occasionally in stressed position) like the **a** in *about*	**aso** (dog) **pagod** (fatigue)
b	Like **b** in *bed*	**bata** (child)

k	Like **k** in *kite* Between vowels, similar to **ch** in German *Bach*	**kamay** (hand) **ako** (me)
d	Like **d** in *dog*, but with the tongue against the back of the teeth When followed by **y**, like **j** in *judge*	**dito** (here) **dyan** (there)
e	Like **e** in *hey*, but not as drawn out	**eskrima** (Filipino fencing)
g	Like **g** in *go* Between vowels tends to soften, such that the airflow doesn't come to a complete stop	**ganda** (beauty) **bago** (new)
h	Like **h** in *house*	**habang** (while)
i	Like **ee** in *bee* When unstressed, like **i** in ship or **e** in rest	**isa** (one) **kasi** (because)
l	Like **l** in *light*	**lola** (grandmother)
m	Like **m** in *more*	**mata** (eye)
n	Like **n** in *new*	**nobyo** (boyfriend)
ng	Like **ng** in *bang*	**ngayon** (now)
o	Like **o** in *row*, but not as drawn out When unstressed, like **oo** in book	**opo** (yes) **aso** (dog)
p	Like **p** in *put*, but with no puff of air	**pangalan** (name)
r	Like **r** in *ladder*	**restawran** (restaurant)
s	Like **s** in *salad* When followed by **y**, like **sh** in *ship*	**sakit** (sick) **telebisyon** (TV)
t	Like **t** in *tip*, but with the tongue against the teeth, and no puff of air When followed by **s** or **y**, like **ch** in *chew*	**tatlo** (three) **tsaa** (tea), **tyan** (stomach)
u	Like **oo** in *food*	**umaga** (morning)
w	Like **w** in *wax*	**wakas** (end)
y	Like **y** in *yellow*	**yamang** (since)

Elementary Tagalog

The Tagalog Language

Tagalog is classified as an Austronesian language and is spoken by 90 million Filipinos in the Philippines as well as more than a million in Saudi Arabia and the United States. The primary language in the Central and Southern Luzon regions of the Philippines, Tagalog has been spoken historically in and around Manila, the capital of the Philippines, and the eight provinces that first rose up in arms against Spanish colonial rule. It is the basis of the national language, Filipino. Linguistically, Filipino and Tagalog share the same syntax, morphology, and phonology. Tagalog uses the Pilipino alphabet, composed of twenty letters, while Filipino uses the Filipino alphabet, which is composed of twenty-six letters from the English alphabet plus the Tagalog letter **ng** and the Spanish letter *ñ* to accommodate borrowed words from Spanish and English, not to mention the names Filipinos give themselves that utilize foreign letters. The term *Tagalog* for the language has more currency among foreign-language learners and even among Filipinos than the term *Filipino*.

The word *Tagalog* derives from the words **taga**, meaning "from," and **ilog**, meaning "river"; thus its original meaning was "river dwellers." Before the arrival of the Spanish, almost all Tagalog speakers were able to read and write Tagalog in the **baybayin** script, a system of writing with borrowings from Sanskrit. Spanish colonization of the Philippines beginning in the late sixteenth century changed the written form of the language. Spanish friars Romanized the orthography of Tagalog using both **baybayin** and the Latin alphabet in the first book published in the Philippines, entitled *Doctrina Cristiana*, in 1593. Since then, Tagalog speakers have continued to use the Latin alphabet to read and write in the language, while **baybayin** gradually fell into disuse.

The first orthography in the Philippines, which was used up until the Spanish colonization of the Philippines

In addiion to the use of Latin letters, Tagalog adopted many Spanish words during the almost four centuries of Spanish colonial rule. About 40 percent of Tagalog words today are derived from Spanish. Many English words have also penetrated the Tagalog vernacular due to more than a hundred years of formal and informal American colonization of the Philippines.

Yet there are many ways in which Tagalog is very different from the European languages that have influenced it. Unlike in English and Spanish, in Tagalog the third-person singular personal pronouns are gender-neutral, with no masculine or feminine forms. For example, **siya**, a third-person personal pronoun, can mean "he" or "she." Another characteristic of the language is the traditional use of the words **ho** and **po** as polite forms to address elders and/or superiors in a professional setting. For example, "**Kinain ko ang kanin.**" ("I ate the rice.") becomes "**Kinain ko po ang kanin.**" ("I ate the rice, sir/ma'am.") when speaking to someone older than yourself.

At a more fundamental level, with regard to word order Tagalog places emphasis on the predicate rather than the subject. Hence, the most common way of forming a sentence is predicate/subject rather than subject/predicate. For example, **Mabait siya** translates literally as "Kind he/she." This sentence can also be stated using the subject/predicate word order where the predicate is preceded by the marker **ay**, as in **Siya ay mabait**. (He/She is kind.) However, this subject-predicate word order is mostly used in formal settings.

Other distinctive features of the language are linkers and particles, such as the marker just mentioned, but the heart of the language is in the use of affixes. Affixes turn a stem or root word into a noun, an adjective, or a verb. Affixes used to form verbs in different time frames signal different types of focuses, such as actor, object, location, and direction, to name a few. A firm grasp of the various affixes will increase your vocabulary exponentially, throwing wide open the portal to learning the Tagalog language and Filipino way of perceiving the world.

In regard to pronunciation, the rule is "how you write the word is how you pronounce it." So for example, **baka** (cow) is pronounced "ba-ka" ("bah-ka," without the "h" sound). The "a" sound is similar to the "a" in **ah**. The two exceptions to this rule are the words **ng** (a direct object marker, which is not translated, or the possessive marker, which translates as "of") and **mga** (the plural marker), the equivalent of **s, -es, -ies,** or the irregular form of plural nouns in English. Some examples of the use of **mga** are: **mga baka** (cows) **and mga bata** (children). **Ng** is pronounced "nang," with the open "a" sound as in *none* combined with the final velar "ng" sound in *sing*. This sound also occurs in Tagalog is the initial velar **ng**, as in **ngayon** (now, today), which does not occur in English. **Mga** is the shortened form of **manga** (*ma-nga*) Both of the *a*'s are pronounced like "ah." The first syllable is pronounced **ma**, like in *mama*, and the second syllable is pronounced like the sound of "ng" in *sing* plus "a." The trick to pronouncing **nga** is to say "si" in *sing* silently and then voice the "ng" and add "a."

There are four major stresses in Tagalog. With **malumay** (*gentle*), the stress is on the second-to-last syllable; **malumi** (*grave*) is a combination of the **malumay** plus a glottal stop; with **mabilis** (*fast*), the stress is on the last syllable; and **maragsa** (marked with a circumflex accent in old Tagalog books) is a combination of **mabilis** and a glottal catch on the vowel sound. Hence, both **malumi** and **maragsa** words only end in vowels, never on a consonant. There is also a fifth stress called **mariin** (emphatic, or having an acute accent on the last syllable or an oxytone), which may be a combination of two of the four major stresses previously mentioned. Learning how to pronounce the words is crucial, since there are quite a number of Tagalog words that have the same spelling but different meanings when pronounced with a different stress, as for example in **basa** (*malumay stress*) "read" and **basâ** (*maragsa stress*) "wet." In the past, written language utilized accent marks, but now the stress marks are no longer used. You will have to rely on the accompanying online audio recordings for the correct pronunciation of the words used in the exercises.

Mga Pagbati
Greetings

An Overview of Mga Pagbati *Greetings*

Objectives
• Express greetings and good-byes
• Express politeness using the appropriate terms in Filipino social etiquette

Vocabulary
• Common Greetings and Expressions

Dialogue: Magandang Umaga Po! *Good Morning, Sir/Madam!*

Dialogue Comprehension

Activities
Activity 1: Greetings
Activity 2: Role-Play
Activity 3: Fill in the Blanks

Vocabulary 🎧 (00–1)

The following are common expressions for greeting someone and saying good-bye.

Expressions

Magandang umaga (ho/po).	Good morning (sir/madam).
Magandang umaga din naman (ho/po).	Good morning to you too (sir/madam).
Magandang tanghali (po/ho).	Good noon (sir/madam).
Magandang tanghali din naman (po/ho).	Good noon to you too (sir/madam).
Magandang hapon, Marco.	Good afternoon, Marco.
Magandang hapon din naman, Karla.	Good afternoon to you too, Karla.
Magandang gabi, Mike.	Good evening, Mike.
Magandang gabi din naman, Patrick.	Good evening to you too, Patrick.
Kumusta ka? (informal)	How are you?
Kumusta (po/ho) kayo? (formal)	How are you (sir/madam)?
Ayos lang./Okey lang.	Fine.
Kumusta na?	How's it going?
Heto buhay pa.	Here, still alive.
Kumusta ang trabaho mo?	How is your work?
Mabuti naman.	Good.
Kumusta ang mga klase mo?	How are your classes?
Ayos na ayos/Okey na okey.	Great!
Ano na?	What's up?
Wala naman./Walang bago.	Nothing much./Nothing new.
Ano'ng bago?	What's new?
Gaya pa rin nang dati.	Still the same.
O sige (po/ho).	All right, see you later (sir/madam)./Good-bye.
O sige (po/ho). Ingat ka!	All right, see you later (sir/madam). Take care!

Dialogue: Magandang Umaga Po! *Good Morning!*

Read the dialogues and complete the Dialogue Comprehension activity that follows.

1. Patrick meets his teacher, Mr. Santos. It is morning.

   Patrick: **Magandang umaga po, Sir Santos.**
   Ginoong Santos: **Magandang umaga rin naman. Kumusta ka?**
   Patrick: **Mabuti naman po. Kumusta po kayo?**
   Ginoong Santos: **Ayos naman. Kumusta ang mga klase mo?**
   Patrick: **Ayos naman po.**
   Ginoong Santos: **O sige.**
   Patrick: **O sige po. Ingat po kayo.**

Note: When one is talking to an elderly person or someone who holds a high position, **po** or **ho** must be used. These words are comparable to *sir* and *madam* in English. When speaking to elderly person, the person must also be addressed by his or her title, such as **lolo/lola** (grandfather/grandmother), **a-ling/mang** (miss/mister), **kuya/ate** (big brother/big sister), etc. On the other hand, **po** or **ho** and terms of address are not necessary when talking with friends or someone close to your age.

2. Sandra meets her friend, Katherine. It is evening.

Sandra: **Magandang gabi, Katherine!**

Katherine: **Magandang gabi rin naman. Kumusta na?**

Sandra: **Ayos naman. Kumusta ang trabaho mo?**

Katherine: **Okey lang!**

Sandra: **O sige!**

Katherine: **O sige! Ingat ka!**

Dialogue Comprehension

Now that you have read the dialogue, place a check mark in the appropriate blank opposite the statement, depending on whether the statement is true, **Tama**, or false, **Mali**.

	TAMA	MALI
1. Patrick greeted Mr. Santos with "Good afternoon."	_____	_____
2. Patrick is doing great.	_____	_____
3. Patrick's classes are all good.	_____	_____
4. Sandra is not doing okay.	_____	_____
5. Katherine's work is good.	_____	_____

Activities

Activity 1

Choose the appropriate expression or expressions to greet the following people. Put a check mark in the blank if the greeting is appropriate and an X if it is inappropriate.

1. Your Tagalog teacher, Professor Maria Manalo

    _____ 1. **Magandang umaga po, Maria!**

    _____ 2. **Kumusta na po, Manalo?**

    _____ 3. **Magandang umaga po, Prop. Manalo.**

2. Your friend, Katherine Cruz

    _____ 1. **Katherine, kumusta ka na?**

    _____ 2. **Katherine, ano na po'ng bago?**

    _____ 3. **Magandang umaga po, Katherine.**

3. Your grandfather, Lolo Bert

    _____ 1. **Magandang hapon po, Lolo.**

    _____ 2. **Ano na, Lolo?**

    _____ 3. **Kumusta po kayo?**

4. An elderly stranger

    _____ 1. **Magandang umaga.**

    _____ 2. **Kumusta po kayo?**

    _____ 3. **Kumusta na?**

Activity 2

Work with a partner and act out the following scenarios. What would you say in these situations? Refer to the vocabulary at the beginning of the unit if you need to.

1. It is 10:00 a.m. You meet your classmate, Joseph. How do you greet him?

_____

2. It is 12:00 p.m. You meet your friend's mother, Edna. How do you greet her?

_____

3. It is 3:00 p.m. You meet your Tagalog professor, Mr. Cruz. How do you greet him?

_____

4. It is 7:00 p.m. You meet your roommate, Martha. How do you greet her?

_____

Activity 3

You run into Mr. Cruz, your old neighbor. Fill in the blanks with the appropriate response.

```
┌─────────────────────────────────┐
│           Word Bank             │
│                                 │
│  mga magulang mo   your parents │
└─────────────────────────────────┘
```

Marco: _____ (Good afternoon, Mr. Cruz.)

Ginoong Cruz: _____ (Good afternoon to you, too. How are you?)

Marco: _____ (I'm great. How are you, sir?)

Ginoong Cruz: _____ (I'm well. How are your parents?)

Marco: _____ (Good, sir.)

Ginoong Cruz: _____ (All right, goodbye.)

Marco: _____ (All right, goodbye. Take care, sir.)

UNIT 1
TUNGKOL SA SARILI
About Self

Culturally, in their personal behavior and social interactions, Filipinos tend to emphasize the collective as opposed to the individual. According to the late University of the Philippines professor Virgilio G. Enriquez, who is known as the father of Philippine psychology, **kapwa**, meaning "both" or "the self in the other," is the core value among Filipinos. One cannot think of oneself without thinking about the other, and vice versa. This core value is manifested in a variety of ways. For example, a person will not cross or dispute with members of her or his **barkada**, or "peer group," if it means burning bridges. This is also why many Filipinos are very family- and community-oriented. Other Filipino values stem from this concept of **kapwa**, for example **pakikisama** or **pakikipagkapwa-tao** (getting along with the group or treating another as a fellow human being) and **bayanihan** (collective spirit). Hence, the self is seeing yourself in your fellow-human being.

A group of Filipino friends playing basketball, a typical leisure activity in the Philippines.

A woman makes sure her mother's needs are attended to, illustrating the concept of **utang na loob**.

Hiya, or "shame," is another concept that is central to the Filipino identity. People will go to great lengths to avoid being shamed or having shame fall on their family, even if doing so is beyond their means financially. For example, if a person is planning to host a large party, such as a wedding, the guest list has to include almost everyone that the person knows, regardless of whether she or he can afford it, for fear of being shamed by others. To be known as having no shame, or **walang hiya**, will ruin your and your family's reputation.

Humor is often used as a tool to strengthen **kapwa**, for example, to diffuse tension between arguing friends. Humor can also be self-deprecating or gently mocking. By transforming a mistake into a light moment, one can relieve the other person of the embarrassment of having to correct her- or himself and allow that person to take responsibility for the error in a way that saves face.

A Filipino system for keeping relationships and communal ties intact is known as **utang na loob**, literally "debt of one's inner self" or "debt of gratitude." **Utang na loob** can be understood as reciprocity. Simply put,

put, if someone has done a favor for you, in the context of Filipino culture, it is advisable to "repay" that person in a socially acceptable way. Failure to fulfill this moral debt subjects you to being labeled **walang hiya** (no shame) and thus ostracized from the collective.

Bahala na, literally translated as "leave it to God" or "come what may," is another common value among Filipinos. Said to be derived from **Bathala**, the pre-Hispanic term for "Supreme Being," **bahala na** is the recourse that remains when you are faced with a difficult challenge and have exhausted every solution, without success. You go forth, trusting that events will follow their natural course, essentially "leaving it in God's hands." However, Virgilio Enriquez interpreted **bahala na** as the Filipinos' courage and owning up to the consequences of an action or situation in the face of uncertainty.

Unang Araw ng Klase

The First Day of Class

An Overview of Lesson 1

Objectives
- Ask questions using the interrogative pronouns **sino** (who) and **ano** (what)
- Respond to inquiries using short and long responses
- Construct identificational and predicational statements

Vocabulary
- Majors/Courses
- Professions and Occupations
- Religion
- Markers
- Nationalities
- Marital Status
- Pronouns
- Idioms and Expressions
- Officials
- Gender
- Adverbs

Dialogue: Kumusta Ka? *How Are You?*

`Dialogue Comprehension`

Activities
Activity 1: Interview
Activity 2: Interview
Activity 3: Fill in the Blanks

Grammar
Definition of Terms: Sentence, Subject, Predicate, Markers, **Ang** Marker in an **Ang** Phrase, **Ang** Pronouns, **Ang** Form, Interrogative Pronouns, Identificational Sentence, Predicational Sentence, Proper Noun, and Common Noun

Examining Form
I. **Sino** (Who): Interrogative Pronoun **Sino** (Who)
  Grammar Presentation: The Interrogative Pronoun **Sino** and the Identificational Sentence
  Grammar Notes
II. **Ano** (What): Interrogative Pronoun **Ano** (What)
  Grammar Presentation: The Interrogative Pronoun **Ano** and the Predicational Sentence
  Grammar Notes

Practice
I. Speaking Practice   II. Reading Practice   III. Writing Practice   IV. Listening Practice

Vocabulary 🎧 (01–1)

The vocabulary below will help you speak about yourself and participate in the activities in this lesson. Memorize the vocabulary words before proceeding to the dialogue.

Majors/Courses

Abogasiya	Law
Arkitektura	Architecture
Ingles	English
Kasaysayan	History
Literatura	Literature
Matematika	Math
Medisina	Medicine
Narsing	Nursing
Wika	Language

Nationalities

Aleman	German
Amerikano/a	American
Hapones	Japanese
Kastila	Spanish
Koreano/a	Korean
Pilipino/a	Filipino
Tsino	Chinese

Officials

alkalde	mayor
gobernador/a	governor
presidente	president
pulis	policeman
senador	senator

Professions and Occupations

abogado/a	lawyer
arkitekto	architect
artista	actor/actress
dentista	dentist
doktor	doctor
estudyante	student
inhinyero/a	engineer
kusinero/a/tagaluto	chef/cook
mananayaw	dancer
manganganta	singer
manunulat	writer
musikero/a	musician
negosyante	businessman
titser/guro	teacher
yaya	nanny

Marital Status

binata	single male
dalaga	single female
diborsyado/a	divorced
may-asawa	married

Gender

babae	female
lalaki	male

Religion

Budista	Buddhist
Katoliko	Catholic
Protestante	Protestant

Pronouns

ako	I
ano	what
ikaw/ka	you
kami	we (exclusive; not including the listener)
kayo	you (plural)
ko	my
mo	your (possessive)
sila	they
sino	who
siya	he/she
tayo	we (inclusive; including the listener)

Adverbs

ngayon	now

Markers

ang	marks singular common nouns and proper names of places or things
ang mga	marks one or more common nouns and proper names of places or things
si	marks the name of a singular person or animal
sina	marks the name of two or more persons or animals

Idioms and Expressions

Kita na lang tayo mamaya.	See you later.
O sige! Kita tayo mamaya.	All right! See you later.
siyanga pala	by the way
talaga	really

Dialogue: Kumusta Ka? *How Are You?*

The dialogue illustrates how to use the words and expressions you studied above. Read it aloud with a partner and complete the Dialogue Comprehension activity that follows.

Patrick: **Magandang umaga, Mike!**
Mike: **Magandang umaga din naman, Pat. Kumusta ka na?**
Patrick: **Ayos naman. Ikaw?**
Mike: **Ayos lang. Heto, buhay pa. Ikaw, ano na'ng bago?**
Patrick: **Wala naman. Siyanga pala ano ang klase mo ngayon?**
Mike: **Tagalog.**
Patrick: **Talaga? Sino ang titser mo sa Tagalog?**
Mike: **Si Propesor Santos. Ikaw? Ano ang klase mo ngayon?**
Patrick: **Math.**
Mike: **Sino ang titser mo sa Math?**
Patrick: **Si Propesor Smith.**
Mike: **Ah, o sige. Kita na lang tayo mamaya.**
Patrick: **O sige. Ingat ka!**

Dialogue Comprehension

For each of the following statements about the dialogue, place a check mark in the appropriate blank, depending on whether the statement is true, **Tama**, or false, **Mali**.

	TAMA	MALI
1. Patrick greeted Mike with "Good morning."	_____	_____
2. Mike is taking Tagalog.	_____	_____

3. Professor Santos teaches Tagalog.

_____   _____

4. Patrick is taking Math.

_____   _____

5. Professor Smith teaches Math.

_____   _____

Activities

Activity 1

Work with a partner. Write down all the classes you are taking this semester or quarter, then interview each other in order to exchange information about your professors or teachers and teaching assistants for each class. The example below illustrates how to use **sino** (who) in your interview.

EXAMPLE:
Q: **Sino ang propesor (titser) mo sa Kasaysayan?** Who is your professor (teacher) in History?
A: **Si Propesor Bonus.** Professor Bonus.
Q: **Sino ang TA mo sa Kasaysayan?** Who is your TA in History?
A: **Si Eric.** Eric.

Using the chart below, write your classes in column 1, the names of the professors in column 2, and the names of the teaching assistants in column 3. Then practice using **sino** in questions and responding appropriately.

Mga Klase	Propesor	Teaching Assistant
1. **Kasaysayan**	A: **Si Propesor Bonus.**	A: **Si Eric.**
2.	A:	A:
3.	A:	A:
4.	A:	A:
5.	A:	A:

Activity 2

This time, use the interrogative **ano** (what) to obtain the information. Work with a partner, and ask each other the questions listed below. Using complete sentences, record your partner's responses in the space provided. After filling in all the information, report your findings to the class.

EXAMPLE:
Q: **Ano ang kurso mo?** What is your course?
A: **Narsing ang kurso ko.** My course is nursing.
Q: **Ano ang mga klase _mo_ ngayon?** What are _your_ classes now?
A: **Matematika, Literatura, at Ingles ang mga klase _ko_ ngayon.** _My_ classes now are Math, Literature, and English.

Notice that to answer the question, you simply replace **ano** with the answer and replace **mo** (your) with **ko** (my). Notice too that the word order in Tagalog is PREDICATE/SUBJECT. The predicate comments on the subject or topic of the sentence.

Mga Tanong (Questions)	Mga Sagot (Answers)
Ano ang kurso mo?	
Ano ang mga klase mo ngayon?	
Sino ang mga propesor (titser) mo?	
Sino ang mga TA mo?	

Activity 3

For more practice with the interrogative **sino** (who), take turns with your partner asking who the following people are. For your answers, use the word bank provided below.

EXAMPLE:
Patrick: **Estudyante**
 S1: **Sino si Patrick?** Who is Patrick?
 S2: **Si Patrick ang estudyante.** Patrick is the student.

1. Wolfgang Puck   _____

2. Michael Jordan   _____

3. Beethoven   _____

4. Donald Trump   _____

5. Jose Rizal   _____

Word Bank

musikero
negosyante
manunulat
basketbolista
kusinero

Grammar

Definition of Terms

The grammatical terms below will be used throughout the lessons in this book. Familiarize yourself with them and learn what they mean.

Sentence	A group of words that express a complete thought or idea.
Subject	The part of the sentence that is being talked about.
Predicate	The part of the sentence that comments or tells something about the topic or subject of the sentence. In Tagalog there are sentences without a subject. This will be discussed in subsequent lessons.

Markers	In Tagalog, there are words that tell you that the word that follows is the subject of the sentence. We call them markers. Markers are used to indicate relationships among the parts of a sentence, and there are other kinds of markers besides those that mark the subject.
	EXAMPLES: **Arkitekto *si Mario*.** *Mario* is an architect.
	Doktor *ang lalaki*. *The man* is a doctor.
	The markers in the sentences above are **ang** and **si**, and they are called **ang** markers. They indicate that the following noun or noun phrase—in this case **Mario** and **lalaki**—is the subject of the sentence. Aside from **ang** markers, there are other markers that will be discussed in the later lessons.
Ang Marker in an Ang Phrase	An **ang** phrase is composed of an **ang** marker and a noun. As explained above, the **ang** marker indicates the subject of the sentence. **Ang** markers include **ang**, **ang mga**, **si**, and **sina**. **Ang** and **ang mga** mark common noun subjects, while **si** and **sina** are used before the proper names of people and animals. The singular markers are **ang** and **si**: they mark single items. The plural markers are **ang mga** and **sina**: they mark plural items. See how the subject markers are used below.
	EXAMPLES: **Binata *ang lalaki*.** *The man* is a bachelor.
	Binata *ang mga lalaki*. *The men* are bachelors.
	Dalaga *si Maria*. *Maria* is single.
	Dalaga *sina Maria at Christine*. *Maria and Christine* are single.
Ang Pronouns	Pronouns that substitute for nouns marked by **ang** markers.
	EXAMPLES: **Dalaga *ang babae*.** (ang phrase) *The woman* is single.
	Dalaga *siya*. (ang pronoun) *She* is single.
	Other **ang** pronouns you may encounter are: **ako** (I), **ka** (you), **tayo** (we), **kayo** (*you* plural), and **sila** (they). These pronouns are in the **ang** form or in the case of the subject, which means, they are used as the subject in a sentence. More will be said about pronouns in different cases in subsequent lessons.
Ang Form	Nouns that are marked by an **ang** marker or pronouns that are in **ang** forms.
	EXAMPLES: **ang lalaki** the man
	Ako I
Interrogative Pronouns	These are pronouns used to ask questions.
	EXAMPLES: ***Sino* ang titser mo?** *Who* is your teacher?
	***Ano* ang klase mo?** *What* is your class?

Identificational Sentence	This is a sentence composed of two major elements, a subject and a predicate without a verb. This type of sentence can be compared to a mathematical equation in which the subject is identified with or "equals" the predicate, as in: Subject X = Predicate Y *Si* **Martha** *ang* **titser.** Martha is the teacher. *Ang* **lalaki** *ang* **pulis.** The man is the police. Notice that, in this type of sentence, *both* the subject *and* the predicate are in **ang** form. The identificational sentence is the only structure in Tagalog where two **ang** forms are utilized. This form is normally used to answer **sino** questions.
Predicational Sentence	This is the most common type of sentence in Tagalog. The word order is: predicate followed by the subject. The predicate doesn't have any markers, while the subject is marked by **ang**. EXAMPLES: **Titser** *si* **Martha.** Martha is a teacher. **Pulis** *ang* **lalaki.** The man is a police.
Proper Noun	This is a noun that refers to a particular name of a person, place, event, or thing. EXAMPLES: Martin University of the Philippines
Common Noun	This is a noun that refers to a general name of a person, place, event, or thing. EXAMPLES: man dog university game

Examining Form

Let's review what we have covered so far. Read the sentences below and complete the tasks that follow. Discuss your answers with a partner.

1. Q: **Ano ang klase mo ngayon?**
   A: **Tagalog.**

2. Q: **Sino ang titser mo sa Tagalog?**
   A: **Si Propesor Santos.**

3. Q: **Ano ang klase mo ngayon?**
   A: **Math.**

4. Q: **Sino ang titser mo sa Math?**
   A: **Si Propesor Smith.**

   a. Circle the interrogative pronouns and underline the markers.
   b. Look at the answers in 1, 2, 3, and 4. What do you notice?

c. What are some of the observations you have made regarding the use of markers? In what instances do you use a marker? When is a marker not needed?

Now, in the section that follows, let's analyze the sentence into its parts in order to understand the grammatical forms associated with **sino** and **ano**.

I. Interrogative Pronoun **Sino** (Who)

The interrogative pronoun **sino** is used to ask questions about a person or people. The English equivalent of **sino** is *who*. The basic pattern of a **sino** question is: **Sino** + **ang** PHRASE ? The **ang** phrase is made up of an **ang** marker and the noun it marks.

EXAMPLES:

Sino *ang* **doktor?**
Sino *si* **Mr. Natividad?**

The response to the question, which is the subject of the sentence, comprises an **ang** phrase made up of an **ang** marker and the noun it marks, as shown below:

Sino ang/si _____ ?
The subject comprises the **ang** *marker* and the thing it marks:
 Si + name of a person or animal
 Sina + name(s) of people or animals
 Ang + noun or proper name of a place or a thing
 Ang mga + noun(s) or proper name of a place or a thing

EXAMPLES:

Sino ang estudyante?	Who is the student?
Sina Mike ang estudyante.	Mike is the student.
Ang lalaki ang estudyante.	The man is the student.
Sino ang mga estudyante?	Who are the students?
Sina Mike at Patrick ang mga estudyante.	Mike and Patrick are the students.
Ang mga lalake ang mga estudyante.	The men are the students.

---

1. When responding to a question that uses **sino** (who), it is necessary to use a marker in front of the noun in your response.
    Sino ang titser mo? Who is your teacher?
    Si Dr. Ramos. Dr. Ramos.

 Ang can also be used to mark the proper name of things (objects) and places.
    Ang Malacañang Palace. Malacañang Palace.
    Ang Magnolia ice cream. Magnolia ice cream.

2. An **ang** marker + noun can be replaced with **ang** pronouns. Below is the list of **ang** pronouns.

Ang Pronouns		
	Singular	**Plural**
First Person	**ako**	**tayo** (inclusive) **kami** (exclusive)
Second Person	**ikaw/ka**	**kayo**
Third Person	**siya**	**sila**

The pronouns **ikaw** and **ka** are synonymous. However, they are not interchangeable. In identificational sentences you use **ikaw**, while in predicational sentences you use **ka**. Identificational and predicational sentences are defined above. We will study predicational sentences in the next lesson. Here is an example of each, using **ikaw** and **ka**.

> **Ikaw ang presidente.** (identificational sentence)
> **Presidente ka.** (predicational sentence)

Grammar Presentation

The Interrogative Pronoun **Sino** and the Identificational Sentence

1. The chart below shows the order of words in a question with **sino**. When constructing an interrogative sentence with **sino**, you can follow the structure shown.

Information Question: **Sino**		
Who	**Marker**	**Common Noun**
Sino	**ang** **ang mga**	**estudyante?**
	Marker	**Proper Noun**
	si **sina**	**Patrick?**

EXAMPLES:
Sino ang titser? Who is the teacher?
Sino ang mga lalaki? Who are the men?

2. When responding to an interrogative sentence that uses **sino**, it is mandatory to use **ang** markers or **ang** pronouns.

Short Answers	
Marker	**Proper Noun**
Si **Sina**	**Patrick.**
Marker	**Common Noun**
Ang **Ang mga**	**estudyante.**
Marker	**Pronoun**
	Ako.

EXAMPLES:
Si Mayta. Mayta.
Ang guro. The teacher.
Ikaw. You.

3. Normally, one uses an identificational sentence when responding to a **sino** question or when making an "equation" with a sentence, as shown in the chart below.

Identificational Sentence (Affirmative Sentence)			
Subject		Predicate	
Marker	Noun	Marker	Noun
Si	Patrick	ang	estudyante.
Predicate		Subject	
Marker	Noun	Marker	Noun
Ang	estudyante	si	Patrick.

EXAMPLES:

Si Patrick ang estudyante. Patrick is the student.
Ang estudyante si Patrick. The student is Patrick.
Ako ang estudyante. I am the student.
Sino ang estudyante? Who is the student?
Sina Mike at Greg po ang mga estudyante. Mike and Greg are the students, sir/madam.

Notice that an identificational sentence doesn't require a verb in the predicate to be complete.

Grammar Notes

1. Remember: identificational sentences have **ang** markers in both the subject and the predicate.
    Si Patrick *ang* estudyante.
    *Si Patrick estudyante. (incorrect)
    *Patrick ang estudyante. (incorrect)

2. When employing an identificational sentence structure, you can use either of the following word orders:
    a. (MARKER) SUBJECT + (MARKER) PREDICATE
       Si Patrick ang estudyante.
    b. (MARKER) PREDICATE + (MARKER) SUBJECT
       Ang estudyante, si Patrick.

    Note that, for identificational sentences, the first structure is more common.

3. Use the marker **ang** to mark either common nouns or proper names of objects and places.
    Ang estudyante
    Ang Toyota
    Ang Maynila

    But, saying *si Tagalog is incorrect, because **si** and **sina** are only used before the names of people and animals.

II. Interrogative Pronoun **Ano** (What)

The interrogative pronoun **ano** is used to ask questions about things. The English equivalent of **ano** is *what*.

Ano?	
Ano ang klase mo?	What is your class?
Answer: (no marker) **Kasaysayan.**	History.
Answer: (no marker) **Tagalog.**	Tagalog.

1. When responding to a question that uses **ano** (what), subject markers are not necessary.
    Ano ang klase mo? Tagalog.
    Ano ang kurso mo? Communication.

2. It is very common to employ a question using **ano** to inquire about people's status, profession, religion, nationality, and/or gender.

    Ano si Greg?   **Binata.** (bachelor)
                          Arkitekto. (architect)
                          Katoliko. (Catholic)
                          Kastila. (Spanish)
                          Lalaki. (man)

    Normally, what the speaker is inquiring about can easily be inferred from the context of the conversation.

Grammar Presentation

The Interrogative Pronoun **Ano** and the Predicational Sentence

1. When forming a question with **ano**, you can follow the structure below.

Information Question: **Ano**		
What	**Marker**	**Common Noun**
Ano	ang ang mga	klase mo?
	Marker	**Proper Noun**
	si sina	Patrick?

EXAMPLES:
Ano ang kurso mo? What is your major?
Ano ang trabaho mo? What is your work?
(What do you do?)

←

2. When responding to a question using **ano**, it is NOT necessary to use markers.

Short Answers
Proper name
Tagalog.
Common Noun
Estudyante.

EXAMPLES:
narsing nursing
Aleman German
Budista Buddhist

→ To summarize, when answering a question using **ano**, a predicational sentence can be used. This sentence structure is the most common type of sentence in Tagalog. It is used when stating a piece of information. There are different types of predicational sentences, and these types will be covered in the next lesson. The word order is always: PREDICATE + SUBJECT. Note that the predicate does not take markers, while the subject is always in **ang** form.

Predicational Sentence (Affirmative Sentence)			
Predicate		**Subject**	
Marker	**Noun**	**Marker**	**Proper Noun**
	Tagalog	ang	klase ko.
	Estudyante	si	Patrick.

EXAMPLES:
Tagalog ang klase ko. My class is Tagalog.
Estudyante si Patrick. Patrick is a student.
Ano ang mga klase mo? What are your classes?
Titser siya. He is a teacher.
Estudyante po sina Patrick at Mike. Patrick and Mike are students, sir/madam.

Grammar Notes

1. When responding to **ano** questions, markers are not necessary.
    Ano ang kurso mo? What is your major?
    Narsing. Nursing.
    Ano si Peter? What is Peter? (literal)
    Doktor. Doctor.

2. Predicational statements are formed by using this structure:
    (NO MARKER) PREDICATE + (ANG MARKER) SUBJECT
    Doktor ang lalaki. The man is a doctor.

Practice

I. Speaking Practice
Work with a partner. Referring to the grammar explanation that you have just studied, take turns asking each other about the kind of work done by the people listed below. Use the example to model your dialogue.

EXAMPLE:
Q: **Ano si Nicanor?** What is (the work of) Nicanor?
A: **Negosyante si Nicanor.** Nicanor is a bussinessman.

Pangalan (Name)	Trabaho (Work)
1. Nicanor	A: businessman
2. Precila	A: teacher
3. Maria	A: nanny
4. Cardo	A: engineer
5. Maria Cecilia	A: singer

II. Reading Practice

Read the dialogue between Raul and Miriam and answer the Reading Comprehension questions in Tagalog.

Word Bank

Sino ang kasama mo kahapon?
Who were you with yesterday?

Unibersidad ng Pilipinas
University of the Philippines

Ang galing ah! Impressive!

Raul: **Kumusta ka, Miriam?**
Miriam: **Heto buhay pa. Ikaw, kumusta ka na?**
Raul: **Ayos lang. Siyanga pala, sino ang kasama mo kahapon?**
Miriam: **Si Greg.**
Raul: **Sino si Greg?**
Miriam: **Si Greg ang tagaluto sa Tokyo Grill.**
Raul: **Talaga?**
Miriam: **Oo. Hapon siya at estudyante siya sa Unibersidad ng Pilipinas.**
Raul: **Ah. Talaga? Ang galing ah! O sige.**
Miriam: **O sige. Kita tayo mamaya!**

Reading Comprehension

1. **Sino si Greg?**

---

2. **Ano si Greg?**

III. Writing Practice

Complete the dialogue below in Tagalog. The English equivalent has been provided.

Ted: _____ (How are you, Jed?)

Jed: _____ (I'm great! How about you?)

Ted: _____ (I'm all right!) Siyanga pala, sino ang kasama mo kahapon?

Jed: _____ (I was with Peter.)

Ted: _____ (Who is Peter?)

Jed: _____ (Peter is the singer at the Bom Bom Bar.)

Ted: _____ (Really?)

Jed: _____ (Yeah! He is Korean.)

Ted: _____ (Really? That's great! All right! I'll see you later.)

Jed: _____ (Okay! See you later!)

IV. Listening Practice

Listen to audio file (01–2) and answer the following questions in English.

1. With whom was Eric speaking?

   _____

2. Who was Eric with yesterday?

   _____

3. Who is Mindy and what does she do?

   _____

Pagpapakilala

Introductions

An Overview of Lesson 2

Objectives
• Introduce yourself and others
• Ask and respond to questions eliciting basic biographical information
• Ask and respond to yes-no questions

Vocabulary

• Parts of the House	• Countries	• Adjectives	• Location Markers
• Places	• Verbs	• Pronouns	• Idioms and Expressions

Dialogue: Pagpapakilala *Introductions*

Dialogue Comprehension

Activities

Activity 1: Interview   Activity 2: Interview   Activity 3: Information Gap Activity

Grammar
Definition of Terms: Enclitics and Question Marker **Ba**

Examining Form

I. **Taga Saan** (From Where): Interrogative Pronoun **Taga Saan** (From Where)
    Grammar Presentation: **Taga Saan** and Types of Predicational Sentences: Information Questions;
    Short Answers; Affirmative Statements; Negative Statements; Interrogative Statements; Affirm-
    ative Responses; Negative Responses
    Grammar Notes
II. **Nasaan** (Where): Interrogative Pronoun **Nasaan** (Where)
    Grammar Presentation: The Interrogative Pronoun **Nasaan** and Types of Predicational Sentences
    Grammar Notes
III. **Saan** (Where): Interrogative Pronoun **Saan** (Where)
    Grammar Presentation: The Interrogative Pronoun **Saan** and Types of Predicational Sentences
    Grammar Notes

Practice
I. Speaking Practice   II. Reading Practice   III. Writing Practice   IV. Listening Practice

Vocabulary 🎧 (02–1)

The vocabulary below will help you ask and answer questions and participate in the activities in this lesson. Memorize the vocabulary words before proceeding to the dialogue.

Parts of the House (Mga Bahagi ng Bahay)

banyo	bathroom
balkonahe	porch, balcony
bodega	storehouse, warehouse
garahe	garage
ibaba	downstairs
itaas	upstairs
komedor/ kainan	dining room
kusina	kitchen
kuwarto	bedroom
labahan	laundry room
sala	living room

Interrogative Pronouns

nasaan	where (followed by is/are)
saan	where (followed by an action word)
taga saan	from where

Location Markers

nasa	in, at, on
sa	in, at, on
taga-	from

Idioms and Expressions

Heto si ____, kaklase ko	This is ____, my classmate.
malapit lang sa ____	just close to ____
O sige na muna.	Bye for now.
Pupunta na ako sa ____	I am now going to ____
salamat	thank you

Places (Mga Lugar)

aklatan	library
bangko	bank
bahay	house
barberya	barber shop
botika	pharmacy
dormitoryo	dormitory
eskwelahan	school
kanto	street corner
kapeterya	cafeteria
klinika	clinic
opisina	office
ospital	hospital
otel	hotel
palengke	market
paliparan	airport
panaderya	bakery
pos opis	post office
restawran	restaurant
simbahan	church
sinehan	movie theater
tindahan	store

Countries (Mga Bansa)

Amerika/ Estados Unidos	United States, U.S.A.
Espanya	Spain
Hapon	Japan
Italya	Italy
Mehiko	Mexico
Pilipinas	Philippines
Pransya	France
Timog Korea	South Korea
Tsina	China

Verbs

nag-aaral	is/are studying
nagtatrabaho	is/are working

Adjectives

nakatira	residing

Dialogue: Pagpapakilala *Introductions*

Read the dialogue between Sheila, Janice, and Martha and answer the Dialogue Comprehension questions in Tagalog.

Sheila: **Magandang hapon, Janice.**
Janice: **Magandang hapon din naman, Sheila. Siyanga pala, heto si Martha, kaklase ko.**
Sheila: **Kumusta ka, Martha? Ako si Sheila.**
Martha: **Mabuti naman. Salamat.**
Sheila: **Taga saan ka, Martha?**
Martha: **Taga-Cebu ako. Ikaw, taga saan ka?**
Sheila: **Taga-Maynila ako. Saan ka nakatira sa Maynila?**
Martha: **Nakatira ako sa Eastwood. Ikaw?**
Sheila: **Sa Fort ako nakatira.**
Martha: **Nasaan ang Fort?**
Sheila: **Nasa McKinley Rd. Malapit lang sa Makati. O sige na muna. Pupunta na ako sa klase, ha.**
Martha: **O sige!**
Janice: **O sige, Sheila! Ingat!**

Dialogue Comprehension

1. **Sino ang kaklase ni Janice?**

_____

2. **Taga saan si Martha?**

_____

3. **Taga saan si Sheila?**

_____

4. **Saan nakatira si Martha?**

_____

5. **Nasaan ang bahay ni Sheila?**

_____

Activities

Activity 1

Interview three of your classmates and find out where they are from. Record the information in the chart below, then report your findings to the rest of the class. Use these examples to structure your interviews and sentences:

S1: **Taga saan ka?**
S2: **Taga-** _____ **ako. (Taga-Maynila ako.)**

Pangalan	Lugar (Place)	Pangungusap (Sentence)
1. Nelson	Taipei	Taga-Taipei si Nelson.
2.		
3.		
4.		

Activity 2

Interview two of your classmates using the questions from the following table and record your answers in the space provided. The first question asks the name of your interviewee; record the answer after the word **Pangalan**. Write the response to the second question in the blank after A. Finally, in the third blank, write a complete sentence using the answer furnished by your classmate. The examples below will help you model your interviews and sentences:

Q: **Ano ang pangalan ng lola mo?** What is the name of your grandma?
A: **Susana.** Susana.
Q: **Saan nakatira si Susana?** Where does Susana live?
A: **Sa Bicol.** In Bicol.

Sentence: **Nakatira si Susana sa Bicol.**
              Susana lives in Bicol.

```
┌─────────────────────────────────────────────┐
│                 Word Bank                     │
│                                               │
│         lola mo your grandmother              │
│           nanay mo your mother                │
│            nanay ko my mother                 │
│     kapatid mo your sibling (brother/sister)  │
│     kapatid ko my sibling (brother/sister)    │
└─────────────────────────────────────────────┘
```

Tanong	Kapareha 1 (Partner 1)	Kapareha 2 (Partner 2)
Ano ang pangalan ng lola mo? **Saan nakatira ang lola mo?**	Pangalan: **Susana** A: **Sa Bicol.** **Nakatira si Susana sa Bicol.** Pangalan: _____ A: _____ _____	Pangalan: **Monita** A: **Sa Makati.** **Nakatira si Monita sa Makati.** Pangalan: _____ A: _____ _____
Ano ang pangalan ng nanay mo? **Saan nagtatrabaho ang nanay mo?**	Pangalan: _____ A: _____ _____	Pangalan: _____ A: _____ _____
Ano ang pangalan ng kapatid mo? **Saan nag-aaral ang kapatid mo?**	Pangalan: _____ A: _____ _____	Pangalan: _____ A: _____ _____

Activity 3

This is an information gap activity, and you'll need to work with a partner. The illustration below shows the rooms of a house. Using the nouns and pronouns listed from 1 to 5, place each in a particular room. Ask your partner to guess where you placed the names. The example below will help model your dialogue.

1. **Si Kiko**
2. **Siya**
3. **Ang bata**
4. **Sina Ted**
5. **Sila**

EXAMPLE:
S1: **Nasa sala ba si Kiko?** Is Kiko in the living room?
S2: **Oo, nasa sala si Kiko.** Yes, Kiko is in the living room.
or **Hindi, wala sa sala si Kiko.** No, Kiko is not in the living room.

Nasaan si . . . ?

Grammar

Definition of Terms

Enclitics	Short words that cannot stand by themselves. They must occur with another word or group of words. Enclitics are considered adverbs in Tagalog. They express different meanings depending on the environment where they occur.
	EXAMPLES: **Taga-Pilipinas *po* ang lalaki.** The man is from the Philippines, sir/madam. **Taga-Pilipinas *ba* ang lalaki?** Is the man from the Philippines? In the second sentence above, the enclitic **ba**, which is a question marker, has no equivalent in the English language. We will cover other enclitics, such as **raw/daw** (it is said), **din/rin** (also), **na** (already, my turn, etc.), and **pa** (yet, still) in subsequent lessons.

Question Marker Ba	An enclitic that turns an affirmative sentence into a question.
	EXAMPLES: **Taga-Pilipinas po ang lalaki.** The man is from the Philippines, sir/madam. (affirmative sentence)
	Taga-Pilipinas *ba* **ang lalaki?** Is the man from the Philippines? (interrogative sentence)
	Nagtatrabaho si Sara sa Pilipinas. Sara is working in the Philippines. (affirmative sentence)
	Nagtatrabaho *ba* **si Sara sa Pilipinas?** Is Sara working in the Philippines? (interrogative sentence)

Examining Form

Now let's review. The sentences below illustrate the grammar patterns that are presented in this lesson. Read the sentences and complete the tasks that follow. Discuss your answers with a partner. If necessary, consult the following section to check your answers.

A

1. S1: **Taga saan ka?**
   S2: **Taga-Canada ako.**

2. S1: **Saan ka nakatira?**
   S2: **Nakatira ako sa Fort.**

3. S1: **Nasaan si Martha?**
   S2: **Nasa bahay si Martha.**

B

S1: **Taga saan po kayo?**
S2: **Taga-Canada po ako.**

S1: **Saan po kayo nakatira?**
S2: **Nakatira po ako sa Fort.**

S1: **Nasaan po si Martha?**
S2: **Nasa bahay po si Martha.**

a. Circle the subjects and underline the predicates.
b. Look at the sentences in column A and B. How do they differ?
c. What have you noticed regarding the use of hyphens when using the word **taga**?

I. Interrogative Pronoun **Taga Saan** (From Where)

The interrogative pronoun **taga saan** has a very specific meaning and a very limited use. It serves to ask about a person's origin or place of residence. The English equivalent of **taga saan** is *from where*.

Q: Taga saan?		
A: **Taga** + *Country*	**Taga-Amerika**	From America
+ *State*	**Taga-Haway**	From Hawaii
+ *City*	**Taga-Maynila**	From Manila
A: **Hindi taga** + *Country*	**Hindi taga-Amerika**	Not from America
+ *State*	**Hindi taga-Haway**	Not from Hawaii
+ *City*	**Hindi taga-Maynila**	Not from Manila

1. The prefix taga is always followed by either **saan** or a place.
   Taga saan? From where?
   Taga-Amerika From the U.S.A.

2. Use a hyphen to separate the prefix **taga** and the proper name of a place.

    Taga-Canada From Canada
    Taga-Tsina From China

Grammar Presentation

Taga Saan and Types of Predicational Sentences

1. When constructing an interrogative sentence with **taga saan**, follow the structure below. Notice that when **taga** is followed by **saan**, a hyphen is not used. Also, the subject noun is always in the **ang** form, i.e. is always an **ang** marker followed by a noun or one of the **ang** pronouns.

Information Question: Taga Saan	
Where	**Subject**
Taga saan	ka? siya? kayo? sila? ang phrase?

EXAMPLES:

Taga saan ka? Where are you from?
Taga saan ang nanay mo? Where is your mother from?
Taga saan si Mario? Where is Mario from?

2. When responding to a question formed with **taga saan**, use the structure below. As noted, when **taga** is followed by a place, a hyphen goes between **taga** and the proper noun for the place.

Short Answers	
Nasa	**Place**
Taga-	Pilipinas. Bulacan. Baliwag.

EXAMPLES:

Taga-Pilipinas. From the Philippines.
Taga-Maynila. From Manila.
Taga-Tsina. From China.

    Using this basic response to the question **Taga saan?** as our point of departure, let's now examine some basic types of predicational sentences.

3. One type of predicational sentence is an affirmative statement. It states a piece of information or fact. The word order is: predicate followed by the subject. The predicate does not take any markers, while the subject is always in **ang** form. Below is the pattern.

Affirmative Statements	
Predicate	**Subject**
Taga-Pilipinas	ako. siya. kami. tayo. sila. ang phrase.

EXAMPLES:

Taga-Pilipinas po ako. I am from the Philippines, sir/ madam.
Taga-Cebu si Maria. Maria is from Cebu.
Taga-Amerika ang mga lalaki. The guys are from the United States.

4. Another type of predicational sentence is a negative statement. It is formed by adding **hindi** before an affirmative statement. Notice, however, that when the subject is a pronoun, the word order changes. This is because **hindi** is a pronoun and enclitic magnet, meaning that whenever there are pronouns and enclitics in the sentence, they must immediately follow **hindi**. In the chart below, notice that **Hindi taga-Pilipinas** is followed by an **ang** phrase, but when the subject is a pronoun, the pronoun is placed right after **hindi** and **taga** follows.

Negative Statements		
Negative Marker	**Predicate**	**Subject**
Hindi	taga-Pilipinas	ang phrase.
Negative Marker	**Subject**	**Predicate**
Hindi	ako ka siya tayo/kami kayo sila	taga-Pilipinas.

EXAMPLES:

Hindi taga-Maynila ang babae. The woman is not from Manila.

Hindi kami taga-Pasay. We are not from Pasay.

Hindi po siya taga-Tsina. She/He is not from China, sir/madam.

5. Another type of predicational sentence is an interrogative statement or question that can be answered by yes (**oo**) or no (**hindi**). It is formed using the question marker, **ba**. Since **ba** is an enclitic, it is placed immediately after the predicate. However, in cases where the subject is monosyllabic, like the second-person singular pronoun **ka**, the question marker **ba** occurs right after the subject instead. This is because monosyllabic pronouns like **ka** have more priority than do enclitics in the word order. The chart below illustrates the sentence structure.

Interrogative Statements		
Predicate	**Question Marker**	**Subject**
Taga-Pasig	ba	siya? kayo? sila? ang phrase?
Predicate	**Subject**	**Question Marker**
Taga-Makati	ka	ba?

EXAMPLES:

Taga-Pasig ba siya? Is he/she from Pasig?

Taga-Pilipinas ba ang lalaki? Is the man from the Philippines?

Taga-Makati ka ba? Are you from Makati?

6. **Oo** and **hindi** are short answers. The questions above can be answered simply by yes or no. In addition, affirmative and negative responses can be made using predicational sentences. The affirmative response is formed by adding **Oo/Oho/Opo** before an affirmative statement. The **Oo/Oho/Opo** is punctuated by a period. The negative response is formed by adding **hindi**, followed by a period, before either an affirmative statement or a negative statement. When **hindi** occurs before an affirmative statement, the statement must supply the correct information to the question. By contrast, when **hindi** is followed by a negative statement, that statement restates in negative form the same information as the question. See the chart and examples for the correct word order in affirmative and negative responses.

Affirmative Responses		
Yes	**Predicate**	**Subject**
Oo. Oho. Opo.	Taga-<u>Pasig</u>	ako. siya. kami/tayo. sila. <u>ang</u> phrase.

Negative Responses			
No	**Negative Marker**	**Predicate**	**Subject**
Hindi.	Hindi	taga-Cebu	<u>ang</u> phrase.
No	**Negative Marker**	**Subject**	**Predicate**
Hindi.	Hindi	<u>ang</u> pronoun	taga-Cebu.
No	**Predicate**	**Subject**	
Hindi.	<u>Taga-Pasay</u>	siya.	

EXAMPLES:

Taga-Pasig ba siya? Is he from Pasig?

Oo. Taga-Pasig siya. Yes. He is from Pasig.

Opo. Taga-Pasig po siya. Yes, sir/madam. She/He is from Pasig, sir/madam.

Taga-Cebu ba ang lalaki? Is the man from Cebu?

Hindi. Hindi po taga-Cebu ang lalaki. No. The man is not from Cebu, sir/madam.

Hindi. Taga-Makati po ang lalaki. No. The man is from Makati, sir/madam. (This negative response provides the correct information.)

Grammar Notes

The word order varies in different types of sentences:

1. With respect to word order, monosyllabic pronouns have precedence over the question marker **ba**.
   Taga-Pilipinas ka ba? Are you from the Philippines?
   ***Taga-Pilipinas ba ka?** (incorrect)

2. The negative marker **hindi** placed at the beginning of an affirmative statement transforms it into a negative sentence.
   Taga-Pilipinas si Mike. (affirmative) Mike is from the Philippines.
   Hindi taga-Pilipinas si Mike. (negative) Mike is not from the Philippines.

3. **Hindi** is a pronoun and enclitic magnet. Therefore, whenever **hindi** is used in a sentence, all the pronouns and enclitics in the sentence must occur right after it.
   Hindi *po ako* taga-Pilipinas. I am not from the Philippines sir/madam. (correct)
   ***Hindi taga-Pilipinas *po ako*.** (incorrect)

4. Below are three ways to say "yes" in Tagalog.
   Oo   used to answer in the affirmative between peers, friends, people of the same age, and between an older person, superior to a younger person or a subordinate
   Oho   used out of respect for an older person, superior or stranger; less formal than **opo**
   Opo   a contraction of **oo po** used the same way as **oho**

   Oo. Taga-Maynila sila. Yes. They are from Manila.
   Oho. Taga-Marikina ho ang mga bata. Yes sir/madam. The children are from Marikina, sir/madam.
   Opo. Taga-Pasig po kami. Yes. We are from Pasig, sir/madam.

5. There are two ways to form negative responses using **hindi** in Tagalog sentences. In the first, **hindi** is followed by a negative sentence. In the second, **hindi** is followed by an affirmative sentence. When using the latter structure, keep in mind that the correct information must be supplied in order to answer the question. See the following examples:

Question: **Taga-<u>Pilipinas</u> ba si Jessica?** Is Jessica from the Philippines?
Structure 1: **Hindi. Hindi taga-<u>Pilipinas</u> si Jessica.** No. Jessica is not from the Philippines.
Structure 2: **Hindi. Taga-<u>Amerika</u> si Jessica.** No. Jessica is from America.

6. In casual conversation, short responses are more common when answering these questions. However, in order to better understand Filipino grammatical structure, students are encouraged to learn how to respond with complete sentences.

Question: **Taga saan si Jessica?** Where is Jessica from?
Answer 1: **Taga-Pilipinas.** From the Philippines.
Answer 2: **Taga-Pilipinas si Jessica.** Jessica is from the Philippines.

Question: **Taga-Pilipinas ba si Jessica?** Is Jessica from the Philippines?
Answer 1: **Oo.** Yes.
Answer 2: **Oo. Taga-Pilipinas si Jessica.** Yes. Jessica is from the Philippines.

7. To summarize, the five types of predicational sentences are:

a. Affirmative statement
   Taga-Amerika ang estudyante. The student is from America.

b. Negative statement
   Hindi taga-Amerika ang estudyante. The student is not from America.

c. Question or interrogative statement
   Taga-Amerika ba ang estudyante? Is the student from America?

d. Affirmative response
   Oo/Oho/Opo. Taga-Amerika ang estudyante. Yes. The student is from America.

e. Negative response
   Hindi. Hindi taga-Amerika ang estudyante. No. The student is not from America.
   Hindi. Taga-Hapon ang estudyante. No. The student is from Japan.

Notice that the first negative response uses two **hindi**.

II. Interrogative Pronoun **Nasaan** (*Where*)

As with English *where*, this pronoun is used when asking for the location of something or someone.

Q: **Nasaan?**		
A: **Nasa** + place	**Nasa <u>Pilipinas</u>**	In the Philippines
	Nasa <u>kuwarto</u>	In the room
A: **Wala sa** + place	**Wala sa <u>Pilipinas</u>**	Not in the Philippines
	Wala sa <u>kuwarto</u>	Not in the room

1. Use the response marker **nasa** when responding to the question **nasaan**.
> **Nasaan ang Maynila?** Where is Manila?
> **Nasa Pilipinas.** In the Philippines.
> **Nasaan si Sheila?** Where is Sheila?
> **Nasa kuwarto.** In the room.

2. The negative form of **nasa** is **wala sa**.
> **Wala sa Pilipinas.** Not in the Philippines.
> **Wala sa kuwarto.** Not in the room.

Grammar Presentation

The Interrogative Pronoun **Nasaan** and Types of Predicational Sentences

1. The interrogative pronoun **nasaan** is used when the question refers to the location of an object or person. When constructing an interrogative sentence with **nasaan**, employ the structure below.

Information Question: Nasaan	
Where	**Subject**
Nasaan	<u>ang</u> pronouns? <u>ang</u> phrase?

EXAMPLES:
Nasaan sila? Where are they?
Nasaan ang klinika? Where is the clinic?
Nasaan po ang garahe? Where is the garage, sir/madam?
Nasaan po si Karla? Where is Karla, sir/madam?

2. To respond to a **nasaan** question, use **nasa** in the structure below. Short answers are not complete sentences and therefore should be used only when responding to questions. In the examples, note that **nasa** is followed by a place or location.

Short Answers	
Nasa	**Place**
Nasa	<u>Maynila.</u> <u>bahay.</u> <u>aklatan.</u>

EXAMPLES:
Nasa Maynila po. In Manila, sir.
Nasa bahay. In the house.

3. Affirmative statements start with the predicate followed by the subject. In the predicate, the place or location is marked by **nasa**, and the subject is in **ang** form, as shown in the following chart.

Affirmative Statements	
Predicate	**Subject**
Nasa <u>paliparan</u>	<u>ang</u> pronouns. <u>ang</u> phrase.

EXAMPLES:
Nasa aklatan ako. I am at the library.
Nasa eskwelahan kami. We are at school.
Nasa eskwelahan ang aklatan. The library is in the school.
Nasa paliparan sina Maria. Maria and others are at the airport.

4. The negative form of this predicate-subject structure uses **wala sa** to mark the place or location; the subject follows and is in **ang** form. However, since **wala** is a negative marker like **hindi**, it is immediately followed by pronouns and enclitics, as illustrated in the chart below.

Negative Statements		
Negative Marker	**Predicate**	**Subject**
Wala	<u>sa Seattle</u>	<u>ang</u> phrase.
Negative Marker	**Subject**	**Predicate**
Wala	<u>ang</u> pronouns	<u>sa Pilipinas</u>

EXAMPLES:

Wala sa bahay si Mark. Mark is not at home.

Wala sila sa restawran. They are not in the restaurant.

5. Now that you know how to respond to **nasaan** (where) questions, let's revisit the yes/no question and how an affirmative statement can be turned into a **ba** question. To transform an affirmative statement into a question, simply add the question marker **ba** after the predicate and before the subject. However, if the subject is a monosyllabic pronoun, the subject pronoun precedes **ba**. See the example below.

Interrogative Statements		
Predicate	**Question Marker**	**Subject**
Nasa <u>kusina</u>	**ba**	<u>ang</u> pronoun? <u>ang</u> phrase?
Predicate	**Subject**	**Question Marker**
Nasa <u>kusina</u>	**ka**	**ba?**

EXAMPLES:

Nasa kuwarto ba ang mga bata? Are the children in the room?

Nasa kusina ka ba? Are you in the kitchen?

6. The affirmative response for this kind of question is formed by adding **Oo/Oho/Opo** before an affirmative sentence. The negative response is formed by adding **wala** before an affirmative statement or a negative statement. When **wala** occurs before an affirmative statement, the correct information to the question must be supplied. When **wala** is followed by a negative statement, that statement restates in negative form the information supplied by the question.

Affirmative Responses		
Yes	**Predicate**	**Subject**
Oo. **Oho.** **Opo.**	Nasa kusina	<u>ang</u> pronouns. <u>ang</u> phrase.

Negative Responses			
No	**Negative Marker**	**Subject**	
Wala.	Wala sa kusina	<u>ang</u> phrase.	
No.	**Negative Marker**	**Subject**	**Predicate**
Wala.	Wala	<u>ang</u> pronoun	sa <u>sala</u>.
No.	**Predicate**	**Subject**	
Wala.	Nasa kuwarto	siya.	

EXAMPLES:

Nasa bahay ba ang bata? Is the child at home?

Oo/Oho/Opo. Nasa bahay ang bata. Yes, sir/madam. The child is at home.

Wala po. Wala sa bahay ang bata. No, sir/madam. The child is not at home.

Wala po. Nasa eskwelahan po ang bata. No, sir/madam. The child is at school.

Nasa Pransya ba siya? Is she/he in France?

Oo/Oho/Opo. Nasa Pransya siya. Yes, sir/madam. She/He is in France.

Wala po. Wala po siya sa Pransya. No, sir/madam. She/He is not in France, sir/madam.

Wala po. Nasa Italya siya. No, sir/madam. She/He is in Italy.

Grammar Notes

1. **Wala** is a negative marker. Like **hindi**, it requires that all pronouns and enclitics be placed immediately after it.

   Wala *siya* **sa Seattle.** She/He is not in Seattle.

   Wala po *siya* **sa Seattle** She/He is not in Seattle, sir/madam.

   ***Wala sa Seattle** *siya*.* (incorrect)

2. **Po** and **ho** are enclitics that express politeness or deference in Tagalog. When talking to an older person, superior, or stranger, it is best to use these enclitics.

III. Interrogative Pronoun **Saan** (*Where*)

The interrogative pronoun **saan** is used when asking where an event or an action takes place. Unlike **na-saan**, **saan** is usually followed by a verb. The answer must include **sa**, which can be translated in several ways: as **at**, **in**, or **on**.

Q: **Saan ka** + VERB ?	Where do you + VERB ?
A: **Sa University of Hawai'i**	At the University of Hawaii
Sa Maynila	In Manila
Sa State St.	On State Street
A: **Hindi sa University of Hawaii.**	Not at the University of Hawaii.
Hindi sa Maynila.	Not in Manila.
Hindi sa State St.	Not on State Street.

1. Use **saan** when asking where the action takes place.

   Saan ka nag-aaral? Where do you go to school? (Where are you studying?)

   Saan kayo nakatira? Where do you (plural) live?

2. Use **sa** when responding to a **saan** question.

   Q: **Saan nakatira si Brian?** Where does Brian live?

   A: **Sa Pilipinas.** In the Philippines.

Grammar Presentation

The Interrogative Pronoun **Saan** and Types of Predicational Sentences

1. The interrogative pronoun **saan** is used when the question refers to the location of an action or event. To construct an interrogative sentence with **saan**, follow the structure below.

Information Question: **Saan**		
Where	**Subject**	**Verb**
Saan	<u>ang</u> pronoun	**nagtatrabaho?**
Where	**Verb**	**Subject**
Saan	**nagtatrabaho**	<u>ang</u> phrase?

EXAMPLES:

Saan siya nagtatrabaho? Where does she/he work?

Saan po nagtatrabaho si Mike? Where does Mike work, sir/madam?

2. When responding to a question with **saan**, follow the structure below. The response is formed by marking a place or location with **sa**.

Short Answers	
Sa	**Place**
Sa	Maynila.

EXAMPLES:
Sa kuwarto. In the room.
Sa opisina. In the office.

3. Affirmative statements about a place begin with the predicate followed by the subject and then the place. The structure of the sentence is detailed in the chart below.

Affirmative Statements			
Verb	**Subject**	**Preposition**	**Place**
Nakatira	ang pronouns ang phrase	sa	Baguio.

EXAMPLES:
Nakatira ako sa Baguio. I live in Baguio.
Nakatira po sina Mike at Mila sa Camiguin. Mike and Mila live in Camiguin, sir/madam.

4. Negative statements are formed by adding the negative marker **hindi** before an affirmative statement. Remember that when the subject is a pronoun, the word order changes. Since **hindi** is a pronoun and enclitic magnet, the enclitics and pronouns are placed right after it.

Negative Statements			
Hindi	**Subject**	**Verb**	**Preposition**	**Place**
Hindi	ang pronouns	nag-aaral	sa	U.P.
Hindi	**Subject**	**Subject**	**Preposition**	**Place**
Hindi	nag-aaral	ang phrase	sa	U.P.

EXAMPLES:
Hindi po sila nag-aaral sa U.P. They do not go to the University of the Philippines, sir/madam. (They are not studying at U.P., sir/madam.)
Hindi nag-aaral si Melanie sa U.P. Melanie does not go to the University of the Philippines. (Melanie does not study at U.P.)

5. Remember that questions are formed by adding the question marker **ba** right after the predicate of the sentence. Below are several word orders that one can use when asking a question.

Interrogative Statements (Questions)			
Verb	**Question Marker**	**Subject**	**Place**
Nag-aaral	ba	siya kayo sila ang phrase	sa UST?
Verb	**Subject: Monosyllabic Pronoun**	**Question Marker**	**Place**
Nag-aaral	ka	ba	sa UST?

EXAMPLES:
Nag-aaral ba siya sa UST? Does she/he go to UST?
Nag-aaral ka ba sa UP? Do you go to University of the Philippines?
Nag-aaral ba si Marco sa Ateneo? Does Marco go to Ateneo?

6. Also remember that the affirmative and negative short responses **oo** and **hindi** are answers to **ba** questions. The affirmative short response for this sentence structure is formed by adding **Oo/Oho/Opo** before an adverb of place. In contrast, the negative short response is formed by adding **hindi** before either an adverb of place or a negative marker plus adverb of place. The chart illustrates this.

Short Responses		
Yes	**Adverb of Place**	
Oo. Oho. Opo.	Sa UST.	
No	**Marker**	**Place**
Hindi. Hindi ho. Hindi po.	Hindi sa	UST.
	Sa	

EXAMPLES:

Nag-aaral ba siya sa UST? Does she go to University of Santo Tomas? (Is she/he studying at University of Santo Tomas?)

Opo. Sa UST. Yes, sir. (She/He goes to) UST.
or **Opo. Nag-aaral siya sa UST.** Yes, sir/madam. She/He goes to UST. (Yes, sir/madam. She/He's studying at UST.)

Hindi. Hindi sa UST. No. (She/He does not go to) UST.
or **Hindi. Hindi siya nag-aaral sa UST.** No. She/He does not go to UST.

The response supplying the correct information is as follows:

Hindi. Sa Ateneo. No. (She/He goes to) Ateneo.
or **Hindi. Nag-aaral siya sa Ateneo.** No. She/He goes to Ateneo.

Nakatira po ba kayo sa Dapitan? Do you live in Dapitan, sir/madam?
Oo. Sa Dapitan. or Oo. Nakatira ako sa Dapitan. Yes. I live in Dapitan.

Hindi. Hindi sa Dapitan. No. Not in Dapitan.
or **Hindi. Hindi ako nakatira sa Dapitan.** No. I don't live in Dapitan.

Hindi. Sa Banawe. No. In Banawe.
or **Hindi. Nakatira ako sa Banawe.** No. I live in Banawe.

Grammar Notes

1. When using **saan**, remember these two structures are correct:
   a. **Saan** + PRONOUN + VERB
      Saan siya nag-aaral?
   b. **Saan** + VERB + ANG PHRASE
      Saan nag-aaral si Mike?
      ***Saan nag-aaral siya?** (incorrect)

2. Enclitics except the pronoun **ka** take precedence over **ang** pronouns in sentence word order.
   Nag-aaral ba siya sa UC Berkeley?
   Nag-aaral ka ba sa UC Berkeley?
   ***Nag-aaral ba ka sa UC Berkeley?** (incorrect)

3. When constructing an affirmative sentence, remember that there are three common word orders you can use:

   a. VERB + ACTOR + ADVERB OF PLACE

   Used when stating a fact (not responding to any questions).

   Nakatira si Miguel sa Makati. Miguel lives in Makati.

   b. ADVERB OF PLACE + VERB + ACTOR

   Used when responding to the interrogative pronoun **saan**.

   Q: **Saan nakatira si Miguel.** Where does Miguel live?
   A: **Sa Makati nakatira si Miguel.** Miguel lives in Makati.

   c. ADVERB + ACTOR + VERB

   Used when responding to the interrogative pronoun **saan**. This is preferred when the actor is a pronoun.

   Q: **Saan siya nakatira?** Where does he live?
   A: **Sa Makati siya nakatira.** He lives in Makati.

Practice

I. Speaking Practice

A. Complete the form below with your own information.

Pangalan: _____

Tirahan: _____

Bansa: _____

Eskwelahan: _____

Kurso mo sa kolehiyo: _____

Paborito mong klase: _____

Propesor mo: _____

B. In complete sentences, write questions using the information from the form above. The interrogative pronouns have been provided to help you.

   1. **Ano <u>ang pangalan mo?</u>**

   2. **Saan** _____?

3. **Taga saan** _____?

4. **Saan** _____?

5. **Ano** _____?

6. **Ano** _____?

7. **Sino** _____?

C. Work with a partner. Use the information in your form to ask and answer questions.

Student 1: **Ano ang pangalan mo?**
Student 2: **Ako si *David Cruz.***

1. **Pangalan:** _____

2. **Tirahan:** _____

3. **Bansa:** _____

4. **Eskwelahan:** _____

5. **Kurso mo sa kolehiyo:** _____

6. **Paborito mong klase:** _____

7. **Propesor mo:** _____

II. Reading Practice

Read the dialogue between Patrick and Jamie and answer the comprehension questions in Tagalog.

Patrick: **Magandang umaga! Ako si Patrick. Ikaw, ano ang pangalan mo?**
Jamie: **Ako si Jamie. Kumusta ka, Patrick?**
Patrick: **Mabuti naman ako. Estudyante ka ba dito?**
Jamie: **Oo. Narsing ang kurso ko. Ikaw, ano ang kurso mo?**
Patrick: **Accounting ang kurso ko. Taga saan ka?**
Jamie: **Taga-Bulacan ako. Ikaw?**
Patrick: **Taga-Abra ako. Saan ka nakatira dito?**
Jamie: **Nakatira ako sa *boarding house* malapit sa ekwelahan. Ikaw?**
Patrick: **Sa Merville ako nakatira.**
Jamie: **Nasaan ang Merville?**
Patrick: **Nasa Parañaque. O sige na muna. Pupunta na ako sa klase, ha.**
Jamie: **O sige. Kita tayo mamaya.**
Patrick: **O sige. Ingat ka!**

Reading Comprehension

1. **Ano ang kurso ni Patrick?**

   _____

2. **Taga saan si Patrick?**

   _____

3. **Ano ang kurso ni Jamie?**

   _____

4. **Saan nakatira si Jamie?**

   _____

5. **Nasaan ang Merville?**

   _____

III. Writing Practice

Complete the dialogue below in Tagalog. The English equivalent has been provided for you.

Kiko: _____ (Good afternoon, Ted.)

Ted: _____ (Good afternoon to you too, Kiko!) _____ (By the way)**, heto si Mike, kaklase ko.**

Kiko: _____ (How are you Mike?) _____ (I am Kiko.)

Mike: _____ (I am great. Thank you.)

Kiko: _____ (Where are you from, Mike?)

Mike: _____ (I am from Cavite. You, where are you from?)

Kiko: _____ (I am from Bulacan. Where do you live?)

Mike: _____ (I live in Fort Bonifacio. You?)

Kiko: _____ (I live in Makati.)

Mike: _____ (Where is Makati?)

Kiko: _____ (It's on Roxas Boulevard. It is close to Fort

Bonifacio.) _____ (All right, I have to go to class.)

Mike: _____ (Bye!)

Ted: _____ (Ok! Bye! Take care!)

IV. Listening Practice

 Listen to audio file (02–2) and complete the chart below.

Pangalan	Bansa	Eskwelahan	Tirahan	Trabaho	Lugar
1. **Sophia**				———	———
2. _____		———	———		
3. **Editha**		———			———
4. _____			———	———	

Mga Gusto at Ayaw

Likes and Dislikes

An Overview of Lesson 3

Objectives
• Ask and respond to questions about your likes and dislikes
• Talk about your favorite sports and people

Vocabulary
• Sports and Games   • Adjectives   • **Ng** Pronouns
• Pseudo-Verbs   • Conjunctions   • **Ng** Markers

Dialogue: Ano Ang Gusto Mo? *What Do You Want?*

Dialogue Comprehension

Activities
Activity 1: Interview
Activity 2: Interview
Activity 3: Cultural Experience

Grammar
Definition of terms: Aspect, Inflection, Pseudo-Verbs, Experiencer, Object

Examining Form
I. Pseudo-Verbs and **Ng** Markers and Pronouns
  Pseudo-Verbs with **Ng** Markers Marking the Object
  Grammar Notes
  Grammar Presentation: Pseudo-Verbs with **Ang** Phrases or **Ang** Pronouns as Object
  Grammar Notes

Practice
I.   Speaking Practice
II. Reading Practice
III. Writing Practice
IV. Listening Practice

Vocabulary 🎧 (03–1)

The vocabulary below will help you express likes and dislikes and participate in the activities in this lesson. Memorize the vocabulary words before proceeding to the dialogue.

Sports and Games

arnis	Philippine martial art that uses two rattan sticks
badminton	badminton
baraha	cards
basketbol	basketball
basketbolista	basketball player
beysbol	baseball
manlalaro ng besybol	baseball player
bilyar	billiards
boksing	boxing
boksingero	boxer
boling	bowling
eskrima	fencing
karera ng kabayo	horse racing
pilota	similar to raquet ball
putbol	football
manlalaro ng putbol	football player
sabong	cockfighting
saker	soccer

Pseudo-Verbs

ayaw	does not like; does not want
gusto	like; want
may	has/have

Adjectives

bastos	uncouth, rude
bobo	stupid, dumb
duwag	coward
guwapo/pogi	handsome
mabagal	slow
mabait	kind
mabilis	active, fast
magaling (sa)	good (at)
maganda	beautiful
mahina	weak
malakas	strong
malaki	big
maliit	small, short
mapagkumbaba	humble
matalino; marunong	intelligent, wise
matangkad	tall
matapang	brave, courageous
mayabang	conceited, boastful
nakakainis	annoying
nakakatuwa	delightful, likeable
nakakatawa	funny, comical
pangit	ugly

Conjunctions

kasi	because
at	and

Ng Pronouns

kita	you by me
ko	I
mo	you
namin	we (exclusive, i.e. not including the listener)
natin	we (inclusive, i.e. including the listener)
nila	they
ninyo	you (plural)
niya	he/she

Ng Markers

ng	marks singular common nouns or proper name of a place or thing
ng mga	marks two or more common nouns or proper names of a place or a thing
ni	marks the name of a specific singular person or animal
nina	marks the name of two or more specific persons or animals

Dialogue: Ano Ang Gusto Mo? *What Do You Want?*

Read the dialogue and test your understanding with the Dialogue Comprehension exercise that follows.

Gary: **Mark, may tiket ako para sa basketbol sa Biyernes. Gusto mo ba?**

Mark: **Hindi. Salamat. Ayaw ko ang Ginebra, eh.**

Gary: **Bakit? Sino ang gusto mo?**

Mark: **Gusto ko ang San Miguel Beermen. Pero sa totoo lang, mas gusto ko ng larong beysbol.**

Gary: **Beysbol? Talaga?**

Mark: **Oo naman. Mariners at Dodgers ang mga paborito ko. Ikaw? Gusto mo ba ng beysbol?**

Gary: **Ayos lang.**

Mark: **E, boksing?**

Gary: **Siyempre!**

Mark: **Sino ang gusto mong boksingero?**

Gary: **Siyempre, si Manny Pacquiao.**

Mark: **Bakit?**

Gary: **Kasi magaling at mabilis si Manny Pacquiao.**

Dialogue Comprehension

Based on the dialogue, decide whether these statements are true, **Tama**, or false, **Mali**.

	TAMA	MALI
1. Mark has basketball tickets.	_____	_____
2. Mark doesn't like the San Miguel Beermen basketball team.	_____	_____
3. Mark also likes baseball.	_____	_____
4. Gary's favorite baseball teams are the Dodgers and the Mariners.	_____	_____
5. Gary likes boxing.	_____	_____

Activities

Activity 1

Interview your classmates, and find two students who like the following sports listed below and two who do not. In complete sentences, fill out the chart below based on the information you have gathered.

S1: **Gusto mo ba ng basketbol?** Do you like basketball?
S2: **Oo, gusto ko ng basketbol.** Yes, I like basketball.
  Hindi, ayaw ko ng basketbol. No, I don't like basketball.

Mga Laro	Gusto	Ayaw
Basketbol	1. **Brian** **Gusto ni Brian ng basketbol.** 2. _____ _____	1. **Danny** **Ayaw ni Danny ng basketbol.** 2. _____ _____
Beysbol	1. _____ _____ 2. _____ _____	1. _____ _____ 2. _____ _____
Putbol	1. _____ _____ 2. _____ _____	1. _____ _____ 2. _____ _____
Boksing	1. _____ _____ 2. _____ _____	1. _____ _____ 2. _____ _____

Activity 2

Interview two of your classmates and find out their favorite and least favorite athletes. Ask them to explain why they feel this way. Write their answers in the chart that follows.

Marc: **Sino ang gusto mong manlalaro?** Who is your favorite athlete?
Greg: **Gusto ko si Manny Pacquiao kasi magaling siya sa boksing.** I like Manny Pacquiao because he is good at boxing.

A.

Ang gusto kong manlalaro	Dahilan (Reason)
1. **Manny Pacquiao**	**Gusto ni Greg Manny Pacquiao kasi magaling siya sa boksing.**
2.	
3.	

B.

Ang ayaw kong manlalaro	Dahilan (Reason)
1.	
2.	

Activity 3

Try a cultural experiment. Form a group of five or more and play one of the traditional Filipino games described below.

1. **Takip Silim (Twilight)**

   Takip silim, which literally means "twilight" or "nightfall," is a game similar to tag and is played by three or more players, one of whom is chosen to be "it." The "it" player is blindfolded with a handkerchief or some piece of cloth, then made to turn around three times before pursuing the other players. In order to tease the "it" player, the other players can poke or tickle him or her or call out "It" or some other oral expression in order to give a hint about their location. When the "it" person succeeds in catching or tagging one of the other players, that player is now "it" and the game continues.

2. **Tumbang Preso (Fallen Prisoner)**

   Tumbang Preso means "fallen prisoner," and most Filipino children play this easy game. To play, you need at least 3 participants and a can. Here again, one of the players is "it" and will act as the defender of the can, while the other players try to knock it down without being tagged. Those players can only be tagged while the can has not been knocked down. If they succeed in knocking it down and then are tagged, the tag doesn't count. Players usually use slippers or flip-flops (**tsinelas**) when playing **Tumbang Preso**, but they are allowed no more than two slippers as their weapons. When all the players have used up all their slippers without knocking down the can, the "it" player can chase everyone and tag the one he/she wishes to make the new "it" player. During the chase, other players can knock the can down with their feet or a slipper but cannot touch the can.

Grammar

Definition of Terms

Aspect	The equivalent of tense in English verbs. This is a characteristic of Tagalog verbs expressed by inflection to denote the time frame of an action. The different aspects are: completed (also called perfective); incompleted or habitual (also called imperfective); and contemplated, for an action that will happen in some future time.
Inflection	Any of the forms a verb takes to indicate aspect. *Inflect* simply means to change the form of a word. In the case of the verb, it means to change from infinitive to the completed, incompleted, or contemplated aspect.
Pseudo-Verbs	These verbs are similar to regular verbs but function somewhat differently. Unlike other Tagalog verbs, pseudo-verbs are not inflected for aspect. **Gusto** (like) and **ayaw** (don't like) fall in this category.
Experiencer	This is the part of a **gusto/ayaw** sentence that experiences or undergoes the "liking" or "disliking." The **ng** pronouns and nouns preceded by **ng** markers are the experiencer in these types of sentences.
Object	That part or word in a sentence that receives the action.

Examining Form

The sentences below illustrate the grammar patterns that are presented in this lesson. Review the sentences and complete the tasks that follow. Discuss your answers with a partner. Consult the following section to check your answers.

1. **Gusto ni Gary ng beysbol.**
2. **Gusto nila ng boksing.**
3. (no equivalent)
4. (no equivalent)
5. **Gusto ko ng mga larong Pilipino.**

1. **Gusto ni Gary ang beysbol.**
2. **Gusto nila ang boksing.**
3. **Gusto ko si Manny Pacquiao.**
4. **Gusto ko si Manny Pacquiao.**
5. **Gusto ko ang mga larong Pilipino.**

a. Underline the experiencer and circle the objects.
b. Look for the words **ng** and **ang** in the sentences. When do you use **ng**? When do you use **ang**?

I. Pseudo-Verbs and **Ng** Markers and Pronouns

Gusto and its negative form, **ayaw**, are examples of pseudo-verbs. Unlike regular verbs, pseudo-verbs cannot be inflected for aspect. **Gusto** is used to express likes or wants, while **ayaw** is used to express dislikes or object to something. The experiencer, or the one who experiences the like or dislike, is a **ng** pronoun or a common noun marked by a **ng** marker. Below, the first chart lists the singular and plural forms of **ng** markers for common nouns as well as the singular and plural forms of **ng** markers for proper nouns. The second chart lists **ng** pronouns.

Ng Markers	Example
Ng + <u>Noun</u> marks singular common nouns and singular proper name of a place or a thing	**Ng bata** kid **Ng Magnolia ice cream** Magnolia ice cream
Ng mga + <u>Noun(s)</u> marks two or more common nouns and more than one proper name of a place or a thing	**Ng mga bata** kids **Ng mga Jollibee at Mc Do** Jollibee and Mc Donald's
Ni + <u>Name of a person/animal</u> marks the name of a specific singular person or an animal	**Ni Mike** Mike **Ni Roxy** Roxy
Nina + <u>Name(s) of people/animals</u> marks the name of one or more specific persons or animals	**Nina Mike at Roxy** Mike and Roxy **Nina Mike** Mike and others

Ng Pronouns		
	Singular	**Plural**
First Person	**ko**	**natin** (inclusive) **namin** (exclusive)
Second Person	**mo**	**ninyo**
Third Person	**niya**	**nila**

Grammar Presentation

Pseudo-Verbs with **Ng** Markers Marking the Object

In a sentence with **gusto** (like) and **ayaw** (don't like), the experiencer, as we saw, has to be a **ng** pronoun or a common noun marked by a **ng** marker. **Ng** and **ng mga** are used to mark an unspecific or generic object. The table below illustrates the pattern for this kind of sentence

Pseudo-Verb	Experiencer		Object		
	Marker	**Noun**	**Marker**	**Noun**	
Gusto **Ayaw**		ko natin (inclusive) namin (exclusive) mo ninyo niya nila	**ng/** **ng mga**	**larong Pilipino.**	
	Marker	**Noun**			
	ni **nina**	<u>**Mario**</u>			
	ng **ng mga**	<u>**Lalaki**</u>			

EXAMPLES:

Gusto ko ng boksing. I like boxing.

Gusto ba ni Mark ng boksing? Does Mark like boxing?

Ayaw ni Maria ng bilyar. Maria does not like billiards.

Grammar Notes

1. **Ng** pronouns and **ng** phrases are used to designate the experiencer in this sentence structure as the sentences below illustrate:
   Gusto ko ng mga larong Pilipino. I like Filipino games/sports.
   Gusto ng bata ng mga larong Pilipino. The child likes Filipino games/sports.

2. The markers **ng** and **ng mga** are used when talking about unspecific or generic objects.
   Gusto ko ng mga larong Pilipino. I like Filipino games.

3. **At** (*and*) is used to connect two or more nouns and/or adjectives.
   Gusto ko *ng* boling at arnis. I like bowling and *arnis*.
   Gusto ko *si Manny Pacquiao* kasi magaling *at* mabilis siya. I like Manny Pacquiao because he is good (vigorous/skilled) and fast.

4. **Kasi** is used to express a reason, similar to English *because*.
   Gusto ko siya *kasi* matalino siya. I like her/him because she/he is smart.

Grammar Presentation

Pseudo-Verbs with **Ang** Phrase or **Ang** Pronouns as Object

When the object of **gusto** and **ayaw** is specific or definite, it will be in **ang** form.

Pseudo-Verb	Experiencer		Object	
	Marker	**Noun**	**Marker**	**Noun**
Gusto Ayaw	ko mo niya	natin (inclusive) namin (exclusive) ninyo nila	ang ang mga si sina	bata. Martha. ako tayo (inc.) kami (exc.) ka kayo siya sila

	Object		Experiencer	
	Marker	**Noun**	**Marker**	**Noun**
		ako tayo (inc.) kami (exc.) ka kayo siya sila	ni nina ng ng mga	Gary. lalaki.

EXAMPLES:
Gusto ko siya. I like her/him.
Gusto ba niya ako? Does she/he like me?
Gusto kita I like you.
Ayaw nila siya. They don't like him/her.
Ayaw sila ng bata. The child does not like them.

Grammar Notes

1. **Kita** is a special pronoun equivalent to the second-person singular **ikaw** (**ka**) and the first-person singular pronoun **ko** (I) together. It means "you by me" Use **kita** when the experiencer of the **gusto/ayaw** sentence is the first person (I) and the second person singular (you) is the object, in ther words, where in English the subject of the sentence would be **I** and the object **you**.

> **Gusto kita.** I like you.
> ***Gusto ko ka.** (incorrect)
>
> **Ayaw kita.** I don't like you.
> ***Ayaw ko ka.** (incorrect)

2. Switch the word order when an ang pronoun is the object in a **gusto/ayaw** sentence and use the construction **Gusto/Ayaw** + ANG PRONOUN + NG PHRASE (EXPERIENCER). Remember that pronouns always take priority in sentence word order, as shown in the following sentence.

> **Gusto sila ni Kris.** Kris likes them
> ***Gusto ni Kris sila.** (incorrect)

Practice

I. Speaking Practice
Referring to the table below, describe what each person likes and dislikes.

EXAMPLES:
Gusto nila ng beysbol at baraha.
Gusto nila si Babe Ruth.

		Laro	Manlalaro
1. They	**Gusto**	Baseball and cards	**Babe Ruth**
	Ayaw	Billiards	**Efren "Bata" Reyes**
2. Lea	**Gusto**	Bowling and soccer	**Paeng Nepumuceno**
	Ayaw	Basketball	**Michael Jordan**
3. Student	**Gusto**	Boxing	**Manny Pacquiao**
	Ayaw	Horse racing and baseball	**Ichiro Suzuki**

II. Reading Practice

The messages below are from four different people. Read them and test your understanding by answering the comprehension questions.

```
Word Bank

paborito favorite
musika music
libro book
```

Message 1

Kumusta kayo? Ako si Mei. Taga-Taiwan ako. Ngayon, estudyante ako sa Unibersidad ng Centro Escolar. Ingles ang kurso ko. Nakatira ako sa Maynila malapit sa unibersidad. Gusto ko ng beysbol at bilyar. Si Ichiro Suzuki ang paborito ko.

Message 2

Ano na? Ako si Carlos. Taga-Baguio ako. Estudyante ako sa Unibersidad ng Pilipinas. Literatura ang kurso ko. Gusto ko ng mga libro at ayaw ko ng mga laro.

Message 3

Magandang umaga! Ako si Tanya. Taga-Espanya ako. Medisina ang kurso ko at nag-aaral ako sa Unibersidad ng Santo Tomas. Gusto ko ng mga musika at libro.

Message 4

Kumusta na? Si Joaquin ito. Taga-Mindanao ako. Nag-aaral ako sa Kolehiyo ng San Beda ng abogasiya. Gusto ko ng mga isports. Gusto ko ang bilyar at basketbol.

Reading Comprehension

Fill in the blanks with the correct information according to the four messages above.

Message 1

Name: _____

School: _____

Major: _____

Hometown: _____

Residence: _____

Likes: _____

Dislikes: _____

Message 2

Name: _____

School: _____

Major: _____

Hometown: _____

Residence: _____

Likes: _____

Dislikes: _____

Message 3

Name: _____

School: _____

Message 4

Name: _____

School: _____

Major: _____   Major: _____

Hometown: _____   Hometown: _____

Residence: _____   Residence: _____

Likes: _____   Likes: _____

Dislikes: _____   Dislikes: _____

III. Writing Practice

Select one person from the reading practice and write him/her a message to introduce yourself.

_____

_____

_____

_____

_____

_____

_____

IV. Listening Practice

Listen to audio file (03–2) and complete the chart below.

		Player	Reason
1. Miguel	**Gusto**	Michael Jordan	
	Ayaw		**Mayabang**
2.	**Gusto**		
	Ayaw	Dennis Orcollo	
3. Maria	**Gusto**		
	Ayaw	Mike Tyson	

UNIT 2

PAMILYA
Family

To the average Filipino, family always comes first. He or she may gain many friends or find other communities in life, but the foundation of a Filipino's life is family. As the basic social unit in Philippine society, family takes precedence over all other individuals, including the self.

A contemporary Filipino wedding

In most Filipino families, the parents will stop at nothing to give their children a better future. When the children are grown and able to provide for themselves, they in turn are committed to making the life of their parents easier. Often the children hesitate to leave home even when they are married and have kids of their own. This is consistent with the concept of **utang na loob**, or "debt of the inner self." Parents have sacrificed for their children, so the children are expected to do everything to reciprocate their love and kindness. As a result, sending parents to a retirement facility, a practice common in Western nations, would be out of the question in the Philippines.

Filipinos always show much respect for their parents and the elderly in general. Almost all Filipinos greet the elderly with **mano po**, which, literally translated, means "hand please (sir/madam)." **Mano po** is the physical gesture of taking the hand of an elder and drawing it toward your forehead. This is a sign of respect for the elder and is usually done at the moment of greeting or farewell. In the context of a traditional Filipino home, failure to perform **mano po** would be extremely disrespectful.

Kinship terms in Tagalog have respectful implications and show the hierarchical nature of a Filipino family. Mothers are referred to as **Nanay, Ina**, or **Nanang**. Fathers are referred to as **Tatay, Itay**, or **Tatang**. But because of Western influence, **Mama, Mom**, and **Mommy** for "mother" and **Papa, Dad**, and **Daddy** for "father" are widely used in Metro-Manila and suburban areas. Elder sisters and cousins are referred to as **Ate** or **Manang**, while elder brothers and cousins are referred to as **Kuya** or **Manong** in general. After **ate** and **kuya** as the terms for the eldest sister and brother, **ditse** and **diko** are used for the second eldest, and **sanse** and **sangko** for the third eldest. There is even a term for the wife of the eldest son, **inso**. **Siyaho** is the husband of the eldest daughter. These later terms may show influence from the Chinese with whom natives of the Philippines have had a long-standing relationship since before Spanish colonization. Aunts can be called **Tita** or **Tiya**, and uncles **Tito** or **Tiyo**. Finally, grandmothers and grandfathers are called **Lola** and **Lolo**, respectively.

Pagmamano, *a sign of respect for the elderly*

Filipino families are not restricted to the nuclear family unit. Extended family members are felt to be just as close as nuclear family members by Filipinos. Many relatives live in the same neighborhood or in close proximity to each other, and many children grow up with their cousins as their best friends. It is quite common to have family reunions comprising as many as a hundred people. Even friends of parents are affectionately called "Uncle" or "Aunt" as if they were blood relatives. This practice adds to the communal feeling of many Filipinos.

A typical family gathering is composed of extended families

Being part of a big, close family is experienced differently than in the West, and there are different perceptions about privacy. Don't be surprised if family members ask you how much money you make or that relatives act as chaperones on dates!

Ang Pamilya Ko

My Family

An Overview of Lesson 4

Objectives
- Ask and answer questions about one's age
- Describe family relationships using kinship terms
- Introduce or talk about family members

Vocabulary
- Family Relationships
- Possessive Pronouns
- Demonstrative Pronouns
- Numbers
- Affixes and Enclitics
- Idioms and Expressions

Dialogue: Pagbisita sa Bahay ni Mark *Visiting Mark at His Home*

Dialogue Comprehension

Activities
Activity 1: Family Tree
Activity 2: Interview
Activity 3: Reading

Grammar
Definition of terms: **Ng** Phrase, **Ng** Pronouns, Affix, Prefix, Suffix

Examining Form
I. Possessive Noun Markers and Possessive Pronouns
    Grammar Presentation: Possessive Markers and Pronouns and Demonstrative Pronouns
    Grammar Notes
II. Numbers
    Grammar Presentation: Numbers in Context
    Grammar Notes

Practice
I.   Speaking Practice
II. Reading Practice
III. Writing Practice
IV. Listening Practice

Vocabulary 🎧 (04–1)

The vocabulary will help you speak about family relationships and participate in the activities in this lesson. Memorize the vocabulary words before proceeding to the dialogue.

Kinship Terms and Other Relations

anak	child (son, daughter)
apo	grandchild (grandson, granddaughter)
asawa	spouse, husband, wife
ate	elder sister
bunso	youngest sibling
inaanak	godchild (godson, goddaughter)
kaibigan	friend
kaklase	classmate
kamag-anak	relative
kapatid	sibling (brother, sister)
kuya	elder brother
lola	grandmother
lolo	grandfather
mag-anak	family
magulang	parent
misis	wife
mister	husband
nanay/ina	mother
ninang	godmother
ninong	godfather
pamangkin	nephew, niece
panganay	oldest sibling, eldest child
pinsan	cousin

tatay/ama	father
tita/tiya/tia	aunt
tito/tiyo/tio	uncle

Possessive Pronouns and Plural Interrogatives

anu-ano	what are
ko	my
mo	your
namin	our (exclusive; not including the listener)
natin	our (inclusive; including the listener)
nila	their
ninyo	your (plural)
niya	his/her
sinu-sino	who are

Demonstrative Pronouns

nandito	here
nandiyan	there (near the listener)
nandoon	there (far from both the speaker and the listener)

Numbers

isa	one
dalawa	two
tatlo	three
apat	four
lima	five
anim	six
pito	seven
walo	eight
siyam	nine
sampu	ten
labing-isa	eleven
labindalawa	twelve
labintatlo	thirteen
labing-apat	fourteen
labinlima	fifteen
labing-anim	sixteen
labimpito	seventeen
labingwalo	eighteen
labinsiyam	nineteen
dalawampu	twenty
tatlumpu	thirty
apatnapu	forty
limampu	fifty

Affixes and Enclitics

-pu	added as a suffix to numbers 2 to 9 to indicate group of tens
labing-	added as a prefix to numbers 1 to 9 to indicate numbers 11 to 19
labin-	a variant of **labing**. It is prefixed to words beginning with the letters *d, l, r, s, t.*
labim-	a variant of **labing**. It is prefixed to words beginning with letters *b* and *p.*
na	already

Idioms and Expressions

Halika! Kain tayo.	Come! Let's eat.
Heto ang ____ ko.	Here is my____.
Ilang taon na si ____ ?	How old is ...?
Tuloy ka.	Come in.

Dialogue: Pagbisita sa Bahay ni Mark *Visiting Mark at His Home*

The dialogue illustrates how to use the words and expressions you studied above. Read it aloud with a partner and complete the Dialogue Comprehension activity that follows.

Julian is visiting his friend, Mark.

Julian: **Magandang hapon po! Nandiyan po ba si Mark?**

Tatay: **Oo, tuloy ka. Mark! Nandito na ang kaibigan mo.**

Mark: **O Julian. Halika. 'Tay, heto po ang kaibigan ko, si Julian. Julian heto ang tatay ko.**

Tatay: **O kumusta ka, iho? Halika, kain tayo.**

Julian: **Salamat po, Tito. Mark, sinu-sino ang mga nandito?**

Mark: **Nandito ang lahat ng kamag-anak namin. Nandoon ang mga tito at tita ko. Pagkatapos, nasa itaas naman ang mga pinsan ko at ang mga kapatid ko.**

Julian: **Sino naman ang nasa kusina?**

Mark: **Sina Lola at Lolo at ang mga kaibigan ni Nanay.**

Julian: **Mark, mukhang batang-bata ang lolo at lola mo. Ilang taon na sila?**

Mark: **Animnapu na si Lola at animnapu't dalawa si Lolo. O sige. Kain muna tayo.**

Julian: **O sige.**

Dialogue Comprehension

Based on the dialogue, answer the following questions in Tagalog.

1. **Sino ang kaibigan ni Mark?**

2. **Sinu-sino ang mga nasa bahay nina Mark?**

_____

3. **Nasaan ang mga pinsan ni Mark?**

_____

4. **Ilang taon na ang lolo ni Mark?**

_____

5. **Ilang taon na ang lola ni Mark?**

_____

Activities

Activity 1

A. Work with a partner. First, create a family tree for your immediate family using the spaces provided, then describe your relationship to each person, using complete sentences in Tagalog.

FAMILY TREE

EXAMPLE:

Si Mario ang lolo ko.   **Si Karla ang nanay ko.**

_____   _____

_____   _____

_____   _____

_____   _____

B. Interview

Next, ask a classmate about the people on his or her family tree.

Mga Tanong	Sagot
1. **Pinsan** Q: **Sinu-sino ang mga pinsan mo?**	A: **Sina Maria, Mike at Patricia ang mga pinsan ko.**
2. **Tito at Tita** Q:	A:
3. **Lola at Lolo** Q:	A:
4. **Nanay at Tatay** Q:	A:

Activity 2

A. Based on the information solicited by the chart below, formulate questions using the interrogative pronouns that are provided. Once you have finished, use these questions to interview a classmate. Record your findings in the chart.

EXAMPLE:

Student 1: **Ano ang pangalan ng tatay mo?** What is the name of your father?

Student 2: **Benildo ang pangalan ng tatay ko.** The name of my father is Benildo.

	Tatay	Nanay
Pangalan		
Tirahan		
Trabaho		
Eskwelahan		
Gusto		
Ayaw		

1. **Ano ang pangalan ng tatay mo?** _____

2. **Saan** _____

3. **Saan** _____

4. **Saan** _____

5. **Ano** _____

6. **Ano** _____

B. Report your answers to the class.

EXAMPLE:

Benildo ang pangalan ng tatay ni Marie. The name of Marie's father is Benildo.

Activity 3

Complete the paragraph below using the word bank. You may use the words more than once.

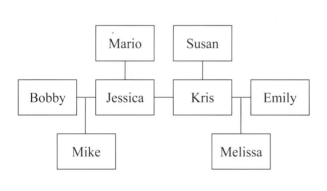

Word Bank

anak child
apo grandchild
asawa spouse
kapatid sibling
pamangkin nephew/niece
pinsan cousin
tito uncle

May dalawang _____ **sina Mario at Susan. Jessica at Kris ang mga pangalan nila.**

May _____ **na si Jessica, Bobby ang pangalan niya. Mike naman ang pangalan ng** _____

nina Jessica at Bobby. Si Kris ang _____ **ni Jessica. May asawa na si Kris. Emily ang pangalan**

ng _____ **ni Kris. May** _____ **na sina Kris at Emily. Melissa**

ang pangalan ng anak nila. _____ **ni Mike si Melissa at mga** _____ **naman nina Mario at**

Susana sina Mike at Melissa. _____ **ni Melissa si Bobby at** _____ **naman nina**

Kris at Emily si Mike.

Grammar

Definition of Terms

Ng Phrase	A **ng** phrase is composed of a **ng** marker and a noun. The **ng** markers examined in this lesson are used to indicate possession or ownership. EXAMPLES: **Tatay <u>ni Mark</u> si Jose.** Jose is Mark's father. **Anak <u>ng kaibigan ko</u> si Jossie.** Jossie is my friend's daughter.
Ng Pronouns	Possessive pronouns that substitute for noun phrases marked by **ng** markers. EXAMPLES: **Tatay <u>ni Mark</u> si Jose** → **Tatay <u>niya</u> si Jose.** Jose is his father. **Anak <u>ni Linda at Boy</u> si Marco** → **Anak <u>nila</u> si Marco.** Marco is their son.
Affix	A syllable that is attached to a word to produce an inflected or derived form.
Prefix	An affix that is added in front of the word.
Suffix	An affix added at the end of the word.

Examining Form

The sentences below illustrate the grammar patterns presented in this lesson. Review the sentences and complete the tasks indicated. Discuss your answers with a partner. Consult the following section to check your answers.

1. **Tay, heto po ang kaibigan ko, si Julian.**
2. **Nandito ang lahat ng kamag-anak namin.**
3. **Mukhang batang-bata ang lolo at lola mo.**
4. **Nandoon sina Lola at Lolo at ang mga kaibigan ni Nanay.**
5. **Animnapu na si lola at animnapu't dalawa na si lolo.**
6. **Limang taon na siya.**
7. **Sampung taon na si Nina.**

    a. Underline all the possessive phrases in numbers 1 to 4.
    b. What is the proper word order in a possessive phrase in Tagalog? Compare it with the proper word order of a possessive phrase in English.
    c. Box all the numbers and circle the subjects in numbers 5 to 7.
    d. Notice that in numbers 6 and 7, the numbers have **-ng** attached to them. Why do you think it is needed?

EXAMPLES:
Tatay <u>ni Mark</u> si Jose. Jose is Mark's father.
Anak <u>ng kaibigan ko</u> si Jossie. Jossie is my friend's daughter.

I. Possessive Noun Markers and Possessive Pronouns

There are noun markers that indicate possession in Tagalog. These noun markers are:

Possessive Noun Markers

Ni + <u>name of a person or animal</u>
Nina + <u>name(s) of persons or animals</u>

Ng + <u>common noun</u>
Ng mga + <u>common noun(s)</u>

Possessive pronouns also indicate possession. The possessive pronouns are:

Possessive Pronouns		
	Singular	**Plural**
First Person	**ko**	**natin** (inclusive) **namin** (exclusive)
Second Person	**mo**	**ninyo**
Third Person	**niya**	**nila**

As in English, one uses these markers and possessive pronouns to indicate:
1. Relationships
   Tatay ni Patrick Patrick's father
   Tatay niya His father

2. Ownership
   Kotse nina Mike at Pat Mike's and Pat's car
   Kotse nila Their car

Grammar Presentation

Possessive Markers and Pronouns and Demonstrative Pronouns

1. In Tagalog, possessive phrases are formed by adding possessive markers or pronouns after the nouns they modify. The table below shows the appropriate word order.

Possessive Markers		
Noun	**Possessive Marker**	**Noun**
Tatay	ni nina	Maria
	Possessive Marker	**Noun**
	ng ng mga	bata
Possessive Pronouns		
Noun	**Possessive Pronoun**	
Nanay	ko **natin** (inclusive) **namin** (exclusive) mo **ninyo** niya **nila**	

EXAMPLES:
Ang pinsan ko My cousin
Ang nanay ng estudyante The student's mother
Ang lolo at lola ni Maria Maria's grandfather
   and grandmother

2. The correct way to use possessive phrases in identificational sentences is illustrated in the table below. As discussed in previous lessons, both the subject and predicate are marked by **ang** markers in an identificational sentence.

Possessive Nouns/Pronouns in an Identificational Sentence				
Subject		**Predicate**		
Marker	**Noun**	**Marker**	**Noun**	**Possessive Noun**
Si	Lydia	ang	nanay	ni Jamie.
Sina	Mark at Susana	ang mga	kapatid	nina Patrick at Jose.
Marker	**Noun**	**Marker**	**Noun**	**Possessive Pronoun**
Si	Mark	ang	anak	ko natin. namin. mo ninyo. niya nila.
Pronoun		**Marker**	**Noun**	**Possessive Noun**
Ako Ikaw Siya		ang	tatay	ng estudyante.
Tayo Kami Kayo Sila		ang mga	magulang	ng mga bata.

The following are some examples of sentences with possessive phrases using **ng** markers and pronouns:

EXAMPLES:

Si Lydia po ang nanay ni Jamie. Lydia is Jamie's mom, sir/madam.
Sina Marco at Paul ang mga kapatid ni Mandy. Marc and Paul are Mandy's siblings.
Siya ang tatay ng bata. He is the child's father.
Sinu-sino ang mga kamag-anak ninyo? Who are your relatives?
Sina Mark, Justin, Minda at Geline ang mga kamag-anak ko. Mark, Justin, Minda, and Geline are my relatives.

3. The correct way to use possessive phrases in predicational statements is shown in the following table.

Possessive Nouns/Pronouns in a Predicational Sentence			
Predicate	**Subject**		
Adverb	**Marker**	**Noun**	**Possessive Noun**
Nandito	ang	nanay	ni Patrick. nina Patrick. ng bata. ng mga bata.
Adverb	**Marker**	**Noun**	**Possessive Pronoun**
Nandoon	ang	tatay	ko natin namin mo ninyo niya nila

EXAMPLES:
Nasaan ang nanay ni Patrick?
Where is Patrick's mom?
Nandito ang nanay ni Patrick.
Patrick's mother is here. (near the person speaking)
Nandiyan ba ang anak ko?
Is my child there? (near the person addressed)
Nandoon po ang anak ninyo.
Your child is over there, sir/madam. (The child is far from both the speaker and the person addressed.)

The predicates in these particular sentences are demonstrative pronouns, specifically **nandito** (in the place where the speaker is), **nandiyan** (in the place where the person spoken to is), and **nandoon** (which refers to a person who or a thing that is there or in a place far off from both the speaker and the person spoken to). These demonstrative pronouns might be used in response to a **nasaan** (where) question, when talking about the location of an object or a person. They can also be used to make simple declarative statements.

Grammar Notes

1. **Ng** possessive pronouns and markers always come after the noun they modify.

   Tatay ni Mark. Mark's father.
   Tatay ko. My father.
   *Ni Mark tatay (incorrect)
   *Ko tatay. (incorrect)

2. Possessive pronouns replace possessive nouns. They agree in number with the noun they replace.

   Si Maria ang nanay *nina Patrick*. Maria is Patrick's and his siblings' mother.
   Si Maria ang nanay *nila*. Maria is their mother.

3. The third-person singular pronoun **niya** is pronounced **n'ya**, and the second-person plural **ninyo** is pronounced **n'yo**.

   Niya → **N'ya**
   Ninyo → **N'yo**

4. The interrogative pronoun **sinu-sino** (who are) is used when the speaker is seeking a plural answer. The response must use the response marker **sina** followed by a series of names. The last name in the series is preceded by the conjunction **at** (and). In the same manner, when the interrogative pronoun **anu-ano** (what are) is used, the speaker expects a plural answer. The response can be a series of nouns, and the last noun is conjoined by **at**.

   Q: **Sino ang kamag-anak mo?** Who is your relative?
   A: **Si Maria ang kamag-anak ko.** Maria is my relative.
   Q: **Sinu-sino ang mga kamag-anak mo?** Who are your relatives?
   A: **Sina Matt, Anne, at Paul ang mga kamag-anak ko.** Matt, Anne, and Paul are my relatives.

5. The adverbs **nandito**, **nandiyan**, and **nandoon** are used to respond to a **nasaan** (where) question and indicate location.

   nandito here (close to the speaker)
   nandiyan there (close to the listener)
   nandoon there (far from both the speaker and listener)
   Nasaan ang tatay ko? Where is my father?
   Nandoon siya. He is over there.
   Nandito po ba si Lolo? Is Grandfather here?
   Wala. Nasa loob ng bahay si Lolo. No. Grandfather is inside the house.

II. Numbers

The table below indicates the cardinal numbers from 1 to 99. Cardinal numbers can be used to answer the questions **ilan** (how many), **gaano** (how much), and **magkano** (how much does it cost).

		Labing		Pu		Pu't	
isa	1	labing-isa	11	dalawampu	20	dalawampu't isa	21
dalawa	2	labindalawa	12	tatlumpu	30	tatlumpu't dalawa	32
tatlo	3	labintatlo	13	apatnapu	40	apatnapu't tatlo	43
apat	4	labing-apat	14	limampu	50	limampu't apat	54
lima	5	labinlima	15	animnapu	60	animnapu't lima	65
anim	6	labing-anim	16	pitumpu	70	pitumpu't anim	76
pito	7	labimpito	17	walumpu	80	walumpu't pito	87
walo	8	labingwalo	18	siyamnapu	90	siyamnapu't walo	98
siyam	9	labinsiyam	19				
sampu	10						

Grammar Presentation

Numbers in Context

The table below illustrates how to say one's age. In the first structure, the number is in the predicate position followed by an enclitic **na**, which literally means "already" or "now," and this is followed by the subject. In the second structure, the number is also in the predicate position but is used as a modifier of the word **taon**. Notice that there is a **-ng** in between the number and the word **taon** (year) when the number ends in a vowel. The suffix **-ng** functions as a linker, a concept that will be discussed in subsequent lessons. For now, it is best to memorize the structure as a chunk.

Numbers			Enclitic	Subject
Labingwalo			na	si <u>Karla</u>. (**ang** phrase)
Numbers	Linker	Year	Enclitic	Subject
Sampu	**-ng**	taon	na	ang <u>bata</u> (**ang** phrase)

EXAMPLES:

Ilang taon na ang nanay mo? How old is your mother now?

Limampu't walo na si Nanay. Mom is already fifty-eight.

Ilang taon na po kayo? How old are you now, sir/madam?

Animnapu't limang taon na ako. I am already sixty-five years old.

Ilang taon na ang lolo at lola mo? How old are your grandfather and grandmother now?

Pitumpu't siyam na si Lolo at pitumpu't walo si Lola. Grandfather is already seventy-nine, and grandmother is seventy-eight.

Grammar Notes

1. **Labi** is added as a prefix to numbers 1 to 9 in order to make the numbers 11 to 19. The prefix **labing** has two variants:

Labin-	before numbers that begin with the letters **d, l, r, s,** and **t**
Labim-	before numbers that begin with the letters **b** and **p**
Labing-	before numbers that begin with a vowel, for example, **isa** (one), **apat** (four), and **anim** (six)

Labin*dalawa*	twelve
Labim*pito*	seventeen
Labing-*isa*	eleven

2. **Pu** is added as a suffix to numbers 2 to 9 to indicate a group of tens.

   Apatnapu = "four tens" = forty

3. Use **m** and **na** to connect the suffix **pu** to numerals.
   m: occurs after vowels

dalawa*m*pu	twenty
tatlu*m*pu	thirty
lima*m*pu	fifty
pitu*m*pu	seventy
walu*m*pu	eighty

   Notice that the letter **o** in the numerals **tatlo, pito,** and **walo** changes to **u**.
   na: occurs after consonants

apat*na*pu	forty
anim*na*pu	sixty
siyam*na*pu	ninety

4. To say the numbers 21 to 99 requires the conjunction **at**. However, in everyday speech, **at** is often contracted.

   77 (= 70 + 7)
   Pitumpu at pito
   Pitumpu't pito (everyday speech)

5. When asking and responding to questions pertaining to age, the enclitic **na** is usually used. Literally, it means "now" or "already."

   Ilang taon ka <u>na</u>? How old are you (now)?
   Dalawampu't isa <u>na</u> ako. I am twenty-one years old now.

Practice

Now let's practice using the structures we have just learned.

I. Speaking Practice

Answer the chart below and then work with a partner. Referring to the grammar explanation that you have just studied, take turns asking each other the age of each person listed in the first column. Use the example below to model your dialogue.

EXAMPLE:

S1: **Ilang taon ka na?** How old are you now?

S2: **Dalawampu't walo na ako.** I am now twenty-eight years old.

S1: **Ano ang pangalan ng kaibigan mo?** What is the name of your friend?

S2: **Martha.** Martha.

S1: **Ilang taon na si Martha?** How old is Martha now?

S2: **Dalawampu na si Martha.** Martha is now twenty years old.

Pangalan	Taon
1. Pangalan mo Pangalan: _____	
2. Pangalan ng kaibigan mo Pangalan: _____	
3. Pangalan ng nanay mo Pangalan: _____	
4. Pangalan ng tatay mo Pangalan: _____	

II. Reading Practice

Read Mario's story about his family and then answer the Reading Comprehension questions in Tagalog.

```
Word Bank

kasama with someone
ilarawan describe
```

Ang Pamilya ni Mario Cruz

Siya si Mario Cruz. Dalawampu't limang taon na siya. Nakatira siya sa Parañaque. Taga-Maynila ang nanay ni Mario at taga-Cebu naman ang tatay niya. Nars ang nanay niya at abogado naman ang tatay niya. Kasama ni Mario ang tatay at nanay niya sa bahay nila. May asawa na si Mario, Lita ang pangalan. Nagtatrabaho si Lita sa bangko. Doktor naman si Mario. May dalawa silang anak, si Paolo at si Joan. Third year high school na si Paolo sa St. Mary's Academy at nasa elementarya pa lang si Joan sa Sacred Heart. Mababait at matatalino ang mga anak nina Mario.

Reading Comprehension

1. Ilang taon na si Mario?

   _____

2. Saan siya nakatira?

   _____

3. Ano ang trabaho ng nanay at tatay niya?

   _____

4. Ano ang pangalan ng asawa niya?

   _____

5. Ilarawan ang mga anak nina Mario.

   _____

III. Writing Practice

Write a short paragraph about your family. Use the paragraph above as a model for your essay.

_____

_____

_____

_____

_____

_____

IV. Listening Practice

Listen to audio file (04–2) and answer the following questions in English.

EXAMPLE:

You will hear: **Ano ang pangalan ng nanay mo?**

You write: **Editha ang pangalan ng nanay ko.**

1. _____

2. _____

3. _____

4. _____

5. _____

Paglalarawan ng mga Miyembro ng Pamilya

Describing Members of the Family

An Overview of Lesson 5

Objectives
• Describe people using **ma-**adjectives
• Describe people using the **naka-** prefix

Vocabulary

• Clothing and Accessories   • Adjectives   • Prefixes
• Hair and Parts of the Face   • Colors

Reading Text: Ang Pamilya Ko *My Family*

Reading Comprehension

Activities

Activity 1: Sentence Completion
Activity 2: Guess Who?
Activity 3: Family Portrait

Grammar

Definition of Terms: Adjectives, Adjectival Phrase, Inflection, Linkers, Reduplication

Examining Form

I.   Adjectives and Linkers
     Grammar Presentation: Adjectives and Linkers
     Grammar Notes
II. **Naka-** Modifiers
     Grammar Presentation
     Grammar Notes

Practice

I.   Speaking Practice
II.   Reading Practice
III. Writing Practice
IV.   Listening Practice

Vocabulary 🎧 (05–1)

The vocabulary will help you describe yourself, family members, and others and participate in the activities in this lesson. Memorize the vocabulary words before proceeding to the reading.

Clothing and Accessories

amerikana	suit
bestida	dress
blusa	blouse
damit	clothes (can also refer to a T-shirt)
hikaw	earrings
kuwintas	necklace
maong	jeans, denim
medyas	socks
palda	skirt
pantalon	pants
polo	button-down shirt
pulseras	bracelet
relos	watch
salamin	glasses
sando	sleeveless undershirt
sapatos	shoes
singsing	ring
sinturon	belt
sumbrero	hat, cap
tsinelas	slippers, slipper

Hair and Parts of the Face

bibig	mouth
buhok	hair
kilay	eyebrow
ilong	nose
mata	eyes
mukha	face
ngipin	teeth
tenga	ears

Adjectives

bata	young
bilog	round
guwapo	handsome, good-looking
kalbo	bald
kalmado	calm
kulot	curly
kuwadrado	square
mabuti	fine, good
magalang	polite
magulo	disorderly, rowdy, mischievous
mahaba	long (length)
mahinhin	modest, refined
mahiyain	shy
maikli	short (length)
mainitin ang ulo	short-tempered
maingay	noisy
maitim	dark-complexioned
makapal	thick
malaki	big
malikot	restless, wriggly; naughty, mischievous
malilimutin	absent-minded
malungkot	sad
manipis	thin, not dense
mapagmahal	loving
maputi	fair-complexioned
mataba	stout, fat
matanda	old

matangos	pointed (referring to the nose)
pahaba	long
pango	flat (referring to the nose)
payat	thin
singkit	narrow-slit or slanting (referring to eyes)
suplado/a	snobbish
tahimik	quiet

Colors

asul	blue
berde	green
dilaw	yellow
itim	black
kayumanggi	brown (only used to describe skin color)
kulay	color
pula	red
puti	white
rosas	pink

Prefixes

naka-	expresses the idea of wearing the article designated by the root

Reading Text: Ang Pamilya Ko *My Family*

The text below utilizes some of the vocabulary words that you've studied for this lesson. Read the text and complete the Reading Comprehension activity.

Word Bank

likod behind
tabi next to

Ito ang pamilya ko. Ako ang bunso sa pamilya. May manika ako sa litrato at naka-asul na bestida ako. Nasa likod ko ang pamilya ko. Mabait at mapagmahal sila. Nasa kanan si Lolo. Nakaasul na pantalon siya. Nasa tabi ni Lolo si Tatay. Matapang at guwapo siya. Nasa harap ni Tatay ang kapatid ko. Jojo ang pangalan niya. Matalino at masipag siya. Nasa tabi ni Tatay si Nanay. Maganda at mahinhin siya. Nasa harap ni Nanay si Lola. Nakaberdeng palda at nakahikaw siya. Nasa tabi ni Lola si Mario. Tito ko si Mario. Mabait at guwapo siya.

Reading Comprehension

For each of the following statements about the reading, place a check mark in the appropriate blank, depending on whether the statement is true, **Tama**, or false, **Mali**.

	TAMA	MALI
1. In the photograph, the author is holding a doll.	_____	_____

2. Her father is strong and handsome.   _____   _____

3. Her mother is beautiful and caring.   _____   _____

4. Her brother is smart and hard-working.   _____   _____

5. Her grandfather is wearing blue pants.   _____   _____

Activities

Activity 1

Choose an appropriate adjective from the vocabulary page to describe each person listed below. When you have finished, write a complete sentence using all the information you have. Remember to use **ang** markers for your subjects.

EXAMPLE:

1. **Mabait**   **nanay ko.**
   Mabait ang nanay ko. _____

2. _____ **Lola.**

   _____

3. _____ **Tatay.**

   _____

4. _____ **kapatid ko.**

   _____

5. _____ **kaibigan ko.**

   _____

Activity 2

In the spaces provided below, write a description of one of your classmates using five different adjectives. Be sure to construct complete sentences. When you're done, read the description to the class and have them guess who the person is. Use the example below to model your sentences and your dialogue with the class.

EXAMPLE:

S1: **Mahaba ang buhok niya. Matangkad siya. Matangos ang ilong niya. Nakadilaw siya at nakasala-min siya.** She has long hair. She's tall. Her nose is prominent. She's wearing yellow, and she wears glasses.

S2: **Si Kristine ba siya?** Is it (she) Kristine?

S1: **Oo, si Kristine siya./Hindi. Hindi siya si Kristine.** Yes, it is Kristine./No. It is not Kristine.

1. _____

2. _____

3. _____

4. _____

5. _____

Activity 3

Work in small groups. Sketch each member of your family on a separate sheet of paper, then take turns with your partners describing the people in your sketches. Here is an example of a description.

Student: **Siya ang tatay ko. Matangkad at payat ang tatay ko. Puti at itim ang buhok niya. Matangos ang ilong niya. Makapal ang kilay niya. Maitim siya. Mabait at tahimik siya.**

He is my father. My father is tall and thin. His hair is salt and pepper. His nose is pointed. His eyebrows are thick. He is dark. He is kind and quiet.

Grammar

Definition of Terms

Adjectives	Words that describe a person or thing in the sentence. EXAMPLE: *Mabait* **ang bata.** The kid is *nice*.
Adjectival Phrase	Composed of an adjective, a linker, and a noun. EXAMPLE: *Malaking lalaki* **si Edward.** Edward is a *big man*.
Inflection	The modification of a word to express different grammatical categories such as aspect, number, etc. EXAMPLE: **Mabait na bata si Mario.** Mario is a nice child. *Mababait* **na mga bata sina Mario.** Mario and others *are nice children*.
Linkers	Words that are used to connect one word to another. EXAMPLE: **Mabait** *na* **bata** Nice kid, child **Bata***ng* **mabait** Nice kid, child

Reduplication	A process by which the root of a word, or part of it, is repeated. In the example below, the reduplication of the consonant and vowel combination **ba** makes the adjective plural.
	EXAMPLE: **Mabait na bata si Mario.** Mario is a good child. <u>**Mababait**</u> **na mga bata sina Mario.** Mario and others are good children.

Examining Form

The sentences below illustrate the grammar patterns that are presented in this lesson. Review the sentences below and complete the tasks that follow. Discuss your answers with a partner. Consult the following section to check your answers.

1. **Matalino at masipag siya.**
   Matatalino at masisipag sila.
2. **Maganda at mahinhin si Nanay.**
   Magaganda at mahihinhin sina Nanay at Lola.
3. **Nakaberdeng bestida at nakasalamin si Lola**
4. **Naka-asul na bestida ako.**
5. **Masipag na bata ang kapatid ko.**
6. **Pilyong bata ang lalaki.**

a. Underline all the modifiers and/or descriptive words in the sentences above and circle the linkers.
b. When is the linker **-ng** used? When is the linker **na** used?
c. Look at the first two examples. The modifiers **matatalino, masisipag, magaganda,** and **mahihinhin** are the inflected forms of **matalino, masipag, maganda,** and **mahinhin.** When do you inflect adjectives?
d. In numbers 3 and 4, notice that some nouns and adjectives have the prefix **naka-.** What happens when this prefix is attached?

I. Adjectives and Linkers

Whenever adjectives are used to modify common nouns, linkers follow or are added to the end of either the noun or the modifier. Below are the three linkers used in Tagalog:

na	follows a noun or a modifier when it ends in a consonant.
	EXAMPLE: **matangos** *na* **ilong** pointed nose
-ng	is attached to the end of the noun or modifier if it ends in a vowel.
	EXAMPLE: **mahaba***ng* **buhok** long hair
-g	is attached to the end of the noun or modifier if it ends in **n.**
	EXAMPLE: **ngipi***ng* **maputi** white teeth

Grammar Presentation

Adjectives and Linkers

1. When an adjective is the predicate of a sentence, you can use the predicational sentence structure. To create this sentence, place your adjective in the predicate position, then add the subject in **ang** form.

Adjective as Predicate	
Predicate	**Subject**
Mahaba	ang buhok niya.

EXAMPLES:
Mahaba ang buhok niya. Her hair is long.
Makapal ba ang kilay ng lalaki? Are the man's eyebrows thick?
Maliit ang mga tenga ni Maria. Maria's ears are small.

2. There are two word orders when forming an adjectival phrase: a) NOUN + LINKER + ADJECTIVE; b) ADJECTIVE + LINKER + NOUN. As stated above, the linkers **na**, **-ng**, and **-g** are used to connect the adjectives (modifier) and the nouns (modified).

Adjective as Modifier					
Predicate	**Subject**				
	Marker	**Adjective**	**Linker**	**Noun**	
Kapatid niya	ang ang mga	maingay	na	lalaki.	
		mayaman	-g	lalaki.	
		maginoo	-ng	lalaki.	
		Noun	**Linker**	**Adjective**	
		lalaki	-ng	maingay.	

EXAMPLES:
a) **Kapatid niya** *ang maingay na lalaki.* The loud guy is his/her brother.
b) **Kapatid niya** *ang lalaking maingay.*

a) **Kaibigan mo ba** *ang mahinhing babae?* Is the refined woman your friend?
b) **Kaibigan mo ba** *ang babaeng mahinhin?*

a) **Pinsan ko po** *ang mabait na bata* The nice kid is my cousin, sir.
b) **Pinsan ko po** *ang batang mabait.*

3. There are two ways to make the adjectival phrase plural: a) by reduplication of the consonant vowel of the root word of the adjective; and b) by placing the plural marker **mga** before the noun or adjective. Note that reduplication can only be used when adjectives have a **ma-** prefix.

   To make the subject plural using reduplication, reduplicate the first syllable or consonant and vowel combination of the root word. The root word in this case is **bait**. **Ma-** is a prefix that turns a root word to an adjective.

   EXAMPLES: **Mabait** → **Ma ba bait** → **Mababait**

   To make the subject plural using **mga**, add **mga** after the marker **ang**.
   EXAMPLES: **Ang mabait na bata** → **Ang *mga* mabait na bata.**

Pluralization	
Reduplication	**Mga**
Pinsan ko ang mababait na bata.	**Pinsan ko ang mga mabait na bata.**

Here are some examples of the two ways to make the subject plural:

a) **Pinsan ko ang mga mabait na bata.** The nice children are my cousins.
b) **Pinsan ko ang mababait na bata.**

a) **Kapatid ni Martha ang mga matangkad na lalaki.** The tall guys are Martha's brothers.
b) **Kapatid ni Martha ang matatangkad na lalaki.**

a) **Kaibigan mo ba ang mga magandang babae?** Are the beautiful women your friends?
b) **Kaibigan mo ba ang magagandang babae?**

4. When the subject of the adjectival phrase is a pronoun, the word order changes. The example below shows how to create this sentence structure.

Pronoun as Subject			
Adjective	**Pronoun**	**Linker**	**Noun**
Mabait	ako tayo kami ka kayo siya sila	**-ng**	**kapatid.**

EXAMPLES:
Mabait akong kapatid. I am a good brother.
Mabuti ba siyang kaibigan? Is he/she a good friend?
Magalang po siyang bata. He is a polite kid, sir/madam.

5. To form a negative sentence, you use either of the two structures outlined below, depending on the subject:

a. **Hindi** + SUBJECT (PRONOUN) + PREDICATE (ADJECTIVAL PHRASE)
b. **Hindi** + PREDICATE (ADJECTIVAL PHRASE) + SUBJECT (PROPER NAME/COMMON NOUN)

Negative Sentence				
Hindi	**Subject Pronoun**	**Adjective**	**Linker**	**Noun**
Hindi	ako tayo kami ka kayo siya sila	**masama**	**-ng**	**kaibigan.**
Hindi	**Adjective**	**Linker**	**Noun**	**Subject Proper/Common Noun**
Hindi	**mabait**	**na**	**anak**	**si Janice.** **sina Janice at Minda.** **ang bata.** **ang mga bata.**

EXAMPLES:

Hindi siya mabait na kaibigan. He/She is not a good friend.

Hindi mabait na kaibigan si Pedro. Pedro is not a good friend.

Hindi siya mabait na bata. He is not a nice kid.

Hindi mabait na bata ang anak niya. Her/His child is not a nice kid.

Grammar Notes

1. Linkers are not necessary when the adjective functions as a predicate.
   Masipag ang lalaki. The man is hardworking.

2. Use linkers when the adjective modifies a noun.
   Taga-LA <u>ang mabait na lalaki.</u> The nice man is from LA.

3. The adjectival phrase can be structured in two ways:
   a. ANG MARKER + NOUN + LINKER + ADJECTIVE
      Ang estudyanteng mabait
   b. ANG MARKER + ADJECTIVE + LINKER + NOUN
      Ang mabait na estudyante

4. There are two ways to make the adjectival phrase plural:
   a. Reduplication, which is to reduplicate the first syllable of the root word
      Ang mababait na estudyante.
      ***Ang tatahimik na estudyante.** (incorrect)

      → Note: Reduplication can be used only for adjectives with a **ma-** prefix.

   b. **Mga**: The second way is to add **mga** after the marker **ang**.
      Ang mga mabait na estudyante.

II. Naka- Modifiers

The prefix **naka-** expresses the idea of wearing the article of clothing, accessory, or color that is designated by the noun that **naka-** attaches to.

naka + <u>any type of clothing</u>
naka + <u>any type of accessories</u>
naka + <u>any color</u>

naka + <u>clothing</u>
naka<u>pantalon</u>   wearing jeans/pants
naka<u>bestida</u>   wearing a dress

naka + <u>accessories</u>
naka<u>salamin</u>   wearing glasses
naka<u>kuwintas</u>   wearing a necklace

naka + <u>color</u>
naka<u>puti</u>   in white; wearing white
naka<u>itim</u>   in black; wearing black

Naka- Modifiers

To create sentences using the **naka-** prefix, simply put **naka-** and the clothing/accessory/color word in the predicate position. This predicate is followed by the subject marker **ang** and the subject.

Predicational Sentence	
Predicate	**Subject**
Nakapantalon	
Nakahikaw	**ang** phrase.
	ang pronoun.
Nakaputi	

EXAMPLES:

Nakapantalon si Lolo. Grandfather is wearing pants.
Nakadilaw ba si Marcus? Is Marcus in yellow?
Hindi ho nakasumbrero ang kapatid ko. My sibling is not wearing a hat, sir.

1. **Naka-** does not mean anything by itself and must always be attached to a noun that designates any form of clothing or clothing accessory.
   Nakapantalon ang lalaki. The guy is wearing jeans.
   *****Naka ang lalaki.** (incorrect)

Practice

I. Speaking Practice

This is an information gap activity. You must work with a partner. You will be Student A, and your partner will be Student B and will use Worksheet B. The illustration below shows several people and their names. Choose one of the people. Without disclosing the name, describe to your partner how that person appears in the drawing, using **naka-** modifiers and what you have learned from previous lessons. The object is to have your partner guess the name of the person you're describing. Take turns.

Worksheet A for Student A

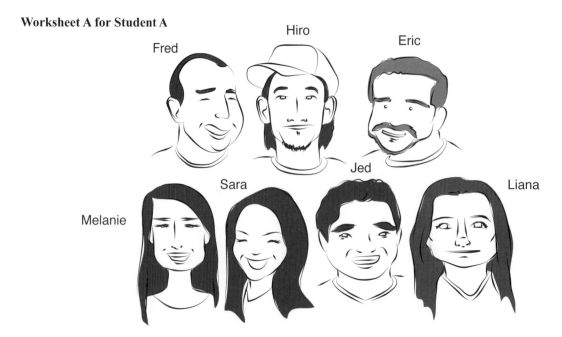

Worksheet B for Student B

Use the boxes in this worksheet to write down the information your partner is giving you to describe each person. Afterwards, try to guess the name of the person your partner is describing.

II. Reading Practice

Read the personal ads from two different people and answer the Reading Comprehension questions in Tagalog.

Message 1

Kumusta kayo? Ako si Jayson. Dalawampu't tatlong taon na ako. Nakatira ako sa Makati. Estudyante ako sa Unibersidad ng De La Salle. Abogasiya ang kurso ko. Maikli ang buhok ko, makapal ang kilay ko, matangos ang ilong ko, at singkit ang mga mata ko.

Gusto ko ng mahinhing mga babae at ayaw ko ang mga suplada.

Message 2

Magandang umaga! Sandra ang pangalan ko. Tatlumpu't isang taon na ako. Kulot ang buhok ko at maputi at matangkad ako. Ngayon, nakatira ako sa Maynila kasama ang isa kong anak. Brandon ang pangalan niya. Walong taon na siya at nag-aaral siya sa Sacred Heart Elementary School.

Gusto ko ang magalang na mga lalaki at ayaw ko ang mga tahimik na lalaki.

Reading Comprehension

Fill in the blanks with the correct in formation according to the two messages above.

1. **Saan nakatira si Jayson?**

_____

2. **Ilarawan si Jayson.**

_____

3. **Ano ang gusto at ayaw ni Jayson?**

_____

4. **Ilang taon na si Sandra?**

_____

5. **Ilarawan si Sandra.**

_____

6. **Ano ang pangalan ng anak ni Sandra?**

_____

7. **Ano ang gusto at ayaw ni Sandra?**

_____

III. Writing Practice

Now, let's put together everything we've learned so far in this lesson. Use the space below to write your own personal advertisement for a dating agency. You can place your photo or sketch yourself in the box. Use adjectives to describe yourself and your personality.

```
+-----------------------------+
|                             |
|                             |
|                             |
|                             |
|                             |
|                             |
+-----------------------------+
```

_____

_____

_____

_____

IV. Listening Practice

 Now let's practice listening. The audio file (05–2) describes Melinda and Edgar. Listen carefully to each description. In the chart below, note down the adjectives given for each person's traits (**katangian**), *hair* (**buhok**), *eyes* (**mata**) *nose* (**ilong**), *height* (**taas**), and *body built* (**katawan**).

> **Word Bank**
>
> **matangkad** tall
> **maliit** short

Pangalan	Katangian	Buhok	Mata	Ilong	Taas	Katawan
Melinda						
Edgar						

Pag-uusap Tungkol sa Pamilya

Talking about Family

An Overview of Lesson 6

This lesson combines all the vocabulary and grammar rules that we have studied and learned so far from Lessons 1, 2, 3, 4, and 5.

Objectives

• Read and write short biographical texts
• Ask and answer basic biographical questions about people

Vocabulary

• Nouns	• Existential Particles	• Markers
• Names of the Months	• Prefixes	• Idioms and Expressions
• Adjectives	• Enclitics	

Reading Text: Ang Pamilya ni Josie *Josie's Family*

Reading Comprehension

Activities

Activity 1: Interview
Activity 2: Speaking Practice
Activity 3: Interview

Grammar

Definition of terms: Existential Particles

Examining Form

I. The Existential Particles **May**, **Mayroon**, and **Wala**
    Grammar Presentation: Sentence Structures with **May**
    Grammar Notes
    Grammar Presentation: Sentence Structures with **Mayroon** and **Wala**
    Grammar Notes
II. The Prefix **Ika-**
    Grammar Notes

Practice

I. Speaking Practice   II. Reading Practice   III. Writing Practice   IV. Listening Practice

Vocabulary 🎧 (06–1)

The vocabulary will help you speak about your family and home and participate in the activities in this lesson. Memorize the vocabulary words before proceeding to the Reading Text.

Nouns

alaga	pet
aso	dog
baboy	pig
bahay-bakasyunan	vacation house
ibon	bird
isda	fish
kabayo	horse
kotse	car
kuneho	rabbit
loro	parrot
manok	chicken
matalik na kaibigan	best friend
pagong	turtle
pera	money
pusa	cat
tandang	rooster
tao	person

Markers

noon(g)	past time marker

Names of the Months

Enero	January
Pebrero	February
Marso	March
Abril	April
Mayo	May
Hunyo	June
Hulyo	July
Agosto	August
Setyembre	September
Oktubre	October
Nobyembre	November
Disyembre	December

Adjectives

mahirap	poor
malinis	clean
malungkot	sad
marumi	dirty
masaya	happy; cheerful
masipag	hard working
matapat	honest
matiyaga	patient
mayaman	rich
sinungaling	liar
tamad	lazy

Existential Particles

may	to have; there is/are/was
mayroon	to have; there is/are/was
wala	to not have; there is/are/was no

Prefixes

ika-	turns a cardinal number into an ordinal number

Enclitics

daw/raw	they say
din/rin	also; either
pa	still

Idioms and Expressions

Most of the expressions below should now be familiar to you. In previous lessons we have analyzed and studied their grammatical structure. One of the goals of this book is for you to master asking such basic biographical questions without having to think about their form. Here is a brief review of the most common questions that might occur when you meet someone.

Ano ang mga gusto at ayaw mo? What are your likes and dislikes?

Ano ang mga pangalan ng mga kapatid mo? What are the names of your siblings?

Ano ang mga pangalan ng mga alaga mo? What are the names of your pets?

Ano ang pangalan ng mga magulang mo? What are the names of your parents?

Ano ang trabaho nila? What do they do for a living?

Ilang taon ka na? How old are you?

Ilan ang kapatid mo? How many siblings do you have?

Ilarawan mo sila. Describe them.

May kapatid ka ba? Do you have siblings?

May mga alaga ka ba? Do you have pets?

Mayroon ka bang trabaho? Do you (have) work?

May matalik na kaibigan ka ba? Do you have a best friend?

Saan ka nakatira? Where do you live?

Saan ka nag-aaral? Where do you go to school?

Saan ka nagtatrabaho? Where do you work?

Sino ang matalik mong kaibigan? Who is your best friend?

Taga saan ka? Where are you from?

Reading Text: Ang Pamilya ni Josie *Josie's Family*

The text below utilizes some of the vocabulary words that you learned in the preceding lessons. Read the text and complete the Reading Comprehension activity.

Siya si Josie. Ipinanganak siya noong ikadalawampu ng Agosto. Nakatira siya ngayon sa Cavite kasama ang pamilya niya. Mayroon siyang masipag na asawa at dalawang mababait na anak. Eric ang pangalan ng asawa niya. Apatnapung taon na si Eric at nagtatrabaho siya sa St. Mary's Academy. Sina Chino at Sophia ang mga anak nina Josie at Eric. Siyam na taon na si Chino at pitong taon naman si Sophia. Mayroong mahaba at kulot na buhok si Sophia at may maikling buhok naman si Chino.

Mayroon ding alagang aso sina Josie. Bantay ang pangalan niya. Maliit si Bantay at may malaki siyang tenga. Wala silang pusa.

Reading Comprehension

For each of the following statements about the reading, place a check mark in the appropriate blank, depending on whether the statement is true, **Tama**, or false, **Mali**.

	TAMA	MALI
1. Josie is thirty-eight and she lives with her family in Cavite.	_____	_____
2. Josie is married to Eric who is a student in St. Mary's Academy.	_____	_____
3. They have two kids, Chino and Sophia.	_____	_____
4. Sophia has short hair.	_____	_____
5. They have a dog named Bantay, who is short and has small ears.	_____	_____

Activities

Activity 1

Interview your classmates to find out whether they have the items listed in the first column of the table below. Model your interview using the sample dialogue, and record your classmates' responses. At the end of the activity, tally who has and who does not have the items listed in the first column.

EXAMPLE:

S1: **Mayroon ka bang <u>aso</u>?** Do you have a dog?

S2: **Oo, may <u>aso</u> ako.** Yes, I have a dog.

or **Wala. Wala akong <u>aso</u>.** No. I don't have a dog.

Alaga/Bagay/Kaibigan	Mayroon/May	Wala
1. aso		
2. pusa		
3. kotse		
4. bahay-bakasyunan		
5. matalik na kaibigan		

Activity 2

Work with a partner. Study the table below, and, using the existential particles **may** and **wala**, discuss who has or does not have the pets listed in the first column. You may need the enclitics **din** and **rin** to indicate whether Edison, they, grandfather or Jose's child own the same pet. A smiley face indicates possession, and a sad face indicates non-possession. Use the examples to model your sentences. Don't forget the linkers!

EXAMPLE:

S1: **Walang <u>pagong</u> si Edison.** Edison has no turtle.

S2: **Wala rin silang <u>pagong</u>.** They also don't have a turtle.

S1: **May <u>pagong</u> si Lolo.** Grandpa has a turtle.

S2: **May <u>pagong</u> din ang anak ni Jose.** Jose's child has a turtle too.

Bagay	Edison	They	Grandfather	Jose's child
1. pagong	☹	☹	☺	☺
2. tandang	☹	☹	☺	☹
3. isda	☺	☹	☹	☺
4. pusa	☺	☺	☹	☺
5. aso	☺	☺	☺	☹

Activity 3

Find a classmate for each month of the year and record their names and birthdates in the table. Use the example to model your interview.

EXAMPLE:

S1: **Kailan ka ipinanganak?** When were you born?

S2: **Ipinanganak ako noong ikadalawampu ng Enero.** I was born on the 20th of January.

Petsa	Pangalan at Petsa	Petsa	Pangalan at Pesta
Enero		Hulyo	
Pebrero		Agosto	
Marso		Oktubre	
Abril		Setyembre	
Mayo		Nobyembre	
Hunyo		Disyembre	

Grammar

Definition of Terms

Existential Particles	Particles that express the existence of something or the state of having something.
	EXAMPLE:
	May aso sa bahay. There is a dog in the house.
	May aso ako. I have a dog.

Examining Form

The sentences below illustrate the grammar patterns that are presented in this lesson. Read the sentences and complete the tasks that follow. Discuss your answers with the class.

1. **Mayroon siyang masipag na asawa at dalawang mababait na anak.**
   Matatalino at masisipag sila.
2. **Mayroong mahaba at kulot na buhok si Sophia.**
3. **Mayroon ding aso sina Josie.**
4. **May masipag siyang asawa at dalawang mababait na anak.**
5. **May mahaba at kulot na buhok si Sophia.**
6. **May aso din sina Josie.**
7. **Wala silang pusa.**
8. **Ipinanganak siya noong ikadalawampu ng Agosto.**
9. **Ipinanganak ang kapatid ko noong ikadalawampu't apat ng Abril.**

   a. Underline all the existential particles and circle the linkers if there are any.
   b. When do we use linkers? When do we not use linkers?
   c. What is the difference between **may** and **mayroon**?

I. The Existential Particles **May, Mayroon,** and **Wala**

In Tagalog grammar books, **may** and **mayroon** are called existential particles because they express the existence of something. **May** and **mayroon** are the equivalent of *there is*, *there are*, or *has/have* in English. Although they mean the same thing, they are not interchangeable in a sentence, as the grammar lesson will show. The negative form of these particles is **wala**, which means the non-existence of something. **Wala** denies the location, existence, or possession of something. It is the equivalent of *none, nothing, absent,* or *there is none* in English. Existential particles are classified as pseudo verbs in Tagalog for the simple reason that **may**, **mayroon**, and **wala** have some verbal qualities but do not inflect for aspect, and aspect is one of the major properties of Tagalog verbs. Though they can be translated into English by the verbs *is* and *have*, the equivalent in Tagalog is not a full-fledged verb.

may/mayroon	has/have there (is, are, was, were, will be)
wala	doesn't have/don't have there (is no, are no, was no, were no, will be no) none/nothing

Note:
- **May** is the proper spelling. **Me** is a colloquial expression and used only in conversation.
- **Mayroon** is the proper spelling. **Meron** is a colloquial expression and used only in conversation.
- **Wala** is the negative form of **mayroon** and **may**.

We will first study the sentence structures associated with **may** and then with **mayroon** and **wala**.

Grammar Presentation

Sentence Structures with **May**

1. **May** can be used in sentences with a subject, as shown in the first sentence below, or in sentences where there is no subject, as in the second sentence.

May (has/have)	Object Phrase (Noun)	Subject (Possessor)
May	<u>aso</u>	**ang** phrase. **ang** pronoun.

May (there is/are)	Object Phrase (Noun)	Prepositional Phrase
May	<u>aso</u>	<u>sa bahay.</u>

EXAMPLES:
May bahay-bakasyunan ako sa Baguio. I have a vacation house in Baguio.
May ibon sa balkonahe. There is a bird on the balcony.

2. The first sentence below illustrates how to ask a question with **may** using the second-person singular pronoun **ka** and the question particle **ba**. In this sentence structure, other enclitics can occupy the same position as **ba**, as for example **raw** (they say) in the second sentence.

May (has/have)	Object Phrase (Noun)	Prepositional Phrase/ Subject/Possessor	Enclitic
May	pusa	ka	ba? raw/daw. din/rin. na.

EXAMPLES:
May pera ka ba? Do you have money?
May kotse ka raw. They say you have a car.

3. The chart below illustrates the placement of enclitics in a **may** question. Note that the enclitic is in the third position after **may** and the noun or object phrase.

May (there is/are)	Object Phrase (Noun)	Enclitic	Prepositional Phrase/ Subject/Possessor
May	kotse	po ba raw/daw din/rin na	ang phrase./? ang pronoun./? sa garahe ninyo./?

EXAMPLES:

May alaga din po si Mike. Mike has a pet too, sir/madam.

May ibon po sa balko-nahe ninyo. There is a bird on your balcony, sir/madam.

Grammar Notes

1. **May** and **mayroon** are synonyms. However, **mayroon** can stand by itself. **May** must always be fol-lowed by a noun.

    Q: **May tao ba sa labas?** Is there a person outside?
    A: **Oo, mayroon.** Yes, there is.
    A: *Oo, may. (incorrect)

2. When the possessor or subject is not mentioned, the meaning conveyed by **may** and **mayroon** is "there is/are" rather than "has/have." Compare the two sentences below:

    May kotse ako. I have a car.
    May kotse sa bahay There is a car at the house.

3. Enclitics always come after the first unit of a sentence. However, when several enclitics occur at the same time, there is an order of priority among enclitics, which is as follows:

1	**na**	already, anymore
1	**pa**	still, yet
2	**din/rin**	also
3	**daw/raw**	they say, supposedly
4	**po**	polite particle
5	**ba**	question marker

    Note that **din** and **daw** are used when the preceding word ends with a consonant, while **rin** and **raw** are used when the preceding word ends with a vowel.

    May aso pa rin daw po ba kayo? Dod they say you still have a dog, sir/madam?
    May aso na raw po ba kayo? Did they say you have a dog already, sir/madam?
    *May aso ba po din kayo? (incorrect)

    In the first sentence, **May aso** is the first unit of the sentence. The word order of the enclitics **pa, rin, daw, po ba** is fixed. (Notice that the translation of **daw** in English is at the beginning of the sentence.) Likewise, in the second sentence, the word order of **na raw po ba** cannot occur in any other order. We will study enclitics more fully in a later chapter.

4. **May** is always immediately followed by an object phrase. The subject or the possessor always oc-curs after the object phrase.

    May isda sa itaas. There are fish upstairs.
    May isda si Mike. Mike has a fish.
    *May sa itaas isda. (incorrect)
    *May si Mike trabaho. (incorrect)

5. The object phrase does not require the use of markers.
> **May kotse sa bahay.** There is a car at the house.
> **May kotse si Mike.** Mike has a car.
> ***May ang kotse sa labas.** (incorrect)
> ***May ang trabaho si Mike.** (incorrect)

6. The possessor is always an **ang** phrase.
> **May bahay-bakasyunan <u>si Mike</u>.** Mike has a vacation house.
> **May bahay-bakasyunan <u>ang lalaki</u>.** The man has a vacation house.

Grammar Presentation

Sentence Structures with **Mayroon** and **Wala**

1. Unlike **may**, **mayroon** and **wala** require linkers between them and the following noun or object phrase. The chart shows the elements of **mayroon** and **wala** sentences and where the linkers occur.

Mayroon (has/have) Wala (doesn't have)	Linker	Object Phrase (Noun)	Subject (Possessor)	
Mayroon Wala	-g -ng	<u>bahay-bakasyunan</u>	ang <u>lalaki</u>. ang mga <u>lalaki</u>.	si <u>Patrick</u>. sina <u>Pat at Mike</u>.
Mayroon (there is/are) Wala (there is/are no)	**Linker**	**Object Phrase (Noun)**	**Prepositional Phrase**	
Mayroon Wala	-g -ng	<u>kotse</u>	sa <u>garahe</u>.	

EXAMPLES:
Mayroong aso sina Mike at Carlos. Mike and Carlos have a dog.
Mayroong pagong sa garahe. There is a turtle in the garage.
Walang alagang aso si Maria. Maria doesn't have a pet dog.

2. In the following chart, the enclitic comes second in the sentence and the linker is attached to the enclitic.

Mayroon	Linker	Object Phrase (Noun)	Object Phrase (Noun)	Subject (Possessor)
Mayroon Wala	po ba na	-ng	<u>kotse</u>	ang <u>lalaki</u>./? ang mga <u>lalaki</u>./? si <u>Patrick</u>./? sina <u>Patrick at Mike</u>./?
Mayroon/Wala	**Particle**	**Linker**	**Object Phrase (Noun)**	**Prepositional Phrase**
Mayroon Wala	po ba na	-ng	<u>kotse</u>	sa <u>bahay</u>./?

EXAMPLES:
Mayroon daw loro ang tita mo. They say your aunt has a parrot.
Wala pong tao sa bahay. There's no one in the house, sir/madam.
Wala nang pera si Miguel. Miguel doesn't have money anymore.

3. In the chart below, **mayroon** and **wala** are immediately followed by the subject/topic in the form of an **ang** pronoun. In this structure, the linker is attached to the pronoun.

Mayroon (has/have) Wala (doesn't have)	Subject (Possessor) Pronoun	Linker	Object Phrase (Noun)
Mayroon Wala	ako tayo kami ka kayo siya sila	-ng	<u>bahay-bakasyunan.</u>

4. In the last word order, an enclitic follows **mayroon** or **wala**, and then the subject/topic follows in the form of an **ang** pronoun to which the linker is attached, followed by the object.

Mayroon/Wala	Enclitic	Subject (Possessor) Pronoun	Linker	Object Phrase (Noun)

Mayroon
 	
Wala
	po
	ba
	raw/daw
	din/rin
	na
		ako tayo
		       kami
		       kayo
		siya sila
			-ng	<u>kotse./?</u>

EXAMPLES:

Mayroon po ba kayong bahay-bakasyunan sa Subic? Do you have a vacation house in Subic?

Mayroon din bang mga manok sa bahay ni Lola? Are there chickens also in grandmother's house?

*Walang na akong pera. (incorrect) I don't have money anymore.

Grammar Notes

1. **Mayroon** and **wala** pull the enclitics and pronouns toward the beginning of the sentence, much like **hindi**. **May** does not.
   Mayroon na siyang pusa. He/She already has a cat.
   Wala na siyang pusa. He/She doesn't have a cat anymore.
   *Walang pusa na siya. (incorrect)

2. In most cases, linkers must be used with **mayroon** and **wala**. When both enclitics and pronouns are used to modify the noun, a linker is attached to the end of the word that comes right before the noun.
   Mayroon na siya*ng* pusa. He/She already has a cat.
   Wala na siya*ng* pusa. He/She doesn't have a cat anymore.
   *Wala*ng* na siya pusa. (incorrect)

   Mayroon na*ng* pusa si Mike. Mike already has a cat.
   Wala na*ng* pusa si Mike. Mike no longer has a cat.
   *Mayroo*ng* na pusa si Mike. (incorrect)

   The first set of examples above uses the pronoun **siya** to indicate who has or doesn't have a cat, while the second set of examples uses the noun **Mike** to indicate who has or doesn't have a cat. In both set of examples, the placement of the linker **-ng** is determined by the position of the noun. The pronoun comes before the object being possessed (which is the cat), whereas the noun comes after the object.

3. If the pronoun or enclitic ends with a consonant, there is no need to use a linker.

> **Mayroon daw pusa si Mike.** They say Mike has a cat.
> **Wala raw kotse ang lalaki.** They say the man has no car.
> *Mayroon raw na pusa si Mike. (incorrect)

II. The Prefix Ika-

1. The prefix **ika-** is affixed to numbers to form ordinal numbers. The chart below shows ordinal numbers from first to the twentieth, then increments of ten, from twenty-first to other ordinal numbers up to ninety-eighth.

Ordinal Numbers							
Una	1st	ikalabing-isa	11th	ikadalawampu	20th	ikadalawampu't isa	21st
Ikalawa	2nd	ikalabindalawa	12th	ikatatlumpu	30th	ikatatlumpu't dalawa	32nd
ikatlo	3rd	ikalabintatlo	13th	ikaapatnapu	40th	ikaapatnapu't tatlo	43rd
ikaapat	4th	ikalabing-apat	14th	ikalimampu	50th	ikalimampu't apat	54th
ikalima	5th	ikalabinlima	15th	ikaanimnapu	60th	ikaanimnapu't lima	65th
ikaanim	6th	ikalabing-anim	16th	ikapitumpu	70th	ikapitumpu't anim	76th
ikapito	7th	ikalabimpito	17th	ikawalumpu	80th	ikawalumpu't pito	87th
ikawalo	8th	ikalabingwalo	18th	ikasiyamnapu	90th	ikasiyamnapu't walo	98th
ikasiyam	9th	ikalabinsiyam	19th				
ikasampu	10th						

2. Below is an example of a date using the ordinal number along with the name of the month, in this case August.

Ordinal Number	Ng	Date
Ikadalawampu	ng	Agosto

EXAMPLES:
> **Ikapito ng Enero** the seventh of January
> **Ikadalawampu't walo ng Abril** the twenty-eighth of April

3. The chart below shows a predicational sentence stating the birthday of someone indicated by an **ang** pronoun or an **ang** phrase. This type of sentence can also serve as a response to the question "When were you born?"

Verb	Subject	Adverbial Phrase
Ipinanganak	**ang** pronoun **ang** phrase	noong ikadalawampu ng Agosto.

EXAMPLES:
Kailan ka ipinanganak? When were you born?
Ipinanganak ako noong ikadalawampu't apat ng Abril. I was born on the twenty-fourth of April.

Grammar Notes

1. The use of Tagalog numbers for dates is typically viewed as formal and most often reserved for print, TV, and radio and such formal occasions as announcements in church. In everyday speech, Spanish numbers are usually preferred instead. We will learn more about this in later lessons.
   Ipinanganak siya noong ikalabing-isa ng Enero. He/She was born on the eleventh of January.
   Ipinanganak siya noong a-onse ng Enero. He/She was born on the eleventh of January.

Practice

I. Speaking

Translate the following questions into Tagalog using the spaces provided below. Afterwards, interview a classmate using these questions. Record the classmate's answers in the space provided.

EXAMPLE:
S1: **Ano ang pangalan mo?**   S2: **Brandon ang pangalan ko.**
A: **Brandon ang pangalan niya.**

1. What is your name? _____

   A: _____

2. Where are you from? _____

   A: _____

3. Where do you live? _____

   A: _____

4. How old are you? _____

   A: _____

5. Where do you go to school? _____

   A: _____

6. Do you have a job? _____

   A: _____

   (If yes) Where do you work? _____

7. What are your parents' names? _____

A: _____

8. What do they do for a living? _____

A: _____

9. Describe them. _____

A: _____

10. Do you have siblings? _____

A: _____

11. How many siblings do you have? _____

A: _____

12. What are their names? _____

A: _____

13. Describe them. _____

A: _____

14. Do you have a best friend? _____

A: _____

15. Who is your best friend? _____

A: _____

16. Describe him/her. _____

A: _____

17. Do you have pets? _____

A: _____

18. What are their names? _____

A: _____

19. Describe them. _____

    A: _____

20. What are your likes and dislikes? _____

    A: _____

II. Reading

Read the dialogue between Cherry, Aling Maria, and Marc and then answer the Reading Comprehension questions in Tagalog.

```
                        Word Bank

                         pero but
              Maiwan ko na muna kayo. I'll get going.
```

Cherry: **Nanay, ito po ang kaibigan ko, si Marc. Marc, ito ang nanay ko.**
Marc: **Kumusta po kayo, Tita?**
Aling Maria: **Mabuti naman. Taga saan ang pamilya mo, Marc?**
Marc: **Taga-Bicol po.**
Aling Maria: **May kamag-anak ka ba dito sa Maynila?**
Marc: **Opo. Nandito po ang pamilya ko.**
Aling Maria: **May mga kapatid ka ba?**
Marc: **Opo. Pero nasa Bicol po siya.**
Aling Maria: **Mayroon din ba kayong bahay sa Bicol?**
Marc: **Wala po kaming bahay sa Bicol. Nakatira po ang kapatid ko sa bahay ng lola ko.**
Aling Maria. **Talaga? O sige. Maiwan ko na muna kayo. Magpupunta na ako sa trabaho.**
Marc: **O sige po tita.**

Reading Comprehension

1. **Ano ang pangalan ng kaibigan ni Cherry?**

   _____

2. **Taga saan ang pamilya ng kaibigan ni Cherry?**

   _____

3. **May kamag-anak ba ang kaibigan ni Cherry sa Maynila?**

   _____

4. **Mayroon bang kapatid ang kaibigan ni Cherry?**

_____

5. **Mayroon bang bahay ang kaibigan ni Cherry sa Bicol?**

_____

III. Writing

Using the existential particles **may**, **mayroon**, and **wala**, write five to ten complete sentences based on the information in the chart on a separate piece of paper.

```
Word Bank

libro book
```

Name	Jose Rizal
Date of birth	June 19th
Place of birth	Calamba, Laguna
Parents	Francisco at Teodora
Number of siblings	Ten
University	University of Santo Tomas
Major	Medicine
Famous works	Two books
Friend	Ferdinand Bluementritt

IV. Listening Practice

 Listen to audio file (06–2) and write the correct information in the spaces provided below.

Pangalan	Kaarawan (Birthday)	Mayroon	Wala
Milo			
Edna			
Cory			
Antonio			

UNIT 3
MGA GAWAIN
Activities

There are plenty of things to do in the Philippines, but among social activities one of the most popular, especially to those who live in or near large cities, is going to the mall. Sure, shopping at the local **palengke**, or market, can be a great cultural experience, but for many urban Filipinos the local mall is the place to be. Malls have replaced the Spanish-built plazas as the central gathering spots for the community, and they attract both tourists and locals. Everything can be found there, from chic art galleries and expensive restaurants to discount stores. And where else can Filipinos escape the intense humidity and the seasonal typhoons than in nicely air-conditioned, water-tight facilities?

"Malling!" A favorite pastime of Filipinos

Local produce sold at the mall

What's remarkable about these shopping centers in the Philippines is their sheer size. Shoe Mart (SM), the largest shopping mall and retail operator in the Philippines, built Megamall, a 331,679 square-meter (3,570,163 square-foot) mall in the Ortigas Center, in 1991. At that time, it was the largest mall in the country and one of the largest ones in the world. It can accommodate a maximum of 4 million people, and there is even an ice skating rink inside—an attraction that one may not expect in a tropical developing country, where the average income of people is limited. Since then, though, SM NORTH EDSA and SM Mall of Asia have surpassed Megamall in size and popularity.

Another popular activity among Filipinos is karaoke. You can find karaoke bars, both high-class and makeshift, all over the country. Karaoke sessions are usually part of family gatherings at clubs and even in the local pool hall. Of course, **pulutan**, or bar food, and lots of beer accompany the karaoke on these occasions. But be mindful, Filipinos take karaoke very seriously, and it should not be seen as mere entertainment. For example, Frank Sinatra's rendition of "My Way" has become a karaoke standard. If you sing it and don't render it correctly, habitués of karaoke clubs and other patrons who see themselves as aficionados won't hesitate to boo or chide you.

Filipinos line dancing for fun and exercise

Singing at a karaoke bar

Dancing is also very popular among Filipinos, and this has been the case since the proliferation of American culture since the early 1900s. Filipinos are known as being among the best dancers in the world, From Latin to ballroom to hip hop, the nation's top dancers regularly compete in some of the most prestigious international dance competitions, and dance clubs are packed with young Filipinos looking for a good time.

Mga Gawain sa Araw-araw

Daily Activities

An Overview of Lesson 7

Objectives
• Be able to talk about daily activities
• Be able to talk about past and future activities

Vocabulary

• Days of the Week	• Adverbs of Time	• Enclitics
• **Mag-** Verbs	• Time	• Idioms and Expressions
• **-Um-** and **Ma-** Verbs	• Adjectives	
• Prefix	• Markers	

Dialogue: Ang Buhay May-asawa *Married Life*

Reading Comprehension

Activities

Activity 1: My Schedule
Activity 2: Interview
Activity 3: Mike's Schedule

Grammar

Definition of Terms: Actor, Focus of the Verb, Direct Object, Transitive Verb, Intransitive Verb, and Inflect

Examining Form

I. **Mag-** Verbs
    Grammar Presentation: Sentence Structures with **Mag-**
    Grammar Notes
II. Telling Time (Formal)
    Grammar Notes

Practice

I.   Speaking Practice
II. Reading Practice
III. Writing Practice
IV. Listening Practice

Vocabulary 🎧 (07–1)

The vocabulary will help you speak about your daily activities in the present, future, and past and participate in the activities in this lesson. Memorize the vocabulary words before proceeding to the dialogue.

Days of the Week

Lunes	Monday
Martes	Tuesday
Miyerkules/	Wednesday
Miyerkoles	
Huwebes	Thursday
Biyernes	Friday
Sabado	Saturday
Linggo	Sunday

Mag- Verbs

mag-ahit	to shave
mag-almusal	to have breakfast
magbasa ng diyaryo	to read newspaper
magbihis	to change clothes
magbuhat	to lift or raise something
magdasal	to pray
maghapunan	to have dinner
maghilamos	to wash one's face
maghugas	to wash something (dishes, hands, etc.)
magkape	to drink coffee
magkita	to meet with someone (pl.)
maglaba	to wash clothes
maglampaso	to mop the floor
maglaro	to play
maglinis	to clean
magluto	to cook
magmaneho papunta sa~	to drive to
magmiryenda/ magmeryenda	to have a snack
magmumog	to rinse or wash one's mouth by gargling
magpabango	to use perfume/ cologne
magpahinga	to take a rest

magpunta sa bahay ng kaibigan	to go to a friend's house
magsaing	to cook rice
magsayaw	to dance
magsimba	to go to church, to hear mass
magsipilyo/ magsepilyo	to brush teeth
magsuklay	comb hair
magsulat	to write
magsuot	to wear something
magtanghalian	to have lunch
magtrabaho	to work
magturo	to teach
mag-usap	to talk with someone (plural actor)

Adverbs of Time

bukas	tomorrow
hanggang	until
kahapon	yesterday
pagkatapos/ tapos	after
tuwing	every

Time

ala una	one o'clock
alas dos	two o'clock
alas tres	three o'clock
alas kuwatro	four o'clock
alas singko	five o'clock
alas sais	six o'clock
alas siyete	seven o'clock
alas otso	eight o'clock
alas nuwebe	nine o'clock
alas diyes	ten o'clock
alas onse	eleven o'clock
alas dose	twelve o'clock

Enclitics

naman	on the other hand

-Um- and Ma- Verbs

(The rules for the inflection of the following -um- and ma- verbs will be discussed in later lessons.)

dumating	to arrive; arrived
dumadating	is arriving
dadating/ darating	will arrive
gumising	to wake up; woke up
gumigising	is waking up
gigising	will wake up
naligo	took a shower, took a bath
naliligo	is taking/takes a shower, taking a bath
maliligo	will take a shower, will take a bath
pumasok	went to work/ school
pumapasok	is going to work/ school
papasok	will go to work/ school
umuwi	to go/come home; went/came home
umuuwi	is going/coming home
uuwi	will go/come home

Adjectives

mahirap	difficult
masuwerte	lucky

Markers

nang	time marker
ng	marks singular direct object
ng mga	marks two or more direct objects
sa	future marker

mag- an affix used to form verbs whose subject or focus is the doer of the action in a sentence, hence actor-focus. **Mag-** means to do what is indicated by the root word.

Idioms and Expressions

Ano'ng ginagawa mo tuwing . . .	What do you do every . . .
(Lunes, ikalawang linggo, Setyembre, atbp.)	(Monday, week, month, etc.)?
Sa palagay ko . . .	I think . . .
Sabihin mo nga sa akin kung ano . . .	Please tell me what . . .
Totoo 'yan.	That's true.

Dialogue: Ang Buhay May-asawa *Married Life*

The interview below utilizes some of the vocabulary words that you've studied for this lesson. Read the interview and complete the Dialogue Comprehension questions.

In this interview, Stephen talks about his typical day at work and as a family man, from the time he wakes up in the morning until nighttime. Notice the use of the respect particle **po** and **ho** in Stephen's responses.

Q: **Magandang umaga, Stephen. Kumusta ka?**

A: **Mabuti naman ho.**

Q: **Sabihin mo nga sa akin kung ano ang tipikal na araw mo?**

A: **O sige po. Gumigising ho ako nang alas sais ng umaga. Pagkatapos naliligo ako at nag-aalmusal. Tapos, nagmamaneho ako papunta sa opisina.**

Q: **Ano'ng oras ka naman dumadating sa opisina mo?**

A: **Dumadating ho ako nang alas otso.**

Q: **Ano'ng oras ka naman umuuwi?**

A: Mga alas singko ho. Tapos naghahapunan kami nang alas sais. Pagkatapos, naglalaro kami ng mga anak namin at nagbabasa kami ng libro hanggang alas otso.

Q: Nagsusulat ka rin ng libro, hindi ba? Kailan mo ito ginagawa?

A: Kadalasan, nag-uusap ho ako at ang asawa ko hanggang alas diyes, pagkatapos, nagsusulat na ako hanggang alas dose.

Q: Tapos gumigising ka nang alas singko ng umaga?

A: Opo, kasi importante na may oras ako sa trabaho at pamilya ko.

Q: Totoo 'yan!

A: Pero sa palagay ko po, mahirap din ang trabaho ng asawa ko, kasi siya ang nag-aalaga ng mga anak namin, naglilinis ng bahay, at nagluluto. Pero masaya naman siya sa trabaho niya.

Q: O sige, talagang masuwerte ka sa pamilya mo.

A: Sa palagay ko rin po.

Dialogue Comprehension

The following questions test your understanding of the interview. Respond in Tagalog to the questions in the blanks provided.

1. Ano'ng ginagawa ni Stephen sa umaga?

   _____

2. Ano ang ginagawa ni Stephen pagkatapos ng trabaho?

   _____

3. Ano ang ginagawa ni Stephen pagkatapos maghapunan?

   _____

4. Kailan nagsusulat ng libro si Stephen?

   _____

5. Ano ang trabaho ng asawa niya?

   _____

Activities

Activity 1

Refer to the tasks listed below and create a schedule showing which tasks you perform on which day or days. Use the example to model your sentences.

EXAMPLES:

Nagsisimba ako tuwing Linggo. I hear (attend) Mass every Sunday.

Nagtatanghalian ako sa labas tuwing Biyernes. I go out to eat lunch every Friday.

Mga bagay na ginagawa ko	
Nagtatanghalian sa labas	Nag-i-email
Naghahapunan sa labas	Naglalaba
Nagkakape	Naliligo
Naglilinis	Nagsusulat
Naglalaro	Nagsasayaw
Nagluluto	Nagpupunta sa bahay ng kaibigan
Nagsisimba	Nagpupunta sa gym
Nag-aaral	Nagpupunta sa parke
Nagbabasa ng libro	Nagpapahinga
Nagbabasa ng dyaryo	Umuuwi sa bahay ng magulang

Araw	Ang mga ginagawa ko sa araw na ito
Lunes	
Martes	
Miyerkules	
Huwebes	
Biyernes	
Sabado	
Linggo	

Activity 2

Now that you have created your own schedule, interview two of your classmates and inquire about their daily activities and tasks. Your classmates will have a chance to interview you as well. Use the example below to model your interview, and record the information you gather in the table provided.

EXAMPLE:
STUDENT 1: **Ano'ng ginagawa mo tuwing <u>Lunes</u>?**
STUDENT 2: <u>**Nag-aaral ako sa bahay tuwing Lunes.**</u>

Pangalan (Name): <u>**James**</u>
Lunes: <u>**Nag-aaral si James sa bahay tuwing Lunes.**</u>

Araw	Pangalan: _____	Pangalan: _____
Lunes		
Martes		
Miyerkules		
Huwebes		

Biyernes		
Sabado		
Linggo		

Reporting

Based on the information you have gathered from your classmates, write in complete sentences what both classmates do each day, using the conjunction **at _____ naman**.

EXAMPLE:

Tuwing Lunes, nag-aaral si Mike sa aklatan *at* nagtatrabaho *naman* si Melissa. Every Monday, Mike is studying at the library *and* Melissa *on the other hand* is working.

Lunes: _____

Martes: _____

Miyerkules: _____

Huwebes: _____

Biyernes: _____

Sabado: _____

Linggo: _____

Activity 3

Below is Mike's schedule from yesterday. In complete sentences, write out each of the activities and tasks he performed.

KAHAPON		Ang Iskedyul ni Mike
8:00	**Nagsipilyo at nagbihis**	
10:00	**Nag-almusal**	
11:00	**Naglinis ng kwarto**	
12:00	**Nagtanghalian**	
1:00	**Nagbasa ng mga libro**	
3:00	**Nag-email sa mga kaibigan**	
5:00	**Naglaro kasama ng mga kaibigan**	
8:00	**Naghapunan**	

1. <u>**Nagsipilyo at nagbihis si Mike kahapon nang alas otso ng umaga.**</u>

2. _____

3. _____

4. _____

5. _____

Grammar

Definition of Terms

Actor	A noun or pronoun that performs the main action of the sentence. In Tagalog, the actor of the verb could be the subject or focus of the sentence.
Focus of the Verb	Refers to the relation of the verb to the subject of the sentence, whether the subject does the action, receives the action, experiences the action, or causes someone to do the action. In the sentence below, Belle, who will do the act of reading, is also the subject of the sentence and the focus of the verb. EXAMPLE: **Magbabasa <u>si Belle</u> ng libro.** <u>Belle</u> will read a book.
Direct Object	A noun that is the receiver of the action of the verb in the sentence. In the sentence above, **libro** receives the action and it is preceded by **ng**.
Transitive Verb	A verb that requires an object. EXAMPLE: **Magbabasa si Belle <u>ng libro</u>.** Belle will read <u>a book</u>.
Intransitive Verb	A verb that does not require an object. EXAMPLE: **Maglalakad ako sa parke.** I will walk at the park.
Inflect	To change the form of a word by inflection, as in conjugating.

Examining Form

Review the sentences below and complete the tasks that follow. Discuss your answers with a partner. Consult the following section to check your answers.

1. **Nagpupunta ako sa bus stop nang alas siyete.**
2. **Naghahapunan kami nang alas sais.**
3. **Nagbabasa kami ng libro.**
4. **Magsisipilyo ng ngipin si Bart.**
5. **Magluluto ng adobo ang asawa ni Stephen.**

6. **Nagbihis siya ng damit.**
7. **Naglinis ng bahay si Stephen.**

   a. Circle the actors and underline the verbs.
   b. The sentences above have **mag-** verbal prefixes. What do you notice about the verbs?
   c. Compare sentences 1, 2, 3, and 6 with sentences 4, 5, and 7. What do you notice about the word order? Why do you think the sentence takes this word order?

I. Mag- Verbs

Generally, a verb in Tagalog has the following elements: a root word or stem word and an affix. The affix indicates the relationship of the verb to the subject or focus of the sentence. It also indicates what kind of action is performed. Verbs in Tagalog are classified according to the affixes that are attached to the stem word, unlike most English verbs, which are single words without affixes, like *run*, *eat*, and *go*. They are also classified as transitive verbs—verbs that have an object receiving the verb's action—and intransitive verbs, which have no object.

The following are some of the most common verbal affixes used in everyday speech and their classification: **mag-**, **-um-** (actor focus); **in-**, **i-** (object focus); **-an** (indirect object focus); **ma-** (experiencer focus); and **magpa-** (causer focus). In this section, we will study only the **mag-** verbs. The other verbal affixes will be discussed in subsequent lessons.

Mag- verbs are actor-focus verbs, which means the subject of the sentence is the one doing the action. The prefix **mag-** means "to do the action indicated by the root word." This prefix can be attached to borrowed words like the example below:

> EXAMPLE: **Nag-tennis sila.** They played tennis.

Another characteristic of Tagalog verbs is aspect. Whatever affix you use, all Tagalog verbs conjugate in the same way. Aspect is a characteristic of some other languages, like Tamil, Russian, or ancient Greek. It is tense in English verbs, which can be present, past, and future. Aspect tells us whether the action has been or will be completed. Tense, on the other, hand tells us whether the action happened in the past or present, or will happen in the future. Aspect makes the distinction between actions that are completed and those that are not. Completed actions are called *perfective*, but for our purposes we will simply call this aspect the completed aspect. Those not completed, or *imperfective*, may be in progress or still being done, continuing, or habitual. We will call this the *incompleted aspect*. For actions that will be completed in some future time, we will use the term *contemplated aspect*.

To summarize, the three aspects are:
a. Completed: the action started and terminated.
b. Incompleted: the action started but is not yet completed and so is still in progress or progressive. The incompleted aspect is also used for habitual past action that continues in the present, as in "Every year, I go to Paris." Here, the action has happened in the past but is repeated in the present.
c. Contemplated: the action has not started but is anticipated

The chart below gives the conjugation of the verbs **mag-aral** (to study) and **magbasa** (to read). The stem or root word that inflects is **aral** (study *or* lesson) and **basa** (read), respectively. To form the infinitive of the verb, add the prefix to the root word:

mag- (verbal prefix) + **aral** (root word)   →   **mag-aral** (verb in the infinitive form)

mag- (verbal prefix) + **basa** (root word)   →   **magbasa** (verb in the infinitive form)

As shown, **mag-** + **aral** results in **mag-aral**. A hyphen is needed between **mag-** and any root word that begins with a vowel. However, **mag-** + **basa** results in **magbasa**, without hyphen. Both **mag-aral** and **mag-basa** are infinitive forms of the verb, which means that they do not show or imply aspect. This form can be used as the command or imperative form of the verb in Tagalog. More about the infinitive form and its uses will be discussed in Units 4 and 5.

Aspect	Inflection	Inflection	Rules
Root Word	**aral**	**basa**	
Infinitive	*mag*-**aral**	*mag*basa	Prefix **mag-** to the root word
Completed	*nag*-**aral**	*nag*basa	From the infinitive, change *m* to *n*
Incompleted	*nag*-**a**aral	*nagba*basa	Take the first two syllables of the completed, plus the root word
Contemplated	*mag*-**a**aral	*magba*basa	From the incompleted, change *n* to *m*

The completed aspect is formed by changing the *m* in **mag-aral** to *n*. The resulting word, **nag-aral** "studied," denotes that the action began in the past and was completed.

The incompleted aspect is formed by reduplicating the first syllable of the root word and attaching the **nag-** form of the **mag-**prefix. In other words, for **aral**: **nag-** plus the vowel **a** that is the first syllable of the root word plus the entire root makes **nag-aaral** (is/was studying/study/studies), which signals that the action is progressive or incompleted.

The contemplated aspect **mag-aaral** (will study) is formed by changing the *n* in the incompleted form to *m*.

Aside from tense, Tagalog verbs do not express person or number of the subject. What the verb expresses is focus, which refers to the verb's relationship to the subject, as was mentioned earlier.

Grammar Presentation

Sentence Structures with **Mag-**

In Lesson 1, we learned to construct **sino** (who) and **ano** (what) questions and how to respond using affirmative and negative statements. We also learned about identificational and predicational sentences where the predicate is a noun. In this section, you will learn another type of predicational sentence, where the predicate is a verb. Because the word order of a sentence in Tagalog is predicate/subject, the sentences that you will see in the following examples have verbs in the initial position.

1. The chart below illustrates how to order the words in a predicational sentence where the predicate used is the verb **magkape** (to take or drink coffee) in its different aspects. Although Tagalog has the subject/predicate structure, the most commonly used and natural way of expression is predicate/subject. The sentences in the chart start with the verb followed by the **ang** phrase (**ang** marker + noun) or **ang** pronoun, and the last element is the location where the action is happening.

   In the following examples of predicational sentences, the verbs in the completed aspect tell us that the action was started in the past and was completed. Notice in the first sentence that the enclitic **na** comes immediately after the verb **nagsaing**. All the verbs mentioned here are intransitive verbs.

Intransitive Verbs			
Verb	**Actor (Ang Phrase)**		**Location**
Mag-	**Markers**	**Nouns**	**Sa**
Nagkape (completed)	si sina	<u>Jamie</u>	
Nagkakape (incompleted)	ang ang mga	<u>bata</u>	<u>sa kapetirya.</u>
Magkakape (contemplated)		ako tayo kami ka kayo siya sila	

EXAMPLES:
Nagsaing na ho ako. I already cooked rice, sir/madam.
Nagtanghalian kami sa Jerry's Grill. We had lunch at Gerry's Grill.

2. The following chart shows the verb **magbasa** (to read) inflected in the different aspects—completed, incompleted, and contemplated—and used in simple sentences with a direct object. The chart illustrates the prescribed word order: VERB + DIRECT OBJECT + SUBJECT (ACTOR) + ADVERB OF TIME + AND LOCATION OF THE ACTION. The verb **magbasa** can be both transitive and intransitive. Notice the different time markers used, corresponding to the aspect: **noong Lunes** (last Monday), **tuwing Lunes** (every Monday), and **sa Lunes** (on Monday).

   Below the chart are examples of sentences with verbs in the incompleted aspect that tell us the action was started in the past and it is still continuing.

Transitive Verb							
Verb	**Direct Object**		**Actor**		**Time**		**Location**
Mag-	**Marker**	**Noun**	**Marker**	**Noun**	**Marker**	**Noun**	**sa**
<u>**Nagbasa**</u> (completed)	ng ng mga	<u>libro</u>	si sina	<u>Patrick</u>	noong	<u>Lunes</u>	sa <u>bahay.</u>
<u>**Nagbabasa**</u> (incompleted)			ang ang mga	<u>bata</u>	tuwing	<u>Lunes</u>	
<u>**Magbabasa**</u> (contemplated)					sa	<u>Lunes</u>	

EXAMPLES:
Nagluluto ng adobo si Bebel. Bebel is cooking adobo.
Naglilinis ng klasrum ang mga estudyante. The students are cleaning the classroom.

Note that *m* is changed to *n* and the first consonant/vowel (CV) of the root word is repeated to denote habitual or ongoing action. In the first sentence, it is the **lu** of **luto** that is repeated.

3. In the chart below, the transitive verb **magluto** has an object, **adobo**, which is the recipient of the action. When the actor (subject) is a pronoun, the word order is as follows: VERB + PRONOUN + DIRECT OBJECT. Compare the word order of these sentences with that of the sentences in the previous chart. Note the use of the time markers **noong** (last) to denote past time, **tuwing** (every) to denote habitual or ongoing time, and **sa** (on) to indicate future time. The location of action, **sa bahay** (at the house), is last in the word order. The sentences below the chart are examples of predicational sentences with verbs in the contemplated aspect as initial words in the sentence.

Transitive Verb							
Verb	**Actor**		**Direct Object**		**Time**		**Location**
Mag-	**Marker**	**Noun**	**Marker**	**Noun**	**Marker**	**Noun**	**Sa**
Nagluto (completed)		ako tayo kami ka kayo siya sila	ng ng mga	adobo	noong	Martes	sa bahay.
Nagluluto (incompleted)					tuwing	Martes	
Magluluto (contemplated)					sa	Martes	

EXAMPLES:

Maglalaba ako ng pantalon ko sa Biyernes. I will wash my pants on Friday.
Mag-aaral ako ng Tagalog bukas. I will study Tagalog tomorrow.

To summarize, the previous two charts show two high-frequency word orders when using **mag**-verbs:

a) VERB + DIRECT OBJECT + ACTOR
   used when the actor is either a proper name or a common noun
b) VERB + ACTOR + DIRECT OBJECT
   used when the actor is a pronoun

4. Now, let's review the interrogative pronoun **sino** with the verb **maglinis** (*to clean*). The chart below shows the correct word order in asking who cleaned, is cleaning, cleans, and will clean the house. The verb in the first sentence after the chart is in the incompleted aspect, **nagmamaneho**, while the verb in the second sentence is in the contemplated aspect, **magpupunta**.

Sino Question					EXAMPLES:
Interrogative	**Ang**		**Verb**	**Direct Object**	
		Mag-	**Marker**	**Noun**	
Sino	**ang**	**naglinis** (completed) **naglilinis** (incompleted) **maglilinis** (contemplated)	**ng** **ng mga**	**bahay?**	

EXAMPLES:

Sino ang nagmamaneho ng kotse? Who is driving the car?
Sino ang magpupunta sa bahay namin? Who will go to our house?

5. Most often, one-syllable enclitics are placed after the verb predicate in a predicational sentence, depending on the context. As mentioned in previous lessons, enclitics in Tagalog are adverbs. Naturally, they are placed near the verbs they modify. The exception to the placement of the enclitics following the verb is the second-person singular pronoun **ka**, which comes before all the other enclitics. **Ka**, the subject of the sentence, immediately follows the verb predicate. The simple explanation for the precedence of **ka**, a one-syllable word, over all one-syllable enclitics is that when you say the sentence with the enclitic before **ka**— for instance, **Nag-aaral na ka ...* or **Nag-aaral ba ka ...*—the resulting sound does not make sense. In the second nonsense sentence, the sound of **ba** and **ka** side by side would mean "cow" (**baka**) in Tagalog.

The chart below shows the word order of this type of sentence. In the examples that follow, the first sentence illustrates the word order of the pronoun **ka** and the enclitic **ba**, which serves as a spoken question mark. The second sentence uses the enclitics **din** (also) and **po**, which signifies respect. The word order of enclitics is fixed according to the context.

Interrogative Sentence					
Verb	Enclitic	Actor		Location	
Mag-		Marker	Noun	Sa	
Nag-aral (completed)	na pa din/rin daw/raw po ba	si sina	Mark	sa aklatan./?	
Nag-aaral (incompleted)		ang ang mga	bata		
Mag-aaral (contemplated)			ako tayo kami ka kayo siya sila		

EXAMPLES:

Nagbasa ka ba ng libro noong Biyernes? Did you read a book on Friday?

Magluluto din po ako ng adobo sa Sabado. I am also cooking adobo on Saturday, sir/madam.

6. What happens when the sentence is negated? There are two possibilities. If the actor is a pronoun, it follows the negative word **hindi** and then is followed by the verb and the direct object marker **ng** and noun object. But if the actor is a noun, **hindi** is followed by the verb and then the direct object marker and noun object, and the actor comes last. Study the chart and examples below.

Negative Sentence					
Negative	Actor		Verb	Direct Object	
	Marker	Noun	Mag-	Marker	Noun
Hindi		ako tayo kami ka kayo siya sila	nagbasa (completed) nagbabasa (incompleted) magbabasa (contemplated)	ng ng mga	libro.

Negative	Verb	Direct Object		Actor	
		Marker	Noun	Marker	Noun
Hindi	nagbasa (completed) nagbabasa (incompleted) magbabasa (contemplated)	ng ng mga	libro	si sina	Mark.
				ang ang mga	estudyante.

EXAMPLES:

Hindi siya nag-ahit. He did not shave.

Hindi nagsipilyo ng ngipin ang bata. The kid did not brush his/her teeth.

Grammar Notes

1. Remember that **hindi** is a pronoun and enclitic magnet. Thus, pronouns and enclitics are always placed right after **hindi**.
      Nag-aral po siya. He/She studied, sir/madam.
      Hindi po siya nag-aral. He/She did not study, sir/madam.
      *Hindi nag-aral po siya. (incorrect)

2. There are two high-frequency word orders when using **mag**-verbs:
      a. VERB + DIRECT OBJECT + ACTOR
          used when the actor is either a proper name or a common noun
      b. VERB + ACTOR + DIRECT OBJECT
          used when the actor is a pronoun.

      Nag-aaral ng Tagalog si Luisa. (preferred)
      Nag-aaral si Luisa ng Tagalog. (acceptable)
      Nag-aaral siya ng Tagalog. (correct)
      *Nag-aaral ng Tagalog siya. (incorrect)

3. Remember the following markers for different parts of the sentence or to convey other grammatical information:
      Subject: **ang** form
      Direct Object: **ng, ng mga**
      Location: **sa**
      Time: **noong** (past time marker)
             tuwing (habitual marker)
             sa (future time marker)

    The examples below illustrate the use of the different markers:
      Nagluluto <u>ang</u> babae. The woman is cooking.
      Nagluluto <u>ng</u> adobo ang babae. The woman is cooking adobo.
      Nagluluto ang babae ng adobo <u>sa</u> kusina. The woman is cooking adobo <u>in</u> the kitchen.
      Nagluto ang babae <u>noong</u> Linggo. The woman cooked <u>last</u> Sunday.
      Nagluluto ang babae <u>tuwing</u> Linggo. The woman is cooking <u>every</u> Sunday.
      Magluluto ang babae <u>sa</u> Linggo. The woman will cook <u>on</u> Sunday.

4. The incompleted aspect in Tagalog could be compared to English grammar's present progressive and simple present:
      a. Simple present: expresses an action that occurs habitually.
      b. Present progressive: expresses an action that is currently happening.

      Naglilinis ako ng bahay tuwing Biyernes. I clean the house every Friday.
      Naglilinis ako ng bahay. I am cleaning the house.

5. The time markers **noong** and **sa** are used only to mark days of the week, months, and year:
      (sa/noong) Lunes   **(sa/noong) Enero**   **(noong) 1898**

6. **Kailan** is the Filipino equivalent of *when*. When responding to a **kailan** question, it is necessary to use time markers. However, for adverbs describing such time concepts as "tomorrow," "yesterday," "later," etc. markers are not used. We will look further into adverbs of time in the following unit.

> **Kailan ka mag-aaral?** When will you study?
> **Sa Biyernes.** On Friday.
> **Kailan nagluto ng adobo si Nanay?** When did mother cook adobo?
> **Noong Sabado ng hapon.** Last Saturday afternoon.

7. Infinitive verbs are used for commands and exhortations. The subject/actor is limited to the following pronouns: **ka** (you, singular, usually placed right after the verb), **kayo** (you, plural), and **tayo** (we/us, including the listener). The concept of **tayo** is comparable to "us" in English, but not in the sense of the speaker and the listener doing the action as in Tagalog. We will cover the uses of the infinitive form in detail in the following unit. The sentences below show the infinitive form **magluto** (to cook) used to express a command with different subject pronouns that are the actors of **mag-** verbs.

> **Magluto <u>ka</u> ng pagkain.** (You, singular) Cook food.
> **Magluto <u>kayo</u> ng pagkain.** (You, plural) Cook food.
> **Magluto <u>tayo</u> ng pagkain.** Let us cook food.

8. The verbs **magkita** (to see each other, meet) and **mag-usap** (converse, speak to each other) are intransitive verbs. Since they describe social activities, these verbs require plural subjects. The sentences below illustrate the plural subjects who are also the actors in the sentences.

> **Nag-usap <u>kami</u> noong Biyernes.** We talked last Friday.
> **Magkikita <u>sina Bob at Paul</u> sa Lunes.** Bob and Paul are going to meet each other on Monday.
> *****Nagkita si Bob ng estudyante.** (incorrect)

9. **Mag-** verbs have this peculiar feature, that **mag-** plus any kind of clothing and/or accessory means to wear that certain article of clothing or accessory. In the following examples an **amerikana** is a suit, a **kuwintas** is a necklace, and a **payong** is an umbrella.

> **mag-amerikana** to wear a suit
> **Mag-aamerikana ka ba bukas?** Are you going to wear a suit tomorrow?
> **magkuwintas** to wear a necklace
> **Nagkuwintas siya kahapon.** She wore a necklace yesterday.
> **magpayong** to use an umbrella
> **Magpayong ka.** (You) Use an umbrella

II. Telling Time (Formal)

The chart below shows the time in Tagalog. If you know Spanish, the words for the hours will be familiar. The reason for this is that the Spaniards brought the concept of twenty-four hours in a day to the Philippines.

Oras					
1:00	Ala una	5:00	Alas singko	9:00	Alas nuwebe
2:00	Alas dos	6:00	Alas sais	10:00	Alas diyes
3:00	Alas tres	7:00	Alas siyete	11:00	Alas onse
4:00	Alas kuwatro	8:00	Alas otso	12:00	Alas dose

EXAMPLES:

Ano'ng oras ka magpupunta sa bahay ko? What time are you coming to my place?

Magpupunta ako sa bahay mo nang alas siyete ng gabi. I will come to your place (house) at seven p.m.

Nag-aral ka ba ng Tagalog kahapon? Did you study Tagalog yesterday?

Oo. Nag-aral ako nang alas sais ng hapon hanggang alas onse ng gabi. Yes. I studied from six p.m. to eleven p.m.

Grammar Notes

1. **Nang** is used to mark the time. The verb aspect determines whether the action has started or ended.
   Nagpunta ako sa parke <u>nang alas otso.</u> I went to the park at 8:00 o'clock.
   Nagpupunta ako sa parke <u>nang alas otso.</u> I go to the park at 8:00 o'clock.
   Magpupunta ako sa parke <u>nang alas otso.</u> I will go to the park at 8:00 o'clock.

2. **Mga** is added after the marker **nang** when one needs to express a time approximation, as in "about."
   Nagluto ang nanay ko ng adobo <u>nang mga alas diyes ng gabi.</u> My mother cooked adobo at around 10:00 pm.
   Mag-aaral si Bonnie <u>nang mga ala una.</u> Bonnie will study at about 1:00 o'clock.

3. In order to indicate whether the time being referred to is in the morning, afternoon, or night, the following phrases are attached after the expressed time: **ng umaga, ng tanghali, ng hapon, ng gabi**.
   Nagsaing ako nang alas onse <u>ng umaga.</u> I cooked rice at 11:00 o'clock in the morning.
   Magluluto ako nang alas kuwatro <u>ng hapon.</u> I will cook at 4:00 o'clock in the afternoon.
   Nagkape siya nang alas dose <u>ng tanghali.</u> He had coffee at 12:00 o'clock in the afternoon.
   Nag-aral siya ng Tagalog nang alas otso <u>ng gabi.</u> He/She studied Tagalog at 8:00 o'clock in the evening.

4. Spanish numbers are usually used when telling time in Tagalog. The Spanish is perceived as more conversational compared to its Tagalog counterpart, which is perceived as more formal.
   Magluluto ako nang alas kuwatro ng hapon. (conversational)
   Magluluto ako nang ikaapat ng hapon. (formal)

5. **Ng tanghali** is used only for 12:00 noon and increments after the noon hour. One p.m. is **ala una ng hapon**.

Practice

I. Speaking Practice

This is an information gap activity to be done by pairs.

WORKSHEET A: What will Freddy do this week? In your worksheet, some information is missing that can be found in Worksheet B. Ask your partner for the missing information. Then compare your activity sheets afterwards.

EXAMPLES:
STUDENT 1: **Ano ang gagawin ni Freddy sa Lunes nang alas nuwebe ng umaga?**
STUDENT 2: **Magkakape si Freddy kasama si Jed.**
STUDENT 1: **Kailan magtatanghalian si Freddy sa bahay ni Brian?**
STUDENT 2: **Sa Lunes nang alas dose ng tanghali.**

Araw	Setyembre
Linggo	9:00- **magkakape kasama si Jed** 12:00- **magtatanghalian sa bahay ni Brian** 4:00- _____
Lunes	_____- **magpupunta sa gym** 5:00- **maglilinis ng kuwarto at kusina** 7:00- _____
Martes	8:00- **magpupunta sa Tagaytay kasama si Melanie** 1:00- _____ _____- **magmamaneho papunta sa bahay**
Miyerkules	10:00- _____ 4:00- **maglalaba sa bahay ng nanay ko** _____- **maghahapunan sa Makati**
Huwebes	9:00- **magbabasa ng libro** 1:00- **magkikita ako at si Patricia** 5:00- **maglilinis ng bahay**
Biyernes	8:00- **mag-aalmusal sa Fort** _____- **maghahapunan sa QC** 10:00- **magpupunta sa bahay ng kaibigan**
Sabado	**Magpapahinga!!!**

WORKSHEET B: What will Freddy do this week? In your worksheet, some information is missing that can be found in Worksheet A. Ask your partner for the missing information. Then compare your activity sheets afterwards.

EXAMPLES:
STUDENT 1: **Ano ang gagawin ni Freddy sa Lunes nang alas nuwebe ng umaga?**
STUDENT 2: **Magkakape si Freddy kasama si Jed.**
STUDENT 1: **Kailan magtatanghalian si Freddy sa bahay ni Brian?**
STUDENT 2: **Sa Lunes nang alas dose ng tanghali.**

Araw	Setyembre
Linggo	9:00- **magkakape kasama si Jed** 12:00- _____ 4:00- **magsisimba**
Lunes	1:00- **magpupunta sa gym** _____- **maglilinis ng kuwarto at kusina** 7:00- **maghahapunan kasama si Tobi**
Martes	8:00- _____ 1:00- **magtatanghalian sa Picnic Grove** 8:00- **magmamaneho papunta sa bahay**
Miyerkules	10:00- **magluluto ng lumpia** 4:00- _____ 7:00- **maghahapunan sa Makati**
Huwebes	9:00- _____ _____- **magkikita ako at si Patricia** 5:00- _____
Biyernes	_____- **mag-aalmusal sa Fort** 5:00- **maghahapunan sa QC** 10:00- _____
Sabado	_____**!!!**

II. Reading Practice

Review Jimmy's schedule for next week and answer the Reading Comprehension questions.

Ang Kalendaryo Ko

Word Bank

pagkain food   **bulaklak** flowers
pasok work   **buo** whole
bino wine
gimikan general term for places like bars and clubs from
the English word "gimmick"
sa palagay mo what do you think, in your opinion

Lunes	Martes	Miyerkules
8:00 **Magtatrabaho ako hanggang alas singko ng hapon.** 5:00 **Magpupunta ako sa grocery para bumili ng bino at bulaklak.** 5:30 **Magpupunta ako sa bahay ng nobya ko.** 7:00 **Anibersaryo namin kaya maghahapunan kami sa isang restawran.**	**Walang pasok!** 9:00 **Magpupunta kami ng nobya ko sa Baguio.** *Magbabaon kami ng mga pagkain.**	**Maraming gawain!** 5:00 **Maggo-grocery at maglilinis ako ng buong bahay namin. Magba-vacuum ako.** 7:00 **Maglalaba ako ng mga damit ko.**
Huwebes	**Biyernes**	**Sabado't Linggo**
5:00 **Magkikita ako, si Theron at ang mga kaibigan ko.** 6:00 **Maghahapunan kami sa Kamay Kainan sa Roxas Blvd.**	7:00 **Magkikita kami ng mga kaibigan ko sa bahay namin. Maglalaro kami ng poker.** 9:00 **Magpupunta kami sa iba't-ibang gimikan sa Malate.**	**Magpapahinga lang ako kasama ang nobya ko.**

1. Magpupunta ba ang nobya ni Jimmy sa bahay niya?
2. Ano ang okasyon sa Lunes?
3. Saan magpupunta sina Jimmy sa Martes?
4. Mayroon bang pasok sa Miyerkules sina Jimmy?
5. Kailan maglilinis ng bahay si Jimmy?
6. Saan maghahapunan si Jimmy at ang mga kaibigan niya sa Huwebes?
7. Ano'ng oras magkikita si Jimmy at ang mga kaibigan niya sa Huwebes?
8. Saan magpupunta si Jimmy at ang mga kaibigan niya sa Biyernes?
9. Sa palagay mo, kailan ang paboritong araw ni Jimmy?
10. Sino ang kasama ni Jimmy sa Sabado at Linggo?

III. Writing Practice

What are your plans for the following week? Write down your schedule in the space provided below. Write at least two to three activities for each day, and try not to use the same verb more than twice.

Araw	Mga Gawain
Linggo	
Lunes	
Martes	
Miyerkules	
Huwebes	

Araw	Mga Gawain
Biyernes	
Sabado	

IV. Listening Practice

Listen to audio file (07–2) and complete the information in the box below.

Sophia			Christian		
Noong Biyernes	Tuwing Linggo	Sa Miyerkules	Noong Agosto	Tuwing Disyembre	Sa Pebrero

Mga Libangan

Hobbies

An Overview of Lesson 8

Objectives

• Be able to talk about one's hobbies and leisure-time activities
• Be able to express preferences regarding activities

Vocabulary

• Nouns	• **Mag-** Verbs	• Adverbs of Time	• **Sa** Markers
• **Sa** Pronouns	• **Ma-** Verbs	• Conjunctions	• Idioms and Expressions

Dialogue: Magsayaw Tayo! *Let's Dance!*

Dialogue Comprehension

Activities

Activity 1: Speaking Activity
Activity 2: My Hobbies
Activity 3: Interview

Grammar

Definition of Terms: Ditransitive Verbs, Indirect Object, Benefactive Complement, Directional Complement, First-Person Plural Inclusive, and First-Person Plural Exclusive

Examining Form

I.   **Sa** Markers and **Sa** Pronouns
     Grammar Presentation: **Sa** Markers and **Sa** Pronouns
II. Usage of **Sa** Markers and **Sa** Pronouns
     Grammar Presentation: Word Order of **Sa** Markers and Pronouns in a Sentence
     Grammar Notes

Practice

I.   Speaking Practice
II. Reading Practice
III. Writing Practice
IV. Listening Practice

Vocabulary 🎧 (08–1)

The vocabulary will help you speak about your hobbies and favorite leisure-time activities and participate in the activities in this lesson. Memorize the vocabulary words before proceeding to the dialogue.

Nouns

bola	ball
gitara	guitar
libro	book
libangan	hobby
piyano	piano
sayaw	dance

Sa Pronouns

sa akin	me
sa amin	us (exclusive)-refers to speaker and company, but excludes the listener
sa atin	us (inclusive)-refers to speaker including the listener
sa inyo	you (plural)
sa iyo	you
sa kanila	them
sa kaniya	him/her

Mag- Verbs

magbakasyon	to take a vacation
mag-bake	to bake
magbaon	to take/bring provision (food, clothes, money etc.)
magbasketbol	to play basketball
magbayad	to pay
magbidyo	to play video games
magbigay	to give
magbisikleta	to ride a bike
magbiro	to crack a joke
magdaan	to drop by/pass by
magdala	to bring
magdram	to play drums
maggitara	to play the guitar
maghanap	to look for

mag-hiking	to go hiking
maghintay	to wait for
mag-ipon	to save, gather, collect
mag-jogging	to go jogging
magkaraoke	to sing along to the accompaniment of recorded music using karaoke
magkompyuter	to use the computer
magkuwento	to narrate a story, tell a story
maglagay	to put/place
magmaneho	to drive
magpasyal	to stroll
magpiyano	to play the piano
magsimula	to start
mag-uwi	to bring/take something home

Ma- Verbs

makinig sa radyo	to listen to the radio
manood ng telebisyon	to watch television
manood ng sine	to watch a movie
matulog	to sleep

Adverbs of Time

Past Time

kagabi	last night
kahapon	yesterday
kamakalawa	two days ago
kamakatlo	three days ago
kanina	earlier
kaninang umaga/ tanghali	earlier this morning/noon

kaninang umaga/ tanghali	earlier this morning/noon
noong isang buwan	last month
noong isang taon	last year
noong nakaraang dalawang buwan	two months ago

Present Time

araw-araw	every day
gabi-gabi	every night
linggu-linggo	every week
oras-oras	every hour
minu-minuto	every minute
maya't maya	every now and then
buwan-buwan	monthly
lagi	always
taun-taon	yearly

Future Time

bukas ng umaga/ hapon/gabi	tomorrow morning/ afternoon/night
mamaya	later
mamayang hapon/gabi	later this afternoon/ later tonight
sa isang taon (buwan, linggo)	next year (month, week)
sa susunod na taon (buwan, linggo)	next year (month, week)
samakalawa	next two days

Conjunctions

pero	but

Sa Markers

sa	marks singular common noun
sa mga	marks two or more common noun
kay	marks one proper name of a person or an animal
kina	marks two or more proper name of a person or an animal

Idioms and Expressions

Alam mo ba na . . .	Do you know that . . .
Parehong kaliwa ang paa ko.	I have two left feet.
Naku!	Oh, my gosh! (literal: Oh, mother!)
O sige na nga.	All right.
Kung may panahon ako	If I have the time

Dialogue: Magsayaw Tayo! *Let's Dance!*

Read the exchange below between Carlos and Vanessa discussing some of their activities, then complete the Dialogue Comprehension activity that follows.

Carlos:	**Kumusta? Alam mo ba na may eskwelahan ng sayaw malapit lang sa bahay mo?**
Vanessa:	**Hindi. Bakit?**
Carlos:	**Magaling daw ang titser doon eh. Nagtuturo raw siya ng sayaw sa mga estudyante sa UST. Mag-aral tayo.**
Vanessa:	**Ay! Hindi naman ako nagsasayaw, eh.**
Carlos:	**Ayos lang! Hindi rin ako nagsasayaw pero sa palagay ko, mabuting libangan ito pagkatapos ng eskwela.**
Vanessa:	**Anu-ano'ng klase ba ng sayaw ang mayroon?**
Carlos:	**May hip-hop, jazz, lyrical, cardio-funk, at mga tradisyunal na sayaw. Ano, gusto mo ba?**
Vanessa:	**Ay! Ayaw ko kasi parehong kaliwa ang paa ko eh.**

Carlos: **Naku! Ayos lang 'yan. Iba-iba naman ang level ng klase, eh. Mayroon para sa mga magaling at mayroon din para sa atin na nagsisimula pa lang.**

Vanessa: **O sige na nga.**

Carlos: **Ayos! Sige, tapos, mag-gym naman tayo tuwing Miyerkules at Sabado.**

Vanessa: **O sige. Magkita tayo bukas sa gym.**

Dialogue Comprehension

For each of the following statements about the dialogue, place a check mark in the appropriate blank, depending on whether the statement is true, **Tama**, or false, **Mali**.

	TAMA	MALI
1. There is a dance school near Carlos's apartment.	_____	_____
2. The dance instructor also teaches at the University of Santo Tomas.	_____	_____
3. The instructor only teaches Filipino traditional dances.	_____	_____
4. Vanessa is not good at dancing.	_____	_____
5. Vanessa and Carlos are going to the gym on Mondays and Sundays.	_____	_____

Activities

Activity 1

Work with a partner. The chart below indicates what Lino and Edna's hobbies are and aren't. The smiley face inside the box indicates that Lino and Edna are doing these activities, and the sad face means they aren't. Write complete sentences naming their hobbies using the incompleted aspect. The example below can serve to model your sentences. Use a separate sheet of paper for your sentences.

EXAMPLES:

*ma*kinig sa radyo: *naki*kinig sa radyo   *mag*-hiking: *nagha*-hiking

Nakikinig si Lino sa radyo.   **Hindi nagha-hiking si Edna.**

Lino listens to the radio.   Edna does not go hiking.

LINO		EDNA	
makinig sa radyo	magluto	magpiyano	mag-hiking
mag-basketball	maglinis ng bahay	mag-aral ng wika	manood ng sine
maggitara	magpunta sa parke	mag-jogging	mag-volleyball
mag-gym	magbisikleta	magkaraoke	magbidyo

Activity 2

Work with a partner. Using the scheduling chart below, list the different hobbies or activities in which you participate. Afterwards, interview some of your classmates and ask them what they do during their leisure hours. Record their names and the information you gathered in the space provided. The example can serve to model your interview and your sentences.

EXAMPLES:

Student 1: **Ano ang libangan mo tuwing umaga?**

Student 2: **Tuwing umaga, nagdya-jogging ako.**

Student 1: **Ah, o sige. Ano naman ang libangan mo tuwing . . .**

Mga Libangan

	Libangan ko	Libangan ni _____
Tuwing umaga		
Tuwing hapon		
Tuwing gabi		
Tuwing Sabado		
Tuwing Linggo		

Activity 3

Complete a survey of what your classmates do in their free time. Write the names of your interviewees on the left and put a check mark if they participate in the activity listed at the top. Use the example below to model your interview.

EXAMPLE:

STUDENT 1: **Nagba-basketball ka ba?**

STUDENT 2: **Oo, nagba-basketball ako.**

STUDENT 3: **Hindi. Hindi ako nagba-basketball.**

Pangalan	mag-shopping	mag-hiking	makinig sa radyo	manood ng sine	mag-gym	magpunta sa parke	magpunta sa bahay ng kaibigan	magbidyo	magluto

Reporting

Based on the information you have gathered, express in complete sentences your classmates' leisure-time activities. Use the example below as a model for your sentences. Make sure you use the incompleted aspect of the verb.

EXAMPLE:

Nagsa-shopping sina Fredy at Nelson.

Mag-shopping

_____

Mag-hiking

_____

Makinig sa radyo

_____

Manood ng sine

_____

Mag-gym

_____

Magpunta sa parke

_____

Magpunta sa bahay ng kaibigan

_____

Magbidyo

_____

Magluto

_____

Grammar

Definition of Terms

Ditransitive Verbs	Verbs that take an actor and two objects. **Nagbigay ako <u>ng bulaklak</u> <u>kay Jamie.</u>** I gave Jamie a flower.

Indirect Object	The recipient of the direct object. It usually answers the questions "To whom?," "From whom?," or "For whom?". EXAMPLES: **Nagtuturo ako ng Tagalog <u>kay Marc</u>.** I am teaching <u>Marc</u> Tagalog.
Benefactive Complement	Shows the beneficiary of the action. EXAMPLE: **Nagluto ako ng pansit <u>para sa iyo</u>.** I cooked *pancit* <u>for you</u>.
Directional Complement	Shows the movement of the direct object toward or away from the actor. EXAMPLE: **Nagbigay ako ng bulaklak <u>kay Jamie</u>.** I gave a flower <u>to Jamie</u>.
First-Person Plural Inclusive	The form of Tagalog pronouns that refers to the person speaking and the listener or listeners in **ang (tayo) ng (natin)**, and **sa (sa atin)**.
First-Person Plural Exclusive	Tagalog pronouns in **ang (kami)**, **ng (namin)** and **sa (sa amin)** that refer to the person speaking and company only, excluding the listener or listeners.

Examining Form

Review the sentences below and complete the tasks that follow. Discuss your answers with a partner. Consult the following section to check your answers.

1. **Nagtuturo raw siya ng sayaw sa mga estudyante sa UST.**
2. **Nagbigay ng bulaklak si Marcus kay Maria.**
3. **Nagluto siya ng pansit para sa amin.**
4. **Nagbe-bake siya ng keyk para sa mga kamag-anak niya.**
5. **Magka-carbonara si Nanay para sa atin.**

   a. Underline all the indirect objects. Write BC after each sentence if the indirect object is a benefactive complement and DC if it is directional complement.
   b. Pay attention to the word order. What are the different word orders? Where is the indirect object usually placed?
   c. Look at the verbs in numbers 4 and 5. How are these verbs conjugated?

I. Sa Markers and Sa Pronouns

In Lesson 2, we encountered **sa** as a place marker equivalent to "in, at, on" in responding to a **saan** (*where*) question asking where an action takes place. In Lesson 7, **sa** is used in sentences as a future-time marker. Aside from being a location and future-time marker, **sa** is also a common-noun marker.

In this lesson, we will study a new set of markers and pronouns called **sa** markers and **sa** pronouns. If **ang** markers + noun (**ang** phrases) and **ang** pronouns are used as subjects of sentences, and **ng** markers + noun (**ng** phrases) are used as objects in sentences, **sa** markers + noun and **sa** pronouns are used as indirect objects. They also can denote location and possession. These, as well as objects of the preposition **to**, are called **sa** forms.

The chart below gives the **sa** markers and **sa** pronouns together with the **ang** and **ng** forms that we covered in Lessons 1, 2, and 3 of Unit 1 for quick reference:

	Ang	Ng	Sa
Noun Marker (singular)	ang	ng	sa
Noun Marker (plural)	ang mga	ng mga	sa mga
Name* Marker (singular)	si	ni	kay
Name* Marker (plural)	sina	nina	kina
I	ako	ko	sa akin
we (including you)	tayo	natin	sa atin
we (excluding you)	kami	namin	sa amin
you (singular)	ka, ikaw	mo	sa iyo
you (plural)	kayo	ninyo	sa inyo
he/she	siya	niya	sa kaniya
they	sila	nila	sa kanila

*proper noun

Grammar Presentation

1. **Sa Markers**: Like **ang** markers and **ng** markers, **sa** markers include proper name markers and common noun markers for singular and plural nouns. **Kay** (singular) and **kina** (plural) markers are for names of people and pets, while **sa** (singular) and **sa mga** (plural) are generally for common nouns. The following examples of **sa** markers + nouns are called **sa** phrases, much like the **ang** phrases and **ng** phrases that we covered in Unit 1.

    kay + proper name of a person or an animal
    kina + proper name of people (more than one person)

    EXAMPLES:
    kay Vera (name of a woman)   to Vera
    kay Tagpi (name of a dog)   to Tagpi

    kina Vita (Vita and company)   to Vita and company
    kina Noel at Jose   to Noel and Jose

    sa + common noun
    sa + name of a place (common noun or proper noun)
    sa mga + common noun (more than one)
    sa mga + proper name
    sa mga + name of a place (common noun)

    EXAMPLES:
    sa bata   to (the) child
    sa kuwarto   to (the) room
    sa United Nations Building   to (the) United Nations Building

sa mga babae	to (the) women
sa mga Dodgers	to (the) Dodgers (name of a baseball team in the U.S.)
sa mga paliparan	to (the) airports

In the examples above, the words **babae** and **paliparan** by themselves are singular. The addition of **sa mga** in front of the word makes the word plural. The concept is similar to the plural endings *-s*, *-es*, *-ies* or irregular nouns like *foot/feet* and *goose/geese* in the English language.

Note: The definite article *the* has no translation in Tagalog. Its closest equivalent is the subject markers **ang** and **ang mga**.

2. **Sa** Pronouns: **Sa** pronouns are possessive pronouns but are also used as indirect objects. In this introductory book, **sa** pronouns used as possessives will not be discussed.

sa akin	my, mine, to me
sa atin	our, ours, to us (inclusive)
sa amin	our, ours, to us (exclusive)
sa iyo	your, yours, to you
sa inyo	your, yours, to you (plural)
sa kaniya	his, hers, to her, to his
sa kanila	their, to their

II. Usage of **Sa** Markers and **Sa** Pronouns

Generally, as was noted earlier, **sa** phrases and **sa** pronouns are used as indirect objects. The indirect object in English is the person or thing to which something is given or for whom something is done.

As a word of caution, the Tagalog language cannot be fully explained or understood using English grammar and terminology, as Tagalog and English belong to two different distinct language families born out of specific geopolitical, economic, religious, cultural, and environmental conditions. Tagalog belongs to the Malayo-Polynesian Austronesian languages, while English belongs to the family of Indo-European languages. These two languages offer two different views into the world. There are some things and concepts that exist in Tagalog and have no equivalent in English, and the same is true for English vis-à-vis Tagalog, as we have seen for instance in the non-existence of the definite article *the* in Tagalog and the absence of predicate/subject word order in English. With this in mind, we would like to explain how to use **sa** forms with the aid of the closest possible concept there is in English, which is the indirect object.

1. **Directional complement:** The directional complement indicates some kind of movement toward or away from someone. In the example below, the object, **limang piso** shows movement away from the actor, **ako**, in the Tagalog sentence and is moving toward the indirect object or the directional complement. which is **kay Mark**.

> **Magbabayad ako ng limang piso *kay Mark*.** I will pay five pesos *to Mark*.
> *I will pay Mark five pesos.*

2. **Benefactive complement:** The benefactive complement is the beneficiary of the action. In this example, Mark is the benefactive complement. Note that when **para** is added before the **sa** marker or **sa** pronouns, it expresses the idea of doing something for someone. **Para** comes from the Spanish word for "for." It is possible that this is a Spanish borrowing.

Nagluto ng manok ang nanay *para kay Mark*. Mother cooked chicken *for Mark.*

Supposing we put **para** in the first example:

Magbabayad ako ng limang piso *para* kay Mark. I will pay five pesos *for* Mark.

The meaning of the sentence is altered simply because of the addition of the word **para**. And if we remove **para** in the second sentence:

Nagluto ang nanay ng manok kay Mark. Mother cooked chicken on Mark.

The sentence would elicit laughter from a native Tagalog speaker.

Grammar Presentation

Word Order of **Sa** Markers and Pronouns in a Sentence

1. The predicational sentences in the chart below use the verb **magbayad** in its different aspects. The chart shows what shape a sentence might take when a **mag-** verb has two objects, one receiving the action directly (PhP 500) and the other indirectly affected by the action of the verb (Jamie, **babae**, and the different **sa** pronouns). When the subject of a **mag-** verb with two objects is a pronoun, the word order is VERB + ACTOR + DIRECT OBJECT + INDIRECT OBJECT.

Directional Complement						
Verb	**Actor**		**Object**		**Indirect Object (Location/Direction)**	
Mag- Verb	**Marker**	**Noun**	**Marker**	**Noun**	**Marker**	**Noun**
Magbayad (infinitive)		ka kayo tayo			kay kina	Jamie.
Nagbayad (completed)		ako tayo kami ka kayo siya sila	ng ng mga	Php500	sa sa mga	babae.
Nagbabayad (incompleted)					sa	akin. atin. amin.
Magbabayad (contemplated)						iyo. inyo. kaniya. kanila.

The sentences below illustrate the position of the indirect objects.

EXAMPLES:

Nagtuturo ho sila ng Tagalog kina Matt at Michael. They are teaching/teach Matt and Michael Tagalog.

Sino ang nagtuturo ng Tagalog kina Matt at Michael? Who is teaching/teaches Matt and Michael Tagalog?

Kailan siya magtuturo ng Tagalog sa akin? When will she/he teach me Tagalog?

2. This time the direct object comes second in the word order after the verb. The doer of the action is indicated by an **ang** phrase and follows the direct object. As usual, the directional complement or indirect object comes last.

Directional Complement						
Verb	Object		Actor		Indirect Object (Location/Direction)	
Mag- Verb	Marker	Noun	Marker	Noun	Marker	Noun
Nagbigay (completed)	ng ng mga	**bulaklak**	si sina ang ang mga	**Patrick** **bata**	kay kina	**Jamie.**
Nagbibigay (incompleted)					sa sa mga	**babae.**
Magbibigay (contemplated)					sa	akin. atin. amin.
Magbibigay (contemplated)						iyo. inyo. kaniya. kanila.

The sentences below illustrate the word order in questions, or interrogative sentences, using the **ba** question marker and the interrogative pronouns **sino** and **kailan**. The verb implies a movement of the object, **pagkain**, to the indirect object, Pepito.

EXAMPLES:

Nagdadala ba ng pagkain si Nenita kay Pepito? Does Nenita bring food to Pepito?/Is Nenita bringing food to Pepito?

Sino ang magdadala ng pagkain kay Pepito? Who will bring food to Pepito?

Kailan ka nagdala ng pagkain kay Pepito? When did you bring food to Pepito?

3. The chart below shows the indirect object marked by **para kay**, **para kina**, **para sa**, and **para sa mga** for nouns and **para sa** for pronouns. In each case, the doer of the action, which is also the subject of the sentence, is an **ang** pronoun.

Benefactive Complement						
Verb	Actor		Object		Indirect Object (Benefactive Complement)	
Mag- Verb	Marker	Noun	Marker	Noun	Marker	Noun
Magluto (infinitive)		ka kayo tayo	ng ng mga	**pagkain**	para kay para kina	**Jamie.**
Nagluto (completed)		ako tayo kami ka kayo siya sila			para sa para sa mga	**babae.**
Nagluluto (incompleted)					para sa	akin. atin. amin. iyo. inyo. kaniya. kanila.
Magluluto (contemplated)						

In the following sentences, the indirect objects are marked by **para** (*for*).

EXAMPLES:

Nagluto ho ba siya ng adobo para kay Melinda? Did she/he cook adobo for Melinda, sir/madam?

Sino ang nagluluto ng adobo para sa lola? Who is cooking/cooks adobo for grandmother?

Kailan kayo magluluto ng adobo para sa akin? When will you cook adobo for me?

4. In the chart below, notice the different word order when the actors are **ang** phrases. The direct object comes second after the ditransitive verb and is followed by the actor and the benefactive complement or indirect object.

Di-transitive Verb						
Verb	**Object**		**Actor**		**Indirect Object (Benefactive Complement)**	
Mag-	**Marker**	**Noun**	**Marker**	**Noun**	**Marker**	**Noun**
Nag-bake (completed)	ng ng mga	pagkain	si sina ang ang mga	Patrick bata	para kay para kina	Jamie.
Nagbe-bake (incompleted)					para sa para sa mga	babae.
Magbe-bake (contemplated)					para sa	akin. atin. amin. iyo. inyo. kaniya. kanila.
Magluluto (contemplated)						

5. The following sentences reflect several grammar points that we have already taken up: predicational sentence, word order of enclitics, direct-object markers, subject markers, benefactive markers, **mag**-prefixed to a borrowed word, and the interrogative pronouns **sino** and **kailan**.

EXAMPLES:

Nagbe-bake raw ng keyk si Mindy para kay Marco. They say Mindy is baking a cake for Marco.

Sino ang magbe-bake ng keyk para kay Marco? Who will bake a cake for Marco?

Kailan ho nag-bake ng keyk si Nanay? When did Mom bake a cake, sir/madam?

Grammar Notes

1. Notes on **mag**-verbs
   a. **mag** + <u>sports</u> means to play the sport expressed.
   b. **mag** + <u>musical instrument</u> means to play the musical instrument expressed.
   c. **mag** + <u>food</u> means to either cook or eat the food expressed.
   d. **mag** + <u>restaurant</u> means to eat at the restaurant expressed.

   Nagte-tennis is Mike araw-araw. Mike plays tennis everyday.
   Magda-drums sila sa bahay mamaya. They will play drums at the house later.
   Nag-adobo si Nanay kanina. Mother cooked adobo a while ago.
   Magdya-Jollibee kami bukas. We (exclusive) will eat at Jollibee tomorrow.

2. In cases where the first syllable of borrowed words that begin with the letters *c, f, j, q, v,* and *z* need to be reduplicated, use the corresponding Tagalog letters to replace the sounds of each borrowed letter or syllable.

c → k	**mag**-carbonara	→	**nagka**-carbonara; **magka**-carbonara
f → p	**mag**-football	→	**nagpu**-football; **magpu**-football
j → dy	**mag**-jogging	→	**nagdya**-jogging; **magdya**-jogging
q → kw	**mag**-quiznos	→	**nagkwi**-quiznos; **magkwi**-quiznos
v → b	**mag**-volleyball	→	**nagba**-volleyball; **magba**-volleyball
z → s	**mag**-ziti	→	**nagsi**-ziti; **magsi**-ziti

3. Definite adverbs of time are adverbs that give an exact time. When using definite adverbs of time like **kanina**, **araw-araw**, **mamaya**, etc., markers such as **sa**, **tuwing** and **noong** are not used.

   Magba-bike si Mike <u>mamaya</u>. Mike will ride the bicycle later.
   *__Magba-bike si Mike sa mamaya.__ (incorrect)

4. The most frequent word orders when using a ditransitive verb, or a verb that has two objects, are:

   VERB + ACTOR + OBJECT + INDIRECT OBJECT + ADVERB
   VERB + OBJECT + ACTOR + INDIRECT OBJECT + ADVERB

   Nagbigay siya ng pagkain sa akin kahapon. She/He gave me food yesterday.
   Nagbigay ng pagkain si Mark sa akin kahapon. Mark gave me food yesterday.

Practice

I. Speaking Practice

Work with a partner. Look at the picture of each person below and, based on visual clues, consider what their hobbies might be. In at least five sentences, describe each person and his or her hobbies. Share what you have written with the rest of the class.

Greg

Maria

Bogart

II. Reading Practice

Read the text below and answer the Reading Comprehension questions in Tagalog.

Word Bank

makakilala to be able to know someone
dapat should
sayawan dance studio
katabi next to
pwede can
karanasan experience
tumawag to call

Ang Sayawan *The Dance Studio*

Filipinos are fond of dancing. The word for dance is **sayaw**. The suffix **-an** in the word **sayawan** denotes a place where the root word is found. Hence, a place for dancing.

Mahilig ka bang magsayaw? Gusto mo bang makakilala ng mga bagong kaibigan? Kung oo ang iyong sagot, magpunta ka sa sayawan namin sa Makati Ave. katabi ng isang parke sa Pasong Tamo tuwing Huwebes ng gabi mula ala sais ng gabi hanggang alas nuwebe ng gabi. Si Luis Santos ang magtuturo ng sayaw sa inyo. Siya ay nagsasayaw nang mahigit sa sampung taon ng kundiman, pandanggo sa ilaw, itik-itik, at tinikling. Pwedeng mag-aral kahit sino, may karanasan o wala.

Para sa direksyon, presyo at iba pang impormasyon *tumawag* **sa: 0917 891 0905**

Reading Comprehension

1. What kind of article is this?

_____

2. Who is teaching the class?

_____

3. Where is the class being held?

_____

4. What time is the class?

_____

III. Writing Practice

On a sheet of paper, illustrate the verbs listed in the Word Bank, following the model of the drawing below. Afterwards, write a sentence using the following sentence structure: VERB + ACTOR (**AKO**) + DIRECT OBJECT + INDIRECT OBJECT. You can use different aspects of the verb to form your sentences.

```
┌────────────────────────────────────────┐
│              Word Bank                  │
│                                         │
│    magluto    mag-bake    magbigay      │
│    magturo    magdala     magpasyal     │
└────────────────────────────────────────┘
```

1. **Kung may panahon ako, nagluluto ako ng mga pagkain para sa mga kaibigan ko at sa pamilya ko.**

2. _____

3. _____

4. _____

5. _____

6. _____

IV. Listening Practice

Listen to audio file (08–2) and answer the following questions. Circle **Oo** if the answer is true and **Hindi** if it is false. Stop the audio clip as often as necessary.

```
┌────────────────────────────────────────┐
│              Word Bank                  │
│                                         │
│           mahilig fond of               │
│           kasama with                   │
│           pagkatapos after              │
└────────────────────────────────────────┘
```

1. **Mahilig bang magbisikleta si Theron?**
    Oo   **Hindi**

2. **Nanood ba si Theron ng sine noong linggo?**
    Oo   **Hindi**

3. **Nagbasketball ba si Theron kasama ang mga kaibigan niya noong Lunes?**
    Oo   **Hindi**

4. **Nagpunta ba si Theron sa club kahapon?**
    Oo   **Hindi**

5. **Mamaya, magbe-bake ba si Theron ng keyk para sa kaibigan niya?**
    Oo   **Hindi**

Pamimili

Shopping

An Overview of Lesson 9

Objectives
• Use appropriate expressions in the context of shopping
• Engage in small talk about shopping

Vocabulary
• Numbers and Nouns   • **-Um-** Verbs   • Affixes
• Adjectives   • **Mag**-Verbs   • Idioms and Expressions

Dialogue: Magkano Ito? *How Much Is This?*

Dialogue Comprehension

Activities
Activity 1: I Like Your Dress
Activity 2: Role Play
Activity 3: Information Gap

Grammar
Definition of Terms: Aspect, Verb Focus, Actor-Focus Verbs, Infix, Prefix, Intransitive Verb, Transitive Verb, Ditransitive Verb, and **-Um-** Verbs

Examining Form
I.   **-Um-** Verbs
    Grammar Presentation: **-Um-** Verbs
II. Numbers: **Daan at Libo** (Hundred and Thousand)
    Grammar Notes

Practice
I. Speaking Practice
II. Reading Practice
III. Writing Practice
IV. Listening Practice

Vocabulary 🎧 (09–1)

The vocabulary below will help you speak about shopping and make small talk—and to participate in the activities in this lesson. Memorize the vocabulary words before proceeding to the dialogue.

Numbers and Nouns

isang daan	one hundred
dalawang daan	two hundred
tatlong daan	three hundred
apat na raan	four hundred
limang daan	five hundred
anim na raan	six hundred
pitong daan	seven hundred
walong daan	eight hundred
siyam na raan	nine hundred
isang libo	one thousand
dalawang libo	two thousand
tatlong libo	three thousand
apat na libo	four thousand
limang libo	five thousand
anim na libo	six thousand
pitong libo	seven thousand
walong libo	eight thousand
siyam na libo	nine thousand
sampung libo	ten thousand
barya	loose change
bayad	payment
manggas	sleeves
mamimili	buyer
presyo	price
sukat	size
sukli	change
tela	fabric, cloth, textile
tindero/a	merchant, storekeeper, seller, clerk

Adjectives

bago	new
baligtad	upside-down, inside-out
kaunti	few, little
luma	old
mabigat	heavy
magaan	light (weight)
mahaba	long
mahal	expensive
maikli/maiksi/ maigsi	short
makapal	thick
makinis	smooth
malambot	soft
malapad	wide
maluwag/ maluwang	loose
manipis	thin
mapusyaw	light color
marami	many, plenty
marumi/ madumi	dirty
matibay	durable
matigas	hard, tough
mura	cheap, inexpensive
pangit	ugly
sira	destroyed, broken
uso	trendy, current style

-Um- Verbs

bumili	to buy
gumastos	to spend
gumamit	to use
humanap	to look for something/ someone
humingi	to ask for something
humiram	to borrow, to check out
kumuha	to get
lumapit	to approach, to get closer
pumasok	to enter
pumunta	to go
tumawag	to call
tumingin	to look at
tumulong	to help
umutang	to borrow money, to buy something on credit
umuwi	to go home

Mag- Verbs

magbenta	to sell
magbukas	to open something
magtinda	to sell

Affixes

daan	a unit of hundred
libo	a unit of thousand
-um-	an actor focus verbal affix

Pronouns

iyan	that (near the listener)
ito	this (near the speaker)
iyon	that (far from the speaker and listener)

Idioms and Expressions

Ang ganda ng damit mo! Bagay na bagay sa 'yo. Your clothes are nice. They really look good on you.

Bago ba 'yan? Saan mo binili iyan? Is that new? Where did you buy it?

Gusto mo bang isukat? Do you want to try it on?

Kasiyang-kasiya lang sa iyo. It really fits you well.

Magkano ang bili mo diyan? How much did you pay for that?

Mayroon kaya sila niyan sa…? Do they have this in . . . ?

Patingin nga ako . . . May I see . . . ?

siyanga ba really

Dialogue: Magkano Ito? *How Much Is This?*

Annie is shopping for a dress at a department store. Read her exchange with a salesperson and answer the Dialogue Comprehension questions that follow.

Saleslady: **Ano po yun, ma' am?**

Annie: **Humahanap ako ng bestida. Nasaan ba ang mga ito?**

Saleslady: **Nandito po. Ano po bang klase ng bestida ang gusto ninyo?**

Annie: **Gusto ko ng pormal na bestida.**

Saleslady: **Heto po. Mahaba at malambot po ang tela ng bestida na ito. Gusto po ba ninyo ito?**

Annie: **Oo. Mayroon ka ba nito sa itim?**

Saleslady: **Opo. Mayroon po kami. Ano ho ang sukat ninyo?**

Annie: *Medium* **lang ako.**

Saleslady: **Ay! Wala na po kami n'yan sa** *medium*, **pero mayroon ho kaming** *small*. **Gusto ho ba ninyong isukat?**

Annie: **O sige.**

      . . . . .

Annie: **Nako! Masikip yata.**

Saleslady: **Hindi po. Kasiyang-kasiya po sa inyo. Maluwag pa nga po.**

Annie: **O sige na nga. Magkano ba ito?**

Salesady: **Isang libo lang po.**

Annie: **O sige. Saan ako magbabayad?**

Saleslady: **Pumunta po kayo doon.**

Annie: **O sige. Salamat, ha!**

Dialogue Comprehension

1. What kind of dress was Annie looking for?

2. What kind of dress did Annie buy?

_____

3. How much was the dress?

_____

4. What was Annie's size?

_____

5. Was Annie's dress too snug?

_____

Activities

Activity 1

Walk around the class and talk to four of your classmates. Comment on what they are wearing. Use the expressions and questions below and fill in the chart as you go.

EXAMPLE:

STUDENT 1: **Ang ganda ng damit mo ah. Bagay na bagay sa iyo!**
Bago ba iyan?

STUDENT 2: **Hindi. Luma na ito.**

STUDENT 1: **Kailan at saan mo binili iyan?**

STUDENT 2: **Noong isang buwan sa Bench.**

STUDENT 1: **Magkanong bili mo diyan?**

STUDENT 2: **Isang libo lang.**

Pangalan	Ano	Saan	Kailan	Magkano
1. Fredy	pantalon	sa Bench	noong isang buwan	Php 1000
2.				
3.				
4.				
5.				

Reporting

Now, using complete sentences, report on the information you have gathered from your classmates.

1. **Bumili si Fredy ng pantalon sa Bench noong isang buwan. Isang libong piso ang pantalon ni Fredy.**

2. _____

_____

3. _____

_____

4. _____

_____

5. _____

_____

Activity 2

Work with a partner. Using the exchange between Annie and the salesperson in the dialogue as a model, create your own dialogue based on one of the following two scenarios. The dialogue should be from twelve to sixteen lines long.

1. You are buying a coat for yourself. You are not sure which one to buy. Ask a salesperson for his or her opinion.

2. You are buying a shirt for your friend. Ask a salesperson if the store has it in medium.

Activity 3

This is an information gap activity. Work with a partner. Carlos went shopping at the different stores in the Philippines. Student 1 will use Activity Sheet 1. Student 2 will use Activity Sheet 2. Some information is missing from each student's receipts. Get the missing information from your partner by asking questions. Do not show your activity sheet to your partner.

Activity Sheet 1

What did Carlos buy yesterday? Ask your partner for the missing information. Then compare your activity sheets after.

Mga Tanong

Ano ang binili ni Carlos sa SM?	Bumili si Carlos ng pabango sa SM.
Magkano ang pabango?	PhP 1500 ang pabango.
Magkano ang ibinayad niya?	PhP 1750 ang ibinayad niya.
Magkano ang sukli?	Wala siyang sukli.

SM

Pabango	1500
Sando	250
Total	1750
Cash	
Sukli	0

Bench

Pantalon……..	2000
Tsinelas………..	
Sinturon……..	750
Total	
Cash	3600
Sukli	

Oxygen

T-shirt,…………	
Kwintas………..	600
Maong………….	2500
Polo……….	
3 Medyas…..	350
Total	5200
Cash	
Sukli	300

Mall of Asia

Pantalon…	
Sapatos….	3250
Total	
Cash	4500
Sukli	250

Robinson's

Relos…………..	3000
Amerikana………	5000
Sumbrero…….	500
Total	8500
Cash	
Sukli	500

Greenhills

Singsing………..	3500
Salamin………..	2050
Total	5550
Cash	6000
Sukli	

Information Gap Activity

Activity Sheet 2

What did Carlos buy yesterday? Ask your partner for the missing information. Then compare your activity sheets after.

Mga Tanong

Ano ang binili ni Carlos sa SM?	Bumili si Carlos ng pabango sa SM.
Magkano ang pabango?	1500 ang pabango.
Magkano ang ibinayad niya?	1750 ang ibinayad niya.
Magkano ang sukli?	Wala siyang sukli.

Information Gap Activity

SM

Pabango	1500
Sando	_____
Total	1750
Cash	1750
Sukli	_____

Bench

Pantalon……..	2000
Tsinelas………..	800
Sinturon……..	_____
Total	3500
Cash	_____
Sukli	50

Oxygen

T-shirt,…………	500
Kwintas………..	600
Maong………….	_____
Polo………..	1250
3 Medyas…..	_____
Total	_____
Cash	5500
Sukli	_____

Mall of Asia

Pantalon…	1000
Sapatos….	_____
Total	4250
Cash	4500
Sukli	_____

Robinson's

Relos…………..	3000
Amerikana………	5000
Sumbrero…….	500
Total	8500
Cash	9000
Sukli	500

Greenhills

Singsing………..	3500
Salamin………..	_____
Total	5550
Cash	_____
Sukli	450

Grammar

Definition of Terms

Aspect	A characteristic of Tagalog verbs that indicates whether the action has started, is continuing, or has been completed; conveyed by inflection using affixes and reduplication of the first consonant vowel of the root word.
Verb Focus	A characteristic of Tagalog verbs that expresses the role of the subject of the verb in a sentence.
Actor-Focus Verb	A verb whose subject is the agent or doer of the action expressed by the verb.
Infix	A syllable that is inserted within the root word.
Prefix	A syllable joined to the beginning of the root word.
Intransitive Verb	A verb that has no receiver of the action.
Transitive Verb	A verb that has a direct object or receiver of the action.
Ditransitive Verb	A verb that has two objects: a direct object and an indirect object.
-Um- Verbs	A class of verbs that are actor-focus.

Examining Form

Review the sentences below and complete the tasks that follow. Discuss your answers with a partner. Consult the following section to check your answers.

1. **Humahanap ako ng bestida.**
2. **Pumunta po kayo doon.**
3. **Titingin ako ng bagong damit sa Greenhills.**
4. **Umutang ng isang libong piso si Joe sa akin.**
5. **Umuuwi si Paloma tuwing Linggo.**

a. Circle the actors and underline the verbs.
b. The sentences above have **-um-** verbal affixes. Identify all the different aspects used.
c. What kind of verbal affix is **-um-**? Is it a prefix, an infix, or both?

I. -Um- Verbs

In this lesson, we will learn about **-um-** verbs, another type of verb that focuses on the actor. As mentioned in Lesson 7, there are many verbal affixes, and **-um-** is one of the most commonly used by verbal roots. Some verbal roots take both **-um-** and **mag-** affixes; some do not. There are no hard-and-fast rules to determine which verbal affixes can be used for verbal root words, save for immersion and familiarization with a lot of verbal roots and how they were used in authentic or real communication. Unlike the verbal prefix **mag-**, which means to perform the act indicated by the root word to which it is attached, the infix **-um-** does not mean anything. Another difference is the formation of the two verbs. Generally, the **mag-** affix can be attached to borrowed words, such as *computer*, to form verbs like **magkompyuter**. As a general rule, the **-um-** affix cannot be attached to a borrowed word from another language.

Two common uses of **um-** verbs are: 1) to denote the action of becoming when attached to adjectives; 2) to denote acts of nature and bodily functions:

-um- + ADJ $\rightarrow$ VERB
pula red
pula + **-um-** $\rightarrow$ **pumula** to become red

ganda beauty
ganda + -um- $\rightarrow$ **gumanda** to become beautiful

-um- + nature

lindol earthquake
lindol + -um- $\rightarrow$ **lumindol** for the earthquake to happen (earthquake happens)

upo sit
upo + -um- $\rightarrow$ **umupo** to sit

For many verbs that have both **-um-** and **mag-** conjugations, the difference in meaning is very slight. or not at all. But some linguists are of the opinion that **mag-** verbs are more purposeful than **-um-** verbs when the meanings are the same.

EXAMPLES:

maglakad to walk   **magpunta** to go
lumakad, to walk   **pumunta** to go

magsayaw to dance   **magsulat** to write
sumayaw to dance   **sumulat** to write

magkain to eat every now and then
kumain to eat

There are instances, though, when the meaning varies completely, as in the examples below. It would seem that the **mag-** verbs express action that is a moving away of an object, whereas the **-um-** verbs indicate simple action indicated by the root word performed by the actor on itself.

EXAMPLES:

mag-alis to remove something   **mag-akyat** to bring something upstairs
umalis to leave   **umakyat** to climb

magbili to sell
bumili to buy

-Um- verbs and **mag-** verbs are actor-focus (subject) verbs. Both verbs can be used in sentences where the verb does not require an object to complete its meaning or when the object is indefinite. An object in a Tagalog sentence is indefinite when a **ng** marker precedes the word.

EXAMPLES:

Tumalon siya. He jumped.
Kumain ako ng kanin. I ate rice.

The -um- verbal affix is an infix. It is attached before the first vowel of the root word, as in **tawag tumawag**. In cases where the root word begins with a vowel, **-um-** might easily be taken to be a prefix.

However, verbs in Tagalog that begin with a vowel have a glottal catch /'/ before the vowel, and this glottal catch is considered a consonant, though it is not visibly marked. The **-um-** infix is placed after the glottal catch: **'utang umutang**.

In the following chart, the root words **utang** (debt) and **bili** (buy) are affixed with **-um-** to form **-um-** verbs. The chart also shows the different completed, incompleted, and contemplated aspectual forms. As we have seen, these are made by affixation and reduplication of the first consonant/vowel of the root word, and that is the case here, although there are differences. For **bili**, the infinitive is **bili** + **-um-** = **bumili**. The completed aspect is the same as the infinitive. The incompleted aspect is **bumibili**, where **bi** is reduplicated and **-um-** is inserted before the first vowel that was reduplicated. In the contemplated aspect, the **-um-** is nowhere to be found. Only the first consonant/vowel of the root word is reduplicated. Among the many Tagalog verb types, only **-um-** verbs have the same form for the infinitive/imperative form and the completed form.

Aspect	Inflection	Inflection	Rules
Root word	Utang	Bili	
Infinitive	*Um*utang	B*um*ili	Place **um** before the first vowel of the root.
Completed	*Um*utang	B*um*ili	Same as the infinitive form.
Incompleted	*Um*uutang	B*um*ibili	Take the first two syllables of the completed aspect, plus the root.
Contemplated	*U*utang	B*i*bili	Take the first syllable of the root, plus the root.

Grammar Presentation

-Um- Verbs

1. The chart below shows the structure of a sentence that uses an **-um-** intransitive verb. It is followed by examples of sentences that use **-um-** verbs in the different aspects.

Intransitive Verbs			
Verb	Actor (Ang Phrase)		Location
-Um-	Markers	Nouns	Sa
<u>Pu</u>masok (infinitive)		ka kayo tayo	
<u>Pu</u>masok (completed) Pu<u>ma</u>pasok (incompleted) <u>Pa</u>pasok (contemplated)	si sina	<u>Jamie</u>	sa <u>botik</u>.
	ang ang mga	<u>bata</u>	
		ako tayo kami ka kayo siya sila	

EXAMPLES:
Lumapit sila sa kaniya. They approached him/her.
Pumupunta ba siya sa Mall of Asia tuwing Linggo? Does she/he go to Mall of Asia every Sunday?
Papasok sina Mike at Carlos sa Bench. Mike and Carlos will go inside Bench (store in the Philippines).

2. The chart below shows the structure of a sentence that uses **bumili**, an **-um-** transitive verb. The actor and the subject of the sentence is an **ang** phrase. Notice that the word order is: VERB + OBJECT + SUBJECT + TIME + LOCATION. This is illustrated by the example sentences below the chart.

Transitive Verb							
Verb	**Object**		**Actor**		**Time**		**Location**
-Um-	**Marker**	**Noun**	**Marker**	**Noun**	**Marker**	**Noun**	**sa**
Bumili (completed)	ng ng mga	damit	si sina	Patrick	noong	Lunes	sa SM.
Bumibili (incomplete)			ang ang mga	bata			
Bibili (contemplated)					sa	Lunes	

EXAMPLES:
Gumastos ng isang daang piso *si Maria* kagabi. Maria spent one hundred pesos last night.
Humahanap ba ng pantalon *si Christine* sa Mega Mall? Is Christine looking for a pair of jeans at Mega Mall?
Bibili raw po ng sapatos *sina Bobby at Kevin* sa Glorieta. They say Bobby and Kevin will buy shoes at Glorieta, sir/madam.

3. The chart below shows the structure of a sentence that uses **kumuha** (to get), an **-um-** transitive VERB. The actor and the subject of the sentence is an ang pronoun. Notice that the word order is: VERB + PRONOUN-SUBJECT + OBJECT + TIME + LOCATION. The example sentences below the chart illustrates this structure in the different aspects.

Transitive Verb							
Verb	**Actor**		**Object**		**Time**		**Location**
-Um-	**Marker**	**Noun**	**Marker**	**Noun**	**Marker**	**Noun**	**Sa**
Kumuha (infinitive)		ka kayo tayo	ng ng mga	damit	sa	Lunes	sa bahay.
Kumuha (completed)		ako tayo kami ka kayo siya sila			noong	Lunes	
Kumukuha (incompleted)							
Kukuha (contemplated)					sa	Lunes	

EXAMPLES:

Bumili *sila* **ng pulseras sa Greenhills noong isang linggo.** They bought a bracelet at Greenhills last week.

Gumagastos ba *kayo* **ng limang daang piso araw-araw?** Do you (plural) spend five hundred pesos every day?

Hahanap na *ako* **ng bagong sumbrero sa Robinson's Place bukas.** I will now look for a new cap at Robinson's Place tomorrow.

4. To ask a question about the person performing an action described by **-um-** verb, use **sino**.

Sino Question				
Interrogative	Ang	Verb	Object	
		-Um-	Marker	Noun
Sino	ang	humiram (completed) humihiram (incompleted) hihiram (contemplated)	ng ng mga	damit?

EXAMPLES:

Sino ang bumili ng blusa? Who bought the blouse?

Sino ang humahanap ng hikaw ko? Who is looking for my earring?

Sino ang kukuha ng amerikana ko? Who will get my suit?

5. As stated in previous lessons, the negative marker hindi is always followed by pronouns in a negative statement. When the actor-subject is an ang phrase, the word order is: **Hindi** + **-um-**VERB + SUBJECT + DIRECT OBJECT.

Negative Sentence					
Negative	Actor		Verb	Object	
	Marker	Noun	-Um-	Marker	Noun
Hindi		ako tayo kami ka kayo siya sila	umutang (completed) umuutang (incompleted) uutang (contemplated)	ng ng mga	pera.

Negative	Verb	Actor		Object	
		Marker	Noun	Marker	Noun
Hindi	umutang (completed) umuutang (incompleted) uutang (contemplated)	si sina	Mark	ng ng mga	pera.
		ang ang mga	estudyante		

When there are adverbs of time in sentences like the ones in the chart, they are usually the last unit in the sentence.

EXAMPLES:

Hindi siya bumili ng mga damit *kahapon.* She/He did not buy clothes yesterday.

Hindi po gumagastos ng isang daang piso si Mike *araw-araw.* Mike does not spend one hundred pesos every day.

Hindi raw sila tumitingin ng damit sa SM. They say they are not looking for clothes at Shoe Mart.

II. Numbers: **Daan at Libo** (Hundred and Thousand)

The word for "hundred" in Tagalog is **daan**, and the word for "thousand" is **libo**. When shopping in the Philippines, or even plain counting, the English numerals are used for bigger numbers, and, at least in Metro Manila, the numbers in hundreds and thousands listed in the chart below are never used. Filipinos prefer English and Spanish numerals over Tagalog numbers, maybe by force of habit, although another possible reason is the sheer length of the Tagalog numerals. Take for instance 40,000. The Tagalog numeral **apatnapung libo** (6 syllables) is quite a mouthful compared to the Spanish and English: *cuarenta mil* (4 syllables) and *forty thousand* (4 syllables). But the main reason for this preference for the Spanish and English numerals is Spanish colonization of the Philippines for over 350 years and American occupation for 50 years. The natives had to transpose their way of counting into Spanish and English, the languages of power, government, and commerce in order to participate and do bussiness with their colonial masters. And thus the native way of counting fell into disuse.

You may wonder why one needs hundreds and thousands to shop in the Philippines. The reason is simple. The Philippine peso has suffered devaluation and inflation as the consequences of a third-world country trying to survive in this global economy after colonization. See the table below for examples of "hundreds" and "thousands" in Tagalog.

Daan				Libo	
Isang daan	100	Isang daan at lima	105	Isang libo	1000
Dalawang daan	200	Dalawang daan at labinlima	215	Dalawang libo limang daan	2500
Tatlong daan	300	Tatlong daan at dalawampu	320	Tatlong libo limang daan at walumpu	3580
Apat na raan	400	Apat na raan at tatlumpu't lima	435	Apat na libo siyamnapu	4090
Limang daan	500	Limang daan at apatnapu	540	Sampung libo walong daan	10800
Anim na raan	600	Anim na raan at limampu't lima	655	Apatnapung libo at limampu't lima	40055
Pitong daan	700	Pitong daan at animnapu	760	Limampung libo siyam na raan at lima	50905
Walong daan	800	Walong daan at walumpu't anim	886	Walumpung libo at walo	80008
Siyam na raan	900	Siyam na raan at siyamnapu't walo	998	Siyamnapung libo pitong daan at isa	90701

Grammar Notes

1. As we have seen, **daan** is the word for a unit of one hundred, and **libo** is the word for a unit of one thoudand. Note that these terms do not express a plural.

Limang daan	five hundred
Walong libo	eight thousand

2. Since numbers function as adjectives, the linkers **ng** and **na** must be employed when using **daan** or **libo**. **-ng-** is attached to numbers ending in vowels. **na** is used when the previous word ends in a consonant.

Is*ang* daan	one hundred
Ani*m* na libo	six thousand

3. **Daan** becomes **raan** when the preceding word ends with a vowel.

Apat n*a* raan	four hundred
Anim n*a* raan	six hundred

4. Use the conjunction **at** when connecting hundreds to tens.

Isang daan at walumpu	one hundred and eighty
Anim na raan at lima	six hundred and five

5. A conjunction is not necessary when connecting thousands to hundreds. However, when connecting thousands to tens, the conjunction **at** must be used.

Isang libo walong daan	one tousand eight hundred
Limampung libo siyam na raan.	fifty thousand nine hundred
Isang libo at walo.	one thousand and eight
Limang libo at dalawampu.	five thousand and twenty

Practice

I. Speaking Practice

Role-Play
The class should be divided into two groups. Half of the class has shopping lists, and the other half will play the role of shop owners. Copy worksheets A and B from below and cut up the cards so that there is an equal number of cards for shoppers (worksheet A) and shop owners (B). The ideal number is four of each.

Worksheet ng mga Mamimili
Shoppers need to find everything on their list and complete their short task. Here is a list of the things that you need to buy today.

Heto ang listahan ng mga dapat mong bilhin ngayong araw.	Heto ang listahan ng mga dapat mong bilhin ngayong araw.
√ kuwintas √ tsinelas √ bestida √ sando √ singsing	√ medyas √ tsinelas √ polo √ salamin √ relos
Heto ang listahan ng mga dapat mong bilhin ngayong araw.	**Heto ang listahan ng mga dapat mong bilhin ngayong araw.**
√ pantalon √ palda √ maong √ pulseras √ sumbrero	√ hikaw √ blusa √ sinturon √ amerikana √ sapatos

Worksheet ng mga Tindero at Tindera

Shop owners need to 1) draw all the products, and 2) decide how much each product costs before starting. You are a variety store owner. The chart below lists all of your merchandise.

1) May tindahan ka ng alahas. Heto ang mga paninda mo:	2) May tindahan ka ng mga sapatos at iba pang gamit. Heto ang mga paninda mo:
√ kuwintas √ relos √ hikaw √ singsing	√ medyas √ sinturon √ sapatos √ tsinelas √ sumbrero
3) May tindahan ka ng damit at salamin. Heto ang mga paninda mo:	**4) May tindahan ka ng damit. Heto ang mga paninda mo:**
√ amerikana √ palda √ maong √ salamin √ bestida	√ pantalon √ blusa √ polo √ sando √ tsinelas

II. Reading Practice

A. Complete the dialogue by choosing one of the sentences marked *a* to below.

Dispatsadora: **Kumusta po sila? May *sale* po kami ngayon sa mga pantalon.**
Jose: _____
Dispatsadora: **Nandito lang po.**
Jose: _____
Dispatsadora: **Heto po.**
Jose: **Nasaan ang *fitting room* ninyo?**

Dispatsdara: _____

_____

Dispatsdora: **Kasya ho ba?**
Jose: _____
Dispatsadora: **Isang libong piso lang po.**
Jose: **O sige. Saan ako magbabayad?**
Dispatsadora: **Doon po sa** *counter*. **May iba pa po kayong gusto?**
Jose: _____
Dispatsadora: **O sige po.**

a: **Nandito po.**
b: **Siyanga ba? Nasaan ang mga ito?**
c: **Wala na. O sige. Salamat.**
d: **Oo. Tamang-tama ang sukat. Magkano ito?**
e: **Gusto ko iyon. Pakikuha mo nga ako ng** *size* **30/30, 30 ang haba, 30 ang bewang.**

B. Now that you have completed the dialogue, answer the following questions about it.

1. **Ano ang naka-sale ngayon?**

_____

2. **Ano ang sukat ni Jose?**

_____

3. **Magkano ang pantalon?**

_____

III. Writing Practice
Interview three classmates and find out the following information:

Kung mayroon kang PhP 5,000   If you have P5,000.00

a. **Ano ang bibilhin mo?**   What will you buy?
b. **Saan mo ito bibilhin?**   Where will you buy it?
c. **Bakit mo ito bibilhin?**   Why will you buy it?

Pangalan: _____

_____

_____

_____

Pangalan: _____

_____

_____

_____

Pangalan: _____

_____

_____

_____

IV. Listening Practice

Listen to audio file (09–2) and answer the following questions about Mario's shopping in Tagalog. Take note of the vocabulary in the word bank, which may help you better understand the audio.

Word Bank

desenyo design

Dialogue Comprehension

Answer the following questions in English.

1. **Anu-ano ang mga klase ng polo?**

   _____

2. **Ano ang usong klase ng polo ngayon?**

   _____

3. **Ano ang sukat ni Mario?**

   _____

4. **Magkano ang polo?**

   _____

5. **Kasya ba ang small kay Mario?**

   _____

UNIT 4

TAHANAN
Home

Homes in the Philippines vary significantly, as one might expect. Rural homes in the provinces may have large backyards and enough space for elaborate gardens and pens for livestock to help sustain the family. On the other hand, many urban dwellings in Manila or Cebu are high-rise condominiums or apartments and tend to be very Western, while homes of the elite are usually Spanish-colonial or American in architectural style. Despite such variation, Filipino homes often share several commonalities.

Bahay Kubo: *A typical native house*

A stone house in one of the affluent exclusive villages in the Philippines

Eighty-three percent of the Philippines is Catholic, so it should come as no surprise to see religious figures such as the Holy Family in Filipino homes, with statues and images of the Virgin Mary and Jesus Christ extremely prevalent. Almost all Catholic Filipino homes have an altar with various types of rosary beads and a Santo Niño, a statue of the child Jesus Christ. Hanging over the dining room or kitchen would probably be a painting of the Last Supper.

Besides religious decoration, another common feature is that many Filipino homes are designed to accommodate a large family. Bedrooms are shared among siblings, and it is not unusual to find children sleeping with their parents. There is also no real distinction between the dining room, living room, and family room in most Filipino households, with the exception of the wealthy. Dinner parties are large, so food is eaten in various places around the house and not just around the dinner table.

A unique quality of the typical Filipino home is the use of two kitchens. There is the main kitchen, where much of the food is prepared and some of the cooking is done. However, many homes also have a "dirty" kitchen, where most of the cooking is done. This is where the cook will fry smelly foods such as fish or **lumpia** (the Filipinos' version of egg roll) in order to avoid the whole house filling with strong and unpleasant cooking odors or smelling of food.

In the dining room, which is the heart of the house, you also might see hung on the wall a giant wooden spoon and fork decoration. Some Westerners find this tacky, but these wall ornaments have become so fashionable that Kaboodle and other large department stores features them on their Web sites. To those with a very fertile imagination, it may seem that the Philippines was once inhabited by well brought-up giants, and these are their artifacts.

A typical middle-class kitchen

Dining room with large wooden spoon and fork on the wall

Ang Aking Bahay

My House

An Overview of Lesson 10

Objectives
• Describe specific location of an object
• List the different objects in the house

Vocabulary

• Things in the House   • Spatial Location Words   • Adverbs
• Adjectives   • Pronouns   • Idoims and Expressions

Dialogue: Ito ang Bahay Ko   *This Is My House*

Dialogue Comprehension

Activities

Activity 1: My House
Activity 2: My Bedroom
Activity 3: Where Is the . . . ?

Grammar

Definition of Terms: Prepositions and Prepositional Phrase

Examining Form

I.   Spatial Location Words
     Grammar Presentation:
     A. **Nasa** and Spatial Location Words
     B. **Sa** and Spatial Location Words
     Grammar Notes

Practice

I.   Speaking Practice
II.   Reading Practice
III.   Writing Practice
IV.   Listening Practice

Vocabulary 🎧 (10–1)

The vocabulary below will help you speak about objects in the house and the location of things. You will need it to participate in the activities in this lesson. Memorize the vocabulary words before proceeding to the dialogue.

Things around the House

aircon	air conditioner
aparador	closet
bangko	bench, stool
banig	mat
basurahan	trash can or garbage container
bentilador	electric fan
bintana	window
bunggalo	bungalow
dingding	wall
hagdan	stair
ilaw	light, lamp
kabinet	cabinet
kalan	stove
kama	bed
kubo	hut
kubrekama	bed spread
kulambo	mosquito net
kumot	blanket
kurtina	curtain
kuwadro	frame
halaman	plant
lampara, ilaw	lamp
libro	book
litrato	picture, photo
mesa	table
orasan	clock
plorera	flower vase
puno	tree
radyo	radio
rep, pridyeder	refrigerator
salamin	mirror
silya	chair
sopa	sofa, couch
tabo	water dipper
tokador	dresser
unan	pillow
up-and-down	two-story house
walis	broom

Adjectives

kakaiba	unusual
komportable	comfortable
pahaba	elongated
pakuwadrado	squared
pabilog	circular
mababa	short (height)
madilim	dark
makaluma	traditional
mahaba	long
mainit	hot
maingay	loud
maikli	short (length)
magulo	messy
malaki	big
malamig	cold
maliit	small
maliwanag	bright
maluwang	spacious
mataas	tall
masikip	cramped
moderno	modern
sira	broken
sira-sira	dilapidated
tahimik	quiet
walang laman	empty

Spatial Location Words

gitna	in between
harap	in front
ibaba	downstairs, below
ibabaw	on top of
ilalim	under
itaas	upstairs, above
kaliwa	left
kanan	right
kanto	corner
labas	outside
likod	behind
loob	inside
tabi	next to
tapat	across

Pronouns

Ilan	how many

Adverbs

banda	direction, toward or towards; at about a certain time

Idioms and Expressions

Akin na lang ang . . . ?	Can I have . . . ?
Pasensya ka na.	I'm sorry.
Magulo dito.	It's messy here.
mula sa	from
Saan mo nabili ito?	Where did you buy this?
Teka, tingnan mo ang . . .	Wait, look at . . .
Tuloy ka.	Come in.

Dialogue: Ito ang Bahay Ko *This Is My House*

In the dialogue below, Lando is visiting Berto at his apartment. Read their exchange and answer the Dialogue Comprehension questions in Tagalog.

Berto: **O Lando. Tuloy ka! Pasensya ka na at magulo dito ah!**

Lando: **Hindi! Ayos naman. Gusto ko nga ang apartment mo, eh.**
          Gusto ko ang mga painting sa dingding mo. Saan mo nabili ito?

Berto: **Sa Baguio. Teka, tingnan mo ang kuwarto ko.**

Lando: **Ang laki-laki! Ilan ang kuwarto lahat dito?**

Berto: **Dalawa lang. Tapos, dalawa rin ang CR namin.**

Lando: **Hindi ko alam na mahilig ka sa mga litrato. Gusto ko ang mga litrato sa ibabaw ng mesa mo at ang mga kuwadro sa tabi ng kompyuter mo.**

Berto: **Oo, mula sa Tagaytay ang mga litrato na iyan.**

Lando: **Eh ang mga sumbrero sa loob ng kabinet mo? Saan mo nakuha ang mga ito?**

Berto: **Koleksyon ko iyan ng mga paborito kong mga baseball team. May dalawampu akong sumbrero.**

Lando: **Ang galing! Akin na lang ang isa.**

Berto: **O sige!**

Lando: **Talaga? Salamat ah!**

Dialogue Comprehension

1. **Nasaan sina Berto at Lando?**

2. **Saan nabili ni Berto ang mga *painting*?**

3. **Ilarawan ang apartment ni Berto.**

4. **Saan nabili ni Berto ang mga litrato?**

_____

5. **Ano ang koleksyon ni Berto? Ilan ang koleksyon niya?**

_____

Activities

Activity 1

Use the chart below to list the different rooms in your house. Give a brief description of each room and mention the different items that you would find there.

EXAMPLE:

Sala

Maluwag at maliwanag sa sala ko. Mayroong sopa, mesa, halaman, bentilador, kwadro at telebisyon sa sala ko.

Kuwarto	Mga Bagay at Paglalarawan

Activity 2

Draw the layout of your bedroom and describe it to a classmate. Use the previous activity to model your description.

Activity 3

Study the picture below and answer the following questions.

1. **Nasaan ang libro?**

_____

2. **Ano ang nasa ibabaw ng tokador?**

_____

3. **Ano ang nasa likod ng** *shopping bag*?

_____

4. **Ano ang nasa ibabaw ng kama?**

_____

5. **Nasaan ang bintana?**

_____

6. **Nasaan ang lampara?**

_____

7. **Ano ang nasa tabi ng lampara?**

_____

8. **Ano ang nasa loob ng aparador?**

_____

9. **Ano ang nasa tabi ng kama?**

_____

10. **Ano ang nasa ilalim ng salamin?**

_____

Grammar

Definition of Terms

Prepositions	For the purposes of this lesson, prepositions are words that describe the position of a noun or pronoun in relation to another element of the sentence. In the example below, the question asking where a person is, **nasaan**, is answered by **nasa**, which translates as _in_, _inside_, _within_, or _on_. We encountered **sa** and **nasa** earlier, in Lesson 2. EXAMPLE: Q: **Nasaan si Maria?** Where is Maria? A: **Nasa loob ng kwarto si Maria.** Maria is inside the room.
Prepositional Phrase	A group of words containing a preposition (for example, **nasa** or **sa**) and a noun or noun phrase to indicate location. EXAMPLES: **Nasa loob ng kwarto si Maria.** Maria is inside the room. **Nasa labas si Mario.** Mario is outside.

Examining Form

Review the sentences below and complete the tasks that follow. Discuss your answers with a partner. Consult the following section to check your answers.

1. **Gusto ko ang mga litrato sa ibabaw ng mesa mo**
2. **Gusto ko rin ang mga kwadro sa tabi ng kompyuter mo.**
3. **Nasa loob ng kabinet mo ang mga sumbrero ng beysbol.**
4. **Nasa dingding mo ang mga painting.**

a. Each sentence contains a prepositional phrase. Underline the prepositional phrase, circle the noun, and box the preposition in each sentence.
b. Notice that in numbers 1 and 2 **sa** introduces a specific place, whereas in 3 and 4, it is **nasa**. When do you use **sa** and when do you use **nasa**?

I. Spatial Location Words

In Tagalog grammar books, a preposition (**pang-ukol**) is defined as a word or words used to indicate that a certain person, thing, place, or event is "intended or reserved for" another person thing, place, or event. It also relates a noun or pronoun to the other words in a sentence. **Pang-ukol** is a coined word for "preposition," and its essence comes from the meaning of the root word **ukol**, which means "intended for or reserved for." As we have seen, some aspects of the English grammar do not correspond neatly to the Tagalog language. The preposition in English is one of them. Each language uses prepositions differently. In Tagalog, the word **sa**, which is a location marker, a singular common noun marker in the **sa** form, and a future time marker, is the most widely used equivalent of a preposition in English. **Sa** is the equivalent of *in*, *on*, *at*, *from*, *to*, *of*, *between*, and other prepositions all at once. Therefore, at times translating an English sentence into Tagalog can be ambiguous. Let's take a look at the examples below:

Tumalon siya *sa* mesa. He jumped *over* the table.
Tumalon siya *sa* mesa. He jumped *off* the table.
Tumalon siya *sa* mga mesa. He jumped *in between* the tables.

As the examples show, the Tagalog preposition **sa** cannot capture, by itself, the exact meaning of all English prepositions, and this is why Tagalog uses spatial location words. Spatial location words denote specific places such as **itaas** (upper floor, upper story), **ibabaw** (top, as of a table), **ilalim** (bottom; the space below or underneath something), **ibaba** (underneath), **tapat** (in front of, the place in front; that which is across), **harap** (front), **likod** (back, reverse side), **gitna** (middle, center), **loob** (inside), **kanan** (right), and **kaliwa** (left).

In the same vein, just because a preposition is needed in English does not mean one is needed in Tagalog, and the reverse is also true. Do not simply translate word for word when an English verb is linked to a certain preposition, as translation software often does. This can lead to grammar mistakes.

EXAMPLES:

English:	**Tagalog:**
to smile at	**ngitian:** no preposition because the meaning of the English preposition *at* is supplied by the verbal suffix **-an** in **ngiti** (smile)
to look for (find)	**hanapin:** no preposition because the meaning of the preposition *at* is expressed in suffix **-in** of the verb

For this lesson, the only location markers we will study are **sa**, the equivalent of *to*, *at*, *from*, *in*, and *on*; **nasa**, which is also considered an adverb in Tagalog and is the equivalent of *in*, *on*, *inside*, and *within*; and **nasa**'s negative form, **wala sa**. The chart below displays the location markers **sa** and **nasa** with words indicating specific locations that may follow.

		gitna
		harap
		ibaba
		ibabaw
SA	+	**ilalim**
or		**itaas**
NASA	+	**kaliwa**
		kanan
		kanto
		labas
		likod
		loob
		tabi
		tapat

The following section will help you in constructing predicational sentences where the predicate is a prepositional phrase.

A. **Nasa** and Spatial Location Words

Use **nasa** or its negative form, **wala sa**, plus a specific location word when there is no action word such as **kumakain** (eating), **nagtatrabaho** (working), etc. in the sentence and you want to talk about the specific location of a person or an object.

The chart below illustrates the possible structure of sentences when a prepositional phrase is the predicate. In the example in the chart, the predicate is the entire phrase **nasa ibabaw ng mesa**, which comments on where the food is located. Notice that there are no action words in the sentence. If you wish to refresh your memory on the usage of **nasa** and **wala sa**, refer to Unit 1, Lesson 2.

Predicate				Subject	
Nasa	**Spatial Location**	**Possessive Marker**	**Noun**	**Subject Marker**	**Common Noun**
	gitna **harap**	ng ng mga	<u>mesa</u>	ang ang mga	<u>pagkain.</u>
	ibaba **ibabaw** **ilalim**	ni nina	<u>Mike</u>	si sina	<u>Patrick.</u>
	itaas	**Ng** Pronoun		**Ang** Pronoun	

Nasa	**kaliwa**
	 kanan
	 kanto
	 labas
	 likod
	 loob
	 tabi
	 tapat
		ko natin
		      namin
		 mo ninyo
		 niya nila
				ako. tayo.
				      kami.
				      kayo.
				 siya. sila.	

EXAMPLES:

Nasa loob ba ng kuwarto si Maria? Is Maria inside the bedroom?

Hindi. Wala siya sa loob ng kuwarto. No. She is not inside the bedroom.

Nasa gitna ng sopa at telebisyon ang mesa. The table is in between the couch and the television.

Nasa ibabaw ng mesa ang libro. The book is on top of the table.

Nasa tabi ng mesa ang halaman. The plant is beside the table.

B. Sa and Spatial Location Words

Use **sa** plus a specific location word when there is an action word or pseudo verb in the sentence. Recall that pseudo verbs include **may** (has, have, there is/are), **mayroon** (a variant of **may**), **wala** (negative form of **may**), **gusto**, and **ayaw**, among others.

1. With a Verb

For our purposes, a Tagalog verb inflects for aspect and will have an infinitive form and a completed, incompleted, contemplated, and recently completed aspect. The last aspect, also known as the recent perfective, will not be studied in this book and is mentioned here only for informational purpose. It refers to an action that has just been completed, and its form is **kaka** + ROOT WORD. To take the example of **bili** (buy), the recent perfective form would be **kakabili**, which translates into English as "just bought." All Tagalog verbs regardless of focus have this form.

The chart below shows how to construct a sentence using **sa** + SPATIAL LOCATION WORD.

Predicate	Subject	Prepositional Phrase			
Verb	Actor	Sa	Spatial Location	Possessive Marker	Noun
Nagpunta	<u>siya</u>	sa	gitna harap ibaba ibabaw ilalim itaas kaliwa kanan kanto labas likod loob tabi tapat	ng ng mga	bahay.

EXAMPLES:

Bumili ako ng pagkain sa harap ng bahay natin. I bought food in front of our house.

Kumuha siya ng pagkain sa ibabaw ng rep. She/He took some food on top of the fridge.

Natutulog ang aso sa ilalim ng sopa. The dog is sleeping under the couch.

2. With a Pseudo-Verb

As explained in the previous lesson, pseudo-verbs are words that function like a verb but do not exhibit all the characteristics of a real verb, like being able to inflect for different time aspects. Among the pseudo-verbs that we have covered are **gusto**, **ayaw**, **may**, **mayroon**, and its negative form, **wala**. For an explanation of the **may** and **mayroon** construction, refer to Unit 2, Lesson 6, and see the dialogue in Lessons 8 and 9, respectively, where **may** and **mayroon** were used. When the possessor or owner is not known or not mentioned, **may** and **mayroon** simply mean "there is/are." For a recap on using **gusto** and **ayaw** in a sentence, revisit Unit 1, Lesson 3.

The chart below shows the structure of a sentence with a prepositional phrase and the existential particle **may**. The example sentences following the chart illustrate the use of **mayroon** and **wala**. Notice that the sentences have no subject, and the spatial locations are marked with **sa**.

May (There is/are)	Object Phrase (Noun)	Prepositional Phrase			
May		**Sa**	**Spatial Location**	**Possessive Marker**	**Noun**
May	pusa	sa	gitna harap	ng ng mga	mesa.
			ibaba ibabaw ilalim itaas kaliwa kanan kanto labas likod loob tabi tapat	ni nina	Patrick.

EXAMPLES:

Mayroong pusa sa loob ng kuwarto ko. There is a cat inside my room.
Mayroon bang pagkain sa loob ng rep? Is there food inside the fridge?
Oo. Mayroon. Yes. There is.
Wala pong tao sa labas ng bahay natin. There is no one outside our house, sir/madam.

The following chart and example sentences show the structure of a sentence with a prepositional phrase and **gusto** and **ayaw**. Notice that the experiencer is always in **ng** form, while the object can be either an **ang** form or a **ng** form. Remember to use an **ang** form when the object is specific and a **ng** form for an unspecific or indefinite object.

Pseudo-Verb	Experiencer		Object		Sa	Prepositional Phrase		
	Marker	Noun/Pronoun	Marker	Noun		Spatial Location	Possessive Marker	Noun
Gusto Ayaw	ni/nina	Chino	ang/ang mga ng/ng mga	pagkain	sa	gitna harap ibaba ibabaw ilalim itaas kaliwa kanan kanto likod tabi tapat	ng ng mga	mesa.
	ng/ng mga	bata ko natin namin mo ninyo niya nila						

EXAMPLES:

Gusto ni Vera ang painting <u>sa</u> dingding. Vera likes the painting on the wall.

Ayaw ni Chino ang pagkain sa loob ng rep. Chino does not like the food inside the fridge.

Gusto mo ba ang sumbrero sa ibabaw ng mesa? Do you like the cap on top of the table?

Grammar Notes

1. When using enclitics with this sentence structure, place the enclitic after the **nasa** phrase.

   Nasa ibabaw _ba_ ng mesa ang libro? Is the book on top of the table?

   <u>Nasa</u> gilid po _ng_ kompyuter ang litrato. The picture is by the side of the computer, sir/ma'am.

2. The negative form of **nasa** is **wala sa**.

   Nasa ibabaw ng mesa ang libro. The book is on top of the table.

   <u>Wala sa</u> ibabaw ng mesa ang libro. The book is not on top of the table.

   In the above example, **nasa** means "on or in the location." We first encountered **nasa** in Lesson 2 in connection with the place markers **sa** and **taga**, the interrogative **nasaan**, and the corresponding answers **nandito, nandiyan, nandoon**, which are demonstrative pronouns. **Nasa** as a response to a **nasaan** question cannot stand alone. It has to be followed by a noun location. **Wala sa**, on the other hand, means that "something, a person, a thing, or event is not in a certain location." The place marker **sa** following the existential particle signals a location.

3. **Wala** is a negative marker. When it is placed in front of an affirmative statement, the sentence becomes negative. When the subject of the affirmative statement is a pronoun, for example **sila** in the sentence below, the pronoun is placed after **wala** and the specific location, **sa loob**, follows.

   Nasa loob _sila_ ng bahay.

   Wala <u>sila</u> _sa_ loob ng bahay. (correct)

   *Wala sa loob ng bahay <u>sila</u>. (incorrect)

Practice

I. Speaking Practice

Draw a picture of your living room. In Tagalog, describe what you have drawn to a classmate without showing him or her the drawing. Be clear and thorough in your description. Your classmate will try to draw a copy of the picture based solely on your words. Your partner may ask questions in Tagalog to help with the drawing. When your partner has finished, show him or her your drawing and compare the two. Then switch roles.

Draw your living room in the box provided below.

Draw your partner's living room in the box provided below.

II. Reading Practice

Read the text below and sketch what is being described in the box provided below.

Sa gitna ng kahon bandang ibaba magdrowing ka ng telebisyon. Sa harap ng telebisyon mayroong mesa. Mahaba ang mesa na ito. Nasa kaliwa ng mesa ang isang maliit na sopa. Nasa kanan ng mesa ang isang *recliner*. Nasa harapan ng mesa ang isang mahabang sopa. Nasa gilid, bandang kaliwa ng mahabang sopa ang isang maliit na mesa. Nasa kanan ng mahabang sopa ang isang halaman.

III. Writing Practice

You made friends with a Filipino online. She's asking you about student life in your country and the typical set-up in a classroom at your school. First, draw a picture of your classroom and the things that you can find there, then write a detailed description of your classroom so she could picture it on her mind. Use the box provided below for your drawing and the lines below for your description.

Ang Klase ko

_____

_____

_____

_____

_____

IV. Listening Practice

Listen to audio file (10–2) and make a sketch of what is being described.

Ang Paborito Kong Lugar

My Favorite Place

An Overview of Lesson 11

Objectives

• Express preference about various places
• Describe and provide basic information about different locations

Vocabulary

• Nouns	• Affixes	• Natural Elements
• Adjectives	• Seasons	• Topography

Reading Text: Ang mga Paborito Kong Lugar *My Favorite Places*

Reading Comprehension

Activities

Activity 1: My Favorite Place
Activity 2: Interview
Activity 3: Where Should They Live?

Grammar

Definition of Terms: Root Word, **Ma-**, Adjective, Comparative, Superlative, Intensifier

Examining Form

I.   Positive, Comparatives, and Superlatives
     Grammar Presentation
     Grammar Notes
II. Intensifier
     Grammar Presentation
     Grammar Notes

Practice

I.   Speaking Practice
II. Reading Practice
III. Writing Practice
IV. Listening Practice

Vocabulary 🎧 (11–1)

The vocabulary below will help you express preferences and describe locations and participate in the activities in this lesson. Memorize the vocabulary words before proceeding to the dialogue.

Nouns

alikabok	dust
araw	sun
asó	smoke
bahaghari	rainbow
bato	rock
bayan	town
bituwin	star
buhangin	sand
bukid; palayan	field, farm, rice field
buwan	moon
daan	road
daungan	port
hamog	dew
langit	sky, heaven
lawa	lake
madaling araw	dawn, sunrise
nayon	village
putik	mud
tabing-dagat	beach
takipsilim	twilight
tanawin	view, scenery
ulap	cloud

Seasons

tag-init	summer
tag-ulan	rainy season
taglagas	fall
taglamig	winter
tagsibol	spring

Adjectives

bago	new
kulay tsokolate	chocolate-colored, brown
luma	ancient, old
maalikabok	dusty
maaga	early
madilim	dark
mahangin	windy
mainit	hot, warm
makabago	modern
makaluma	traditional
makasaysayan	historical
mapayapa	peaceful
maputik	muddy
matao	crowded
matulungin	helpful
maulan	rainy
maulap	cloudy
palakaibigan	friendly
sariwa	fresh
tahimik	calm, quiet
tanghali	late
umido	humid
walang tao	deserted

Natural Elements

alon	wave
ambon	drizzle
apoy	fire
bagyo	storm
hangin	air, wind
kidlat	lightning
kulog	thunder
lindol	earthquake
tubig	water
ulan	rain

Topography

bulkan	volcano
bundok	mountain
burol	hill
dagat	ocean
disiyerto	desert
gubat	forest
ilog	river
isla/pulo	island
kuweba	cave
lambak	valley
sapa	small brook or rivulet, small stream
talon	falls

Affixes

mas-	turns an adjective into higher degree; from Spanish meaning "more"
magkasing-	turns an adjective into equal degree
napaka-	turns an adjective into intensified degree
pinaka-	turns an adjective into superlative degree

Reading Text: Ang mga Paborito Kong Lugar *My Favorite Places*

The Philippines, a tropical country in the Far East, is composed of 7,100 islands. Mark traveled there during the summer break and sent Vanessa a postcard telling her about his vacation. Read Mark's messages about some of the beautiful places he visited, then complete the Reading Comprehension activity that follows.

Word Bank

ginawa made
katutubo indigenous
hilaga north
nagtatanim planting
palay rice

Luzon: Banawe Rice Terraces

Kumusta na, Vanessa?
Ang *rice terraces* sa Banawe ang isa sa mga paborito kong lugar sa Luzon. Napakalaki at napakataas ng hagdan-hagdang palayan na ito. Ginawa raw ito ng mga katutubong Pilipino at dito sila nagtatanim ng palay. Gusto ko ang lugar na ito kasi sariwang-sariwa ang hangin at mapayapa ang lugar na ito.

O sige,
Mark

Visayas: Chocolate Hills

Vanessa,

Ang Chocolate Hills sa Bohol ang pinakapaborito kong lugar sa Visayas. Mayroong isang libo dalawang daan at animnapu't walong burol ang makikita dito. Magkas-inlaki ang bawat burol dito at kung tag-ulan, berde ang mga burol at kung tag-init, nagiging kulay tsokolate ang mga burol. Gusto ko ang lugar na ito kasi napakasariwa ng hangin dito at tahimik na tahimik dito.

Sige,
Mark

Mahal kong Vanessa,

Ang Camiguin ang pinakamaliit na siyudad sa hilagang Mindanao. Sa lugar na ito, makikita ang pinakamagandang tabing-dagat. Bukod dito, ang mga tao dito ay napakarelihiyoso, matulungin at palakaibigan.

Sige,
Mark

Mindanao: Camiguin

Reading Comprehension

Based on what you've read, provide descriptions of each place in English in the box below.

Rice Terraces	Chocolate Hills	Camiguin

Activities

Activity 1

Think of your favorite place in the world. Make a sketch of it on a separate sheet of paper and describe it to a classmate in Tagalog.

Activity 2

Think of two specific places in your area that you like most and in the space provided explain why. When finished, interview two classmates about their favorite places and report your findings in the chart below.

EXAMPLE:

Student 1: **Ano ang paborito mong lugar?**

Student 2: **Gusto ko ang Subic Bay kasi malinis na malinis ang lugar na ito. Sa Subic, mayroong maraming *beach resort*, tindahan, at mga lugar para sa turista.**

A. **Pangalan ng Lugar:**_____

_____

_____

B. **Pangalan ng Lugar:**_____

_____

_____

Classmates' Favorite Places

Pangalan ng Kaklase	Unang Lugar at Dahilan	Pangalawang Lugar at Dahilan
1. _____	_____ _____ _____ _____ _____	_____ _____ _____ _____ _____
2. _____	_____ _____ _____ _____ _____	_____ _____ _____ _____ _____

Activity 3

Imagine that you work for a real-estate agency and four people come to you seeking your advice as to the best place for them to live. Read the brief information about each person, and then help each find the perfect place to live. Write at least three sentences explaining why this is the perfect place for them. Try to use adjectives in your explanation.

Word Bank

kakatapos/katatapos just finished
gimikan clubs or bars, literally from the word gimmick
makipagkilala to know someone, meet someone
pag-akyat sa bundok mountain climbing
pamimingwit fishing

Mga tao:
Andrea Smith

Nag-PhD si Andrea sa Sikolohiya sa Univesity of California sa Berkeley. Tatlumpung apat na taong gulang na siya at kasalukuyang dalaga. Hindi mahilig si Andrea na magpunta sa klab. Kadalasan, nagsusulat lamang siya at nagri-reseach para sa kaniyang bagong libro.

Lugar: _____

Dahilan: _____

Anthony Michaels

Dalawampu't dalawang taong gulang na si Anthony at kakatapos lamang niya sa kolehiyo. Computer Science ang kurso niya. Kasalukuyang binata si Anthony at nakatira siya sa bahay ng mga magulang niya sa Melbourne, Australia. Mahilig magpunta si Anthony sa mga gimikan at gustong-gusto niyang makipagkilala sa mga tao.

Lugar: _____

Dahilan: _____

Sarah Lopez

Apatnapu't limang taong gulang na si Sarah. May asawa at tatlong anak si Sarah. Kasalukuyang nasa elementarya pa lamang ang tatlong anak niya. Akawntant si Sarah at abogado naman ang asawa niya. Mahilig sa mga outdoor na aktibiti ang pamilya ni Sarah tulad ng pag-akyat sa bundok at pamimingwit.

Lugar: _____

Dahilan: _____

Oscar Santos

Retirado na si Oscar at ang asawa niya. May sarili nang pamilya ang lahat ng mga anak nila. Wala nang obligasyon sa buhay ang mag-asawa. May problema sa puso si Oscar, Nag-eehersisyo at nagdya-jogging siya sa labas ng bahay nila araw-araw.

Lugar: _____

Dahilan: _____

Grammar

Definition of Terms

Root Word	The basic Tagalog word or stem, without affixes.
Ma-	The prefix used to form descriptive words or adjectives.
Adjective	A word used to describe a noun or a pronoun. In English, adjectives generally do not change form. In Tagalog, adjectives change form by means of affixes.
Comparative	An adjective used to compare the quality or attribute of two different nouns or pronouns. The comparison can be greater or equal.
Superlative	An adjective expressing the quality of the noun or pronoun in the highest degree.
Intensifier	An adjective equivalent to the English *very*, *too*, or *so*. Some intensifiers in Tagalog would be the equivalent of an adverb in English.

Examining Form

Review the sentences below and complete the tasks that follow. Discuss your answers with a partner. Consult the following Grammar Form section to check your answers.

1. **Napakalaki at napakataas ng hagdan-hagdang palayan na ito.**
2. **Ang Camiguin ang pinakamaliit na siyudad sa hilagang Mindanao.**
3. **Gusto ko ang lugar na ito kasi sariwang-sariwa ang hangin dito.**
4. **Sa lugar na ito, makikita ang pinakamagandang tabing-dagat.**
5. **Napakasariwa ng hangin dito**
6. **Magkasinlaki ang bawat burol dito.**

   a. Underline the nouns and circle the adjectives.

b. Identify and write down all the different prefixes attached to the adjectives.

c. Discuss with a partner how each prefix changes the meaning of the adjective.

I. Positive, Comparatives, and Superlatives

Adjectives, words that describe a noun or a pronoun, change form in Tagalog through the use of affixes, which attach to a root word. There are several adjectival affixes. One of the most common is **ma-**, which means "full of the quality indicated by the root word." There are also adjectives that are themselves root words (a descriptive word that has no affix), like **pula** "red." In the examples below, the adjectives are used as predicates in a predicational sentence. The adjective in the first example has a prefix, **ma-**: ma + **ganda** (beauty). The translation of **maganda** in English is "beautiful." In the sentences below, notice that the helping verb *is* has no equivalent in Tagalog.

EXAMPLES:

Maganda ang siyudad. The city is beautiful.

Asul ang damit. The dress is blue.

Adjectives can express different degrees of having a quality. Ordinary adjectives associate a quality with a noun, and this we call a positive degree. Comparatives denote an equal or greater degree of the quality, and superlatives denote the greatest degree of the qualtiy. Note that *greater* is a comparative in English, and *greatest* is a superlative.

Comparative Degree: When expressing the idea of "greater" in comparative degree, the prefix **mas-** is used before the adjective. When expressing the idea of "equal," use **magkasing-** before the root word of the adjective. In the example below, the root word is **ganda** (beauty). The comparative adjective of greater degree is **mas maganda** (more beautiful). The translation of "than" in Tagalog is **kaysa**. The comparative adjective of equal degree is **magkasingganda** (equally beautiful, as beautiful).

EXAMPLES:

Mas maganda ang Baguio kaysa sa Tagaytay. Baguio is more beautiful than Tagaytay.

Magkasingganda ang Baguio at Tagaytay. Baguio and Tagaytay are equally beautiful.

In the first example, **kaysa** (than) is followed by the place marker **sa** before the proper name of a place, **Tagaytay**. When the word following **kaysa** is the name of a person or pet, the marker used is **kay**. Remember the **sa** forms from Lesson 8. A note on pronunciation: the word **Baguio** is pronounced "**bag-yo**".

Superlative Degree: When expressing the idea of the greatest or highest degree, the prefix **pinaka-** is attached to the positive or ordinary form of the adjective.

EXAMPLE:

Pinakamaganda ang Baguio sa lahat. Baguio is the most beautiful of all.

The chart below gives the different degrees of comparison of adjectives: positive, comparative equal, comparative higher, and superlative. The root words are **ganda** and **bago**, respectively. The first adjective has a prefix **ma-**, and the second has no affix. Notice that the **-ng** in **magkasing** becomes *m* before **bago**.

Positive	Comparative (Equal Degree)	Comparative (Greater Degree)	Superlative (Greatest Degree)
maganda	magkasingganda	mas maganda	pinakamaganda
bago	magkasimbago	mas bago	pinakabago

Grammar Presentation

1. An adjective expressing a quality can be used as a predicate in a sentence. The chart below shows the adjective **maganda** (beautiful) as predicate preceding possible subjects of the sentence, namely an **ang** phrase (**ang** + NOUN) or any of the **ang** pronouns.

Positive Adjective	
Predicate	**Subject**
maganda	<u>ang</u> phrase. <u>ang</u> pronoun.

An adjective expressing a quality can also be used in a sentence that has no subject. The sentence **Malamig sa Baguio** states literally "In **Baguio** is cold." Idiomatically, this is translated as "It is cold in Baguio." Contrast this statement with the examples below the box.

Subjectless Sentence		
Predicate	**Preposition**	
Adjective	**Marker**	**Noun**
<u>Malamig</u>	sa	<u>Baguio.</u>

EXAMPLES:

Makasaysayan ang Corregidor.
Corregidor is historical

This sentence has a subject.

Mahangin ba sa labas?
Is (it) windy outside?

This sentence has no subject, though the pronoun *It* is usually supplied in the English translation.

Mainit po sa Pilipinas.
(It is) hot in the Philippines, sir/madam.

This sentence is a statement of fact but has no subject.

2. The following chart details the use of the comparative prefix **magkasing-**. Note the changes that occur when the prefix is attached to words beginning with the letters *d, l, r, s, t, b, p*. **Magkasin-**, **magkasing-**, and **magkasim-** signify that the quality of the nouns being compared is equal. Both have equal attributes indicated by the PREFIX + ROOT WORD. This is the equivalent of "as + ADJECTIVE + as" in English.

Magkasing- Prefix	**When to use**	**Example**
magkasin-	Occurs before /d/ /l/ /r/ /s/ /t/	**magkasinlamig** **magkasintahimik**
magkasim-	Occurs before /b/ /p/	**magkasimbilis** **magkasimputi**
magkasing-	all other instances	**magkasingganda** **magkasing-ingay**

As with the positive degree, the comparative degree of an adjective can serve as a comment or predicate of a sentence. The sentences below show comparatives of an equal degree.

Comparative Sentence (Equal Degree)		
Predicate	**Subject**	
Adjective	**Ang-phrase/Pronoun**	
	Marker	**Noun**
Magkasingganda	sina	Jamie at Maria.
	ang mga	tabing dagat.
		tayo. kami. kayo. sila.

EXAMPLES:

Magkasinsariwa ang hangin sa Boracay at ang hangin sa bukid. The air in Boracay and the air in the field are equally fresh.

Magkasindilim ang kuwarto ko at ang kusina. My room and the kitchen are equally dark.

Magkasintahimik ba ang klase ninyo at ang aklatan? Are your classroom and the library equally quiet?

3. The chart and the examples below shows comparatives of a greater degree as predicates. Note the use of the word **kaysa** (than) followed by the **sa** noun marker. As mentioned earlier, when the noun is a common noun, **sa** is used before it, and when the noun is the proper name of a person or pet the marker is **kay** (for one person) or **kina** (for more than one person). Notice that for the proper names of places like Boracay, the subject marker **ang** is used. Since the markers are **sa** forms, naturally, **sa** pronouns are the substitutes for these nouns.

Comparative Sentence (Greater Degree)						
Adjective		**Subject**		**Predicate**		
		Ang Phrase		**Sa Phrase**		
Mas	**Adjective**	**Ang Marker**	**Noun**	**Kaysa**	**Sa Marker**	**Noun/Pronoun**
Mas	maganda	si sina	Jamie	kaysa	kay kina	Sheila.
		ang (ang mga)	Boracay		sa (sa mga)	Hawaii.

		ako tayo
		       kami
		ka kayo
		siya sila
					sa	akin. atin.
						        amin.
						iyo. inyo.
						kaniya. kanila.

EXAMPLES:

Mas sariwa ang hangin sa Boracay <u>kaysa</u> sa hangin sa bukid. The air in Boracay is fesher than the air in the field.

Mas madilim ang kuwarto ko <u>kaysa</u> sa kusina. My room is darker than the kitchen.

Mas tahimik ba ang klasrum ninyo <u>kaysa</u> sa aklatan? Is your classroom more quiet than the library?

4. The chart below shows the superlative prefix **pinaka-** attached to **maganda**. Note that the complete predicate of the sentence is the superlative plus the **sa** phrase that follows the subject. In the first sentence structure, **Pinakamaganda si Jamie sa lahat** (Jamie is the most beautiful of all), the complete predicate is **Pinakamaganda sa lahat**. However, the word order **Pinakamaganda sa lahat si Jamie**, a declarative sentence, is also correct.

Superlative Degree				
Adjective	**Subject**		**Predicate**	
	Ang Phrase		**Sa** Phrase	
Pinaka	**Ang** Marker	**Noun**	**Kaysa**	**Sa** Marker
Pinakamaganda	si sina	<u>Jamie</u>	sa	lahat.
	ang ang mga	<u>Boracay</u> <u>sapatos</u>		

		ako tayo
		         kami
		ka kayo
		siya sila
				akin. atin.
				               amin.
				iyo. inyo.
				kaniya. kanila.

EXAMPLES:

Pinakasariwa ang hangin sa Boracay. The air in Boracay is the freshest.

Pinakamadilim na lugar ang kuwarto ko sa bahay namin. My room is the darkest place in our house.

Pinakatahimik na lugar ang aklatan sa eskwelahan. The library is the quietest place at school.

Grammar Notes

1. The prefix **magkasing-** is added before an unaffixed adjective or the root word of **ma-** adjectives.
   magkasingganda
   *** magkasingmaganda** (incorrect)

2. **Magkasing** has two other variants:
   magkasin- occurs before the sounds "d," "l," "r," "s," "t."
   magkasim- occurs before the sounds "b" and "p."
   magkasing- occurs in all other instances.

magkasintangkad	of the same height
magkasimbango	of the same degree of fragrance
magkasingganda	of the same beauty

3. The subject of the **magkasing** adjective is always plural.
   Magkasingganda <u>ang Paris at New York.</u> Paris and New York are equally beautiful.
   Magkasinsikip <u>ang Los Angeles at Tokyo.</u> Los Angeles and Tokyo are equally crowded.

4. The superlative degree is generally expressed by the prefix **pinaka-** and the adjective. **Pinaka-** occurs before **ma-**adjectives and non **ma-**adjectives.
   pinakamaganda most beautiful
   pinakamatangakad tallest
   pinakabago newest

II. Intensifiers

The intensifier in Tagalog can be expressed in two ways: by reduplicating the adjective and by using the prefix **napaka-**. With the prefix **napaka-**, only the root word of the adjective is used.

Reduplication	Napaka- (prefix)
magandang-maganda	napakaganda
malinis na malinis	napakalinis

When the intensifier is made by reduplicating the adjective, a linker is used between the two instances of the adjective. The form of the linker is determined by whether the preceding word ends in a vowel or a consonant, as shown in the following examples:

EXAMPLES:

malinis na malinis very clean (The first word ends in a consonant.)

bagong-bago very new (The first word ends in a vowel.)

mayamang-mayaman very rich (The first word ends in the letter *n*.)

The alternative way to form the intensifier is with the prefix **napaka-** plus the root word of the adjective.

EXAMPLES:

napakaganda very beautiful

napakalinis very clean

napakabago very new

Grammar Presentation

1. The chart below shows the two forms of intensifiers: the reduplicated form and the form using the prefix **napaka-** and the root word. The first adjective is the **ma-** adjective **mataas** (tall), which ends in a consonant, *s*, and the word is reduplicated. The second adjective, **bago** (new), is a root word that ends in a vowel, *o*, and is also reduplicated. When **napaka-** is affixed to both, only the root word is used.

Ma Adjective/Non-ma Adjective	Reduplication	Napaka
Mataas	Mataas na mataas	Napakataas
Bago	Bagong-bago	Napakabago

2. The intensifier can be a predicate in a sentence with a noun or pronoun as subject, as shown in the chart below.

Predicate	Subject	
Adjective	Marker	Noun/ Pronoun
Magandang-maganda	ang ang mga	siyudad.
	si sina	Jamie.
		ako. tayo. kami. ka. kayo. siya. sila.

EXAMPLES:**Lumang-luma ang mga bahay sa probinsya.** The houses in the province are <u>very old</u>.
Madilim na madilim ang bahay sa likod ng bahay ninyo. The house behind your house is <u>very dark</u>.
Magandang-maganda ang tanawin dito. The view here is <u>very beautiful</u>.

3. As we've seen, sentences in Tagalog can have no subject. In the chart below, an intensifier is the predicate in a subjectless sentence, which can be translated literally as "In Seattle is very beautiful." or "(It) is very beautiful in Seattle." *It is* will always serve to translate these sentences.

Subjectless sentence		
Predicate	Prepositional Phrase	
Adjective	Marker	Noun
Magandang-maganda	**sa**	**Seattle.**

EXAMPLES:
Mainit na mainit sa Pilipinas tuwing tag-init. It is very hot in the Philippines every summer.
Maputik na maputik sa bukid. It is very muddy in the farm.
Mataong-matao sa siyudad. It is very crowded in the city.

4. The intensified adjective with the **napaka-** prefix is always a subjectless sentence, as the chart below illustrates. This is only true for the Tagalog structure. The English equivalent has a subject.

Napaka Structure		
Adjective	Marker	Noun
Napakaganda	**ng** **ng mga**	**siyudad.**
	ni **nina**	**Jamie.**
		ko. **natin.** **namin.** **mo.** **ninyo.** **niya.** **nila.**

EXAMPLES:
Napakalinis ng tubig sa lawa. The water in the lake is very clean.
Napakalakas ng hangin sa labas. The wind is very strong outside.
Napakaganda ng tanawin sa probinsya. The scenery in the province is very beautiful.

Grammar Notes

1. The intensified degree of quality denoted by an adjective is expressed by the following forms:
   a. Reduplication, in which the adjective is repeated with the linker **na/-ng**.
   b. Attaching the prefix **napaka-** to the unaffixed adjective or the root word of a **ma-** adjective.
   magandang-maganda
   mataas na mataas
   mayamang-mayaman

   napakaganda
   napakataas
   napakayaman

2. **Napaka-** requires the replacement of the subject's **ang** phrase with a **ng** phrase. Hence, there is no subject in the Tagalog sentence.
   Napakaganda ng Seattle.
   *Napakaganda ang Seattle.** (incorrect)

Practice
I. Speaking Practice
In groups of three, choose and discuss four of the most beautiful places in the world and sketch them in the boxes below. Afterwards, present what your group has discussed and sketched to the rest of the class.

<table>
<tr><td></td><td></td><td></td></tr>
</table>

II. Reading Practice

Mila and Malou are reminiscing about their favorite places in the Philippines. Read their description of the places and answer the questions about them in Tagalog.

> **Word Bank**
>
> **makakita** to be able to see
> **tumingin** to look at
> **paglubog ng araw** sunset
> **lumaki** to be raised, grew up
> **sasakyan** vehicle
> **puwede** can

Ang Parke

Ang Parke sa bayan ang paborito kong lugar. Dito ako *nakakakita* ng katahimikan kaya nakakapagbasa ako dito ng mga libro. Sa umaga, marami kang makikitang taong naglalakad. Ang iba ay may kasamang anak at ang iba nama'y kasama ang kanilang mga mahal sa buhay. Pagdating ng hapon, gustong-gusto kong *tumingin* sa lawa para tingnan ang *paglubog ng araw*.

1. What is the article about?

    _____

2. What are the different things that can be seen at the park?

    _____

Ang Probinsiya Ko

Lumaki ako sa isang probinsiya sa Pilipinas. Sa probinsiya namin, kaunti lang ang mga tao pati na ang mga *sasakyan*. Talagang kapansin-pansin na sariwang-sariwa ang hangin. At ang mga dagat, ilog, at lawa naman ay maraming mga isda at malinis na malinis ang tubig. *Pwede* ditong maligo. Isang araw *natatandaan* ko na nagpunta ako sa tabing-ilog kasama ang nanay ko. Naglaba ang nanay ko habang naliligo naman ako. Masayang-masaya ang araw na iyon.

1. What is the article about?

    _____

2. Describe the lake.

    _____

3. What is the author's favorite memory by the lake?

    _____

III. Writing Practice

Draw a picture of your favorite place in your hometown and write a short paragraph about it. Use a separate sheet of paper for the drawing and the lines below for your paragraph.

_____

_____

_____

_____

_____

_____

IV. Listening Practice

Listen to audio file (11–2) and answer the following questions. Circle **Oo** if the answer is true and **Hindi** if it is false. Stop and repeat the audio clip as necessary for better comprehension.

1. **Sariwang-sariwa ba ang tubig sa dagat sa Boracay?**
   Oo   **Hindi**

2. **Nagpupunta ba sila sa Boracay tuwing tag-init?**
   Oo   **Hindi**

3. **Nagbabakasyon ba sila sa Boracay nang isang buwan?**
   Oo   **Hindi**

4. **Naglalaro ba ng buhangin ang mga bata?**
   Oo   **Hindi**

5. **Nagpa-parasailing ba sila sa hapon?**
   Oo   **Hindi**

LESSON 12

Ang Bayan Ko

My Hometown

An Overview of Lesson 12

Objectives
• Give and ask for directions
• Express simple requests and commands

Vocabulary
• Nouns   • **-Um-** Verbs   • **Mag-** Verbs   • Idioms and Expressions

Reading Text: Imbitasyon sa Aking Bahay *An Invitation to My House*

Reading Comprehension

Activities
Activity 1: Role Play
Activity 2: Where Am I?
Activity 3: How Do I Get to . . .?

Grammar

Examining Form
I.   Imperatives
     Grammar Presentation
     Grammar Notes
II. **-Um-** Verbs
     Grammar Presentation

Practice
I.   Speaking Practice
II. Reading Practice
III. Writing Practice
IV. Listening Practice

Vocabulary 🎧 (12–1)

The vocabulary below will help you make requests or commands and give or ask for directions. You will need it to participate in the activities in this lesson. Memorize the vocabulary words before proceeding to the dialogue.

Nouns

direksiyon	direction
eskinita	alley
gusali	building
hilaga	north
kalye	street
kanluran	west
kanto	corner
mapa	map
pamilihan	market
rotonda	roundabout, rotary, intersection
silangan	east
timog	south

-Um- Verbs

bumaha	to flood
bumalik	to go/return/come back
bumagyo	to storm, to have a typhoon
bumaba	to go/come down
dumaan	to pass by
dumalaw	to visit
dumiretso	to go straight
humangin	to blow, as wind
huminto	to stop
kumaliwa	to turn left
kumanan	to turn right
kumidlat	to flash, as lightning
kumulog	to thunder
lumabas	to go out
lumayo	to go far away, to stay away
lumiko	to make a turn
lumipat	to move
lumindol	to quake
pumasyal	to stroll
pumunta	to go
sumakay	to ride
sumunod	to follow
umatras	to back up
umabante	to go forward
umakyat	to climb
umambon	to drizzle
umaraw	to become sunny
umikot	to turn around
umulan	to rain

Mag- Verbs

magbangka	to take a boat
magbarko	to take a ship
magbisikleta	to ride on a bicycle
magbus	to take a bus
magdyip	to take a jeep
mag-eroplano	to take an airplane
magkalesa	to ride on a horse-drawn rig
magkotse	to take a car
magmotorsiklo	to ride on a motorcycle
magtanong	to ask a question
magtren	to take a train
magtrak	to ride on a truck

Idioms and Expression

Makikita mo ang...	You will see the . . .
Sana makarating ka!	Hope you can make it!
Mawalang-galang na po.	Excuse me; pardon me, sir/ma'am.
Walang anuman.	You're welcome!
Nawawala po ako.	I am lost.

Reading Text: Imbitasyon sa Aking Bahay *An Invitation to My House*

Read Sandra's letter to her friend Martha, inviting her to her new apartment and answer the Reading Comprehension questions that follow.

Mahal Kong Martha,

Kumusta ka na, Martha? Lumipat na ako ng bagong apartment dito sa Makati. Pumunta ka naman at pumasyal tayo dito. May maraming sinehan, pamilihan at kainan dito. Kaya kung hindi ka okupado sa susunod na Biyernes, dumalaw ka naman sa akin at manood tayo ng bagong sine at kumain sa isang masarap na restawran dito.

O heto ang direksiyon papunta sa bahay ko:

Mula sa bahay mo, magbus ka papunta sa Alabang. Pagkatapos, bumaba ka sa Ayala Ave. Pagkatapos, kumaliwa ka sa Rada at kumanan ka sa Legaspi. Dumiretso ka lang dito at makikita mo ang apartment ko sa kaliwa. 543 ang numero ng gusali.

O sige. Sana makarating ka!

Nagmamahal,
Sandra

Reading Comprehension

1. **Saan lumipat si Sandra?**

---

2. **Ano ang mga plano ni Sandra?**

_____

3. **Para pumunta kay Sandra, kakaliwa ba si Martha sa Rada?**

_____

4. **Para pumunta kay Sandra, sasakay ba si Martha sa dyip?**

_____

5. **Mula sa Legaspi, nasa kanan ba ang apartment ni Sandra?**

_____

Activities

Activity 1

Read the dialogue below and use it as a model to write your own version, changing the location being described. Write a dialogue in each of the boxes below.

> ## Word Bank
>
> **kailangan** necessity, need to
> **ngayon** now
> **pambahay** housedress, (clothes) for home use
> **tapos** then

Modelong Dayalogo
Student 1: **Excuse me ho. Pwede hong magtanong?**
Student 2: **Oo naman. Ano ba iyon?**
Student 1: **Alam ho ba ninyo kung paano pumunta sa Mall of Asia?**
Student 2: **Madali lang iyan, nasa Roxas Boulevard ka ngayon. Kumaliwa ka sa EDSA, tapos kumaliwa ka sa Diokno Boulevard, tapos kumanan ka sa Marina Way. Nasa kanan mo na ang Mall of Asia.**
Student 1: **Salamat po!**
Student 2: **Walang anuman.**

Pagpunta sa pinakamalapit na kainan Going to the nearest restaurant

Student 1	Excuse me ho. Pwede hong magtanong?
Student 2	Oo naman. Ano ba iyon?

Student 1	Alam ho ba ninyo kung paano pumunta sa…
Student 2	
Student 1	Salamat po!
Student 2	Walang anuman.

Pagpunta sa bus stop Going to the bus stop

Student 1:	Mawalang galang na ho. Alam ho ba ninyo kung nasaan ang bus stop?
Student 2:	
Student 1:	
Student 2:	Oo, tama! Mag-ingat ka!

Activity 2

Angelo is from the Philippines but is new to Manila. Since he does not know his way around, help him by responding to each of his inquiries regarding the whereabouts of the given location using the map.

"Nawawala ako! Heto ang mapa ko!"

1. "Nasa Mall of Asia ako. Kailangan kong magpunta sa Ninoy Aquino International Airport."

_____

2. "Nasa Soriano at Bocobo ako. Kailangan kong bumili ng mga puting damit para pambahay. Paano ako pupunta sa pamilihan?"

_____

3. "May malaki akong problema, kailangan kong pumunta sa ospital mula sa Rizal Park. Paano ako pupunta doon?"

_____

Activity 3

Work with a partner and practice giving directions. Use the example below as a model for your directions.

EXAMPLE:

Going to the movie theater

- **Kumaliwa ka sa Quezon Ave.**
- **Kumanan ka sa Carlos St.**
- **Dumiretso ka lang hanggang sa Rizal St.**
- **Kumanan ka sa Rizal St.**
- **Nasa kanan mo ang sinehan.**

From your current location, give directions to the closest pharmacy.

_____

_____

From your current location, give directions to the closest church or place of worship.

_____

_____

Grammar

Examining Form

Review the sentences below and complete the tasks that follow. Discuss your answers with a partner. Consult the following section to check your answers.

1. **Pumunta ka naman at pumasyal tayo dito.**
2. **Dumalaw ka naman sa akin.**
3. **Mula sa bahay mo, magbus ka papunta sa Alabang.**

4. **Manood tayo ng bagong sine at kumain tayo sa isang masarap na restawran.**

   a. Circle the actors and and underline the verbs.
   b. What are the different verb forms? What kinds of conjugations are used for each verb?
   c. How do we form imperatives?

I. Imperatives

In Lessons 7 and 8 we studied the conjugation and use of **mag-** verbs, and here we will build on what you already know about them and about Tagalog verbs in general.

In Tagalog, the infinitive form of the verb is used to form the imperative, which is used to express a command, a request, or an exhortation. In English, the infinitive form of the verb, for example *to do*, is made up of *to* + the unaffixed present tense of the verb. The infinitive in English has no tense and does not reflect person or number. In Tagalog, the infinitive is a root word with the attachment of a verbal affix. It has no aspect, and the action it expresses has not happened yet but has a possibility of happening. There are several major verbal affixes, among them **mag-**, **ma-**, **-um-**, **i-**, and **-in-**, and the following examples show infinitives formed with two of them.

EXAMPLES:

mag- (verbal prefix) + root word   →   *mag***bus** (infinitive)
ma- (verbal prefix) + root word   →   *ma***nood** (infinitive)

The meaning of the infinitive is determined by the root word. A root word is a unit of language that communicates meaning. Tagalog words can be divided into content words (noun, pronoun, verb, adjective, and adverb) and function words that connect words in a sentence to help create meaning (preposition, marker, conjunction, and linker). Words that inflect or change forms in Tagalog are the content words—namely nouns, verbs, and adjectives—except for pronouns. Pronouns do not inflect. There are distinct and specific affixes for each of the content words. In cases where an affix is used for both verbs and adjectives, for example the prefix **ma-** that is used in both **maganda** (beautiful) and **maligo** (to take a bath), what determines whether the word formed is an adjective or a verb is the meaning of the root word and common usage. In the case of **maganda**, the root word **ganda** is a descriptive word, and that results in an adjective. With **ma-** + **ligo** (bath), the result is a verb. The verbal prefix **ma-** can be a bit tricky in this respect.

In Tagalog, any content word can be changed into a noun, verb, or adjective through the use of affixes. For instance, the negative marker **hindi** and the affirmative answer **oo** can both be changed into a verb by using the affix **-um-**. You will learn how to conjugate the **-um-** verb in the next section.

EXAMPLES:

hindi (negative marker) + **-um-** (affix)   →   **humindi** (to say no)
oo (affirmative response) + **um-** (affix)   →   **umoo** (to say yes)

In previous lessons, you have used the words **manood** (to watch, as in a show, movie, television, stage play), **makinig** (to listen), and **maligo** (to take a bath). You may wonder how you would know whether the root word is a descriptive word or whether it can signify action. Or a more basic question is: "How do I know whether to use an **-um-** verb, a **mag-** verb, or a **ma-** verb? To learners new to the language, the best way is to use the dictionary and immerse yourself in the language and culture through reading, watching movies, listening to songs and actually singing Tagalog songs, and, most importantly, being around native speakers and using the language with them in conversation.

For **-um-** verbs, the thing to remember is this: the affix **-um-** is placed before the first vowel of the root word. The examples below show how to form the infinitive/imperative with **-um-**. In the first example, the root word or base word is **sakay** (passenger, load). The first vowel in **sakay** is **a**. Since there is a consonant before the vowel, **-um-** acts as an infix and is affixed inside the word, between the initial consonant and the **a**. For words beginning with a vowel, **-um-** is a prefix. We will discuss this more in later sections.

EXAMPLES:

sakay (passenger, load) + **-um-**   →   **s<u>um</u>akay** (to ride)
lakad (walk) + **-um-**   →   **l<u>um</u>akad** (to walk)
iyak (cry) + **-um-**   →   **<u>um</u>iyak** (to cry)

Grammar Presentation

The chart below illustrates the use of **mag-** and **ma-** imperative forms in giving directions using predicational sentences. It is obligatory in Tagalog to indicate whether the actor (subject) is singular or plural. This has nothing to do with agreement in number and person between the verb and the actor. It is just a matter of making clear what person is to execute the action, whether a singular or plural "you." In English, "you" is not stated, and both the singular and plural forms of the second-person personal pronoun are you, so no distinction has to be made.

Note also that the first infinitive is made from the root word *bus*, a term borrowed from English. Borrowed words in Tagalog have been incorporated in the language to signify things or events that did not exist in the culture like **kompyuter** (computer); **elektrisidad** and **oras** from Spanish (**electricidad** = *electricity*; **hora** = *hour*); **siomai** from Chinese (a kind of dumpling); and **karaoke** from Japanese. Filipinos have acquired such words through encounters with foreign cultures in trade and commerce and past colonization; from living and working abroad; through the media and the Internet; and from the effects of globalization in today's world.

Imperatives						
Verb	**Actor**		**Object**		**Location**	
	Marker	**Noun**	**Marker**	**Noun**	**Marker**	**Noun**
Magbus		ka			sa	<u>Quirino.</u>
D<u>u</u>miretso		kayo			sa	**Rizal St.**
Manood		tayo	ng ng mga	<u>sine</u>	sa	<u>SM.</u>

EXAMPLES:

Magtaksi ka papunta sa eskwelahan. (You, singular) Take the cab to school.
Dumalaw kayo sa akin. (You, plural) Visit me.
Gumawa ka ng imbitasyon. (You, singular) Make an invitation.

Grammar Notes

1. Use imperatives to give commands, instructions, or directions or make exhortations.
   Kumuha ka ng pagkain sa bahay. Get food at the house.
   Umuwi kayo sa bahay. (You, plural) Go home.
   Kumaliwa ka. (You) Turn left.

2. We use **naman** in commands and instructions to make imperatives more polite. It softens the command or direction for the person addressed.
   Kumuha ka naman ng pagkain sa bahay.
   Umuwi naman kayo sa bahay.

3. When using imperatives, the actor for **-um-** and **mag-** verbs is always either **ka** (**ang** pronoun for *you* singular) or **kayo** (ang pronoun for *you* plural)
   Umuwi ka sa bahay ninyo. (You, singular) Go home to your (plural) house.
   Umuwi kayo sa bahay ng lola ninyo. (You all, plural) Go home to the house of your (plural) grandmother.
   Maglinis ka ng kuwarto mo. (You, singular) Clean your (singular) room.
   Maglinis kayo ng buong bahay. (You all, plural) Clean the whole house.

II. -Um- Verbs

When used with a verbal root word, the **-um-** verbal affix forms an actor-focus verb. The **-um-** affix usually attaches to root words that express the following: direction, natural occurrences or acts of nature, and bodily functions, While there are verbal root words that can be turned into an action word, keep in mind that there are also root words that cannot be turned into a verb. For example, **papaya**, the name for a fruit, cannot be turned into an action word.

Direction:
Kumanan ka sa Rada. Turn right on Rada Street.
Kumaliwa kayo sa kanto. Make a left on the corner

Natural Occurrences:
Umuulan ngayon dito. It is now raining here.
Bumagyo raw kahapon sa Pilipinas. They said it rained yesterday in the Philippines

Bodily Functions:
Kumain ako ng adobo. I ate adobo.
Iinom ako ng gatas. I will drink milk.
Sumakit ang tiyan ko. I had a tummy ache. (Literally, My stomach ached.)

Grammar Presentation

1. **Um-** verbs can serve to give directions when in the imperative form. It so happens that the infinitive/ imperative and the completed aspect of **-um-** verbs is the same. This is the only class of Tagalog verb where the infinitive and completed aspect share the same form.

Direction			
Verb	**Actor (Ang Phrase)**		**Location**
-um-	**Markers**	**Nouns**	**Sa**
Lumiko (infinitive)		ka kayo tayo	sa kanto.
Lumiko (completed)	si sina	Jamie	
Lumiliko (incompleted)	ang ang mga	bata	
Liliko (contemplated)		ako tayo kami ka kayo siya sila	

2. Declarative sentences with **-um-**verbs can describe movement or displacement in space. The last example is a **ba** question with an **-um-** verb in the contemplated aspect.

EXAMPLES:

Kumaliwa sila sa Espanya. They turned left on España.

Bumabalik ako sa bahay tuwing hapon. I go back to my place every afternoon.

Kakanan ba sina Marcus at Glen sa Dapitan? Will Marcus and Glen turn right on Dapitan?

3. Acts of nature or natural occurrences are expressed with **-um-** verbs, as shown in the chart below with the verb **bumagyo** (to storm) in the different aspects. Among the different kinds of verbs, only **-um-** verbs can be used to express acts of nature. In this lesson, our focus is on the use of infinitives as imperatives, and we show the aspects only for the purpose of recognizing the verb. You will learn how to conjugate **-um-** verbs in a later lesson.

Natural Occurances (Subjectless Sentence)	
Verbs	**Location**
-um-	**sa**
Bumagyo (completed)	sa Maynila.
Bumabagyo (incompleted)	
Babagyo (contemplated)	

Some other examples of **-um-**verbs depicting acts of nature or natural occurences are:

Umulan sa amin kagabi. It rained in our place last night.

Bumabaha sa Maynila tuwing tag-ulan. (It) Floods in Manila every rainy season.

Aaraw ba bukas? Will it be sunny tomorrow?

4. Another use of **-um-**verbs is to express bodily functions.

Bodily Function							
Verb	**Object**		**Actor**		**Time**		**Location**
-um-	**Marker**	**Noun**	**Marker**	**Noun**	**Marker**	**Noun**	**sa**
Kumain (completed)	ng ng mga	prutas	si sina	Patrick	noong	Lunes	sa bahay.
Kumakain (incompleted)			ang ang mga	bata			
Kakain (contemplated)					sa	Lunes	

EXAMPLES:

Tumakbo ang bata papunta sa nanay niya. The kid ran toward his/her mother.

Umiinom ka ba ng gatas tuwing gabi? Do you drink milk every night?

Kakanta ako mamaya. I will sing later.

5. Supplemental Vocabulary

-Um- Verbs			
bumangon	to rise or get up, as from bed or a lying position	**sumayaw**	to dance
bumasa	to read	**sumulat**	to write
gumawa	to do, to make	**tumalon**	to jump
gumising	to wake up from sleep	**tumakbo**	to run
humindi	to say no	**tumayo**	to stand up
humiga	to lie down	**tumawa**	to laugh
kumain	to eat	**umayaw**	to decline; to refuse
kumanta	to sing	**uminom**	to drink
kumita	to make money, to earn, to gain	**umiyak**	to cry
lumakad	to walk	**umupo**	to sit down
ngumiti	to smile	**umoo**	to say yes

Practice

I. Speaking Practice

Give the Tagalog equivalent for the following exchange in English and then act it out in Tagalog with a classmate. Use a separate piece of paper to write your answers.

Marco	Excuse me, sir. May I ask you a question?
Juan	Yeah, sure. What is it?
Marco	Do you know how to get to U.S.T., sir?
Juan	Oh! That's easy. You are on Recto right now. Make a right on Loyola, then turn left on P. Noval. Then turn right on Dapitan. U.S.T. will be on your right.
Marco	Thank you, sir. So, I will turn right on Recto. Then I will make a right on Loyola. Then I will make a left on P. Noval. Afterwards, I will turn right on Dapitan. Is that correct, sir?
Juan	Yes.
Marco	Okay. Thank you so much, sir.
Juan	You're welcome.

II. Reading Practice

Read about the misadventures of Hiro below and answer the Reading Comprehension questions in Tagalog.

Word Bank

maghulog to drop off, to mail
makipagkita to meet with
malambot flat
gulong tire
pambomba air pump
bumuhos to pour
tumila to stop (for rain)
papunta in the direction of
pauwi in the direction of one's home, toward one's home

Ang Mahabang Biyahe ni Hiro *Hiro's Long Journey*

Nakatira si Hiro malayo sa siyudad. Ngayong araw na ito, pupunta si Hiro sa Downtown para bumili ng pagkain, *maghulog* ng mga sulat sa pos opis at *makipagkita* sa kaibigan niya.

Pagkatapos niyang kumain ng almusal, handa na si Hiro para sa mga gawain niya ngayong araw na

ito. Sumakay siya sa trak niya pero wala na itong gasolina. Sumakay siya sa vespa niya pero *malambot* ang *gulong* nito. Malaki ang problema ni Hiro. Sa wakas, nakita niya ang bisikleta niya!

Hindi pwedeng dumaan si Hiro sa freeway, *kaya* sa kalye lang siya nag-bike. Nag-bike nang nag-bike si Hiro nang maraming oras. Pagkalipas ng dalawang oras, nakarating na rin si Hiro sa pamilihan. Bumili siya agad ng mga kailangan niya. Pagkatapos, nagpunta na siya agad sa pos opis. Naghulog siya ng mga bills niya. Ngayon, papunta na si Hiro sa bahay ng kaibigan niya. Ang problema, hindi pamilyar si Hiro sa bagong tirahan ng kaibigan niya. Nagtanong siya sa tindero pero hindi alam nito. Naghanap si Hiro ng iba pang tao at nakita niya ang drayber ng bus. Nagtanong siya kung alam ba niya kung paano magpunta sa Arlington. At ang sabi ng drayber, "Oo, dumiretso ka lang sa Roscoe at kumanan ka sa Wyoming at tapas, kumaliwa ka sa simbahan. Nagpasalamat si Hiro sa drayber at nagpunta sa bahay ng kaibigan niya. Nagkita sina Hiro at ang kaibigan niya. Buong araw silang nag-usap. Masayang-masaya silang dalawa.

Noong uuwi na si Hiro, nakita niya na malambot ang gulong ng bisikleta niya. Humiram sila ng *pambomba* ng gulong sa kapitbahay dahil wala ang kaibigan niya. Sa wakas, maayos na ang bisikleta ni Hiro pero ilang sandali humangin nang malakas at *bumuhos* ang ulan. Hindi *tumitila* ang ulan kaya nagpasiya si Hiro na magbus na lang pabalik sa bahay niya. Pagod na pagod si Hiro ngayong araw na ito.

Reading Comprehension

1. **Saan nagpunta si Hiro ngayong araw na ito?**

   _____

2. **Saan sumakay si Hiro at bakit?**

   _____

3. **Sino ang nagbigay ng direksyon kay Hiro papunta sa bahay ng kaibigan niya?**

   _____

4. **Paano magpunta sa bahay ng kaibigan ni Hiro?**

   _____

5. **Ano ang problema ni Hiro sa bisikleta niya noong pauwi na siya?**

   _____

6. **Bakit hindi nagbisikleta si Hiro pauwi sa bahay niya?**

   _____

7. **Saan sumakay si Hiro pauwi sa bahay niya?**

   _____

III. Writing Practice

You are organizing a get-together at your home next week. Prepare an invitation for a friend, giving details about the events as well as precise directions to arrive at your house from his or hers.

_____

_____

_____

_____

_____

_____

IV. Listening Practice

Listen to audio file (12–2) and answer the following questions in English.

1. **Paano pumunta sa bahay ni Marc?**

_____

2. **Paano pumunta sa pamilihan?**

_____

3. **Paano pumunta sa simbahan?**

_____

4. **Paano pumunta sa eskwelahan?**

_____

5. **Paano pumunta sa koreo?**

_____

UNIT 5

KALUSUGAN
Health

For a nation that supplies so many workers to the medical industries of Western nations, it is a wonder that most Filipinos do not follow the conventions of Western medicine. They don't for a number of reasons. While the hospitals in Metro Manila and other large cities are among the best in the world, often they are out of reach for ordinary Filipinos. Either the care is too expensive, or the hospitals are simply not in close proximity to those who need them. The Philippines is an archipelago composed of 7,107 islands, with three major islands, Luzon, Visayas, and Mindanao. A greater part of the underserved rural areas are not easily accessible by land or water due to poor roads and unavailable transportation. In the provincial regions of the Philippines, a sick person would most likely seek out the local faith healer, or **albularyo**, rather than a doctor for economic reasons or because of the scarcity of Western-trained medical practitioners, who have become part of the brain-drain phenomenon in the Philippines. Aside from lack of personnel and supplies used in Western medicine, other factors contributing to a reliance on folk healers are low level of education and the lack of governmental funding to open public health clinics, train health workers, and create awareness of the availability of health services. There is no universal health care system in the Philipines, and only less than half of the population has health insurance. Reportedly, copayments are high.

Yet, besides low average incomes and the wide dispersion of the population in rural areas, it is also true that folk practices regarding health care tend to slow the inroads of Western medicine. When a farmer goes to a folk healer, he need not pay a fixed fee to access health care. He can give a small donation in cash or in kind. This health care system and its methods of healing date back to the precolonial era. Folk medicine relies on the great abundance of plants and herbs and other natural sources for healthy recovery rather than on Western pharmaceuticals. Going to a **manghihilot**, a local healer who administers a type of therapeutic massage to relieve pain, assists in birthing, and restores dislocated bone or bones is a common alternative to modern medicine.

A local **hilot**

Whitening products from local pharmacies

The tradition of faith healing stems from the belief that spirits and other supernatural beings control peoples' lives. Consequently, much faith healing focuses on ridding the body of unwanted spirits. Healers act as mediums between the patient and the spirit causing the pain. They recite chants and prayers in an effort to communicate with the supernatural realm and propitiate the spirit. Other techniques include blessing the body with holy water, laying of hands on the patient, and anointing with oil, all of which are consistent with the Catholic tradition of charismatic healing.

One of the most dramatic forms of faith healing is "psychic surgery," in which a healer purports to insert her or his fingers inside the patient's body and remove various tissues or organs. However, many international medical practitioners as well as foreign media have debunked claims of miraculous healing from this type of intervention.

While Filipinos' faith in indigenous healing suggests a rejection of modern techniques of medicine, the ideals of beauty pursued by urban Filipinos are, on the other hand, heavily reliant on Western medical methods. Skin lightening or whitening is very common among Filipinos who wish to shed their brown skin for lighter shades. Some people attempt to lengthen their nose in order to compensate for not having a nose bridge like white Europeans or Americans. Recently, plastic surgery to widen ones eyes has been gaining in popularity among more well-off Filipinos and Filipinos who live abroad.

Mga Iba't ibang Sakit

Various Illnesses

An Overview of Lesson 13

Objectives
- Talk about the physical symptoms of common ailments
- Develop the language skills to suggest possible remedies
- Use helping verbs and negative commands in a sentence

Vocabulary
- Nouns
- Parts of the Body
- Adjectives
- Verbs
- Helping Verbs
- Phrases

Reading Text: Isang Paalala *A Reminder*

Reading Comprehension

Activities
Activity 1: Things You Can and Cannot Do
Activity 2: Asking for Permission
Activity 3: Description

Grammar
Definition of Terms: Helping Verbs, Main Verbs

Examining Form
I.   Helping Verbs and Negative Markers
     Grammar Presentation: Helping Verbs and Negative Markers
     Grammar Notes

Practice
I. Speaking Practice
II. Reading Practice
III. Writing Practice
IV. Listening Practice

Vocabulary 🎧 (13–1)

The vocabulary below will help you speak about health matters and participate in the activities in this lesson. Memorize the vocabulary words before proceeding to the reading text.

Nouns

balinguyngoy	nosebleed
bulutong-tubig	chicken pox
dalandan	orange, citrus
gamot	medication, medicine
hika	asthma
kalamansi	citrus, small acidic fruit
katas	juice
kolera	cholera
lagnat	fever
lugaw	porridge
lunas	treatment
malaria	malaria
paalala	notice, reminder
pakiramdam	feeling
sakit	ailment, illness, disease
sakit ng ulo	headache
sakit ng ngipin	toothache
sinat	slight fever
sintoma	symptom
sipon	cold
sopdrink	soda
suha	grapefruit, pomelo
sugat	wound
tigdas	measles
trangkaso	flu
ubo	cough

Parts of the Body

balat	skin
balikat	shoulder
binti	leg
braso	arm
daliri	finger
hita	thigh
kamay	hand
katawan	body
lalamunan	throat
leeg	neck
likod	back
paa	foot
siko	elbow
tiyan	stomach
tuhod	knee
ulo	head

Adjectives

makati	itchy
maga	swollen
mahapdi	burning feeling
malalambot	soft (plural)
mapula	red
masakit	painful
mabigat	strenuous
nakakapagod	tiring, tiresome

Verbs

alam (object focus)	to know something
bumisita	to visit
dumudugo	bleeding
magpahinga	to rest
nahihilo	feeling nauseous/ feeling dizzy
nagtatae	having diarrhea
sumasakit	aching
tandaan	remember (object-focus verb)
uminom	to take (medicine); to drink
yumuko	to stoop

Helping Verbs

bawal	forbidden, prohibited
dapat	should
huwag	don't
puwede	can

Phrases

ayon sa	according to
kung may sakit	if sick/when sick

Reading Text: Isang Paalala *A Reminder*

It's flu season, and John, an exchange student to the Philippines from Canada, was not feeling well. His friend brought him to the clinic. The nurse gave them some health materials in Tagalog. Read the leaflet and help John understand by answering the Reading Comprehension questions.

> ### Word Bank
>
> **paalala** reminder
> **sumusunod** following

ISANG PAALALA

Ikaw ba ay mayroong lagnat at nakakaramdam ng anuman sa mga sumusunod? a) masakit na lalamunan, b) masakit na katawan, at c) ubo. Kung oo ang iyong sagot, ikaw ay may trangkaso. Heto ang ilang paalala na dapat tandaan.

[BAWAL]
1. Huwag kang lumabas ng bahay.
2. Huwag kang gumawa ng mga nakakapagod na gawain.
3. Bawal kang kumain ng mga matatamis na pagkain tulad ng kendi at tsokolate.
4. Bawal kang uminom ng mga malamig na inumin.

[PUWEDE]
1. Dapat kang uminom ng gamot.
2. Dapat kang magpahinga.
3. Puwede kang kumain ng lugaw at iba pang malalambot na pagkain.
4. Puwede kang uminom ng mga katas ng prutas tulad ng kalamansi, dalandan, at suha.

Reading Comprehension

1. Ayon sa paalala, anu-ano ang mga sintoma ng trangkaso?

_____

2. Anu-ano ang mga bawal gawin kung may trangkaso?

_____

3. Kung may trangkaso, puwede bang gumawa ng mga nakakapagod na gawain?

_____

4. Anu-ano ang mga puwedeng gawin kung may trangkaso?

_____

5. Kung may trangkaso, bawal bang magpahinga?

_____

Activities

Activity 1

Decide whether you can or cannot do the following activities under the following circumstances. Discuss your answers with a partner.

	Bawal	Puwede
1. Maligo kung may lagnat.	_____	_____
2. Pumasok sa eskwela kung masakit ang ngipin.	_____	_____
3. Uminom ng sopdrink kung may ubo.	_____	_____
4. Kumain ng tsokolate kung masakit ang lalamunan.	_____	_____
5. Yumuko kung may balinguyngoy.	_____	_____

Activity 2

Write a question using **puwede** to ask permission in each of the following scenarios. Provide explanations and, when appropriate, use polite enclitics. The example can serve to model your sentences.

```
Word Bank

amo boss
humiram to borrow
permiso permission
sandali a short time
umalis to leave
```

1. **Nasa trabaho ka. May appointment ka sa doktor. Humingi ka ng permiso sa amo mo para pumunta sa doktor.**

   <u>May appointment po ako ngayon sa doktor. Puwede po ba akong umalis sandali?</u>

   _____

   _____

2. **Nasa ospital ka at kailangan mo ng bolpen. May bolpen ang lalaki na nasa harap mo. Humiram ka ng bolpen sa kanya.**

   _____

   _____

3. **Nasa ospital ka. Bibisita ka sa kaibigan mong si Fredy pero hindi mo alam kung nasaan ang kuwarto niya. Magtanong ka sa nars kung nasaan ang kuwarto ni Fredy.**

   _____

   _____

4. **Nasa bahay ka. Kailangan mong pumunta sa ospital. Humiram ka ng kotse sa kaibigan mong si Marco.**

   _____

   _____

Activity 3

In the space provided, list all the physical symptoms that are associated with each of the ailments in the table below. Also include all the activities that one should or shouldn't do to alleviate the pain. Remember to use **dapat** and **huwag**.

Mga Sakit	Mga Nararamdaman	Dapat at Huwag
1. Lagnat	Mabigat ang katawan. Mainit ang pakiramdam.	Dapat kang kumain. Dapat kang uminom ng gamot. Huwag kang maglaro. Huwag kang pumasok sa opisina o eskwela.
2. Sakit ng ulo		
3. Hika		
4. Sipon		
5. Sakit ng ngipin		

Grammar

Definition of Terms

Helping Verbs	Modify the meaning of the main verb to express any of the following: negative commands, the ability to perform or carry out an action, or the necessity or obligation to do something. EXAMPLES: ***Dapat* kang uminom ng gamot.** You *should* take medication. ***Huwag* kang magtrabaho nang mabigat.** *Do not* do strenuous work. ***Bawal* kang lumabas ng bahay.** You are *forbidden* to go outside the house. ***Puwede* ka nang pumasok sa eskwela.** You *can* now go to school.

Main Verbs	Express the main action or state of being of the subject in the sentence. The verbs used are in the infinitive form.
Infinitive	Verb form consisting of an affix and a root word, but uninflected for aspect.
Root Word	The basic word in Tagalog without affixes or changes. EXAMPLES: **Dapat kang *uminom* ng gamot.** You should *take* medication. **Bawal kang *lumabas* ng bahay.** You are forbidden *to go outside* the house. **Puwede ka nang *pumasok* sa eskwela.** You can now *go to school*.
Actor-Focus Verbs	Verbs in which the actor, which is also the subject of the sentence, is **ang** form; **-um-** and **mag-** verbs are actor-focus verbs.
Enclitics	Adverbial particles that change in meaning depending on the context of their usage in a sentence. They are usually placed right after the predicate of a sentence. EXAMPLES: **Umalis *na* siya** He/She left *already*. **Alas dose *na*.** It is *now* 12:00 o'clock. **Wala *na* siya.** He/She is not here *anymore*. **Wala *pa* siya.** He/She is not *yet* here. **Kumain *pa* si Ana.** Ana ate *more* (had a second helping).

Examining Form

Review the sentences below and complete the tasks that follow. Discuss your answers with a partner. Consult the following section to check your answers.

Column A	Column B
1. **Huwag kang lumabas ng bahay.**	**Lumabas ka ng bahay.**
2. **Bawal kang uminom ng malamig na inumin.**	**Uminom ka ng malamig na inumin.**
3. **Dapat kang magpahinga.**	**Magpahinga ka.**
4. **Puwede kang kumain ng lugaw.**	**Kumain ka ng lugaw.**

1. Underline all the actors and enclitics, draw a box around the helping verbs and the negative markers, and circle the main verbs.
2. What happens with the order when using helping verbs and the negative command, **huwag**?
3. List all the differences and similarities in structure in column A and column B.

I. Helping Verbs and Negative Markers

Helping verbs in Tagalog do not by themselves show action, as verbs like **kumain** (to eat), **maligo** (to take a shower), and **pumunta** (to go) do. Instead, helping verbs in some way provide assistance to the main verbs as they show action. These helping verbs are also known as pseudo-verbs because they do not inflect for aspect as regular verbs do. In this lesson, we will study the following four helping verbs, shown here with their equivalent in English:

bawal	it is forbidden/not permitted to (helping verb)
dapat	should, ought to (helping verb)
puwede	can, be able to (helping verb)
huwag	don't (negative command)

There are rules for correctly using helping verbs and the negative command **huwag**, and there is a mnemonic to help remember the rules. The mnemonic is the acronym HIL. It works like this: Normally, the word order in a Tagalog sentence is PREDICATE (VERB) + ENCLITIC + SUBJECT (ACTOR). However, when helping verbs are present, the enclitic and pronoun actor are "hauled" in front of the main actor-focus verb, such as a **mag-** or **-um-** verb, so that the order is now HELPING VERB + ENCLITIC + PRONOUN ACTOR + MAIN VERB. Hence, the first rule is called HAUL.

H = **HAUL**

What is HAUL? This simply means that all **ang** and **ng** pronouns, and enclitics should be placed immediately after the helping verb and in front of the main verb. In the example below, the pronoun **ka** is placed right after the negative marker **Huwag**, followed by the main verb, **lumabas**. We will discuss the use of **ng** pronouns as actors with object-focus verbs in a later lesson. The second sentence below is just for illustration.

Huwag *ka*ng lumabas ng bahay. Don't go outside the house.
Huwag mong ilabas ang aso. Don't bring the dog outside.

In the next example, the helping verb **Dapat** is followed by the enclitic **na** and the pronoun **kayo** before the main verb **magpahinga**.

Dapat *na kayo*ng magpahinga. You (plural) should now take a rest.

I = **Infinitive form**

This brings us to the next rule, which is that the main verb has to be in the infinitive form. **Lumabas** and **magpahinga** are both infinitives, comprised of the root word plus the verbal affix. As we saw above, in English grammar the equivalent of the Tagalog infinitive form is the "to" form, in other words, *to go outside* or *to take a rest*.

Huwag kang *lumabas* ng bahay. Don't go outside the house.
Dapat na kayong *magpahinga*. You (plural) should now take a rest.

L = **Linker**

Linkers, either **-ng** or **-g**, must be attached to the pronoun or enclitic that precedes the main verb. Notice that **-ng** is attached to words ending in vowel: for example, **ka** and **kayo**. If the the word preceding the main verb ends in *n*, such as the enclitic **din/rin** (also), **-g** is attached to it.

Huwag ka*ng* lumabas ng bahay. Don't go outside the house.
Dapat na kayo*ng* magpahinga. You (plural) should now take a rest.
Puwede ri*ng* magpunta sa ospital. (You) Can also go to the hospital.

When you are using a helping verb or negative command and the subject actor is not a pronoun, the rules are slightly different, as will be explained below.

Grammar Presentation

Helping Verbs and Negative Markers

1. When using the helping verbs **bawal**, **dapat**, and **puwede** in a predicational sentence, remember to use the HIL mnemonic: that is, when a pronoun is the subject, be sure to "haul" it before the main verb, put the main verb in the infinitive form, and use a linker. The chart below illustrates the word order in sentences where the actor that is the subject of the sentence is not a pronoun but an **ang** phrase. This order is HELPING VERB + INFINITIVE + SUBJECT + DIRECT OBJECT.

Predicational Sentence						
Helping Verb	Linkers	Main Verb	Actor		Direct Object	
			Marker	Noun	Marker	Noun
Bawal Dapat		uminom	si sina	Sheila	ng ng mga	gamot.
Puwede	-ng		ang ang mga	bata		

Notice the different word order in the examples below, where the actor of the verb is also a noun, or **ang** phrase:

EXAMPLES:

1. HELPING VERB + ENCLITIC + INFINITIVE + SUBJECT + PREPOSITIONAL PHRASE
   Bawal hong pumasok <u>ang anak</u> ninyo sa eskwelahan. Your child is not allowed to go to school, sir/madam.

2. HELPING VERB + ENCLITIC + INFINITIVE + DIRECT OBJECT + SUBJECT
   Dapat daw uminom ng gamot <u>si Patrick</u>. They say Patrick should take medicine.

3. HELPING VERB + ENCLITIC + INFINITIVE + DIRECT OBJECT + SUBJECT
   Puwede ho bang kumain ng malamig na pagkain <u>ang kapatid ko</u>? Can my sibling eat cold food, sir/madam?

2. The chart below illustrates the word order in sentences where the actor that is the subject of the sentences is an **ang** pronoun as opposed to **ang** phrase. Notice the difference.

Predicational Sentence					
Helping Verb	**Actor**	**Linker**	**Main Verb**	**Direct Object**	
				Marker	**Noun**
Bawal Dapat Puwede	ako tayo kami ka kayo siya sila	**-ng**	<u>uminom</u>	ng ng mga	<u>gamot.</u>
Negative Command	**Actor**	**Linker**	**Main Verb**	**Direct Object**	
				Marker	**Noun**
Huwag	ka kayo	**-ng**	<u>uminom</u>	ng ng mga	<u>gamot.</u>

EXAMPLES:

Bawal kang pumasok sa eskwelahan. You are not allowed to go to school.

Dapat daw siyang uminom ng gamot. They say he/she should take medicine.

Puwede ho ba akong kumain ng malamig na pagkain? Can I eat cold food, sir/madam?

Huwag kang maglaro sa labas. (You) Don't play outside.

Grammar Notes

1. You only use the linker **-ng** when the word it attaches to ends in a vowel, and **–g** when the word before the main verb ends in **_n_**. When the word before the main verb ends with a consonant (except **_n_**), do not use any linkers.
    EXAMPLES:
    Bawal ka_ng_ uminom ng dyus. You are forbidden to drink juice.
    Bawal uminom dito. It is forbidden to drink here.
    *__Bawal_ na_ uminom ng dyus.** (incorrect)

2. When using helping verbs and/or the negative marker **huwag**, remember the HIL rule:
    H for **Haul**: All pronouns and enclitics should be placed immediately after the helping verb.
    EXAMPLES:
    Bawal _ka na_ng uminom ng dyus. You are forbidden to drink juice now.
    Dapat _siya_ng magpahinga. She/He should take a rest.

    I for **Infinitive**: The main verb has to be in the infinitive form.
    EXAMPLES:
    Bawal ka nang _uminom_ ng dyus. You are forbidden to drink juice.
    Dapat siyang _magpahinga_. She/He should take a rest.

    L for **Linker**: The linkers **-ng** or **-g** must be attached to the pronoun or enclitic that precedes the main verb.
    EXAMPLES:
    Bawal ka na_ng_ uminom ng dyus. You are forbidden to drink juice.
    Dapat siya_ng_ magpahinga. She/He should take a rest.

3. **Huwag** is a negative form of a command. Thus the subject of **huwag** used with actor-focus verbs such as **mag-** and **-um-** is always second-person singular, **ka**, or second-person plural, **kayo**.

    EXAMPLES:

    Huwag *ka*ng maglaro. (You) Don't play.

    Huwag *kayo*ng maglaro. (You plural) Don't play.

Practice

I. Speaking Practice

In the chart below, describe symptoms of common ailments associated with the parts of the body listed in the first column. Then, choosing a partner, describe what you have written and ask your partner to recommend two possible remedies. Take turns for each body part. Use the example below to model your sentences and your dialogue with your partner.

    STUDENT 1: **Masakit na masakit ang mata ko. Mapulang-mapula ito at magang-maga din ito.**

    STUDENT 2: **Huwag kang pumasok sa eskwelahan. Dapat kang maglagay ng eyedrops.**

Bahagi ng Katawan	Paglalarawan ng Sakit o Sintoma
Ulo **(mata, tainga, ilong)**	
Balat	
Leeg at likod	
Braso, kamay, binti, at paa	

II. Reading Practice

Read Rose's entry in her diary when she was eight years old, then complete the activity that follows.

> ### Word Bank
>
> **nagkaroon** had
> **nakita** saw

Nagkasakit Ako

Tandang-tanda ko pa, noong walong taong gulang ako, *nagkaroon* ako ng sakit. Napakataas ng lagnat ko at masakit na masakit ang buong katawan ko. Wala noon sina Nanay at Tatay; nasa Maynila sila. Ang mga kapatid ko lang ang nasa bahay. Hindi nila alam ang gagawin nila para tumulong sa akin. Tumawag sila sa telepono nina Nanay at Tatay pero hindi sila sumagot. Pumunta ang mga kapatid ko sa bahay nina Lolo at Lola, pero walang tao sa bahay nila. Problemadong-problemado sila. Noong bumalik ang mga kapatid ko sa bahay, *nakita* nila na dumating na sina Nanay at Tatay. Masayang-masaya sila at nawala na ang takot nila.

Supply the main sentence or missing words based on Rose's entry in her diary

1. **Noong walang taong gulang ako . . .** _____

2. **Nagkaroon ako ng lagnat at masakit . . .** _____ .

3. **Tumawag ang mga kapatid ko sa . . .** _____ **pero . . .** _____ .

4. **Pumunta ang mga kapatid ko sa . . .** _____ **pero . . .** _____ .

5. **Buti na lang, noong bumalik ang mga kapatid ko . . .** _____ .

III. Writing Practice

Following the example of Rose's story, write a paragraph on a separate sheet of paper about a day that you were sick. You may use the questions below as prompts for writing your paragraph:

   a. **Ano ang sakit mo?**
   b. **Anu-ano ang naramdaman mo?**
   c. **Anu-ano ang ginawa mo para bumuti ang pakiramdam mo?**
   d. **Sinu-sino ang tumulong sa iyo noong may sakit ka?**
   e. **Ano ang unang ginawa mo noong bumuti na ang pakiramdam mo?**

IV. Listening Practice

Listen to audio file (13–2) and answer the following questions. Use the box below to write your answers.

Word Bank
maligamgam lukewarm **huminga nang malalim** to take a deep breath

Hika	Trangkaso	Sipon	Sakit ng Ulo
Anu-ano ang dapat gawin kung may hika?	Anu-ano ang mga bawal gawin kung may trangkaso?	Anu-ano ang mga puwedeng gawin kung may sipon?	Anu-ano ang hindi dapat gawin kung may sakit ng ulo?

Pagbisita sa Doktor

Going to the Doctor

An Overview of Lesson 14

Objectives

• Use appropriate expressions in the context of a doctor's consultation
• Describe minor aches and pains

Vocabulary

• Nouns	• Verbs	• Adverbs	• Idioms and Expressions
• Time	• Adjectives	• Prefixes	

Dialogue: Pagbisita sa Doktor *Visiting the Doctor*

Dialogue Comprehension

Activities

Activity 1: Fill in the Blanks
Activity 2: Role-Play
Activity 3: Fill in the Blanks

Grammar

Definition of Terms: **Magka-** Verbs, **Magkaroon** Verbs, Experiencer, Object Phrase, and Adverb

Examining Form

I. **Magka-** and **Magkaroon**
    Grammar Presentation: The Completed, Incompleted, and Contemplated Aspect of **Magka-** and
    Magkaroon
    Grammar Notes
II. Telling Time (Informal)
    Grammar Notes

Practice

I. Speaking Practice
II. Reading Practice
III. Writing Practice
IV. Listening Practice

Vocabulary 🎧 (14–1)

The vocabulary below will help you express yourself when consulting a doctor and to participate in the activities in this lesson. Memorize the vocabulary words before proceeding to the dialogue

Nouns

bakuna	vaccine
beses	times
klinika	clinic
masakit ang lalamunan	sore throat
pampatak sa mata	eyedrops
pampawala ng sakit	pain reliever
pamahid sa kati	anti-itch ointment
pamahid sa sugat	anti-bacterial ointment
pantal	welt, insect bite
gamot sa pagtatae	medicine for diarrhea
gamot sa mga pantal	medicine for insect bites
pamahid sa sugat	treatment for wounds
panahon	weather/season
pasyente	patient
reseta	prescription
tag-init	summer
taglagas	fall; autumn
taglamig	winter
tagsibol	spring
tag-ulan	rainy season

Time

ala una y singko	1:05 the "y" comes from Spanish *y*, meaning "and"
alas dos diyes	2:10
alas tres kinse	3:15
alas kuwatro bente	4:20
alas singko bente singko	5:25
alas sais trenta/ y media	6:30
alas siyete trenta'y singko	7:35
alas otso kuwarenta	8:40
alas nuwebe kuwarenta'y singko	9:45
alas diyes singkwenta	10:50
alas onse singkwenta'y singko	11:55
alas dose y medya	12:30

Prefix

magka-	to have/ to develop

Verbs

dumalaw	to visit
kumunsulta sa doktor	to consult a doctor
magkaroon	to have/to develop
magkasipon	to have a cold
maglagay	to apply/to put
magpabakuna	to get a shot, vaccine
magreseta	to prescribe
nahihilo	feeling dizzy
napilay	has/have/had sprain
nagsusuka	(is) vomiting
sinisipon	has/have a cold

Adjectives

kada	per, each
malala	severe, serious
masuwerte	lucky
malas	unlucky

Adverbs

halos	almost
kinabukasan	the following day
linggu-linggo	every week, each week
noong isang buwan	the past month

Idioms and Expressions

Ano ang iniinom mo ngayon?	What medications are you taking right now?
dahil sa ...	because of ...
Mukhang hindi po bumubuti.	It doesn't seem to be getting better, sir/madam.
May sumasakit ba sa iyo?	Are you feeling any pain or discomfort?
O sige.	Okay./I see. Expression of affirmation of what was said, then something may or may not follow, an action word, or an adverb
simula po noon . . .	since then . . .
Wala naman po.	Not that I know of.
Wala pong epekto.	It doesn't seem to be helping.

Dialogue: Pagbisita sa Doktor *Visiting the Doctor*

Ricky went to see Dr. Natividad regarding his chronic illness. Read the dialogue below between Ricky and the doctor and answer the Dialogue Comprehension questions that follow.

Word Bank

Neozep a popular medicine taken when one has a cold
nawala literally, lost, disappeared
nararamdaman feeling something
maraming tubig plenty of water
dati former, previous

Doktor: **Kumusta ho kayo? Ano ho ang problema?**

Pasyente: **Dok, halos linggu-linggo po akong nagkakasipon.**

Doktor: **Ilang linggo ka nang nagkakasipon?**

Pasyente: **Mga limang linggo na po. Nagkaroon po kasi ako ng trangkaso noong isang buwan tapos, simula po noon hindi na *nawala* ang sipon ko.**

Doktor: **May iba ka pa bang *nararamdaman* ngayon? May sumasakit ba sa iyo?**

Pasyente: **Wala naman po.**

Doktor: **Ano ang iniinom mo ngayon?**

Pasyente: **Umiinom lang po ako ng kalamansi dyus araw-araw at *Neozep*.**

Doktor: **Anong oras ka uminom ng gamot?**

Pasyente: **Mga alas dos y medya po.**

Doktor: **Mabuti iyan! Ngayon gusto ko ring magpahinga ka at uminom ka rin ng maraming tubig.**

Pasyente: **O sige po dok!**

Doktor: **O sige! Kapag hindi bumuti ang pakiramdam mo, bumalik ka sa akin at magrereseta ako sa iyo ng gamot.**

Pasyente: **Maraming salamat po, dok.**

Dialogue Comprehension

1. **Ano ang sakit ng pasyente?**

   _____

2. **Ilang linggo nang may sakit ang pasyente?**

   _____

3. **Ano ang dating sakit ng pasyente?**

   _____

4. **Ano ang iniinom ng pasyente?**

   _____

5. **Ano ang reseta ng doktor?**

   _____

Activities

Activity 1

Chester is suffering from some ailment and went to see the doctor for a cure. Working with a partner, help Chester say what he has to and understand what the doctor said by filling in the blanks with the information supplied in the parenthesis. When you are finished, act out this dialogue with your partner.

D → Doktor   **P → Pasyente**

> **Word Bank**
> **bumalik** to return, come back
> **nangangati** have itch

D: **Kumusta po kayo?** _____(Now, what seems to be the problem?)

P: **Mayroon po akong** _____ (itch on my arm)

D: **Ilang** _____ (weeks) **ka nang** _____ (have itch)?

P: Mga _____ (one week) **na po.**

D: **Umiinom ka ba ng** _____ (medication)?

P: _____ (put) **po ako ng cream pero** _____ (it doesn't seem to be helping).

D: _____ (I see). **May** *allergy* **ka ba sa mga** _____ (medicine)?

P: _____ (Not that I know of).

D: _____ (I'm going to prescribe) **ng pampahid sa kati. Gusto kong maglagay**

ka ng pamahid nang _____ (three times a day). **Bumalik ka sa akin sa isang**

linggo, kung hindi ito bumubuti.

Activity 2

You have returned from an outing at a botanical garden near the beach, where you and your friends ate exotic food and enjoyed magnificent views of the mountains and sea. After the outing, you felt sick. Work with a partner and create your own dialogue between a doctor and a patient similar to the one from the previous activity.

D → **Doktor**   **P** → **Pasyente**

D: _____

P: _____

D: _____

P: _____

D: _____

P: _____

D: _____

P: _____

D: _____

P: _____

Activity 3

From the word bank below, choose the appropriate **gamot** to treat the **sintoma** listed in the following table.

Word Bank

pampatak sa mata eyedrops
pampawala ng sakit pain reliever
gamot sa pagtatae medicine for diarrhea
gamot sa mga pantal medicine (ointment or cream) for welts
pamahid sa sugat ointment or cream for wounds

Sintoma	Gamot
Gamitin mo ang gamot na ito kung nadapa ka at nagkaroon ka ng gasgas o sugat.	
Gamitin mo ang gamot na ito kung mapula, makati o namamaga ang iyong mga mata.	
Gamitin mo ang gamot na ito kung sumasakit ang ulo mo.	
Gamitin mo ang gamot na ito kung malambot ang iyong dumi at kung madalas ang iyong pagdumi.	
Gamitin mo ang gamot na ito kung nakagat ka ng mga insekto o di kaya kung mapula ang iyong balat.	

Grammar

Definition of Terms

Magka- Verbs	Verbs that mean "to have, or to come into possession of something" (expressed by the noun attached to the prefix **magka-**). With respect to "having a sickness," which is the subject of this lesson, this verb "experiences" the action of the verb rather than does the action.
Magkaroon Verbs	Consist of **magkaroon** followed by **ng** and then a noun object. These are synonymous with **magka-** verbs. Translates into English as *has*, *have* or *had*.
Experiencer	The subject of a **ma-** verb in a sentence. May be a person, an animal, living things like plants or inanimate objects like a cup.
Object Phrase	A noun following the direct object marker **ng**
Adverb	A word or words that modifies or describes a verb, an adjective, or another adverb. It indicates manner, degree, place, time, or frequency.

Examining Form

Review the sentences below and complete the tasks that follow. Discuss your answers with a partner. Consult the following section to check your answers.

Column A	Column B
1. **Nagkakasipon ako.**	**May sipon ako.**
2. **Nagkaroon ako ng trangkaso noong isang buwan.**	**Mayroon akong trangkaso.**
3. **Nagkaroon ng ubo ang bata kahapon.**	**Mayroong ubo ang bata.**
4. **Magkakasakit ang mga bata dahil sa panahon.**	**May sakit ang mga bata.**
5. **Pumunta ka dito nang alas kuwatro y medya.**	**Pumunta ka dito bukas.**
6. **Iinom ako ng gamot nang alas diyes ng umaga.**	**Iinom ako ng gamot mamaya.**
7. **Naglalagay ako ng gamot tuwing alas nuwebe.**	**Naglalagay ako ng gamot tuwing gabi.**

For numbers 1–4
1. Underline all the verbs and circle all the object phrases.
2. When do we use linkers? When do we not use linkers?
3. What is the difference between **magka** and **may** and **magkaroon** and **mayroon**?

For numbers 5–7
4. Underline all the adverbs of time.
5. Notice the words before each adverb of time. When do we use **nang** and **tuwing**?

I. Magka- and Magkaroon

Magka- and **magkaroon** are synonyms. Both are used to form verbs meaning "to have," "to acquire," or "to get." Though synonyms, they differ in some aspects of their use in a sentence, which we will go into later. The prefix **magka-** is a variant of **magkaroon**. Both are inflected for the completed, incompleted, and contemplated aspects like all Tagalog verbs. You may have noticed that these verbs have the same meaning as the existential particles **may** and **mayroon** (have). However, **may** and **mayroon** differ in that they do not inflect for aspect and have a connotation of "the state of having" or possessing. This so-called "state" does not connote action, since these words are not verbs. It simply is—a person or condition or thing has it. On the other hand, **magka-** and **magkaroon** suggest that the subject of the sentence is experiencing whatever is attached to **magka-** or named as object in **magkaroon ng** _____. The subjects of both **magka-** and **magkaroon** are **ang** pronouns and **ang** phrases.

The chart below shows the different aspectual forms of the verbs **magkaubo** (to have a cough) and **magkaroon ng sakit** (to have an illness).

Aspect	Inflection	Inflection
	Magka-	**Magkaroon**
Infinitive	magkaubo	magkaroon ng sakit
Completed	nagkaubo	nagkaroon ng sakit
Incompleted	nagkakaubo	nagkakaroon ng sakit
Contemplated	magkakaubo	magkakaroon ng sakit

Here are some features to remember about **magka-** and **magkaroon**:

1. Unlike **may** and **mayroon**, **magka-** and **magkaroon** can be conjugated for aspect as illustrated above.
2. **Magka-** is prefixed to the noun object.

EXAMPLES:

Prefix   Noun

nagka-   +   **tigdas**   →   **nagkatigdas** (had measles)

Nagkatigdas na ako at ang kapatid ko noong bata pa kami. My sibling and I had measles already when we were kids.

nagka-   +   **lagnat**   →   **nagkalagnat** (had fever)

Nagkalagnat ang bata noong isang linggo. The child had fever last week.

3. Unlike the **magka-**, a verbal affix, **magkaroon** is a verb that stands alone. It requires the object marker **ng**, while **magka-**prefixes to the object and requires no object marker.

EXAMPLES:

Nagkaroon na ako ng bulutong tubig noong bata pa ako. I already had chicken pox when I was little.

Nagkaroon ako ng lagnat kamakalawa. I had fever two days ago.

Grammar Presentation

1. The Completed Aspect

When using **magka-** and **magkaroon** in the completed form, several different predicational sentence structures are possible. For **magkaroon**, the word order changes depending on whether the subject is an **ang** phrase or an **ang** pronoun. The chart below illustrates the possible sentences using **magkaroon ng sakit** and **magkasakit** (to become sick).

Completed Form				
Verb + Noun	**Subject (Possessor)**	**Time Marker**		
Nagkasakit	ang <u>bata</u> si <u>Patrick</u> ang mga <u>bata</u> sina <u>Patrick</u>	<u>dati.</u>		
	ako tayo kami ka kayo siya sila	**Past Marker**		**Noun**
		noong		<u>Linggo.</u>

Verb	**Subject (Possessor)**	**Object Phrase**		**Time Marker**	
Nagkaroon	ako tayo kami ka kayo siya sila	**Marker**	**Noun**	<u>dati.</u>	
		ng ng mga	<u>sakit</u>	**Past marker**	**Noun**
				noong	<u>Linggo.</u>

Verb	**Object Phrase**		**Subject (Possessor)**	**Time Marker**	
	Marker	**Noun**		**Past Marker**	**Noun**
Nagkaroon	ng ng mga	<u>sakit</u>	ang <u>bata</u> ang mga <u>bata</u>	noong	<u>Linggo.</u>
			si <u>Patrick</u> sina <u>Patrick</u>	<u>dati.</u>	

The meaning of the **magka-** and **magkaroon** verbs used in the sentences in the chart is basically the same. However, to modify the ailment expressed in the verb **magkasakit** (to get sick), for example, one would use an adverb expressed as **nang malala** (gravely), which does not translate well in English. To express the same thing in the sentence with the verb **magkaroon ng sakit**, the modifier would be an adjective, **malala** (severe, serious, grave), modifying the noun **sakit** (sickness). That is the only difference between the two verbs.

In the examples below, notice that the last sentence uses the enclitics **po**, denoting respect, and **ba**, the question marker, and that, as we've learned, because they are one-syllable words they immediately follow the first word of the sentence in a fixed sequence.

EXAMPLES:

Nagkalagnat ang bata noong isang buwan. The kid had a fever last month

Nagkaroon po ng trangkaso ang anak ko kahapon. My child had the flu yesterday, sir/madam.

Nagkaroon po ba siya ng ubo noong isang linggo? Did she/he have a cough last week, sir/madam?

2. The Incompleted Aspect

When using **magka-** and **magkaroon** in the incompleted form to indicate habitual action, the following sentence structures are possible. Notice again how the word order changes depending on the subject. The example sentences also illustrate the difference in meaning between **nagkaka-** and **nagkakaroon** on the one hand and the existential partcles **may** and **mayroon** on the other.

Incompleted Form			
Verb + Noun	**Subject (Possessor)**	**Time Marker**	
Nagkakasakit	ang <u>bata</u> si <u>Patrick</u> ang mga <u>bata</u> sina <u>Patrick</u> ako tayo kami ka kayo siya sila	<u>tuwing tag-init.</u>	

Verb	**Subject (Possessor)**	**Object Phrase**		**Time Marker**
		Marker	**Noun**	
Nagkakaroon	ako tayo kami ka kayo siya sila	ng ng mga	<u>sakit</u>	<u>tuwing tag-init.</u>

Verb	**Object Phrase**		**Subject (Possessor)**	**Time Marker**
	Marker	**Noun**		
Nagkakaroon	ng ng mga	<u>sakit</u>	ang <u>bata</u> ang mga <u>bata</u> si <u>Patrick</u> sina <u>Patrick</u>	<u>tuwing tag-init.</u>

EXAMPLES:

Nagkakaroon ng sipon ang mga bata tuwing taglamig. The children get a cold every winter.

Nagkakaroon sila ng trangkaso tuwing Disyembre. They get the flu every December.

May sipon ang mga bata tuwing Disyembre. The kids have flu every December.

May trangkaso sila tuwing Nobyembre. They have the flu every November.

Nagkakabalinguyngoy si Lydia tuwing tag-init. Lydia gets nosebleeds every summer.

*May balinguyngoy si Lydia tuwing tag-init. (incorrect)

In the last sentence above, the native speaker's way of expressing "having nosebleeds every summer" is to use the obect-focus **-in-** verb **binabalinguyngoy**, which we will study in a subsequent lesson.

3. The Contemplated Aspect

When using **magka-** and **magkaroon** in the contemplated form, the following sentence structures are possible. Notice that the adverbs of time are all placed toward the end of the sentence.

Completed Form				
Verb + Noun	**Subject (Possessor)**	**Time Marker**		
Magkakasakit	ang <u>bata</u> si <u>Patrick</u> ang mga <u>bata</u> sina <u>Patrick</u> ako tayo kami ka kayo siya sila	<u>bukas</u>		
		Future Marker		**Noun**
		sa		<u>Linggo.</u>

	Verb	**Subject (Possessor)**	**Object Phrase**		**Time Marker**		
			Marker	**Noun**	**bukas**		
	Magkakaroon	ako tayo kami ka kayo siya sila	ng ng mga	<u>sakit</u>			
					Future marker		**Noun**
					sa		<u>Linggo.</u>

Verb	**Object Phrase**		**Subject (Possessor)**	**Time Marker**	
	Marker	**Noun**		**Future Marker**	**Noun**
Magkakaroon	ng ng mga	<u>sakit</u>	ang <u>bata</u> ang mga <u>bata</u>	sa	<u>Linggo.</u>
			si <u>Patrick</u> sina <u>Patrick</u>	<u>bukas.</u>	

EXAMPLES:

Magkakasipon si Mike. Mike will get a cold.

Magkakaroon ng sakit sa ngipin ang bata kasi hindi siya nagsisipilyo. The child will get a toothache because he/she does not brush his/her teeth.

Magkakaroon ako ng sipon dahil sa panahon. I will get a cold because of the weather.

Grammar Notes

1. When there is an adjective modifying a noun, it is preferable to use **magkaroon** instead of **magka-**.
   Nagkaroon ako ng malalang sakit. I had a severe sickness.
   *****Nagkamalalang sakit ako.** (incorrect)

2. **Magkaroon** pulls the pronouns and enclitics to the front.
   Nagkaroon ng trangkaso si Martha. Martha had the flu.
   Nagkaroon po siya ng trangkaso. She/He had the flu, sir/madam.

3. The existential particle **may** expresses a state of having or of existing currently or presently in time. Because it expresses a state rather than an action, **may** is commonly employed to express having sickness, just like **magka-** and **magkaroon** verbs. The first two sentences below indicate that the subject is sick presently even without there being an adverb of time. From the point of view of the native speaker, having the sickness (**may sakit**) is in the present time unless an adverb of time indicates otherwise. In the last two sentences, the words **kahapon** (yesterday) and **noong isang linggo** (last week) do just that, changing the meaning to the "state of having sickness or being sick in the past."

   May sakit siya. She/He is sick.
   May sakit ang mga bata. The children are sick.

   May sakit siya kahapon. She was sick yesterday.
   May sakit ang mga bata noong isang linggo. The children were sick last week.

4. **Nagkaka-** is used when something occurs habitually—whether yearly, monthly, weekly, or otherwise.
   Nagkakasakit sila tuwing tag-init. They get sick every summer.
   Nagkakaroon ng sakit ang mga bata tuwing taglamig. The children get sick every fall.

II. Telling Time (Informal)

Before the Spaniards came, the natives of the islands reckoned time by the position of the sun in the firmament and through other signs in nature, such as the crowing of the rooster. The clock and the concept of the twenty-four-hour day were introduced and inculcated in the Filipino population by the Spanish during their more than 350 years of colonization of the islands from 1565 to 1898. **Oras**, the Tagalog term for hour and time comes from the Spanish word *hora*. In Tagalog, **oras** is both singular and plural. Tagalog also uses the Spanish *y* (and) in time expressions like **alas tres y medya** (3:30), where it retains the Spanish pronunciation and sounds like "e" in *English*. The word for "quarter," as in "quarter till (the hour)," was also borrowed from Spanish and is now spelled the Tagalog way: **kuwarto**. So 1:45 or "15 minutes before two o'clock" is **menos kuwarto para alas dos**.

The table below shows how to say the time in hours and minutes. Memorize the different ways and notice how they're used in the example sentences. The last sentence illustrates the use of **oras** to mean "hours."

	Oras
1:05	**Ala una y singko**
2:10	**Alas dos diyes**

3:15	**Alas tres kinse**
4:20	**Alas kuwatro bente**
5:25	**Alas singko bente singko**
6:30	**Alas sais trenta**
7:35	**Alas siyete trenta'y singko**
8:40	**Alas otso kuwarenta**
9:45	**Alas nuwebe kuwarenta'y singko**
10:50	**Alas diyes singkuwenta**
11:55	**Alas onse singkuwenta'y singko**
12:30	**Alas dose y medya**

EXAMPLES:

Anong oras na? What time is it?

Alas singko bente. It's 5:20

Anong oras ka pupunta sa doktor? What time are you going to the doctor?

Mga alas tres y medya. Around 3:30.

Anong oras ka uminom ng gamot mo? What time did you take your medicine?

Uminom ako ng gamot ko nang alas kuwatro kuwarenta'y singko. I took my medicine at 4:45.

Ilang oras ang papunta sa ospiral? How many hours does it take to go to the hospital?

Grammar Notes

1. **Nang** is used to mark time. It is translated as "at" in English.

   Pupunta ako sa doktor *nang* **alas dos y medya ng hapon.** I will go to the doctor at 2:30 p.m.

   Naglagay ako ng gamot *nang* **alas kuwatro bente singko.** I put on some ointment at 4:25.

2. **Mga**, which is also a plural noun marker, is used when one is unsure about the exact time of occurrence of the event and is positioned before the entire time expression. It is translated as "about" or "around, nearly, approximately."

   Pupunta ako sa doktor nang *mga* **alas dos y medya ng hapon.** I will go to the doctor at around 2:30 p.m.

   Naglagay ako ng gamot nang *mga* **alas kuwatro.** I put on some ointment at around 4:00.

3. **Tuwing** is used when the event happens on a habitual basis.

   Umiinom ako ng gamot ko araw-araw tuwing ala una y medya ng hapon. I take my medication every day at 1:30 p.m.

   Kumakain ako ng almusal araw-araw tuwing alas siyete ng umaga. I eat breakfast every day at 7:00 a.m.

Practice

I. Speaking Practice

Each person listed in the table below is suffering from some kind of injury or ailment. Next to each name, write a story explaining how the person got sick. What were they doing that led to their ailment or injury? Follow the example of the story of Mario and how he got his sore throat.

Pangalan/Karamdaman	Kwento
Mario, masakit ang lalamunan	Ito si Mario, nagkaroon siya ng sakit sa lalamunan kasi kahapon nanood siya ng beysbol. Naglaro ang paborito niyang koponan, ang Seattle Mariners. Habang nanonood siya, sumigaw siya nang malakas na malakas at saka uminom siya ng malamig na malamig na serbesa. Pagkatapos ng laro, wala na siyang boses at ngayon masakit na masakit ang lalamunan niya.
Nelson, nahihilo	_____ _____ _____ _____ _____ _____
Rosario, napilay	_____ _____ _____ _____ _____ _____ _____ _____

II. Reading Practice

This is an information gap activity. Pair up with another student. Student A will read each sentence below silently, then he or she will translate it into English and tell the translation to his/her partner (student B). Student B must then translate student A's English version back into Tagalog and write it down. Compare the two Tagalog texts. What accounts for the differences?

A. Isang Araw na May Sakit Ako

Noong isang taon, nagbakasyon ako sa Pilipinas. Nagkaroon ako ng mataas na lagnat. Masakit ang katawan ko at hindi ako puwedeng kumain. Masuwerte ako dahil may gamot ang mga kamag-anak ng nanay ko. Uminom ako ng gamot nang alas diyes y medya ng gabi at kinabukasan, mabuti na ang pakiramdam ko.

B. Isang Araw na May Sakit Ako

_____

_____

_____

_____

III. Writing Practice

Think about one time when you were sick. In Tagalog, explain what you were doing before you became ill. Don't recount the symptoms of becoming ill.

Karamdaman	Mga Ginawa ko Bago Magkasakit
Nagsusuka	_____ _____ _____ _____ _____ _____
Sinisipon	_____ _____ _____ _____ _____ _____

IV. Listening Practice

 Listen to audio file (14–2) about illness and the medication that was prescribed. Fill in the chart below.

Pangalan	Oras	Petsa	Sakit	Reseta
1.				
2.				
3.				

Mga Iba't ibang Lunas

Various Remedies

An Overview of Lesson 15

Objectives
• Talk about medicinal plants and other non-traditional form of medication
• Express different things that one wants, needs, or does not want to do

Vocabulary
• Nouns
• Experiencer-Focus Verbs
• Idioms and Expressions
• Actor-Focus verbs,
• Object-Focus Verbs,
• Helping Verbs
• Adjective

Dialogue: Pagbisita sa May Sakit *Visiting the Sick*

Dialogue Comprehension

Activities
Activity 1: Things I Like and Dislike to Do When I'm Sick
Activity 2: Different Kinds of Advice When One Is Sick
Activity 3: A Day When I Was Sick

Grammar
Definition of terms: Experiencer-Focus Verbs and Actor-Focus Verbs

Examining Form
I. The Helping Verbs **Gusto**, **Ayaw**, and **Kailangan**
   Grammar Presentation: Helping Verbs
   Grammar Notes
II. Experiencer-Focus **Ma-** Verbs
   Grammar Presentation

Practice
I.   Speaking Practice
II. Reading Practice
III. Writing Practice
IV. Listening Practice

Vocabulary 🎧 (15–1)

The vocabulary below will help you speak about wants and needs and to participate in the activities in this lesson. Memorize the vocabulary words before proceeding to the dialogue. A word of caution: The contents of this lesson describe Filipino culture's approach to alternative medicine and are not to be taken as healthcare advice.

Nouns

albularyo	faith healer
bayabas	guava
bubuyog	bee
buko	bud
dahon	leaf
dyus	juice
gagamba	spider
gumamela	hibiscus
halamang gamot	medicinal plants
kagat	bite
kalamansi dyus	citrus (native) juice
lamok	mosquito
limonada	lemonade
lunas	remedy
manghihilot	healer who treats muscular and joint pains and dislocated bones using massage/local midwife
pantal	welt, insect bite
pagdalaw	visit
pigsa	boil
sabila	aloe vera
surot	bed bugs
tsaa	tea

Experiencer-Focus Verbs

maaksidente	to have an accident
madapa	to fall flat on one's face
madulas	to slip
makagat	to be bitten
magupit	to be cut (with scissors)
mahawa	to be contaminated or infected
mahiwa	to be cut (with a knife)
mahulog	to fall down
maipit	to be caught by the door, or pressed between two objects
maospital	to be hospitalized

Actor-Focus Verbs

lumala	to get worse
magdikdik	to pulverize; to pound
magmumog	to gargle
magpakulo	to boil
magtitimpla	will mix (will make juice)
tumubo	to grow

Object-Focus Verbs

ilagay	to put
inumin	to drink
pakuluin	to bring to a boil
tandaan	to remember

Helping Verbs

gusto	like; want
ayaw	dislike; do not want
kailangan	need

Adjectives

maligamgam	lukewarm
magang-maga	very swollen, really swollen

Idioms and Expressions

Mawawala rin ito.	This (I) will get better.
Tamang-tama gutom na ako.	Good, I am really hungry.
Ano ka ba?	What's the matter with you?

Dialogue: Pagbisita sa May Sakit *Visiting the Sick*

Jayson has come to pay Hiro a visit at his home. Read the dialogue between Jayson and Hiro about how to take care of oneself to prevent illness from getting worse, then answer the Dialogue Comprehension questions that follow.

Jayson: **Oy kumusta ka na?**

Hiro: **Ayos lang. Pero, nahawa ako ng sipon sa kaibigan ko.**

Jayson: **O eh, kumusta naman ang pakiramdam mo? Ayos ka lang ba?**

Hiro: **Medyo hindi. Lumalala ang sipon ko at masakit na masakit na ang lalamunan ko ngayon. Magang-maga na ito.**

Jayson: **O eh, uminom ka ng gamot para hindi ka na maospital.**

Hiro: **Hindi na. Mawawala rin ito bukas. Kailangan ko lang magpahinga.**

Jayson: **Ano ka ba! Baka lumala pa lalo 'yan, bahala ka. O sige, may sopas ako para sa iyo.**

Hiro: **Tamang-tama gutom na ako.**

Jayson: **O sige. Tandaan mo na kailangan mong kumain para lumakas ka. Tapos, pagkatapos mong kumain, magmumog ka ng *mouthwash*.**

Hiro: **Ay, wala akong *mouthwash* dito, eh.**

Jayson: **Kung wala, puwede kang magmumog ng maligamgam na tubig na may asin. Pagkatapos, uminom ka ng limonada o kalamansi dyus.**

Hiro: **O sige, magtitimpla na ako ng limonada. Gusto mo rin bang uminom ng limonada?**

Jayson: **Salamat pero ayaw kong uminom ng dyus, siguro iinom na lang ako ng tsaa mamaya.**

Hiro: **Salamat sa tulong at sopas, ha.**

Jayson: **Oo. Ayos lang 'yan.**

Hiro: **O sige. Salamat ulit at ingat ka!**

Dialogue Comprehension

> **Word Bank**
>
> **ibinigay** gave
> **payo** advice

1. **Ano ang sakit ni Hiro?**

   _____

2. **Ilarawan ang pakiramdam ni Hiro.**

   _____

3. **Ano ang ibinigay** (gave) **ni Jayson kay Hiro?**

   _____

4. **Pumunta ba si Hiro sa ospital? Bakit?**

   _____

5. **Ano ang payo** (advice) **ni Jayson kay Hiro?**

   _____

Activities

Activity 1

In the table below, make a list of things you like (**gusto**) and don't like (**ayaw**) to do when you have one of these ailments. Use the example to model your answers.

Mga Sakit	Gusto	Ayaw
SIPON	**Gusto _kong_ uminom ng tsaa kung may sipon ako.**	**Ayaw _kong_ lumabas ng bahay kung may sipon ako.**
LAGNAT		
UBO		

Activity 2

Use the helping verb **kailangan** to suggest a list of remedies for the following ailments. The example can serve to model your responses.

Mga Sakit o Karamdaman	Mga Unang Lunas
Sipon	Kung magkakasipon ka o kung mayroon ka nang sipon, kailangan mong magmumog ng maligamgam na tubig na may asin o magmumog ng mouthwash nang limang minuto. Pagkatapos mong magmumog, uminom ka ng mainit na tsaa o limonada. Pagkatapos, puwede ka nang magpahinga o matulog.
Sugat	
Sakit ng tiyan	

Activity 3

Think about a day when you were sick and, on a separate sheet of paper, explain what steps you took to make yourself feel better. Draw a picture to accompany your text.

Grammar

Experiencer-Focus Verbs	Verbs whose subjects "experience" the action that may or may not be done to them from without, as in **Naaksidente ako**. "An accident happened to me." For example, **ma**-verbs.
Actor-Focus Verbs	Verbs whose focus or subject is the actor, doer of the action, or originator of the action in **ang** form. For example, **mag-** and **–um-** verbs.

Examining Form

The sentences below illustrate the grammar patterns that are presented in this lesson. Review the sentences and complete the tasks that follow. Discuss your answers with a partner. Consult the following section to check your answers.

Column A	Column B
1. **Kailangan ko lang magpahinga.**	**Magpapahinga lang ako.**
2. **Kailangan mong kumain para lumakas ka.**	**Kumain ka para lumakas ka.**
3. **Gusto mo rin bang uminom ng limonada?**	**Iinom ka ba ng limonada?**
4. **Ayaw kong kumain.**	**Iinom ako ng dyus.**
5. **Nahawa ako ng sipon sa kaibigan ko.**	
6. **Uminom ka ng gamot para hindi ka na maospital.**	
7. **Nakagat ng aso ko si Mike.**	
8. **Nahiwa ko ang daliri ko.**	

For numbers 1–4
1. Underline all the actors and enclitics, box the helping verbs, and circle the main verbs.
2. What happens with the word order when using these helping verbs?
3. List all the differences in structure in column A and column B.

For numbers 5–8
4. Circle the verb, underline the actor, and box the experiencer.
5. Notice that in numbers 7 and 8, there are two **ng** forms after the verb. How do these two **ng** forms function in the sentence?

I. The Helping Verbs **Gusto, Ayaw,** and **Kailangan**

In the first lesson in this unit, Lesson 13, we studied the helping verbs **bawal, dapat, puwede,** and **huwag** and learned the HIL rule. In this lesson, we will reprise the HIL rule for a different set of helping verbs. They are:

> **gusto** want, like
> **ayaw** don't want, don't like
> **kailangan** need

For this group of verbs, the possessive form **ng** is the actor. To remind us that the actor of these verbs is in the possessive form, we will expand the acronym HIL to include the letter P, making it the PHIL rule.

P = Possessive: The actor has to be a **ng** form.

H = Haul: All pronouns and enclitics should be placed immediately after the helping verb.

I = Infinitive form: The main verb has to be in infinitive form.

L = Linker Linkers, either **-ng** or **-g**, must be attached to the word before the main verb.

Grammar Presentation

Helping Verbs

1. When using the helping verbs **gusto**, **ayaw**, and **kailangan** in a predicational sentence, where the actor is a **ng** phrase, the word order is **Ayaw** + INFINITIVE + **ng** ACTOR + DIRECT OBJECT.

   For **gusto** and **kailangan**, the word order is **Gusto/Kailangan** + LINKER + INFINITIVE + **ng** ACTOR + DIRECT OBJECT. See the chart below for other possible sentence structures.

Predicational Sentence						
Helping Verb	Linkers	Main Verb	Actor		Direct Object	
			Marker	Noun	Marker	Noun
Ayaw		uminom	ni nina	Sheila	ng ng mga	gamot.
Kailangan Gusto	-g -ng		ng ng mga	bata		

EXAMPLES:

Ayaw pumunta ng bata sa doktor. The child does not want to go to the doctor.

Kailangan po*ng* magpahinga ni Berto. Berto needs to rest, sir/madam.

Gusto ba*ng* dumalaw nina Melody at Janice kay Mario? Do Melody and Janice want to visit Mario?

Notice that the first and last example sentences have indirect objects, **sa doktor** in the first sentence and **Mario** in the last sentence. **Mario** is marked by **kay**, a proper-name **sa** marker. The second sentence has an enclitic (**po** + linker) before the infinitive **magpahinga**. The actor in the sentence is **Berto**, preceded by the proper-name **ng** marker, **ni,** which makes it a **ng** form.

2. When **ng** pronouns are the actors of the verb, remember to place them before the main verb in the infinitive form. Use the PHIL rule in forming your sentences.

Predicational Sentence						
Helping Verb	Actor		Linker	Main Verb	Direct Object	
					Marker	Noun
Gusto Ayaw Kailangan	ko natin namin mo ninyo niya nila		-g -ng	uminom	ng ng mga	gamot.

EXAMPLES:

Gusto *kong* magpahinga buong araw. I want to take a rest the whole day.

Ayaw <u>daw</u> *nilang* bumisita kay Marc sa ospital. They say they don't want to visit Marc at the hospital.

Kailangan *ko* <u>po</u> <u>bang</u> uminom ng gamot? Do I need to take medicine, sir/madam?

Grammar Notes

1. We learned in previous lessons that –**um**- verbs are actor-focus verbs and that the actor is also the subject, which necessitates that the actor be in the **ang** form. However, in the sentences below, you will observe that, although the main verb, **uminom** (to drink), is actor-focus, the one doing the action is a **ng** form instead of **ang**. This is an anomaly associated with this sentence structure. Just remember that, generally, when using **gusto**, **ayaw**, and **kailangan**, you must bear in mind the PHIL rule. Study the application of the PHIL rule in the sentences below. In all of these sentences, the main verb is in the infinitive form.

   EXAMPLES:

   P: **Ayaw <u>kong</u> uminom ng gamot.**
   (The actor is Possessive, although **uminom** is actor-focus.)

   H: **Ayaw <u>kong</u> uminom ng gamot.**
   (Haul the pronoun actor **ko** forward so that it comes right after **Ayaw** and is in front of the main verb.)

   But: **Ayaw uminom ng gamot <u>ni Patrick</u>.**
   (We apply the HAUL rule only with pronouns. Thus, "**ni** Patrick," which is a **ng** phrase, goes after the verb.)

   I: **Ayaw <u>uminom</u> ng gamot ni Patrick.**
   (In all of these sentences, the main verb is in the Infinitive form)

   L: **Ayaw ko<u>ng</u> uminom ng gamot.**
   (A linker is attached to the word before the main verb)

2. Use the linker -**ng** with **gusto** and -**g** for **kailangan**. However, when the word that precedes the main verb ends with a consonant (except *n*), no linker is needed.
   Ayaw ko*ng* uminom ng gamot.
   Kailanga*ng* uminom ni Mike ng gamot.
   *****Ayaw na uminom ng dyus.** (incorrect: this translates to "The juice no longer wants to drink")

II. Experiencer-Focus **Ma-** Verbs

Certain **ma**- verbs refer to some kind of accident or disaster experienced by the subject. Experiencer-focus verbs mostly express actions that are involuntary, unintentional, or not purposeful. Their subjects or focus are not doing the action, and instead the action happens to them. The experiencer/subject of the sentence or verb may be a person, an animal, living things like plants, or sometimes inanimate objects like a cup. These verbs conjugate for aspect, but since they are non-volitional, there can be no imperative form. The high frquency **ma**- experiencer-focus verbs are the following:

maaksidente	to have an accident happen to the subject
madapa	to fall flat on one's knees, stomach, face accidentally while walking or running
madulas	to slip involuntarily

makagat	to be bitten by a dog, cat, bird, snake, person, etc., accidentally
mahawa	to have a disease transfered to another person
mahiwa	to be cut by a knife accidentally
magupit	to be cut by a pair of scissors accidentally
maospital	to be hospitalized
malunod	to drown accidentally
mahulog	to fall accidentally

EXAMPLES:

Naaksidente kami. An accident happened to us.

Nadapa siya. He stumbled face forward accidentally.

Nakagat ako ng aso. A dog bit me accidentally. (In this sentence, the verb has an actor—the dog— and **ako** "I" experienced the dog bite. The dog's biting happened to "I.")

Nalunod ang pamangkin ko sa lawa. My nephew drowned in the lake accidentally.

Nahulog ang baso. The glass fell by accident.

Natumba ang puno. The tree fell accidentally.

The **ma-** verb follows the same aspect formation as the **mag-**verb. *N* replaces the *m* of the prefix for the started action, and the first consonant-vowel or vowel of the root is reduplicated for action not terminated. The chart below shows the inflection of the verbs **mahawa** (to transfer a disease from one person to another) and **madapa** (to fall or stumble face down acccidentally).

Aspect	Inflection	Inflection	Rules
Root	**hawa**	**dapa**	
Infinitive	**mahawa**	**madapa**	Prefix **ma-** to the root.
Completed	**nahawa**	**nadapa**	From the infinitive form, change /m/ to /n/.
Incompleted	**nahahawa**	**nadadapa**	Take the first two syllables of the completed aspect, plus the root.
Contemplated	**mahahawa**	**madadapa**	From the incompleted aspect, change /n/ to /m/.

Grammar Presentation

1. The following chart shows the **ma-** verb **madulas** (to slip or slide accidentally) conjugated in its aspects with different subjects in a predicational sentence structure. It is worth noting that the English equivalent usually does not quite capture the accidental or involuntary nature of the action experienced by the subject or focus in this type of Tagalog sentence. For instance, in **Nadulas si Patrick sa hagdan** (Patrick accidentally slipped on the stairs), the idiomatic translation in English, "Patrick fell on the stairs," does not capture the Tagalog nuance of involuntary sliding on the slippery surface, since "fell" or "slip" is active, as though intentional. More examples of experiencer-focus verbs can be found in the sentences following the chart.

Ma- Verb: **Madulas** (No actor)						
Verb	**Actor**		**Subject**		**Preposition**	
Mag	**Marker**	**Noun**	**Marker**	**Noun**	**Marker**	**Noun**
Nadulas (completed)	-	-	si sina ang ang mga	**Patrick** **bata** ako tayo kami ka kayo siya sila	sa	**hagdan.**
Nadudulas (incomplete)						
Madudulas (contemplated)						

EXAMPLES:

Nahawa ng sipon si Mike. Mike caught a cold.

Nahulog ang lalaki sa hagdan. The man fell down the stairs.

Nadulas si Maria sa kusina. Maria slipped in the kitchen.

2. In the chart below, the **ma-** verb requires an actor to complete its meaning. Notice that the actor is **ng** form. The chart illustrates the different sentence patterns for when the subject or focus is an **ang** phrase (**si Patrick**) or an **ang** pronoun.

Ma- Verbs (with **Ng** Actor)						
Verb	**Actor**		**Subject/Experiencer**		**Preposition**	
Ma	**Marker**	**Noun**	**Marker**	**Noun**	**Marker**	**Noun**
Nahiwa (completed)	ni nina ng ng mga	**Marc** **bata** ko natin namin mo ninyo niya nila	si sina ang ang mga	**Patrick** **lalaki**	sa	**kamay.**
Nahihiwa (incomplete)						
Mahihiwa (contemplated)						
Verb	**Subject/Experiencer**		**Ng Actor**		**Preposition**	
Ma	**Marker**	**Noun**	**Marker**	**Noun**	**Marker**	**Noun**
Nahiwa (completed)		ako tayo kami ka kayo siya sila	ni nina ng ng mga	**Marc** **lalaki**	sa	**kamay.**
Nahihiwa (incomplete)						
Mahihiwa (contemplated)						

EXAMPLES: **Nakagat <u>ng aso</u> si Mike sa binti.** Mike got bitten on the leg by a dog.
Nahiwa <u>ko</u> ang daliri ko kanina. I cut my finger earlier.

Supplementary Vocabulary	
mabasag	to be broken (glass, mirror, etc.)
masira	to be destroyed, broken; to become spoiled, as cooked food
masunog	to be burned
matapon	to be spilled
mawala	to be misplaced
mahuli	to be late
maligaw	to be lost (pertaining to direction)
matrapik	to be caught in traffic

Practice

I. Speaking Practice

Work with a partner and discuss what you would each do in the following situations. Be sure to use the helping verbs that you have learned in this lesson.

Sakit o Aksidente	Gusto, Ayaw, at Kailangang Gawin
1. **Nakagat ng lamok**	
2. **Nahawa ka ng sipon**	
3. **Naospital**	
4. **Naipit sa pinto**	
5. **Nadapa**	

II. Reading Practice

Madelaine and Jewel are doing a project on medicinal plants for Botany class and have gone to Quiapo in Manila, where vendors sell herbs with medicinal qualities. Read the labels of the packages, then do the Reading Comprehension activity that follows in order to help them with their research.

Mga Halaman	Paglalarawan
	Katas ng Sabila (Aloe Vera) **Mabuting gamot ang katas ng sabila para sa mga paso** (burns) **at sa mga sugat. Ginagamit din ito para tumubo ang buhok.** **Paano gamitin?** **Kunin ang katas ng dahon at ipahid sa anit** (scalp) **o sa sugat.**

DAHON NG BAYABAS (Guava leaves)

Mabuting gamot ang dahon ng bayabas para sa mga sugat at sa pagtatae.

Paano gamitin?

Magpakulo ng tubig at ilagay ang dahon ng bayabas. Para sa sugat, kailangan mong linisin ang sugat gamit ang maligamgam na tubig na may dahon. Para sa pagtatae, kailangang uminom ng maligamgam na tubig na may dahon.

GUMAMELA (Hibiscus)

Mabuting gamot sa pigsa ang gumamela.

Paano gamitin?

Kailangang magdikdik ng buko ng bulaklak na may kaunting asin at ilagay ito sa pigsa. Gawin ito nang madalas.

Reading Comprehension

For each of the following statements about the medicinal plants, place a check mark in the appropriate blank, depending on whether the statement is true, **Tama**, or false, **Mali**.

	TAMA	MALI
1. Ginagamit ang gumamela para sa buhok.	_____	_____
2. Gamot sa pigsa ang katas ng gumamela.	_____	_____
3. Magdikdik ng dahon ng sabila para sa sugat.	_____	_____
4. Gamot ang dahon ng bayabas sa pagtatae.	_____	_____
5. Kailangang uminom ng katas ng gumamela para sa pagtatae.	_____	_____

III. Writing Practice

What medicinal plants and nontraditional medications do you use or are you familiar with? Draw a picture of that plant or remedy and explain what it is for and how it is used. Take the text from the previous activity as a model. If you do not use or are not familiar with medicinal plants and non-traditional medications, research them on the Internet.

Mga Halaman	Paglalarawan
	_____ _____ _____ _____ _____
	_____ _____ _____ _____ _____

IV. Listening Practice

Listen to audio file (15–2) and answer the following questions. Circle **Oo** if the answer is true and **Hindi** if it is false. Pause the audio as needed.

1. **Kailangan bang gumamit ng gamot sa pantal kung nakagat ka ng aso?**
   Oo   Hindi

2. **Kung nagkasugat ka, kailangan mo bang gumamit ng katas ng gumamela?**
   Oo   Hindi

3. **Kung masakit ang lalamunan mo kailangan mo bang kumain ng tsaa?**
   Oo   Hindi

4. **Kung hindi malala ang hika mo, kailangan mo bang pumunta sa ospital?**
   Oo   Hindi

5. **Kung may sakit ka, puwede ka bang gumamit ng mga halamang gamot?**
   Oo   Hindi

UNIT 6

PAGKAIN
Food

If it is close to a mealtime and you encounter a Filipino friend or colleague, often the greeting will be "**Kumain ka na ba?**" ("Have you eaten yet?"). If you are entering a Philippine home, this greeting will often be accompanied by an offer of food. It is considered polite to graciously decline the first offer by saying, "**Salamat po pero busog pa po ako**" ("Thank you, ma'am/sir, but I'm still full."). If a second offer is made, this one should also be graciously declined. However, if you are offered food a third time, you should say, "**O sige na nga po**" ("Okay, ma'am/sir.") and enjoy the delicious food and warm hospitality of the Filipino table. In the Philippines, food is a celebration, and a celebration is meant to be shared.

A typical Filipino celebration

Though Filipino food shares some things with other Southeast Asian cuisines like the use of **tanglad** or lemon grass, ginger, and other spices, **patis** (a sauce made from fermented fish), and a wide variety of rice dishes, it also shows influences from Spanish and Mexican cuisine due to the long-standing trade between Manila and Acapulco during the Spanish colonial period. Between the seventeenth and nineteenth centuries, ships passed regularly between the two colonies carrying from Mexico the basis for a number of classic Filipino dishes, including **menudo** (a pork and liver stew), **apritada** (a tomato-based stew), and of course, the world-renowned **adobo** (chicken or pork or both cooked in soy sauce and vinegar and seasoned with bay leaves and garlic). Philippine cuisine also bears the marks of the large Chinese population in the Philippines, as evidenced in everything from **pancit** (rice noodles) to **lumpiya** (egg rolls). Despite such influences, however, Filipino food retains flavors and ingredients unlike any other.

Since the Philippines is surrounded by water, it is no surprise that seafood plays a large role in the diet of many Filipinos. Fried, stewed, or stuffed (**relleno**), fish appears on almost every menu. Alongside fish, pork is probably the most popular meat in Philippine cuisine, and almost the whole pig is used in various ways, from the skin and fat in **chicharron** to the cheeks and snout in **sisig**. One of the most famous is **lechon**, a whole roasted pig that is served at many large Filipino celebrations.

Fresh fruits and vegetables rich in vitamins, minerals, and antioxidants abound in the Philippines the whole year round. Fruits and vegetables provide health benefits and cleanse the body as well as give it nourishment. They can be bought at the lowly **sari-sari** store, a small neighborhood variety store, from itinerant vendors peddling their produce in the streets in push carts, in the wet market or local **palengke**, or at a Western-style supermarket. There are large, sweet, and aromatic mangoes; red, yellow, and orange varieties of watermelon (**pakwan**); pineapples and different varieties of bananas than the ones raised and exported abroad by Dole and Del Monte, the biggest banana- and pineapple-plantation owners in the Philippines; avocados; and **langka** or jackfruit, said to be the largest fruit, depending on the variety. You can buy **lanzones**, a small yellow fruit that has a sweet, white, translucent flesh, by the kilo. Some fruits you can just solicit from neighbors who have a tree in their backyard, such as **chico**, a small round, brown fruit; **sinigwelas**; **santol**; **duhat** (a black berry that looks like a kind of olive); guavas; and **macopa** and other tropical fruits that are not available in other parts of the world. Other fruits endemic to the region and that we share with the rest of Southeast Asia are the purple **mangosteen**, called the queen of fruits, and **durian**, the king of fruits; pomelos, called **suha**; **atis** (sugar apple or custard apple); and tamarind, called **sampalok** in Tagalog. With such a diverse supply of fruits available, Filipino creativity has concocted unique ice cream flavors such as **ube** (purple yam), **Quezo Real** (cheese), **halo-halo** (inspired by a Filipino dessert made of crushed ice mixed with banana, **kaong** (immature seeds of sugar palm tree), **nata de coco** (a sweetened, clear white gelatinous substance formed from fermented coconut water), and sweet beans. Other unique dessert flavors are **nangkasoy**, a combination of jackfruit and cashew; sweet corn with real corn in it; **macapuno**, a variety of coconut that has thick, soft meat and almost no liquid inside the nut; and **buko pandan**, a blend of coconut and the essence of **pandan** leaf, an aromatic leaf used in boiled rice and sweets.

Among vegetables, Filipinos eat the flowers of squash, young leaves of bitter melon and sweet potato, and all the vegetables and seeds mentioned in the folk song "**Bahay Kubo**" ("Nipa Hut"): jicama, eggplant, winged beans, peanuts, string beans, kidney beans, kinds of gourds, squash, white radish, etc., all of which have local names.

For beverages, the Philippines can boast of locally distilled spirits like **lambanog**, made from distilled coconut water; **tapuy**, rice wine; and **duhat**, wine made from the **duhat** fruit. Favorite juices are concocted from **calamansi**, a Philippine lime; avocado; **buko** (young coconut); **guyabano** (soursop fruit); pineapple; and mango.

Lumpiya *(egg roll) and other Filipino foods*

Sa Palengke

At the Market

An Overview of Lesson 16

Objectives
- Use appropriate expressions in the context of shopping
- Engage in small talk about shopping

Vocabulary
- Food (Fruits, Vegetables, Meat)
- Units of Measure
- **Ng** Demonstrative Pronouns
- Adjectives
- Adjectives with **Ang**, **Kay**, and **Medyo**
- Idioms and Expressions

Dialogue: Isang Araw sa Palengke *One Day at the Market*

Dialogue Comprehension

Activities
Activity 1: My Fridge
Activity 2: Making Lumpia and Pancit
Activity 3: Role Play

Grammar
Definition of terms: Full Reduplication, Partial Reduplication

Examining Form
I.   Moderative Adjective Forms and Exclamatory Sentences
     Grammar Presentation
     Grammar Notes

Practice
I.   Speaking Practice
II. Reading Practice
III. Writing Practice
IV. Listening Practice

Vocabulary 🎧 (16–1)

The vocabulary below will help you express yourself and make small talk when shopping—and participate in the activities in this lesson. Memorize the vocabulary words before proceeding to the dialogue.

Food (Fruits, Vegetables, Meat)

ampalaya	bitter melon	prutas	fruit
baboy	pork	repolyo	cabbage
baka	beef	saging	banana
bawang	garlic	sampalok	tamarind
bayabas	guava	serbesa	beer
buko	coconut	sibuyas	onion
inumin	drinks, beverage	sili	pepper
itlog	egg	sitsaro	snow pea
isda	fish	sopdrinks	soda, soft drinks
kabute	mushroom	suha	pomelo, grape-fruit
kalabasa	squash		
kamatis	tomato	talong	eggplant
kamote	sweet potato	tinapay	bread
karot	carrot	toge	bean sprouts
keso	cheese	tubig	water
kintsay	Chinese celery	ubas	grape
gatas	milk	ube	purple yam
gisantes	sweet peas		
gulay	vegetable		
langka	jackfruit		
letsugas	lettuce		
luya	ginger		
mais	corn		
mangga	mango		
manok	chicken		
mansanas	apple		
mantekilya	butter		
pakwan	watermelon		
pagkain	food		
patatas	potato		
pinya	pineapple		
pipino	cucumber		

Units of Measure

dosena/dusena	dozen
galon	gallon
kada	each
kalahati	half
kilo	kilogram
libra	pound
litro	liter
pares	pair

Ng Demonstrative Pronouns

nito	this (near the speaker)
niyan	that (near the listener)
niyon/noon	that (far from both the speaker and the listener)

Adjectives

bulok	spoiled, rotten
hilaw	raw, unripe
hinog	ripe
luto	cooked
maalat	salty
maanghang	spicy
maasim	sour
makunat	chewy
mainit	hot
mamantika	oily
malambot	tender
malamig	cold
malamig-lamig	cool, some-what cold
malansa	fishy
malata	soggy, soft
matigas	hard
malutong	crispy
mapait	bitter
masarap	delicious
masustansiya	nutritious
matabang	bland, taste-less
matamis	sweet
matigas	tough, hard
sariwa	fresh
sunog	burnt

Adjectives with **Ang, Kay,** and **Medyo**

ang + adjective	may denote intensive degree of quality of noun
kay + adjective	denotes quality equivalent to "very extremely" or "how!" as in "how beautiful!"
medyo + adjective	somewhat; to some extent, to some degree of quality of noun indicated by the adjective

Idioms and Expressions

Ano ang lulutuin mo?	What are you going to cook?
Bigyan po ninyo ako ng . . .	Please give me some . . .
Kay/Ang mahal naman po!	That's too expensive, sir/ma'am!
Magkano po ang lahat-lahat?	How much are all these?
Nakalimutan ko ang . . .	I forgot the . . .
Wala na po bang tawad?	Can I get a discount, sir/ma'am?

Dialogue: Isang Araw sa Palengke *One Day at the Market*

Linda is at the **palengke** (market) buying the ingredients she will need for cooking. Read her exchange with the **tindera** (saleslady) and answer the Dialogue Comprehension questions.

Linda: **Kumusta po? Magkano ang repolyo ninyo?**

Tindera: **Tatlumpung piso kada kilo.**

Linda: **Ang mahal naman po. Wala na po bang tawad?**

Tindera: **O sige. Dalawampu't limang piso na lang para sa iyo. Ano pa ang kailangan mo?**

Linda: **Mayroon din ba kayong karot?**

Tindera: **Oo. Heto.**

Linda: **Ay. Medyo maliit po ang mga ito. Mayroon po ba kayong malaki-laki?**

Tindera: **Pasensiya na. Iyan lang ang mayroon ako, eh.**

Linda: **O sige, ayos na 'yan. Bigyan po ninyo ako ng isang kilo ng karot.**

Tindera: **O sige. Heto. Ano ang lulutuin mo, iha?**

Linda: **Magtsa-chop suey po ako.**

Tindera: **Ah. Ang sarap-sarap naman. O teka. May sitsaro ka na ba?**

Linda: **Ay! Nakalimutan ko po 'yan. Salamat po. O sige, bigyan po ninyo ako ng kalahating kilo.**

Tindera: **Heto, iha.**

Linda: **Magkano po ang lahat-lahat?**
Tindera: **Limampu't limang piso lahat-lahat.**
Linda: **Kay mahal naman po. Pwede bang limampung piso na lang ang lahat?**
Tindera: **O sige.**
Linda: **O heto po ang bayad. Salamat po.**
Tindera: **Salamat din.**

Dialogue Comprehension

1. **Magkano ang bili ni Linda sa repolyo?**

   _____

2. **Malaki ba ang mga karot?**

   _____

3. **Ano ang lulutuin ni Linda?**

   _____

4. **Ano ang nakalimutan ni Linda?**

   _____

5. **Magkano ang bayad ni Linda?**

   _____

Activities

Activity 1

List all the food that you have in your fridge, and then ask two of your classmates what's inside their fridge right now. Use the chart below to jot down your items.

EXAMPLE:
Student 1: **Ano ang laman ng rep mo ngayon?**
Student 2: **May tubig, sopdrinks, keso, at gatas sa loob ng rep ko ngayon.**

Ang Rep Ko	Ang Rep ni _____	Ang Rep ni _____

Activity 2

List all the ingredients you need to make **lumpiya** and **pansit**. For the last column, choose any Filipino food you wish and list all the ingredients for that as well.

EXAMPLE:

Para magluto ng tinola, kailangan ko ng <u>manok, papaya, bawang, sibuyas, at tubig</u>.

Lumpiya	Pansit	_____

Activity 3

Choose a partner and create a dialogue that responds to one of the scenarios listed below. Don't forget to use polite particles when appropriate.

Scenarios:

1. **Magluluto ka ng adobo, pero bago ka magluto kailangan mo munang bumili ng mga sumusunod: manok at baboy. Pumunta sa tindahan at bilhin ang mga sangkap na ito. Huwag kalimutang humingi ng tawad.**

2. **Kailangan mong bumili ng mga matatamis na prutas. Magtanong sa tindera kung matamis at hinog ang mga prutas niya. Pagkatapos, bumili ng mga ito.**

Grammar

Definition of Terms

Full Reduplication	The reduplication of an entire word or the root word in order to make an exclamation about the intensity of degree.
	EXAMPLES:
	matamis (tamis) sweet
	Ang *tamis-tamis!* How sweet!
	maalat (alat) salty
	Kay *alat-alat!* How salty!

Partial Reduplication	The reduplication of part of the word or root word in order to make an exclamation about the intensity of degree.
	EXAMPLES: **masustansiya (sustansiya)** nutritious **Ang *susta-sustansiya!*** How nutritious! **mamantika (mantika)** oily **Ang *manti-mantika*** How oily!

Examining Form

Review the sentences below and complete the tasks that follow. Discuss your answers with a partner. Consult the following section to check your answers.

1. **Ang mahal naman po.**
2. **Medyo maliliit po ang mga ito.**
3. **Mayroon po ba kayong malaki-laki?**
4. **Ang sarap-sarap naman.**
5. **Kay mahal naman po.**

    a. Circle all the adjectives.
    b. Identify and write down all the different markers, adverbs, and affixes attached to the adjectives.
    c. Discuss with a partner how each marker, adverb, and affix changes the meaning of the adjective.

I. Moderative Adjective Forms and Exclamatory Sentences

1. Moderative Adjective Forms: As we have seen, adjectives are descriptive words used to modify a noun or a pronoun. In sentences, an adjective can be a predicate. In Lesson 11, we introduced the degrees of comparison of adjectives: positive (ordinary adjectives), comparative (**mas** + adjective), superlative (**pinaka-** + adjective), and intensive (**napaka-** + root word of adjective). A fourth type of degree of comparison is called adjectives of moderate degree of quality. Moderative adjective forms convey the idea of an increment, as in "somewhat" or "a little bit."

    The examples below illustrate two ways to form moderative **ma-** adjectives to express the quality of a noun in the moderate degree according to what is indicated in the root word or base word of the adjective. The first, **maliit-liit**, is formed by reduplicating the base word (**liit**) of the adjective **maliit** (small). A hyphen is used after the adjective **maliit**. When the root word has more than two syllables, only the first two syllables are reduplicated. The second way of forming moderative adjectives is by placing the word **medyo** in front of the **ma-** adjective:

maliit-liit	a little bit small
medyo maliit	a little bit small
matali-talino	somewhat intelligent
medyo matalino	somewhat intelligent

2. Exclamatory sentences express surprise, awe, anger, wonder, vehemence, and other deep emotions. They are formed using the following structure:

> **Ang** followed by a descriptive base word or a root word.
> **Ang liit!**　　　How small!
> **Ang liit.**　　　It is small.
>
> **Kay** followed by a descriptive base word or a root word.
> **Kay tamis!**　　How sweet!
> **Kay tamis.**　　It is sweet.

The exclamatory sentence can be intensified by reduplicating the first two syllables of the adjective, The reduplicated adjective preceded by **ang** or **kay** can be used to form the following kinds of sentences:

> **Ang liit-liit!**　　　It is very small! or How very small!
> **Kay sarap-sarap!**　　It is very delicious! or How very delicious!

Intensified adjectives express an extreme degree of whatever quality is denoted by the root word. The noun need not be stated. It is assumed that the person spoken to knows what the speaker is referring to.

In Lesson 11 we studied the intensifier made from the prefix **napaka-** plus the root word of the adjective. In this lesson, we will study how to intensify an exclamatory sentence that uses **ang** or **kay** (very), as in **ang tamis** (very sweet) or **kay dami** (very many) or an interjection in exclamatory sentences like **Ang sarap!** (How delicious) **Kay alat!** (How salty!).

Generally, an intense degree of the quality denoted by an adjective is conveyed through reduplication of an adjective, with a linker, **na/-ng**, placed between the two words or attached to the first instance of the adjective ending in a vowel and preceding the second instance. **Ma-** adjectives and adjectives made up of root words can be given intensified meaning by repetition. The intensive form is equivalent to the English *very*.

masarap (delicious)	→	**masarap** *na* **masarap** very delicious
sariwa (fresh)	→	**sariwa***ng*-**sariwa** very fresh

Any adjective that can be intensified by **napaka-** in a sentence may also be intensified by using this structure:

> **ang** + reduplication of an adjective
> **kay** + reduplication of an adjective

EXAMPLES:
kay sarap-sarap/ang sarap-sarap　very delicious/how delicious!
kay susta-sustansiya/ang susta-sustansiya　very nutritious/how nutritious!

Notice that, in the first example, the root word is reduplicated in its entirety. This process of reduplication is called full reduplication. This is used when the adjectival root has two syllables, like **masarap** (delicious). The root word **sarap** has two syllables; thus, when reduplicated it becomes **sarap-sarap**. However, when an adjectival root has three or more syllables, only the first two syllables are reduplicated. For example, **matalino** (smart) becomes **matali-talino**. This process of reduplication is called partial reduplication.

3. The chart on the left below summarizes the rules governing the formation of adjectives of moderate degree by reduplication and the use of the word **medyo**. In the first example, **sikip** (tight, crowded) is the base word or root word. For **ma-** adjectives like **masikip**, moderation is indicated by reduplication of the root, as in **masikip-*sikip*** (somewhat tight or rather tight, a little tight). Another way of expressing a moderate degree of the quality by an adjective is by placing **medyo** (from the Spanish for "half, semi-, somewhat, to some extent, in some degree, rather") in front of the adjective, as in **medyo masikip** (somewhat tight).

Moderative Expressions		Exclamatory Sentences with Adjectives	
Reduplication	**Rules**	**Ang/Kay**	**Rules**
masikip-sikip **mabigat-bigat** **matali-talino**	Take the first three syllables of the **ma-** adjective followed by a hyphen plus root.	**ang sarap** **kay sarap**	**ang** + <u>root word</u> **kay** + <u>root word</u>
Medyo	**Rules**	**Adjective Intensified by Reduplication**	**Rules**
medyo masikip **medyo mabigat** **medyo matalino**	**medyo** + adjective	**ang sarap-sarap** **kay sarap-sarap**	**ang** + root word–root word **kay** + root word–root word

When inflecting the adjective for moderate degree, you take the first three syllables of the **ma-** adjective plus the root.

> **Matamis-tamis ang prutas.** The fruit is a little bit sweet.
> **Mamanti-mantika ang baboy.** The pork is a little bit greasy.

You can only use **ma**-adjectives to inflect the adjective for moderate degree, Non-**ma**-adjectives cannot be reduplicated.

> **Matamis-tamis ang prutas.** The fruit is a little bit sweet.
> **Mamanti-mantika ang baboy.** The pork is a little bit greasy.
> ***Sunog-sunog ang pagkain** (incorrect)

Compare the adjectives of moderate degree with the adjectives in exclamatory sentences in the chart on the right above. The structure of the exclamatory sentence with **ang** or **kay** is the same, as are their meanings: "How tasty!" In either case, **ang** or **kay** is followed by the descriptive root word **sarap** (tasty, delicious). To intensify the meaning of the exclamatory sentences, the root word made up of two syllables is repeated, and a hyphen is placed between the two root words. Note that, in the first exclamatory sentence, the adjective is marked by a common noun marker **ang**.

1. The chart below illustrates the use of an adjective of moderate degree as the predicate of a sentence.

Moderative Expressions in Predicational Sentences		
Adjective	**Subject**	
Medyo	Marker	Noun/Pronoun
Matamis-tamis **Medyo matamis**	ang ang mga	<u>prutas.</u>
	(ang mga)	ito. iyan. iyon.

The predicate adjective describes the noun or pronoun that is always the subject of the sentence. In this sentence, the fruit (**prutas**) that is the subject of the sentence is described as "a little bit sweet":

Matamis-tamis ang prutas. The fruit is a little bit sweet.
Matamis-tamis ang mga prutas. The fruits are a little bit sweet.
Matamis-tamis ito. This ([fruit] near the person speaking) is a little bit sweet.
Matamis-tamis *ang mga ito*. *These* ([fruits] near the person speaking) are a little bit sweet.

The last two sentences use the demonstrative pronoun **ito**. Note that, when employing demonstrative pronouns like **ito**, **iyan**, and **iyon** for singular nouns, markers are omitted, as illustrated in the third sentence above. However when employing these pronouns to substitute for plural nouns, the plural marker **ang mga** must come before each demonstrative pronoun to indicate plurality.

Malasa *ang isda*. The fish is tasty.
Malasa *ito*. This is tasty.
Malasa *ang mga ito*. These are tasty.
*****Malasa ang ito.** (incorrect)

Here are some more examples of sentences with moderative adjectives used as predicates.

EXAMPLES:
Maalat-alat ang mga ito. These are a little bit salty.
Medyo mainit *pa* **po ang pagkain.** The food is *still* somewhat hot, sir/ma'am.
Hindi ko gusto ang baboy kasi medyo matabang ito. I don't like the pork because it's a little bland.

2. The chart below illustrates the use of intensified adjectives in exclamatory sentences without a subject.

Exclamatory Sentences with Adjectives		
Adjective	**Ng Phrase (Subject in English sentence)**	
	Marker	Noun/Pronoun
Ang <u>asim</u> **Ang** <u>asim-asim</u>	ng ng mga	<u>mangga.</u>
Kay <u>asim</u> **Kay** <u>asim-asim</u>		nito. niyan. niyon.

With exclamatory sentences, the noun being described is marked by **ng** or is a **ng** phrase or in the **ng** form. This is obligatory. In the sentence **Ang asim ng mangga** (The mango is sour), when one asks, "What is sour?", the answer is "mango." This suggests that **mango** functions like an object; hence, it is marked by **ng**. In the English equivalent, the sentence has a subject—the mango—but Tagalog perceives the situation differently.

> **Ang asim ng mangga.** The mango is sour!
> **Ang asim-asim ng mangga.** The mango is very sour./How very sour the mango is! (intensified)
> **Kay asim ng mangga.** The mango is very sour./How sour the mango is!
> **Kay asim-asim ng mangga.** The mango is very, very sour./How very sour the mango is!
> **Kay asim nito.** How sour this is!

There are other uses of intensified adjectives with **ang** and **kay** constructions, but they are not within the scope of this book.

The last sentence uses the demonstrative pronoun **nito**. **Nito**, **niyan**, and **niyon** are **ng** pronouns. This means that these pronouns are used as objects of actor-focus verbs or when the subject is required to be in **ng** form:

> **Nagluto** *nito* **si Maria kahapon.** Maria cooked this yesterday.
> **Kay sarap** *nito*. How tasty this is!

Here are some more examples of exclamatory sentences utilizing intensified adjectives:

EXAMPLES:

> **Ang tamis ng pakwan na nasa rep.** How sweet the watermelon inside the fridge is!
> **Kay anghang-anghang nito.** How spicy this is!
> **Hindi ko gusto ang adobo kasi ang alat-alat nito.** I don't like the adobo because it is too salty.

Grammar Notes

---

1. Remember that in exclamatory sentences with adjectives, there is no subject. Instead, the expression is always followed by a **ng** phrase or **ng** pronoun. In the example below, **nito** substitutes for the noun **mangga** (mango).

   > **Ang tamis** *ng mangga*. How sweet the mangoes are!
   > **Kay tamis** *nito*. How sweet this is!
   > *****Kay tamis** *ang* **mangga.** (incorrect)
   > *****Kay tamis** *ito*. (incorrect)

Practice

I. Speaking Practice

Describe the following fruits and vegetables using moderate and exclamatory adjectives. Write your notes in the chart below.

Prutas	Paglalarawan	Gulay	Paglalarawan
1. Mangga		1. Ampalaya	

Prutas	Paglalarawan	Gulay	Paglalarawan
2. Saging		2. Kamote	

II. Reading Practice

The passages below describe specific fruits or vegetables. Read the passages and identfy the fruit or vegetable, using a term from the word bank.

```
┌────────────────────────────────┐
│          Word Bank             │
│                                │
│            sibuyas             │
│             sili               │
│            pinya               │
│            buko                │
│           bawang               │
│           mangga               │
└────────────────────────────────┘
```

_____ Talagang ang init-init tuwing Marso hanggang Mayo. Kapag ganito, bumibili ako ng inumin na ito at iniinom ko ang malamig na malamig na sabaw. Minsan, matamis-tamis ito dahil sa asukal (sugar) pero mas gusto ko ito kung puro (pure).

_____ Mahilig akong magluto at ito ang paborito kong sangkap (ingredient). Matapang ang lasa (flavor) nito pero nagbibigay ito ng masarap na lasa (flavor) sa pagkain. Ang paborito kong pagkain na mayroon nito ay sinangag (fried rice). Nagpiprito ako nito hanggang sa maging medyo pula ito, pagkatapos inilalagay ko sa ibabaw ng sinangag.

_____ Ito ang paborito kong prutas pagkatapos kong kumain. Maasim-asim ito at manamis-namis. Kung minsan, kung gusto ko ng mas maraming lasa, naglalagay ako ng patis dito. Ang prutas na ito ay kulay berde sa labas pero kulay dilaw naman sa loob.

_____ Maraming iba't-ibang klase nito. May iba't-ibang laki, kulay at anghang. Sa palagay ko, mas maanghang ito kung maliit. Gusto ko ito sa mga sawsawan (dipping sauce). Naglalagay ako nito sa suka at toyo.

_____ Ito ang pinakamasarap na prutas sa lahat. Gusto ko ito kung medyo hilaw at berde pa ang balat nito. Talagang ang asim-asim at ang lutong-lutong nito kung berde pa ito.

III. Practice

In the chart below, provide a description of two of your favorite fruits and vegetables and explain why you like them. Be sure to use a combination of exclamatory adjectives and moderate expressions.

Prutas	Paglalarawan	Gulay	Paglalarawan
1.		1.	
2.		2.	

IV. Listening Practice

Listen to audio file (16–2) and complete the following tasks.

A. You will hear three conversations. Listen to each one and list in Tagalog all the items that the customer bought, the quantity, and the price of each item. Then write the total amount that the customer paid. Use the chart below for taking notes.

	Ano (What)	Gaano karami (Quantity)	Magkano (Price)	Magkano lahat-lahat (Total Price)
1				
2				
3				

Pagkain sa Labas

Eating Out

An Overview of Lesson 17

Objectives

- Order food at a restaurant
- Express preferences regarding food and drink
- Make requests

Vocabulary

- Nouns
- Filipino Foods and Drinks
- Adjectives
- Verb Stems or Root Words

- Object-Focus and Actor-Focus Verbs (**-In-**, **I-**, and **Ma-**)
- Enclitics
- Prefixes
- Idioms and Expressions

Dialogue: Pagkain sa isang Restawran *Eating at a Restaurant*

Dialogue Comprehension

Activities

Activity 1: Filipino Food
Activity 2: Interview
Activity 3: Role-play

Grammar

Definition of Terms: Focus, Object-Focus Verbs, **-In** Verbs, **I-** Verbs, **Paki-**, and Enclitics

Examining Form

I.   Different Ways to Say "Please"
     Grammar Presentation
     Grammar Notes

Practice

I.   Speaking Practice
II. Reading Practice
III. Writing Practice
IV. Listening Practice

Vocabulary 🎧 (17–1)

The vocabulary below will help you express your preferences about food and drink and order in a restaurant. It will also allow you to participate in the activities in this lesson. Memorize the vocabulary words before proceeding to the dialogue.

Nouns

baso	glass
bino	wine
kahera	cashier
kubiyertos/ kubyertos	silverware, tableware
kutsara	spoon
kutsarita	teaspoon
kutsilyo	knife
lutong-bahay	homemade, home-cooked
pampagana	appetizer
pampalasa	seasoning
pitsel	pitcher, jug
platito	saucer, small plate
plato	plate
reklamo	complaint
sangkap	ingredient
sarsa	sauce
sawsawan	condiment, sauce or any liquid to dip food
sukli/barya	change (loose change)
tagapagluto	chef, cook
tasa	cup
tinidor/tenedor	fork
tsit	bill, check
weyter	waiter

Adjectives

nakakadiri	awful (taste); disgust or distaste for something dirty
ubod ng sarap	very delicious
pagkasarap-sarap	very delicious
ang sarap-sarap	very delicious
napakasarap	very delicious
malinamnam	very tasty or savory
nakakagutom	appetizing; literally means "makes one hungry"
tuyo	dry

Enclitics

lang	just, only
naman	please
nga	please

Prefixes

paki-	verbal prefix equivalent to English "please"

Object-Focus and Actor-Focus Verbs

Object-Focus -In Verbs	Actor-Focus	Definition
abutin	**mag-abot**	to reach
bilhin	**bumili**	to buy
dalhin	**magdala**	to bring, to take
gamitin	**gumamit**	to use
hingin	**humingi**	to ask for something
inumin	**uminom**	to drink
kainin	**kumain**	to eat
linisin	**maglinis**	to clean
tanungin	**magtanong**	to ask
tawagin	**tumawag**	to call
ubusin	**umubos**	to finish
yayain	**magyaya**	to invite

I- Verbs	Actor-Focus	
ibaba	**magbaba**	to take/bring something down
ibigay	**magbigay**	to give
iabot	**mag-abot**	to pass, to hand over
isauli	**magsauli**	to return

Ma- Verbs	
maalala	to remember

Filipino Foods and Drinks

adobo	typical dish of chicken and pork with garlic, bay leaf, soy sauce, and vinegar
buko dyus	coconut juice
goto	rice porridge with tripe
halo-halo	mixture of shaved ice, milk, and various preserved fruits
kalamansi dyus	calamansi juice
kaldereta	stew (originally goat meat)
lumpiya	Filipino eggroll
mais con yelo	mixture of shaved ice, milk, and corn
manggo dyus	mango juice
paksiw	a fish or meat dish cooked in vinegar with salt, ginger, or garlic
pandan iced tea	pandan iced tea from aromatic leaves that gives the drink its flavor
pansit	Filipino noodle dish
pinaupong manok	(literally, "chicken made to sit on salt") roasted chicken
sago at gulaman	a popular drink with agar-agar and tapioca
salabat	ginger tea
sinangag	fried rice
sinigang	tamarind-based soup with meat, fish, or shrimp, and vegetables
siopao	steamed rice bun containing pork and red egg or mongo beans

Idioms and Expressions

ang sarap	yummy
super sarap	very delicious
kadiri	yuck, disgusting, unappealing
Busog na busog na kami.	We are very full.
kaniya-kaniya	separate checks
Pakikuha mo naman ang menu.	Can we see the menu? (lit., Please get the menu.)
Pakidala mo na lang ang tsit namin.	Can we get our bill? (lit., Please bring us our bill.)
Pakiulit mo naman ang . . .	Please repeat . . .

Dialogue: Pagkain sa Isang Restawran *Eating at a Restaurant*

Michael and Sandra are at a restaurant. Read their dialogue with the waiter and answer the Dialogue Comprehension questions.

Weyter: **Magandang gabi po. Marco po ang pangalan ko at ako po ang weyter ninyo ngayong gabi. Ang ispesyalti po namin ngayong gabi ay pinaupong manok. O sige po, babalik po ako para sa order ninyo.**

(The waiter leaves to give Sandra and Michael time to look at the menu. He comes back a few minutes later.)

Weyter: **Alam na po ba ninyo kung ano ang gusto ninyong orderin?**
Sandra: **Oo. Gusto ko ng pinaupong manok.**
Weyter: **Kayo po, sir?**
Michael: **Gusto ko ng pansit.**
Weyter: **Ano po ang gusto ninyong inumin?**
Sandra: **Buko dyus.**
Michael: **Ako, tubig na lang. Boss, *paki*ulit mo naman ang inorder namin.**
Weyter: **O sige po. Isang pinaupong manok, isang pansit, buko dyus, at tubig.**

(The waiter exits to get their food from the kitchen. He comes back a few minutes later.)

Weyter: **Heto na po ang order ninyo.**
Michael: **Salamat.**
Weyter: **Kumusta po ang pagkain?**
Sandra: **Ang sarap-sarap ng lahat.**
Michael: ***Paki*kuha mo naman ang menu para sa dessert.**
Weyter: **Heto po, sir.**

Michael: **Salamat, ha.** (Looks at the menu.)
Weyter: **May gusto po ba kayo?**
Sandra: **Wala na. Busog na busog na kami. *Paki*dala mo na lang ang tsit namin.**
Weyter: **O sige po.**

Dialogue Comprehension

1. **Ano ang ispesyalti ng restawran sa araw na ito?**

    _____

2. **Anu-ano ang mga inorder nina Sandra at Michael?**

    _____

3. **Umorder ba si Sandra ng pansit?**

    _____

4. **Ano ang hiningi ni Michael sa weyter?**

    _____

5. **Umorder ba sila ng dessert? Bakit?**

    _____

Activities

Activity 1

Look over the list of Filipino foods and drinks in the table below. Using complete sentences, state the foods that you like or might like and why. The example below can serve as a model for your sentences.

> EXAMPLE:
>
> S1: **Gusto ko ng adobo kasi masarap ito. Nagluluto ang nanay ko ng adobo lagi at tuwing kumakain ako ng adobo naaalala ko ang pamilya ko.**

Mga Pagkain	Gusto ko	Mga Inumin	Gusto ko
adobo goto kaldereta lumpiya paksiw pansit pinaupong manok sinangag sinigang		buko dyus halo-halo kalamansi dyus mais con yelo manggo dyus pandan iced tea sago at gulaman salabat	

Activity 2

Step 1: Answer the following questions as they pertain to you. Complete the chart with your responses.

Pangalan	Gusto mo bang kumain sa labas?	Ano ang paborito mong restawran?	Ano ang gusto mong bilhin?	Gaano ka kadalas kumain sa labas?
EXAMPLE: **Bogart**	Oo, gusto kong kumain sa labas	'Italiannis' ang paborito kong restawran.	Gusto ko ng manok at pasta.	Siguro, dalawang beses sa isang linggo.

Step 2: Interview three of your classmates using the questions below. List their names and record their responses in the table below.

Pangalan	Gusto mo bang kumain sa labas?	Ano ang paborito mong restawran?	Ano ang gusto mong bilhin?	Gaano ka kadalas kumain sa labas?
1. _____				
2. _____				
3. _____				

Step 3: Based on the information that you have gathered, write a short paragraph about each one of the three classmates you interviewed. The example below can serve to model your paragraph.

1. <u>**Gustong kumain ni Bogart sa labas. 'Italiannis' ang paborito niyang restawran. Gusto niyang orderin ang manok at pasta doon. Kumakain siya sa labas nang dalawang beses sa isang linggo.**</u>

2. _____

    _____

    _____

    _____

3. _____

_____

_____

_____

4. _____

_____

_____

_____

Activity 3

In groups of three or four, write a dialogue that corresponds to one of the following prompts. Be sure to use **paki-** in your dialogue. For the usage of **paki-**, refer to the dialogue on **Pagkain sa Isang Restawran**. Incorporate the lines provided below in your dialogue.

a. **Kumuha ng mesa para sa apat. Humingi ng menu at umorder ng mga pagkain.**

b. **May problema sa pagkain mo; malamig na ang inorder mong soup. Sabihin mo sa weyter na ayaw mo ito at gusto mong initin ng weyter ang order mo.**

_____

_____

_____

_____

_____

Grammar

Definition of Terms

Focus	The expression in the verb of the grammatical role of the subject of the sentence. The role can be actor, object, indirect object, location, instrument, cause, or experiencer.
Object-Focus Verbs	A class of verbs the topic/subject or focus of which is the receiver of the action or the direct object, as opposed to the performer of the action. The object is marked with **ang** markers, and the doers of action are **ng** forms. Object-focus verbs include the following types of verbs: **-in-**, **-an**, and **paki-** verbs. Some object-focus verbs can take on actor-focus affixes like **-um-** and **mag-**, and the meaning may or may not remain the same. (See the Vocabulary at the beginning of the lesson.)
-In Verbs	Indicate that the object of the sentence is in focus. **-In** verbs are transitive and volitional and use the **-in** affix with the verbal root. All object-focus affixes turn the root word into an action on its object.
I- Verbs	A type of object-focus verb that indicates the movement of the object of the sentence. This type of verb uses the **i-** prefix.
Paki-	A prefix attached to verb roots to express a request. The resulting verb is object-focus.
Enclitics	Adverbial partcles in Tagalog that change meaning depending on the context in a sentence. These words usually follow the first word in the context to which they relate. The word order of encltics in a sentence is fixed.

Examining Form

Review the sentences below and complete the tasks that follow. Discuss your answers with a partner. Consult the following section to check your answers.

A

1. *Boss*, **pakiulit mo naman ang order namin.**
2. **Pakikuha mo naman ang menu.**
3. **Pakidala mo na lang ang tsit namin.**
4. **Pakilinis naman ang mesa namin.**

B

1. **Mag-ulit ka ng order namin.** (not commonly used)
2. **Kumuha ka ng menu.**
3. **Magdala ka ng tsit namin.** (not commonly used)
4. **Maglinis ka ng mesa namin.**

a. Underline all the actors and circle the verbs.
b. Identify all the different verbal affixes and enclitics in column A and B.
c. List all the differences in structure in column A and column B.

I. Different Ways to Say "Please"

The following are several ways to say "please" in Tagalog:

> 1. The verbal affix **paki** + VERB + (**naman**)
> 2. Enclitics **naman** and **nga**
> 3. Noun (noun phrase) + **enclitic nga**

1. **Paki- + Verb + (Naman)**

   In this first form, **naman** is not obligatory, and that is why it is inside the parenthesis above. This structure is normally used when there is an object in the sentence. Unlike the verbs that were introduced in the previous lessons, such as **mag-**, **-um-**, and **ma-**, the verbal affix **paki-** requires an **ang** phrase to mark its object and **ng** phrase to mark its actor.

   EXAMPLE

   Paki- + kuha (get) + **naman** *ang* **bag ko.** Please/ Kindly get my bag.

   The prefix **paki-** is attached to the verbal root word **kuha** and immediately followed by the enclitic **naman**.

2. Enclitics **Naman** and **Nga**

   Simply using **naman** or **nga** in imperative sentences makes the command more polite, depending on the intonation or how the statement is delivered. **Naman/nga** can be used for both transitive and intransitive verbs. However, when the verb is intransitive, i.e. does not take an object, **naman** and **nga** is preferable.

   EXAMPLES:

   Maglinis ka ng kusina. Clean the kitchen.
   Maglinis ka naman ng kusina. Kindly/Please clean the kitchen.
   Maglinis ka nga ng isda. Clean the fish. (May be a command depending on the way the sentence is delivered and the context of the conversation.)
   Bumili kayo ng isang kilo ng toge. Buy one kilo of bean sprouts.
   Bumili naman kayo ng isang kilo ng toge. Please buy one kilo of bean sprouts.

3. Noun (Noun Phrase) + Enclitic **Nga**

   Unlike the first and second structures, this construction is used when there is no action word in the sentence. Normally, **nga** is employed when the speaker wants someone to give him or her something. This is handy when buying goods at a **sari-sari** store or at a food court.

   EXAMPLES:

   Coke nga ho. One Coke please, sir/madam.
   Dalawang order ng pansit nga ho. Two orders of *pancit* please, sir/madam.

Grammar Presentation

1. The chart below illustrates how to use **paki-** in sentences to request something politely.

Paki- + Verbal Root						
Verb	**Actor**		**Direct Object Ang Phrase**		**Location/Direction**	
Paki-	**Marker**	**Pronoun**	**Marker**	**Noun**	**Marker**	**Noun**
Pakiabot		(mo) (ninyo)	ang ang mga	pagkain	kay kina	Patrick.
					sa sa mga	lalaki.
					sa	akin. atin. amin. iyo. inyo. kaniya. kanila.
Pakikuha		(mo) (ninyo)	ang ang mga	tsit.		

In the sentence **Pakiabot (mo) ang pagkain kay Patrick**, the direction of the action is toward Patrick, and a **sa** proper-name marker precedes his name. Note that the actors **mo** and **ninyo** in this type of sentence could be omitted.

> **Pakiabot mo ang pagkain kay Patrick.** (You) Please pass the food to Patrick.
> **Pakiabot ang pagkain kay Patrick.** Please pass the food to Patrick.

Here are more examples of request sentences with the enclitics **po** and **naman**.

> EXAMPLES:
> **Nanay, pakihingi naman po ang menu sa weyter.** Mom, please ask for the menu from the waiter.
> **Weyter, pakilinis mo naman ang mesa namin.** Waiter, please clean our table.
> **Pakitawag mo naman ang weyter natin.** Please call our (inclusive) waiter.

2. **Naman** and **nga** are used in the sentences below to express a request. The first word order is: VERB + ONE-SYLLABLE PRONOUN + ENCLITIC + LOCATION.

> **Pumunta ka naman dito** Please come here.

The second word order is: VERB + ENCLITIC + ACTOR + LOCATION.

> **Pumunta naman kayo dito.** Kindly come here.

From these examples, we can observe that one-syllable pronouns have precedence over enclitics in sentences.

Naman/Nga					
Verb	**Actor**		**Please**	**Location**	
	Marker	**Noun**	**Naman/Nga**	**Marker**	**Noun**
Pumunta		ka	naman nga		dito. diyan. doon.
	Please		**Actor**		**Location**	
	Naman/Nga		**Marker**	**Noun**	**Marker**	**Noun**
	naman nga			kayo		dito. diyan. doon.

EXAMPLES:

Bumili ka naman ng manok. Please buy chicken.

Magdala ka nga ng tubig sa amin. Please bring us some water.

Mag-abot ka naman sa kanila ng pagkain. Please hand them over some food.

3. The chart below illustrates the use of **nga** in a phrase without a verb.

Nga + Noun		
Noun	**Please**	**Enclitic denoting respect**
	Nga	**Ho/Po**
Pop Cola	nga	ho/po.

EXAMPLES: **Kendi nga po.** I want some candy, please.

Isa nga pong balut. One duck egg, please.

Lima nga pong isaw. Five chicken intestines, please.

Grammar Notes

1. The verb **paki-** is object-focus; this means its object is the topic of the sentence and is in the **ang** form: an **ang** phrase or an **ang** pronoun.

    Pakiinom mo *ang gatas.* Please drink the milk.

    Pakibigay mo *ang tsit* sa akin. Please give me the bill.

    Pakisundo *siya* sa palengke. Kindly pick him/her up at the market.

2. **Paki-** verbs cannot take an **ang** actor, only a **ng** actor.

    Pakilinis mo ang mesa. Please clean the table.

    ***Pakilinis ka ng mesa.** (incorrect) Please let the table clean you.

    Pakikain nga ninyo ang manok. Please eat the chicken.

    ***Pakikain ka ng manok.** (incorrect) Please let the chicken eat you.

3. No two **ang** forms side by side in **paki-** sentence.

    Pakitawag mo ang weyter. Please call the waiter.

    ***Pakitawag ka ang weyter.** (incorrect)

4. To make imperative statements more polite, add the enclitic **naman** or **nga**.

> **Maglinis ka naman ng mesa.** Clean the table, please.
> **Kumain ka nga ng manok.** Eat some chicken, please.

5. **Paki-** can be combined with the enclitic **naman** or **nga**. Doing so makes the request more polite. The English translation does not capture this nuance in the Tagalog sentence.

> **Pakiinom mo** *naman* **ang gatas.** Please drink the milk.
> **Pakibigay mo** *nga* **ang tsit sa akin.** Please give me the bill.

6. When you want something to be handed to you, or when buying something from the store, you can use this structure:

> NOUN + NGA + HO/PO
> **Coke nga ho.** Please give me a bottle of coke.
> **Isang kilo ng kamatis nga ho.** Please give me a kilogram of tomatoes.

The respect enclitics **po** and **ho** add more politeness to the request.

Practice

I. Speaking Practice

Interview three of your classmates and ask them what they ate, drank, or brought with them for breakfast from home. Fill in their responses in the table below. Use the example to model your interview.

> Student 1: **Ano ang kinain mo kaninang umaga at saan?**
> Student 2: **Kumain ako ng isang mansanas at yogurt kaninang umaga sa bahay.**

Pangalan	Kinain	Ininom	Binaon
1. Nelson	sinangag at itlog sa "Kwatog."	gatas sa bahay.	tinapay sa eskwelahan.
2. _____			
3. _____			
4. _____			

Pagbuo ng Pangungusap (Constructing a Sentence)
Now express in complete sentences what you learned from your classmates. Use the example below to model your sentences. Afterwards, share what you have written with the rest of the class.

1. <u>**Kaninang umaga, kinain ni Nelson ang sinangag at itlog sa 'Kwatog,' ininom niya ang gatas sa bahay at binaon niya ang tinapay sa eskwelahan.**</u>

2. _____

3. _____

4. _____

II. Reading Practice

Below is a review for a Filipino restaurant. Read the review and answer the Reading Comprehension questions that follow.

Word Bank

alaala memory
naisipan thought of
pagpilian (items) to choose from
karamihan most
talaga really
sa palagay ko I think, I believe, in my opinion
nagpasiya decided
sulit worth the money

Kamay Kainan: Ang Paborito Ko Mula Noon Hanggang Ngayon

Isa sa mga paborito kong alaala ay noong nasa kolehiyo ako. Naaalala ko na madalas kaming gumimik at kumain sa labas ng mga kaibigan ko. Isang araw, naisipan naming mag-reunion at nagpasiya kami na kumain sa 'Kamay Kainan' sa may Market Market sa Fort Bonifacio. Mayroon silang Php 300.00 na eat-all-you-can na may tatlumpung iba'tibang pagkain na pwedeng pagpilian.

Karamihan sa mga pagkain doon ay pagkaing Pilipino at sa palagay ko, masarap ang pagkain doon at talagang sulit ang bayad namin. Gusto ko ang lugar na iyon dahil kasinsarap ng luto ng nanay ko ang mga pagkain nila.

Ang mga weyter at tagapagluto doon ay mababait at magagalang. Ibinibigay nila ang pinakamabuting serbisyo na pwede nilang ibigay. Lagi silang pumupunta sa mesa namin para alamin kung mayroon kaming kailangan.

Talagang inirerekomenda ko ang restawran na ito sa lahat. Mura na, masarap pa, at mayroon pa silang magaling na serbisyo.

Reading Comprehension

1. Nasaan ang 'Kamay Kainan'?

_____

2. Magkano ang bayad sa 'Kamay Kainan' para sa *eat-all-you can*?

_____

3. Ilan ang pagkain doon na puwedeng pagpilian?

_____

4. Bakit gusto ng nagrebyu ang mga pagkain sa 'Kamay Kainan'?

_____

5. Ilarawan ang mga weyter at tagaluto.

_____

III. Writing Practice

In the boxes below, write four different requests or questions that one usually makes to a waiter. Be sure to use one of the forms learned in this lesson to say "please."

EXAMPLES:

Kunin mo naman ang menu. Kindly get the menu.

Pakikuha mo nga ang menu.

IV. Listening Practice

Listen to audio file (17–2) and complete the box below.

Mga Pagkain	Mga Inorder	Mga Inumin	Mga Inorder

Pagluluto

Cooking

An Overview of Lesson 18

Objectives
• Give and follow instructions
• Talk about common food preparation techniques in Filipino cooking

Vocabulary
• Nouns
• Object-Focus and Actor-Focus Verbs (**-In-**, **I-**, and **-An** Verbs)
• Adjectives
• Verbal Affixes

Reading Text: Binagoongan *Pork with Shrimp Paste*

Reading Comprehension

Activities
Activity 1: Matching Activity
Activity 2: Puzzle
Activity 3: Recipe

Grammar
Definition of Terms: Object-Focus Verbs, Glottal Stop or Glottal Catch

Examining Form
I.   Looking Back and Looking Forward
II. Object-Focus Verbs (**-In-/I-/-An** Verbs)
     Grammar Presentation: Imperative Sentences with **-In**, **I-**, and **-An** Affixes
     Grammar Notes
III. Interrogative Pronoun **Gaano** (How Much, How Many)
     Grammar Presentation
     Grammar Notes

Practice
I. Speaking Practice   II. Reading Practice   III. Writing Practice   IV. Listening Practice

Vocabulary 🎧 (18–1)

The vocabulary below will help you say and understand instructions and participate in the activities in this lesson. Memorize the vocabulary words before proceeding to the reading text.

Nouns

abrelata	can opener	**kalan**	stove
arina/harina	flour	**kaldero**	pot
asin	salt	**kaserola**	casserole, pan
asukal	sugar	**kawali**	frying pan
bagoong	shrimp paste	**keso**	cheese
banana kyu	deep fried bananas coated in caramelized brown sugar	**kudkuran**	shredder, grater
		gata	coconut milk
		gawgaw	cornstarch
		gulaman	gelatin
bandehado	platter, tray, usually oblong	**gripo**	faucet
		lababo	sink
banilya	vanilla	**liyempo**	pork chop, a cut of meat from the flank or side
baso	glass		
betsin	monosodium glutamate	**mantel**	tablecloth
		mantika	cooking oil
dahon ng lawrel	bay leaf	**mangkok**	bowl
		maruya	banana fritters
kalahati	half	**mesa**	table

palanggana	basin
pamintang buo	peppercorn
paminta	black pepper
patis	fish sauce
salaan	strainer, sifter, colander
sandok	ladle
siyanse	spatula
suka	vinegar
tapsilog	dried or cured beef, fried rice and egg
tsamporado/ sampurado	chocolate rice porridge
toyo	soy sauce

Adjectives

labog	excessively soft or tender, overcooked

Object-Focus and Actor-Focus Verbs

Object-Focus	Actor-Focus	Definition
-In Verbs		
alisin	**mag-alis**	to remove
batihin	**magbati**	to beat
gadgarin	**maggadgad**	to grate
haluin	**maghalo**	to stir
hanguin	**maghango**	to remove from fire
hiwain	**maghiwa**	to slice
ihawin	**mag-ihaw**	to grill
kunin	**kumuha**	to get, take
lutuin	**magluto**	to cook
pakuluin (causative)	**magpakulo**	to boil
palambutin (causative)	**magpalambot**	to make something tender
patayin	**pumatay**	to turn off the light or stove; to, kill
pirasuhin	**magpiraso**	to cut into pieces
pitpitin	**magpitpit**	to pound
pukpukin	**magpukpok**	to pound
putulin	**magputol**	to cut
salain	**magsala**	to strain

tadtarin	magtadtad	to chop into small pieces, dice
tagain	magtaga	to chop
tanggalin	magtanggal	to remove
timplahin	magtimpla	to mix
tuyuin	magtuyo	to dry

I- Verbs

iadobo	mag-adobo	to make adobo
ibabad	magbabad	to soak, marinate
ibuhos	magbuhos	to pour
idagdag	magdagdag	to add, include
igisa	maggisa	to sauté
ihain	maghain	to serve
iinit	mag-init	to heat, microwave
ilagay	maglagay	to put
ipaksiw	magpaksiw	to make or cook fish or meat in vinegar
iprito	magprito	to fry
isalin	magsalin	to pour into another receptacle or container

-An Verbs

balatan	magbalat	to peel
hayaan	(no af verb)	to let
hugasan	maghugas	to wash
takpan	magtakip	to cover

Verbal Affixes

-an   an object-focus suffix that, when added to a root or word base, can mean to perform an act on or toward something

i-   an object-focus prefix that, when added to a root that can take on a **mag-** prefix, means the direct object is the topic or focus

-in   an object-focus affix that can be a prefix, infix, or suffix depending on the aspectual form of the **-in-** verb. **-In** verbs are formed by affixing **-in** to verb root and are the object-focus counterpart of actor-focus **-um-** and **mag-** verbs.

pa-in   affixes that, when attached to verbal roots, form causative object-focus verbs. In this kind of verb, there are two actors: one causes the action, but the other actually performs the action.

Reading Text: Binagoongan *Pork with Shrimp Paste*

Ricky got this recipe for a Filipino dish from the Internet. Read the recipe and help Ricky with the instructions by answering the Reading Comprehension questions that follow.

Binagoongan

Mga Sangkap:
Isa't kalahating tasa ng bagoong
Isang kilo ng liyempo (hiwain nang maliliit)
Isang malaking sibuyas (hiwain nang maliliit)
Dalawang malaking kamatis (hiwain nang maliliit)
Isang kutsara ng asukal
Mantika
Anim na piraso ng bawang (pitpitin)
Kalahating tasa ng gata
Dalawang sili

Tatlong piraso ng dahon ng lawrel
Tatlong tasa ng tubig
Isang kutsarita ng pamintang buo
Kalahating tasa ng suka

Mga Hakbang:
1. **Hugasan mo nang mabuti ang baboy. Ilagay mo ang baboy sa kawali na may tubig, suka, dahon ng lawrel at paminta. Hayaan mong kumulo at maluto ang baboy.**
2. **Hanguin mo ang baboy at iprito sa ibang kawali.**
3. **Tanggalin mo ang baboy sa kawali. Gamit ang parehong kawali, igisa mo ang bawang, sibuyas at kamatis.**
4. **Kung labog na ang kamatis, idagdag mo na ang bagoong, at sili. Gisahin mo ang bagoong.**

5. Ihalo mo ang asukal at gata sa bagoong. Pagkatapos, idagdag mo ang baboy.
6. Takpan mo ang kawali at pakuluan nang tatlong minuto.
7. Hanguin at ihanda.

Reading Comprehension

1. Anu-ano ang mga kailangan para lutuin ang baboy?

_____

2. Paano lutuin ang baboy?

_____

_____

_____

3. Ano ang kailangang ilagay pagkatapos ng bawang?

_____

4. Kailangan ba ng sili para lutuin ang binagoongan?

_____

5. Ano ang huling sangkap na kailangan?

_____

Activities

Activity 1

Match these pictures to their definitions.

Cooking Verbs				
iinit	ihawin	ibuhos	gadgarin	idagdag
lutuin	hiwain	isalin	tadtarin	

Activity 2

Word Search
The words in the word bank are embedded in the puzzle below. Find them, and write the English equivalent of each word in the blank provided.

Word Bank			
Pakuluin	_____	Putulin	_____
Palambutin	_____	Salain	_____
Patayin	_____	Tadtarin	_____
Pirasuhin	_____	Tagain	_____
Pitpitin	_____	Timplahin	_____
Pukpukin	_____	Tuyuin	_____

```
T C I E R Q T T T A G A I N
A B E U N H N I K U P K U P
D B U N I B U M T X N T T S
T N Z I L U W P L I J N A N
A I H T U L O L Y L Y L Y S
R T R U T I N A R N A Y E H
I I V B U G T H K I H Z G I
N P T M P A N I N I D V K I
E T R A P J T N B V V S Y N
W I C L R N I U L U K A P I
B P F A P S U G N U Y Z D U
F H Y P U N L S J T S O V Y
B M L L N I H U S A R I P U
N Y L R X D E Y R O K D L T
```

Choose your favorite snack from the list below and explain how you prepare it to the person sitting next to you. If you do not know how to prepare the food, use the Internet to research the recipe.

> **Maruya**
> **Sinangag**
> **Tapsilog**
> **Tsampurado**
> **Banana kyu**

Grammar

Definition of Terms

Object-Focus Verbs	Verbs that require **ang** markers and/or **ang** pronouns for their direct object, which indicates that the object is specific or defined. The verb and **ang** marker accomplish what a definite article would in English.
Glottal Stop or Glottal Catch	A speech sound produced by momentary complete closing of the glottis or opening between the vocal cords in the larynx.

Examining Form

Review the sentences below and complete the tasks that follow. Discuss your answers with a partner. Consult the following section to check your answers.

Column A	Column B
1. Ilagay mo ang baboy sa kawali.	1. Maglagay ka ng baboy sa kawali.
2. Igisa mo na ang bagoong.	2. Maggisa ka na ng bagoong.
3. Hugasan mo nang mabuti ang baboy.	3. Maghugas ka ng baboy nang mabuti. (not commonly used)
4. Takpan mo ang kawali.	4. Magtakip ka ng kawali. (not commonly used)
5. Hanguin mo ang baboy.	5. Maghango ka ng baboy. (not commonly used)
6. Gisahin mo ang bagoong.	6. Maggisa ka ng bagoong.

    a. Underline all the actors, circle the verbs, and box the object.
    b. What are the different affixes used?
    c. List all the differences in structure in column A and column B.

I. Looking Back and Looking Forward

So far we have covered the **ang**, **ng**, and **sa** forms—that is, the **ang**, **ng**, and **sa** pronouns and phrases—and their use in sentences. As a refresher, **ang** forms are used for subjects/topics of sentences, **ng** forms for direct objects and possession, and **sa** forms for indirect objects or the beneficiary of the action of the verb, as well as location and direction. We have also learned that **ang** forms are doers as well as subjects/topics of actor-focus verbs (**-um-**, **mag-**) and experiencer-focus verbs (**ma-**, **magka-**, **magkaroon** in Lesson 15), which are somewhat similar to active verbs in English, and **ng** forms are agents or performers of the action of object-focus verbs (**-in**, **i-**, **-an**, **pa-in**) and verbs with other focuses, which are somewhat similar to the passive verbs in English, as in the sentence "The banana was eaten by me." "**Kinain ko ang saging**." We also learned about transitive verbs, which require an object; ditransitive verbs, which have two objects; and intransitive verbs, which do not require an object to complete their meaning, Verbs can be purposeful, as in **nagtapon ako** (I threw) and non-purposeful, as in **natapon** (spilled accidentally) or can express acts of nature, as in **Umulan** (It rained), or involuntary and accidental actions, as in **nalunod ako** (I drowned).

Aside form the actor, experiencer, and the object, Tagalog verbs may focus on the location where the action happened or the direction of the action, the indirect object or the one who benefits from the action, as well as the cause and the instrument with which to accomplish the action. Each verb focus (actor, experiencer, object, locative, directional, benefactive, causative, and instrumental) has a distinct set of affixes that are attached to verbal roots that separate and differentiate one from the other. For all these other focuses of verbs, the agent or performer of the action is a **ng** form. **Ng** forms are also the agents of the pseudo-verbs **gusto**, **ayaw**, **dapat**, **pwede**, and **kailangan**, as we have previously encountered in past lessons.

In the last two units of this book, 7 and 8, we will learn more about directional/locational focuses and the uses of infinitives and different aspectual forms of verbs.

It is a good idea at this point to do an inventory and put together everything we have learned in order to help us organize the knowledge we have acquired about the language and the domain of verbs. Doing so will help us understand this very important aspect of the Tagalog language and how affixes affect words and their meanings, specifically verbs. The table below summarizes the different verbs we have covered so far.

Focus of Verbs				
Focus (Subject)/ Kind of Action	**Affixes Used**	**Actor**	**Meaning**	**Example**
Actor/ Deliberate	-um- mag-	**ang** forms	Subject does the action	**Naglakad ako.** (I walked.) **Uminom ako ng dyus.** (I drank juice.)
Actor/ Spontaneous	-um-	none	No subject. The action happens. Nature, i.e. the earthquake, is doing the action itself.	**Lumindol.** (It quaked/The earhquake happened.)
Experiencer/ Accidental & Spontaneous	ma- magka- magkaroon	none	Action happens to subject	**Namatay ang ilaw.** (The light went out accidentally.) **Nagkasipon ako.** (I had a cold.) **Nagkaroon ako ng tigdas.** (I had measles.)
Object/ Deliberate	-in i- -an paki-	**ng** actor	Ng actor does the action to the subject.	**Prituhin mo ang isda.** (Fry the fish.) **Igisa mo ang baboy.** (Sauté the pork.) **Kaliskisan mo ang isda.** (Scrape off the scales of the fish.) **Pakikuha nga ang talong.** (Kindly get the eggplant.)

Aspect of Verbs

The root word, base, or stem word gives the core meaning of the verb. The affixes determine the kind of action the verb has in relation to the subject of the verb. Some verbal root words can take on affixes for actor, object, and location and adjust their meaning accordingly. Tagalog verbs inflect for aspect through the use of affixes and reduplication of the first consonant-vowel of the root word. Tagalog verbs represent action in space and time as a continuum: action possible to happen (infinitives used as imperatives and in pseudo-verbs **gusto**, **ayaw**, **kailangan**, **dapat**); action started and still happening (incompleted); action started and ended (completed); action that has not started but will happen in some future time (contemplated); and action that has just been ended (recently completed), which is not covered in this book.

The chart below illustrates the use of the verbal root word **putol** (cut) with different affixes and their different aspectual forms. The affix has been italicized in each aspectual form. Some of the inflections you are seeing for the first time. The purpose of including them in the chart is primarily for recognition and as an advanced organizer. The meaning of the verb (ROOT WORD + AFFIX) is not provided. But one thing is certain: the core meaning remains "cut." The affix attached to the root word provides the information about how it is done, the subject, who is doing it, who it is being done to, whether the action is accidental, spontaneous, or deliberate, or whether it happens to the subject. Is it a straightforward action, or is it repeated, reciprocal, or possible? In some books, the characteristic of verbs that tells you what kind of action is performed is called mode, and a Tagalog verb is characterized as having focus, aspect, and mode.

In the next part of this lesson, we will study the use of object-focus verbs specifically for cooking. But before that, let's look at the chart below to complete our review of Tagalog verbs. Can you recognize the pattern in the changes?

Verbal Root Word **Putol** with Different Affixes					
Root Word	**Affix**	**Infinitive**	**Completed**	**Incompleted**	**Contemplated**
putol (cut)	-um-	p*u*mutol	p*u*mutol	p*u*m*u*putol	puputol
	mag-	*mag*putol	*nag*putol	*nag*puputol	*mag*puputol
	-in-	putul*in*	p*in*utol	p*in*uputol	puputul*in*
	-an	putul*an*	p*in*utul*an*	p*in*uputul*an*	puputul*an*
	ma-	*ma*putol	*na*putol	*na*puputol	*ma*puputol
	magka-	*magka*putul-putol	*nagka*putul-putol	*nagkaka*putul-putol	*magkaka*putul-putol
	magkaroon	*magkaroon* ng putol	*nagkaroon* ng putol	*nagkakaroon* ng putol	*magkakaroon* ng putol
	pa-in	*pa*putul*in*	p*in*aputol	p*in*apaputol	papaputul*in*
	paki	*paki*putol	p*in*a*ki*putol	p*in*a*kiki*putol	pa*kiki*putol

II. Object-Focus Verbs (-In-/I-/-An Verbs)

Object-focus verbs (OF verbs) are verbs that take the object as the topic or subject of the sentence. The direct object takes, or is marked by, the **ang** phrase, while the actor takes, or is marked by, the **ng** phrase. The infinive form of object-focus verbs can be used in making requests or giving commands that involve an object. See the rules for forming the infinitive of **-an**, **-in**, and **i-** verbs in the chart below.

Root	Infinitive	Verbal Affix	Rules
hugas	hugasan	-an	**-AN** VERBAL AFFIX: add **-an** after the root word.
balat	balatan	-an	
gisa	gisahin	-hin	**-IN** VERBAL AFFIX: add **-in** or **-hin-** after the root word. Use **-in** before root that ends with consonants & vowel with glottal stop; and use **-hin** for vowels.
ihaw	ihawin	-in	
buhos	ibuhos	i-	**I-** VERBAL AFFIX: prefix **i-** before the root word.
lagay	ilagay	i-	

Object-focus verbs are transitive by virtue of the fact that the topic is the object, and this is the reason for their name. There are no subjectless object-focus sentences in Tagalog. Although **-um-** actor-focus verbs may not have an actor, as is the case for acts of nature (for example **Kumikidlat** ("It is lightning," literally translated as "Lightning" and therefore subjectless), the same is not true for object-focus verbs or object-focus sentences. The topic/subject/object is always explicitly stated. The exception would be in response to questions like "**Anong gagawin ko sa baboy?**" ("What am I going to do with the pork?"), as in "**Igigisa mo**" ("You're going to saute [it]"). In responding to the question, especially in conversation, the object is not mentioned, because it is understood: both the speaker and the listener understand what would receive the action.

The Definition of Terms above mentions that the direct object, which is the focus or topic of the sentence, is made specific, similar to what is accomplished by the article *the* in English. Below are sentences that clarify the meaning of a definite and an indefinite object in a sentence.

> **Kumain ako <u>ng</u> manok.** (actor-focus) I ate chicken.
> **Kinain ko <u>ang</u> manok.** (object-focus) I ate *the* chicken.

The first sentence states that the actor **ako** ate chicken, while the second sentence tells us that the actor **ko** ate not just any chicken or any kind of chicken but a specific chicken that is known to the listener.

Object-focus verbs cannot be used when the direct object is not established yet. Let's look at this scenario: Mark comes back to his apartment and has a conversation with his roommate, Pete, that goes as follows:

> Pete: **Mark, binili ko na ang pagkain.** Mark, I already bought the food.
> Mark: **Ano?** What?
> Pete: **Binili ko na ang pagkain.** I already bought the food.
> Mark: **Aling pagkain?** Which food?
> Pete: **Ang pagkain na paborito natin sa Jollibee.** The food that is our favorite at Jollibee.

It is evident from this conversation that Mark does not at first understand what Pete is referring to. Pete used an object-focus verb, but the object he meant was not established or self-evident for Mark. Learners of Tagalog have to understand that when using object-focus verbs, the direct object either needs to be mentioned beforehand or the speaker needs to somehow establish its specificity.

> Pete: **Pumunta ako sa Jollibee kanina at binili ko na ang paborito nating pagkain.** I went to Jollibee a while ago and bought our favorite food.
> Mark: **Magkano ang bili mo?** How much was it?

Or

Pete: **Mark, binili ko na ang pagkain sa Jollibee.** Mark, I already bought the food at Jollibee.
Mark: **Mabuti naman.** That's good

Object-focus verbs are used when the object is specific. Therefore, when the English term you would use for the object is any of the following, use an object-focus verb.
1. The pronoun *it*
2. A possessive pronoun
3. Pronouns
4. The definite article *the* plus a noun
5. Proper names

EXAMPLES:
Imbitahan mo *si Mike.* You invite *Mike.*
Kainin mo. You eat *it.*
Kainin mo *ang pagkain mo.* You eat *your food.*
Kainin mo *ito.* You eat *this.*
Kainin ninyo *ang pagkain.* You (plural) eat *the food.*

The sentences above illustrate the rules for using an object-focus verb. The first sentence, **Kainin mo**, has no specific subject or receiver of the action, so the English translation fills in with the neutral pronoun *it* as the object. Hence, *You eat it.* The objects in the other sentences are also in italics: they receive the action of the verb.

More explanation will be given about object-focus verbs (**-in, i-, -an**) in the following section.

Grammar Presentation

Imperative Sentences with -In, I-, and -An Affixes
The chart below shows the possible shapes of sentences when the object-focus transitive verbs **hiwain** (to cut), **igisa** (to sauté), and **hugasan** (to wash) are used in imperative sentences.

Transitive Verb in Imperative Sentences				
Verb	Actor		Object	
OF Verbs	Marker	Noun	Marker	Noun/Pronoun
Hiwain	**mo** **ninyo**		**ang** **ang mga**	<u>baboy.</u>
Igisa				---------- ito.
Hugasan				iyan. iyon.

EXAMPLES:
Hiwa*in* mo na <u>ang</u> manok. Cut the chicken already.
I*prito* mo <u>ang</u> isda, pagkatapos mong lutu*in* <u>ang</u> mechado. Fry the fish, after you cook mechado.
Pagkatapos mong ihaw*in* ang manok, lutu*in* mo na <u>ang</u> baboy. After you grill the chicken, cook the pork.
Hugas*an* ninyo <u>ang</u> manok. (You, plural) Wash the chicken.

Grammar Notes

1. The following are the rules for forming the imperative/infinitive form of object-focus verbs **-in**, **-an**, and **i-**.

A) **-in**/**-hin** suffix
- Use **-hin** when the root word ends with a vowel.
- Use **-in** when the root word ends with either a consonant or a glottal stop, a sound produced by the abrupt complete closing of the glottis momentarily. Conventionally, the sound is represented as "**unh-unh**" in English.
- When a suffix such as **-in** (or **-an**) is attached to a root word whose last syllable has a letter **o**, the **o** becomes **u**.

EXAMPLES:

Bati<u>hin</u>   The root word **bati** means "act or manner of beating or stirring"; the infinitive means "to beat." The root word ends in **i**, which is a vowel and has no glottal catch when pronounced. Therefore, we add **-hin**.

Patay<u>in</u>   The root word **patay** means "dead, or "; the infinitive means "to kill *or* to turn off." The root word ends in **y**, a consonant. Therefore, we add the suffix **-in**.

Hiwa<u>in</u>   The root word **hiwà** means "cut, slice"; the infinitive means "to cut or to slice." The word ends in a vowel but has a glottal catch at the end when pronounced. Therefore, add the suffix **-in**.

Lutu<u>in</u>   The root word **lutò** has a stress on the second-to-last syllable **lu** when pronounced and also has glottal catch on **o** at the end. The **o** becomes a **u** when the suffix **-in** is attached.

B) **-an**/**-han** suffix
The same rules apply for the **-an**/**-han** suffix as for **-in**/**-hin**.
- Use **-han** when the root word ends with a vowel.
- Use **-an** when the root word ends with either a consonant or a glottal stop.

Punta<u>han</u> (directional-focus verb)   From **punta-** "go"; the infinitive means "to go."

Balat<u>an</u>   From **balat-** "skin, peel"; the infinitive means 'to peel.'

Haya<u>an</u>   From **hayà-** "consenting or toleration of an act"; the infinitive means "to leave one alone."

III. Interrogative Pronoun **Gaano** (How Much, How Many)

The interrogative pronoun **gaano** is used when inquiring about the quantity or quality of something. The English equivalent is *how much, how many*.

> **Gaano + ka** (adjectival root) + subject
>
> EXAMPLES:
> **Gaano katamis ang mangga?** How sweet is the mango?
> **Gaano kainit ang pagkain?** How hot is the food?

Grammar Presentation

Sentences using **gaano** can be constructed in two ways, as shown in the chart below. In the first sentence structure, **gaano**, the interrogative "quantifier," can be followed by an adjective prefixed with **ka-** to denote comparison, for example: **Gaano karami ang sabaw?** (How much soup is (there)?) The meaning of the question depends on the context of the conversation. Supposing that I am cooking and don't know the quantity of liquid I should add to my mixture, the answer might be **Dalawang tasa** (Two cups). The second sentence structure follows **gaano** with the ang demonstrative pronoun and then **ka** + ADJECTIVE.

Gaano Question		
Interrogative	**Ka + Adjective**	**Subject**
		Ang phrase
Gaano	karami	ang sabaw? ang mga
Interrogative	**Subject**	**Ka + Adjective**
Gaano	ito iyan iyon	kasarap?

EXAMPLES:

Gaano kaalat ang adobo? How salty is the adobo?

Gaano katabang ang pagkain mo? How bland is your food?

Gaano kalamig ang sabaw mo? How cold is your soup?

Grammar Notes

1. When using **gaano**, notice that you must prefix the adjectival root with **ka-**.

adjective: **mainit**   root: **init**   → **ka**init

adjective: **malamig**   root: **lamig**   → **ka**lamig

Practice

I. Speaking Practice

Work with a partner. Try to come up with your own version of **Binagoongan**. Match column one with column 2 in the chart below. Put a number (1–5) before each ingredient and step. Then create a sentence using the ingredient and the step that are numbered the same.

EXAMPLE:

<u>1</u> **Baboy**   <u>1</u> **Hiwain**

Hiwain mo ang baboy.

Mga Sangkap	Mga Paraan
_____ baboy	_____ igisa

_____	baboy at sili	_____	ihalo
_____	bawang at sibuyas	_____	ilagay
_____	gata	_____	hiwain
_____	bawang	_____	pitpitin

Ang Sariling Bersyon ko ng Binagoongan

1. _____

2. _____

3. _____

4. _____

5. _____

II. Reading Practice

Trisha is a university student who is staying at a dormitory. She wants to eat adobo, but she does not know how to do it. She called her mom for instructions, but unfortunately her mom was not available, so she searched for the recipe on the Internet. Read the recipe she downloaded and help Trisha cook chicken adobo by answering the Reading Comprehension questions that follow.

Adobo

Mga Sangkap:
Apat na piraso ng manok
Isang tasa ng toyo
Isang tasa ng tubig
Kalahating tasa ng suka
Dalawang piraso ng dahon ng lawrel
Isang kutsarita ng pamintang buo
Limang piraso ng bawang
Asin
Mantika

Mga Hakbang
1. **Ilagay ang mantika sa kawali.**
2. **Idagdag ang bawang.**
3. **Ilagay ang manok at lagyan ng asin. Takpan ang kawali. Maghintay ng lima hanggang pitong minuto.**
4. **Idagdag ang suka, toyo, tubig, at paminta.**
5. **Takpan at pakuluan ng sampung minuto.**
7. **Hanguin at ihanda.**

Reading Comprehension

Q: **Gaano karami ang suka?**
A: **Kalahating tasa ang suka.**

Q: **Gaano karami ang dahon ng lawrel?**
A: **Dalawang piraso.**

1. Q: **Gaano karami ang bawang?**

   A: _____

2. Q: **Gaano karami ang manok?**

   A: _____

3. Q: **Gaano karami ang toyo?**

   A: _____

4. Q: _____

   A: **Isang tasa ang tubig.**

5. Q: _____

   A: **Apat na piraso ang manok.**

III. Writing Practice

You and your friend plan to enter a "Filipino Fusion Cuisine" contest. Choose a partner and create a new Filipino fusion recipe. Make a sketch of your dish on a separate sheet of paper and list the ingredients in the space provided below. You must be creative and innovative in order to win the contest. Afterwards, discuss the following questions with your partner and be ready to present your new creation to the class.

1. What are the different ingredients in your recipe?

   _____

2. How is this different from a typical Filipino food?

   _____

   _____

3. What is the name of your creation?

   _____

4. How do you prepare the food?

_____

Mga Sangkap:

_____ _____	 _____

Paraan ng Pagluluto:

_____

_____

_____

_____

_____

_____

IV. Listening Practice

Listen to audio file (18–2) and answer the questions. Circle **Oo** if the answer is true and **Hindi** if it is false. Stop the audio clip as needed.

> ### Word Bank
>
> **Giniling** Ground

1. **Para magluto ng picadillo, kailangan ba ng isang kilo ng giniling na baboy?**
   Oo   Hindi

2. **Para magluto ng picadillo, kailangan ba ng isang kutsara ng asukal?**
   Oo   Hindi

3. **Kailangan bang gisahin ang bawang, sibuyas at patatas?**
   Oo   Hindi

4. **Kailangan bang idagdag ang limang tasa ng tubig?**
   Oo   Hindi

5. **Kailangan bang lutuin ang picadillo ng limang minuto?**
   Oo   Hindi

PAGLALAKBAY
Travel

Tara na! In English, this phrase translates as "Let's go!" And with the 7,107 islands that comprise the Philippine archipelago, there are many places to visit and things to see. Popular tourist destinations in the Philippines include Baguio in the province of Benguet and Tagaytay in the province of Cavite, both on the island of Luzon. Both cities are located in the mountains and, because of their high elevation, benefit from cooler climates than most parts of the tropical Philippines, which makes them popular resorts in the summer.

Lion Head in Baguio City that welcomes visitors to the City of Pines

Tagaytay is home to Picnic Grove, a sprawling area of lush vegetation where visitors can go zip lining or horseback riding within sight of the Taal Volcano, one of the world's smallest volcanoes. Taal Volcano and the lake that surrounds it can also be viewed from the highest point in Tagaytay, the People's Park in the Sky, a former palace built by President Ferdinand Marcos that is now a tourist attraction because of its superb vistas of the surrounding landscape.

Daniel Burnham, an American architect who served in the United States colonial government in the Philippines from 1898 to 1945, designed the layout of the modern city of Baguio in 1904. Baguio is known as "the Summer Capital of the Philippines" because of its popularity with Filipino tourists during the hottest months, when Baguio remains reasonably cool.

Boracay Beach

Other popular tourist sites include Boracay, an island in the Visayan islands. Considered by many as having some of the best beaches in the world, Boracay has developed into a beautiful resort catering to both local and international travelers who want to snorkel, dive, sail, or just lounge on the white sands and soak up the sun.

The Philippines is home to a wide diversity of cultures and peoples, and festivals are a common way for communities throughout the country to celebrate their heritage and history. For example, the **Ati-Atihan** Festival is celebrated in Kalibo, Aklan Province, on Panay Island. Participants don tribal costumes that reflect the pre-Hispanic cultures of the region and perform dances and music as they parade down the street. Many festivals combine indigenous elements such as costumes and dances with Spanish elements, particularly those from the Catholic tradition, for example the processing of religious icons and performing of special masses.

*"**Hala bira! Puwera Pasma!**" Performers and devotees dancing and chanting during the Ati-Atihan Festival*

Another famous festival where the mixture of cultures can be seen is the Flores de Mayo (Spanish for "Flowers of May"), a month-long celebration in May observed throughout the Tagalog regions of the island of Luzon. The festival was introduced by the Spaniards in honor of the Virgin Mary, whom Filipinos fondly call Mama Mary and lavish with the local flowers in bloom. It has become a colorful celebration that includes the decoration of homes with copious flowers and the building of floral floats and culminates in a parade called **Santacruzan**. During the month of May, children and adults dressed in their Sunday best come together in the afternoons to pray the rosary and offer flowers to Mama Mary. Many villages and towns have their own festivals, with feasts, parades, and beautiful decorations, and these have become favorite attractions for tourists.

Historical sites are also popular among travelers in the Philippines. Cities such as Vigan, Ilocos Sur, Luzon—a UNESCO World Heritage Site for its well-preserved Spanish architecture—and Iloilo City in the Visayas, one of the principal cities during the Spanish colonial period, are a constant draw for fans of history and architecture. The Rice Terraces in Banawe, Ifugao Province (in Tagalog: "Hagdan-hagdang Palayan ng Banawe") are another attraction. They were constructed by the Ifugao people, using only the simplest tools and their own hands. Built over 2,000 years ago and maintained by the Ifugao since that time, the terraces have been called by some the Eighth Wonder of the World.

So, when you visit the Phiippines, plan to explore the many beautiful landscapes and experience the full cultural and historical diversity that this archipelago has to offer. **Tara na!**

Bakasyon

Vacation

An Overview of Lesson 19

Objectives
• Talk about a previous vacation
• Describe places
• Reserve a plane ticket
• Give and ask for directions

Vocabulary
• Travel-Related Nouns
• Verbs (Object- and Actor-Focus Verbs)
• Additional Object- and Actor-Focus Verbs
• Markers

• Adverbs
• Adjectives
• Prefixes
• Idioms and Expressions

Dialogue: Ang Bakasyon ko sa Boracay *My Vacation in Boracay*

Reading Comprehension

Activities
Activity 1: My Vacation
Activity 2: Interview
Activity 3: Story Completion

Grammar
Definition of Terms: **-In-** and **I-** Verbal Affixes, **-In-** Verbs, and **I-** Verbs

Examining Form
I.   Verbal Equivalence: Actor Focus and Object Focus
II. Completed Aspect (**-In-** and **I-** Verbs)
     Grammar Presentation
     Grammar Notes

Practice
I.   Speaking Practice
II.   Writing and Speaking Practice
III. Writing and Reading Practice
IV. Listening Practice

Vocabulary 🎧 (19–1)

The vocabulary below will help you describes places and speak about your travel plans. It will also allow you to participate in the activities in this lesson. Memorize the vocabulary words before proceeding to the dialogue.

Travel-Related Nouns

ale	term of address for a woman, Miss or Mrs.
alis	departure
alon	wave
bahay-bakasyunan	vacation house
bangka	boat
baon	provision or supply of food taken on a trip or vacation
barya	loose change, coins, lower denomination of money
batuhan	reef (for rocks)
biyahe	commute, trip, journey, tour
buhangin	sand
dagat	beach
dating/balik	arrival/return; a going or coming back
daybing	diving
eroplano	airplane
isla	island
isnorkling	snorkeling
istasyon ng bus	bus station
karanasan	experience
kas/kash	cash
korales	corals
lipad	flight
maleta	luggage
mama	mister, a term of address for a man
pasaporte	passport
pasahero	passenger
pasyalan	tourist destination or any place to spend leisure
paliparan	airport
pamasahe	fare
pampang	shore
pasalubong	a present from one's travels given to relatives and friends
pera	money, cash
pitaka	wallet
pulbos	powder
pupuntahan	destination
subenir	souvenir
turista	tourist
upuan	seat

Additional Actor-Focus Verbs

lumangoy	to swim
maglakbay	to travel
magpapalit	to change money
pumayag	to say yes
sumisid	to dive
umakyat ng bundok	to climb a mountain

Markers

'yung	variant of **ang**

Adverbs

kinabukasan	the following day, the next day

paakyat	on the way up, going up
pababa	on the way down, going down
pabalik	on the way back, going back
papunta	toward, going to

Adjectives

malinaw na malinaw	very clear
nakakaantok	makes someone feel sleepy
nakakahilo	nauseating
nakakalibang	entertaining
nakakalula	makes someone feel anxious (due to heights)
nakakalungkot	makes someone feel sad
nakakamangha	amazing
nakakapagod	tiring
nakakarelaks	relaxing
nakakatawa	makes someone laugh
nakakatuwa	makes someone feel happy

Prefixes

nakaka-	adjectival affix meaning making someone feel according to the root word

Verbs

Object-Focus	Actor-Focus	Definition
alukin	mag-alok	to offer something
ayusin	mag-ayos	to repair, organize, fix
basahin	magbasa/bumasa	to read
dalhin	magdala	to bring
hanapin	humanap/maghanap	to look for
hintayin	maghintay	to wait for
hiramin	humiram	to borrow
ibaon	magbaon	to carry or bring provisions or supplies of food
ibigay	magbigay	to give
ikuwento	magkuwento	to be told (as a story)/to tell a story
ilarawan	maglarawan	to describe
kainin	kumain	to eat
nakawin	magnakaw	to steal
sabihin	magsabi	to say
sunduin	sumundo	to pick someone up, to fetch
tanggapin	tumanggap	to receive

Idioms and Expression

Ay nako!	Oh, my gosh!
Buti na lang!	Thank goodness!
Hanggang dito na lang muna ako	Till then
Hinding-hindi ko makakalimutan . . .	I will never forget . . .
Mahal kong . . .	Dear. . . (letter salutation)
Murang-mura ito.	This is/was really cheap.
Pagkagising namin	When (After) we woke up
Sana ay mabuti ka naman.	I hope you are well.

Reading Text: Ang Bakasyon Ko sa Boracay *My Vacation in Boracay*

Read Mario's letter to Emily and answer the Reading Comprehension questions.

Mahal Kong Emily,

Kumusta ka na? Sana ay mabuti ka naman. Ako dito ay ayos naman. Talagang nagkaroon ako ng masayang bakasyon noong isang linggo. Pumunta kami ng pamilya ko sa bahay-bakasyunan ng tito namin sa Boracay. Dalawang oras ang biyahe papunta sa Boracay kaya nagbaon kami ng maraming pagkain. Tatlong araw kaming nandoon. Noong unang araw namin, lumangoy kami ng mga kapatid ko sa dagat nang apat na oras. Ang saya-saya doon at talagang ang ganda-ganda ng dagat. 'Yung buhangin, parang pulbos at 'yung tubig naman, malinaw na malinaw. Pagkatapos naming lumangoy at mamasyal sa tabing-dagat, naglakad kami pabalik sa bahay-bakasyunan ng tito namin. Ay nako! Talagang nakakapagod.

Kinabukasan, pagkagising namin, gutom na gutom kami kaya pumunta kami sa *buffet* na restawran. Kinain namin ang lahat ng klase ng isda at prutas doon. Pagkatapos, pumunta kami sa dagat para lumangoy ulit. Maganda ang dagat—maraming tao at marami ring mga ibon. Pagkatapos nito, nag-*island hopping* kami. Dito, nakita namin ang mga kuweba at ang parte ng dagat na maraming-maraming korales. Talagang masayang-masaya kami noon. Pagkatapos mag-*island hopping*, pumunta kami sa 'D' Mall'. Pamilihan ito sa Boracay. Bibili sana kami ng mga pasalubong para sa mga kamag-anak at kaibigan namin sa Maynila, pero noong hinahanap ko na ang pitaka ko, hindi ko na ito makita. Ninakaw na pala ito.

Sinabi ko sa kapatid ko ang nangyari at buti na lang may pera siya at binigyan niya ako ng isang libo. Kahit na nangyari ito, masaya pa rin ang bakasyon namin.

O sige, hanggang dito na lang muna ako. Magkuwento ka naman.

Nagmamahal,
Mario

Reading Comprehension

1. Saan nagbakasyon si Mario at ang pamilya niya?

   _____

2. Ano ang ginawa nina Mario noong unang araw?

   _____

3. Saan sila kumain noong pangalawang araw?

   _____

4. Ano ang D' Mall?

   _____

5. Ano ang naging problema ni Mario noong bumibili siya ng pasalubong?

   _____

Activities

Activity 1

Think of your most unforgettable vacation, good or bad. Where and when did you go? Who did you go with? What did you do? Sketch one of your memories of this vacation on a separate sheet of paper and talk about your sketch with your partner.

EXAMPLES:

Hinding-hindi ko makakalimutan ang bakasyon ko sa Hong Kong noong isang taon. Pumunta ako doon kasama ang nobya ko. Pumunta kami sa iba't-ibang mga pasyalan at parke doon. Kumain kami sa iba't ibang restawran. Bumili kami ng mga damit at pasalubong sa mga tindahan sa kalye. Ang pinakamasayang ginawa namin sa Hong Kong ay ang pamamasyal sa gabi. Pumunta kami sa ibaba ng otel namin at kumain kami ng mga "street food." Talagang masayang karanasan ito.

Activity 2

Interview two of your classmates. Ask them what their dream vacation is and why? Record their responses in the table below. Use the example to model your interviews and sentences.

S1: **Anong lugar ang gusto mong puntahan sa hinaharap?**
S2: **Gusto kong puntahan ang Italya kasi gusto kong mag-aral magluto ng mga Italyan na pagkain.**

Pangalan at Lugar	Dahilan
1. **Mike: Italya**	**Gustong puntahan ni Mike ang Italya kasi gusto niyang mag-aral magluto ng mga Italyan na pagkain.**
2. _____	
3. _____	

Activity 3

Revisit the Reading Text above and create your own ending to the story that was recounted there. What do you think happened to Mario after he found out that his wallet was missing? Continue the story.

> **"Bibili sana kami dito ng mga pasalubong para sa mga kamag-anak at kaibigan namin sa Maynila, pero noong hinahanap ko na ang pitaka ko, hindi ko na ito makita. Ninakaw na pala ito."**

_____

_____

_____

_____

_____

_____

Grammar

Definition of Terms

-In and I- Verbal Affixes	Affixes that, when attached to verbal roots, make the resulting word an object-focus verb.
-In Verbs	Indicate that the object of the sentence is the focus. **-In-** verbs use the **-in-** affix with the verbal root and are transitive and volitional. All object-focus affixes turn the root word into an action on its object.
I- Verbs	A class of object-focus verbs that give a meaning of movement or transference of the focus or subject/topic to another location.

Examining Form

The sentences below illustrate the grammar patterns presented in this lesson. Review the sentences and complete the tasks that follow. Discuss your answers with a partner. Consult the following section to check your answers.

A	B
Nagbigay ang kapatid ko ng pera sa akin.	Ibinigay ng kapatid ko ang pera sa akin.
Nagbaon kami ng maraming pagkain.	Ibinaon namin ang maraming pagkain.
Kumain kami ng mga isda at prutas.	Kinain namin ang mga isda at prutas.
Naghanap ako ng pitaka ko.	Hinanap ko ang pitaka ko.
Bumili ako ng regalo sa D' Mall.	Binili namin ang regalo sa D' Mall.

1. Compare the sentences in columns A and B. Is there any difference in meaning?
2. Underline the verbs, circle the doers of the action of the verb, and box the object. What differences did you observe in the sentences in columns A and B?
3. Look at all the verbs in column B. How do we form the completed aspect of object focus verbs?

I. Verb Equivalence: Actor Focus and Object Focus

There are varied ways to express the same idea in Tagalog. The focus of the verb makes this possible, as do the different types of sentence—predicational or the subject-**ay** predicate sentence that is the more formal and less common way of using the language. Focus allows Tagalog to give emphasis to the complement, which is the element that completes the verb grammatically. The complement of the verb can be an actor complement, object complement, or indirect-object complement, which is also commonly referred to as the directional complement. Thus sentences in Tagalog can also be classified as actor-focus, object-focus, or indirect object–focus (directional-focus) type of sentences.

The verbs that accept complements are mainly transitive verbs. In Lesson 7, we learned about ditransitive verbs, which take on two types of objects: the direct object marked by **ng** and the indirect object, the one that benefits from the action of the verb and is the receiver of the direct object. The indirect object is marked by **sa** forms. In that same lesson, we presented an overview of Tagalog verbal construction: inflection, focus, and the use of transitive and intransitive verbs in sentences. Here we will summarize the major points covered in the previous lessons regarding verbal aspect and focus before we introduce and move on to a more detailed explanation of verbal construction and equivalences in the current lesson.

The aspect of the verb pertains to the process or flow of an action: whether the action has begun but not been completed, which is conveyed by the incompleted aspect; whether the action has begun and ended, which is conveyed by the perfective or completed aspect; and whether the action has not yet begun, which is conveyed by the contemplated aspect. Aspect is indicated by the change of form in the verb, or inflection. The verb in Tagalog is made up of the verbal root or base plus an affix belonging to particular verb classes that determines the focus of the verb. By inflection, we mean that each aspectual meaning is associated with a different modification of this basic verb form. So far, we have introduced actor-focus verbs (classed as **-um-**, **mag-**, and **ma**-verbs), object-focus verbs (**-in/-hin**, **i-**, and **–an/-han** verbs), and experiencer-focus verbs (**magka-**, **magkaroon**. and **ma-** involuntary verbs). Each verb class has its own set of affixes. The form that we call the infinitive consists of the verbal affix and the verb base or verbal root word. The affix may be a prefix (**mag-**), an infix (**-um-**), a suffix (**-in/-hin**, or **-an/-han**), or a compound affix consisting of both a prefix and a suffix (**pa- -in**, as in the verb **pakuluin** "to let boil," which we encountered in Lesson 18.

Affixes that are used in the predicate verb of a basic sentence, such as **-um-**, **mag- ma-**, **-in**, **i-**, and **-an**, are major affixes, and the verbal roots to which they are attached are major verbs. Other verbal affixes are derived affixes, and the verbs formed with these affixes are derived verbs. We will not cover derived affixes and derived verbs in this lesson. The second element of an infinitive is the core meaning of the verb, indicated by the verbal root word. A verbal root may be used by two or more major verbs as well as a few derived verbs. There is no general rule that could indicate whether a verbal root or base can belong to a particular major verb.

The semantic role of a predicate verb with respect to the subject of a sentence varies with the focus of the verb, which is associated with the affixes used. Affixes in actor-focus (AF) verbs focus on a subject/topic that denotes the doer of the action. Other affixes belong to goal-focus verbs, which are verbs whose subjects express the goal of the action. For the purposes of our lesson, goal focus is a general term for all verbs that are not actor-focus verbs. A major verb, when not actor-focus, may occur in one or two classes of goal-focus verbs: object-focus verbs and indirect object-focus verbs (directional verbs). We will summarize the differences between the three main verb focuses in the next unit.

There is no general rule that can help you figure out if an actor-focus verb has a counterpart with an **-in** or **i-** (object-focus) affix. Conventionally, **-um-** verbs correspond to **-in** verbs, and **mag-** verbs correspond to **i-** verbs. But there is no general rule that can help you ascertain for sure what type of affix from the set of affixes in the object-focus verb class would correspond to the actor-focus set of verbs and their affixes. The only way to know is to use the actor-focus verb in a sentence, and, if it has a direct object and indirect object (directional complements), then there will be corresponding object-focus and indirect object–focus (directional-focus) verbs. But as to what type of affix the corresponding verbs will have, only familiarization with the Tagalog language and Filipino culture will enable you to know. As a general rule, actor-focus verbs have a set of affixes corresponding to object-focus affixes and indirect object–focus affixes. In this lesson, our focus is on the **mag-/i-** and **-um-/-in** correspondence.

Listed below are the general correspondences between the actor-focus affixes **mag-** and **-um-** and the object-focus affixes **i-** and **-in**. The object-focus suffix **-an**, which we encountered in Lesson 18, will not be given a lot of emphasis in this book because it is not highly productive as an object focus.

1. **Mag-** and **I-**

Root word	Affix	Infinitive	Meaning
lagay (put)	mag-	**maglagay**	to put, place (I put)
	i-	**ilagay**	to put something on/in

This verbal root (**lagay**) can be affixed with **-um-** to make **lumagay**, but the meaning changes, as can be illustrated by this sentence: **Lumagay ka na sa tahimik** literally means "Be in a state of silence (quietness) now." Idiomatically, it means "You get married now." For Filipinos, getting married is being in a state of serenity or quietude.

Lagay does not occur with the object-focus affix **-in**. No such verb or word as **lagyin** exists in Tagalog.

2. **-Um-** and **-In/-Hin**

Root word	Affix	Infinitive	Meaning
bili (buy)	**-um-**	**bumili**	to buy (I buy)
	-in/-hin	**bilhin**	to buy something

The root word **bili** can be affixed with **i-**, but the meaning would change to a benefactive focus. **Ibili** means "to buy something for someone."

3. **-Um-**, **Mag-**, and **I-**

Root word	Affix	Infinitive	Meaning
bukas (open)	**mag-**	**magbukas**	to open something
	-um-	**bumukas**	to open (it [object] opened, involuntary)
	i-	**ibukas**	to open something (do to the object)

The root word **bukas** has two actor-focus equivalents, and the meaning differs somewhat depending on the particular affix. When **bukas** is affixed with **mag-**, there is an actor doing the act of opening an object; whereas, when it is affixed with **-um-**, there is no actor doing the act of opening something. Some Tagalog root words that work the same way are the following: **tapon** (**tumapon** "to spill"; **magtapon** "to throw away") and **buwal** (**bumuwal** "to fall down (accidental, no actor)"; **magbuwal** "to fall down"). However, in some cases when the root word is conjugated with **mag-**, the idea is that there's always an actor and an object, while, when it is conjugated with **-um-** there seems to be no object or the actor is doing the action to himself/herself as in the following examples: **akyat** (**umakyat** "to go up"; **mag-akyat** "to bring something up stairs"), **baba** (**bumaba** "to go down"; **magbaba** "to bring something downstairs"), **pasok** (**pumasok** "to go/come inside"; **magpasok** "to bring something inside"), **labas** (**lumabas** "to go/come outside"; **maglabas** "to bring something outside").

Now that we have examined the correspondence of actor-focus verbs and object-focus verbs, let's move on to the completed aspect of the object-focus **-in-** and **i-** verbs, the counterparts of **-um-** and **mag-** verbs, which belong to the actor-focus set of verbs.

II. Completed Aspect (-In/ I- Verbs)

The completed aspect corresponds to the simple past tense in English. Simple past denotes action that started and finished at a specific time in the past. The completed aspect is formed differently in **-in** verbs and **i-** verbs. For **-in** verbs, the root word is the base, and **-in** is inserted in front of the first vowel of the root word. For **i-** verbs, the base is the infinitive form, which is **i-** + ROOT WORD. The completed aspect is formed by inserting **-in-** before the first vowel of the root word. The chart below illustrates how to form the completed aspect in both **-in** and **i-** verbs. Notice that when the root word is conjugated in the completed aspect with **i-**, the **i-** prefix may be omitted. In the next lesson, **Mga Pista**, we will discuss in detail some alternate conjugations of the **i-** verbal affix.

Root	Infinitive	Completed Aspect	Rules for Forming the Completed Aspect
sabi	sabihin	si*n*abi	**-IN-** VERBAL AFFIX: From the root, insert -**in**- before the first vowel.
hanap	hanapin	hi*n*anap	
bigay	ibigay	ibi*n*igay	**I-** VERBAL AFFIX: From the infinitive, insert -**in**- before the first vowel of the root word.
lagay	ilagay	ili*n*agay	

Grammar Presentation

In an object-focus sentence, the word order changes depending on the actor and the direct object, as illustrated in the chart below. Since "object-focus" means the direct object is the focus, we refer to the direct object in an object-focus sentence as the subject or topic. The sentences in the chart use the same verbal roots (**sama** and **sunda**) with the **i-** and **-in-** affixes in the completed aspect, **isinama** and **sinundo**. Notice that when the direct object that is the topic of the sentence is an **ang** phrase (that is, the common-noun marker **ang** with a noun), the actor complement—a **ng** phrase—immediately follows the verb. However, when pronouns are the topic (direct object) of the sentence, these subject pronouns immediately follow the verb and are followed by the **ng** phrase—which is the actor complement or doer of the action in verbs other than actor-focus verbs, as pointed out earlier. In both cases, the place and time may come last in the word order of the sentences; but they could also go before the predicate verb as illustrated in the example sentences below.

Object-Focus Verbs							
Verb	**Actor**		**Direct Object (Subject/Topic)**		**Location/Direction**		**Time**
I-, -In, -An	**Marker**	**Noun/ Pronoun**	**Marker**	**Noun**	**Marker**	**Noun**	**Past Marker**
*I*sinama	ng ng mga ni nina	<u>kuya ko</u> <u>Kardo</u> ko namin mo ninyo niya nila	ang ang mga si sina	<u>kaibigan ko</u> <u>Roel</u>	sa	<u>parke</u> <u>eskwelahan</u>	<u>kanina.</u>
*Si*nundo							

Verb	**Direct Object (Subject)**		**Actor**		**Location/Direction**		**Time**
I-, -In, -An	**Marker**	**Pronoun**	**Marker**	**Noun**	**Marker**	**Noun**	**Past Marker**
*I*sinama	-	ako tayo kami ka kayo siya niya	ng ng mga ni nina	<u>ate ko</u> <u>Ricky</u>	sa	<u>parke</u> <u>eskwelahan</u>	<u>kahapon.</u>
*Si*nundo							

EXAMPLES:

Hiniram ni Mike ang kotse ko noong isang buwan. Mike borrowed my car last month.

Noong isang linggo, ikinuwento niya ang bakasyon niya sa akin. Last week she told me about her vacation.

Ibinigay po niya ang tiket sa akin. She/He gave me the ticket, sir/madam.

Sinundo ako ni Miguel sa paliparan kahapon. Miguel picked me up at the airport yesterday.

Ibinigay mo ba kay Maria ang mapa? Did you give the map to Maria?

What if the actor complement and the topic (direct object) are both pronouns or noun substitutes? How would the word order be? In that case, the **ng** pronouns that are the actors of the sentence come immediately after the verb predicate and are followed by the topic (direct object).

Isinama niya ako. He/She brought me along.

Sinundo nila ako. They fetched me.

Grammar Notes

1. The most frequently occurring word order for sentences with object-focus verbs is:
   VERB + ACTOR + OBJECT + (LOCATION) + (TIME)

   Kinain ni Mike ang mga pagkain. Mike ate the food.
   Kinain nila ang mga pagkain. They ate the food.

   Hinintay ni Sabrina ang mga kaibigan niya. Sabrina waited for her friends.
   Hinintay niya ang mga kaibigan niya. She waited for her friends.

   However, if the direct object is an **ang** pronoun and the actor is either a common or a proper noun, the actor and direct object switch positions:
   VERB + OBJECT + ACTOR + (LOCATION) + (TIME)

   Kinain ito ni Mike. Mike ate this.
   Hinintay sila ni Sabrina. Sabrina waited for them.

2. Normally object-focus verbs are used when the object in English would be any one of the following:
   1. *It.* This has no translation in Tagalog, because there is no neutral pronoun in Tagalog. Sometimes, *it* is translated as the demonstrative pronoun **ito** (this).
   2. A pronoun that is an object of the preposition *for*, which would translate into the **ang** pronoun in Tagalog
   3. A proper noun
   4. The definite article *the* plus a noun
   5. A possessive pronoun followed by a common noun

   The sentences below illustrate these rules:
   Hinintay nila. They waited for *it.*
   Hinintay nila *siya.* They waited for *him.*
   Hinintay nila *si Mike.* They waited for *Mike.*
   Hinintay nila *ang lalaki.* They waited for *the man.*
   Hinintay nila *ang tatay nila.* They waited for *their father.*

> The first two sentences can be a response to a question where both interlocutors know what they are talking about, that is, who the "it" or the pronoun for "him" refer to.
>
> **Hinintay ba nila?** Did they wait?
> **Oo, hinintay nila.** Yes, they waited.

3. Some **-an** verbs are also object-focus, but we will not discuss them here, because **-an** is not highly productive as an object-focus affix. However, in the next unit, **Popular na Kultura**, we will study **-an** as an indirect object-focus (directional) verb.

Practice

I. Speaking Practice

Translate the following questions into Tagalog and write two of your own questions about vacations. Afterwards, use these questions to interview a classmate. Try to apply what you've learned in the grammar lesson.

Have you ever been abroad?   **Nagpunta (Nakapunta) ka na ba sa ibang bansa?**

Where have you been?   _____

Describe your best trip.   _____

Describe your worst trip.   _____

Describe the most interesting person you met on one of your travels.

_____

_____

My Vacation Questions:

1. _____

2. _____

II. Reading Practice

Read the conversation below between two people talking over the phone and answer the Reading Comprehension questions.

A. Pagbili ng tiket sa eroplano
  A: **Hello.**
  B: **Hello. Ano po iyon?**
  A: **Kailangan ko po ng dalawang tiket papunta sa Boracay.**
  B: **O sige po. Kailan po ang lipad ninyo?**

A: Sa isang linggo. Sa Biyernes.

B: Kailan po ang balik ninyo?

A: Sa Lunes. Apat na araw lang kami doon.

B: O sige po. Itsetsek ko po kung may upuan pa ho.

A: Sige. Pwede bang pakihanap mo ako ng upuan malapit sa *exit row*?

B: Sige po.

A: At saka isulat mo naman diyan na kailangan ko ng *vegetarian* na pagkain.

B: Wala pong problema. Confirmed na po ang lipad ninyo sa Biyernes at ang balik po ay sa Lunes.

A: Magkano ang lahat-lahat?

B: Kasama po ang tax. Anim na libo limang daan po.

A: Salamat pero pakitsek mo naman kung mas mura kung sa Martes ang balik.

B: O sige po.

A: Salamat ah.

B: Pareho lang po ang presyo.

A: Ah ganun ba? Sige, bibilhin ko na.

Reading Comprehension

1. **Saan pupunta ang pasahero?**

   _____

2. **Ilang araw sa destinasyon ang pasahero?**

   _____

3. **Magkano ang tiket?**

   _____

4. **Ilan ang tiket na binibili?**

   _____

5. **Anu-ano ang mga gusto ng pasahero?**

   _____

   _____

   _____

B. **Simulation**

   Now work with a partner and act out one of the following scenarios.

   1. **Nagbabakasyon ka sa Maynila. Ang problema, nawala mo ang mapa mo at hindi mo alam kung paano bumalik sa iyong hotel. Humingi ng tulong at alamin ang daan pabalik sa hotel mo.**

2. **Nagreserba ka ng hotel sa Internet. Ang problema, noong dumating ka sa kuwarto mo, napansin mo na smoking ang kuwarto na ibinigay sa iyo. Kausapin mo ang receptionist at sabihin na kailangan mong lumipat ng kuwarto. Ipaliwanag ang iyong sitwasyon.**

III. Writing Practice

Write a letter in Tagalog to a friend telling him or her about your most recent vacation. Use a separate piece of paper for your letter.

IV. Listening Practice

 Listen to audio file (19–2) and complete the box below.

Pasahero	Alis	Balik	Destinasyon	Presyo ng tiket
1.				
2.				
3.				

Mga Pista

Fiestas

An Overview of Lesson 20

Objectives
- Discuss some specific holidays and festivities
- Say dates

Vocabulary
- Nouns
- Holidays
- Spanish-Derived Numbers
- Verbs (**-In** and **I-** Object-Focus and Corresponding **Mag-** and **-Um-** Actor-Focus)
- **Ipag-** Verbs
- **-An** Verbs
- **Mang-** Verbs

Reading Text: Mga Pista *Festivals*

> Reading Comprehension

Activities
Activity 1: Interview
Activity 2: Holiday and Festival Calendar
Activity 3: **Ano Kaya?**

Grammar

Examining Form
I.   Incompleted Aspect (**-In** and **I-** Verbs)
     Grammar Presentation
     Grammar Notes
II. Saying Dates
     Grammar Presentation
     Grammar Notes

Practice
I.   Speaking Practice
II.   Reading Practice
III. Writing Practice
IV.   Listening Practice

Vocabulary 🎧 (20–1)

The vocabulary below will help you say dates and discuss holidays in Tagalog and to participate in the activities in this lesson. Memorize the vocabulary words before proceeding to the dialogue.

Nouns

bayan	town
buhay	life
kasuotan	wardrobe
nayon	village
pagdiriwang	celebration/festival
parada	parade

Holidays

Araw ng mga Ama	Father's Day
Araw ng Kalayaan	Independence Day
Araw ng mga Bayani	National Heroes' Day
Araw ng mga Ina	Mother's Day
Araw ng Manggagawa	Labor Day
Araw ng Pasasalamat	Thanksgiving Day
Araw ng mga Patay	All Souls' Day
Araw ng mga Puso	Valentine's Day (Day of the Hearts, literally)
Bagong taon	New Year's Day
Biyernes Santo	Good Friday
Huwebes Santo	Maundy Thursday
Pasko ng Pagkabuhay	Easter
Pasko	Christmas
Semana Santa	Holy Week
Undas	All Saints Day

Spanish-Derived Numbers

uno	one	tres	three
a-primero	first	kuwatro	four
dos	two	singko	five
		sais	six
		siyete	seven
		otso	eight
		nuwebe	nine
		diyes	ten
		onse	eleven
		dose	twelve
		trese	thirteen
		katorse	fourteen
		kinse	fifteen
		disisais	sixteen
		disisiyete	seventeen
		disiotso	eighteen
		disinuwebe	nineteen
		bente	twenty
		bente uno	twenty-one
		trenta	thirty
		trentay uno	thirty-one

Verbs

Object-Focus	Actor-Focus	Definition
-In Verbs	**Mag-** Verbs	
alalahanin	(no actor-focus)	to remember
basain	magbasâ	to make something wet
buhatin	magbuhat	to lift or carry
laruin	maglaro	to play
tiisin	magtiis	to endure
-In Verbs	**-Um-** Verbs	
bungguin	bumunggo	to hit
gawin	gumawa	to make, fix, do
guluhin	gumulo	to disarrange
habulin	humabol	to chase
kantahin	kumanta	to sing
piliin	pumili	to choose
sayawin	sumayaw	to dance
tugtugin	tumugtog	to play a musical instrument

I- Verbs	Mag- Verbs	
ibalita	**magbalita**	to pass the news
iitsa	**mag-itsa**	to throw, toss
ipatak	**magpatak/pumatak**	to drop

Ipag- Verbs	Mag- Verbs	Definition
ipagdiwang	**magdiwang**	to celebrate

-An Verbs	Mag- Verbs	Definition
binyagan	**magbinyag**	to baptize
protektahan	**magprotekta**	to protect

Mang- Verbs	Definition	
mangyari	to happen	infinitive
nangyari	happened	completed
nangyayari	is/was happening	incomplete
mangyayari	will happen	contemplated
maniwala	to believe	infinitive
naniwala	believed	completed
naniniwala	is/was believing	incomplete
maniniwala	will believe	contemplated

Idioms and Expressions

. . . ang ibig sabihin	It means . . .
ayon sa	according to

Reading Text: Mga Pista *Festivals*

Mark is planning to go on a vacation in the Philippines and he wants to know what celebrations or fiestas that he could attend. Read the following descriptions of some traditional Filipino celebrations and answer the Reading Comprehension questions to help Mark plan his trip.

Word Bank

maskara	mask	**bulag**	blind
pumatak	to drop	**pagsalubong**	act of welcoming, meeting
palaspas	palm leaves	**pintahan**	to color, paint
kalamidad	calamity	**halamang-ugat**	root crop/tuber
tahanan	home	**lumalahok**	participating

Moriones

Sa Marinduque, ang Moriones ang atraksyong nangya-yari tuwing Semana Santa. Ang ibig sabihin ng morion ay helmet. Kaya ang mga taong nagsusuot ng maskara na may kasamang helmet at ng Romanong kasuotan ay tinatatawag na moriones. Sa pagdiriwang na ito, inaalaala ng mga tao ang buhay ni Longhino. Ayon sa kuwento, si Longhino ay bulag sa kaliwang mata at nang pumatak ang dugo ni Kristo sa mata niya ay nakakita siya muli.

Ang Araw ng Palaspas

Tuwing Linggo ng Palaspas o Linggo de Ramos, inaalaala ng lahat ang pagsalubong kay Kristo sa Herusalem. Nag-dadala ang mga tao ng mga palaspas na may mga deko-rasyong papel na bulaklak sa simbahan. Naniniwala ang mga tao na nagpoprotekta ang palaspas sa bahay mula sa mga kalamidad. Sa ibang lugar, ito ay sinusunog at ihinahalo sa tubig at halamang-ugat. Ginagamit ito para sa mga sakit sa tiyan.

Ati-Atihan

Ginagawa ang ati-atihan sa Kalibo, Aklan. Pinipintahan ng mga tao ang katawan nila ng kulay itim at nagsusuot din sila ng mga makukulay na damit habang sila ay su-masayaw at sumisigaw ng "hala bira".

Reading Comprehension

1. **Ano ang nangyayari na atraksyon sa Marinduque tuwing Semana Santa?**

   _____

2. **Ano ang pumatak sa mata ni Longhino?**

   _____

3. **Ano ang inaalaala ng mga tao tuwing Linggo ng Palaspas?**

   _____

4. **Ano ang nagpoprotekta sa mga tahanan sa mga kalamidad?**

   _____

5. **Ano ang ipinagdiriwang sa Kalibo, Aklan?**

   _____

6. **Ano ang isinusuot ng mga lumalahok sa ati-atihan?**

   _____

Activities

Activity I

Work with a partner. Discuss some of the holidays and festivities that happen in your area. In the table below, describe the kinds of activities that take place during these celebrations.

Pista sa Ibang Lugar	Mga Ginagawa
1. **Bagong Taon**	**Masayang-masaya ang araw na ito. Maraming tao ang umiinom kasama ang mga kaibigan habang naghihintay ng alas dose ng hatinggabi.**
2. _____	_____ _____ _____

Pista sa Ibang Lugar	Mga Ginagawa
3. _____	

Activity II

Think about the different holidays that you celebrate throughout the year. Next to the months in the chart below, identify these holidays and describe how each is usually celebrated.

Buwan	Mga Pagdiriwang at Gawain
Enero	Bagong Taon- tuwing a-primero ng Enero, naghahanda ng maraming pagkain ang mga tao at umiinom sila ng mga serbesa at bino sa araw na ito. Iniisip din nila ang mga nangyari noong nakaraang taon at gumagawa sila ng mga listahan ng mga bagay na kailangan nilang baguhin sa darating na taon.
Pebrero at Marso	
Abril at Mayo	
Hunyo, Hulyo, at Agosto	
Setyembre at Oktubre	
Nobyembre at Disyembre	

Activity III

Work with a partner and study the illustrations below, which document specific festivals and celebrations that take place throughout the Philippines. Based on your observations, how do you think each fiesta is celebrated?

Parada ng Kalabaw

Parada ng Lechon

Grammar

Examining Form

The sentences below illustrate the grammar patterns that are presented in this lesson. Review the sentences and complete the tasks that follow. Discuss your answers with a partner. Consult the following section to check your answers.

1. **Ano ang idinaraos na atraksyon sa Marinduque tuwing Semana Santa?**
A. **Idinaraos ang Moriones sa Marinduque tuwing Semana Santa.**
B. **Nagdaraos ang mga tao ng Moriones sa Marinduque tuwing Semana Santa.**

2. **Ano ang pumatak sa mata ni Longhino?**
A. **Pumatak ang dugo sa mata ni Longhino.**

3. **Ano ang dinadala ng mga tao sa simbahan tuwing Linggo de Ramos?**
A. **Dinadala ang mga palaspas na may mga dekorasyong papel na bulaklak sa simbahan.**
B. **Nagdadala ang mga tao ng mga palaspas na may mga dekorasyong papel na bulaklak sa simbahan.**

4. **Ano ang nagpoprotekta sa mga tahanan sa mga kalamidad?**
A. **Nagpoprotekta ang palaspas sa mga tahanan sa mga kalamidad.**

5. **Kailan ipinagdiriwang ang Araw ng mga Puso?**
A. **Ipinagdiriwang ang Araw ng mga Puso tuwing ikalabing-apat ng Pebrero.**
B. **Ipinagdiriwang ang Araw ng mga Puso tuwing a-katorse ng Pebrero.**

6. **Kailan ipinagdiriwang ang Araw ng Kalayaan sa Pilipinas?**
A. **Ipinagdiriwang ang Araw ng Kalayaan sa Pilipinas tuwing ikalabindalawa ng Hunyo.**
B. **Ipinagdiriwang ang Araw ng Kalayaan sa Pilipinas tuwing a-dose ng Hunyo.**

For numbers 1–4
1. Look at questions 1, 2, 3, and 4. Underline all the verbs and identify each verb form.
2. Questions 1 and 3 use object-focus verbs, whereas questions 2 and 4 use actor-focus verbs.
   a.) When do you use actor-focus verbs with the interrogative pronoun **ano**?
   b.) When do you use object-focus verbs with the interrogative pronoun **ano**?
3. Look at all the responses and compare A1 and A2. What are the differences in structure?

For numbers 5–6
4. Underline all the dates in numbers 4 and 5. What is the difference between A and B?

I. Incompleted Aspect (-In/I- Verbs)

The incompleted aspect corresponds to English simple present tense and present progressive tense. In the simple present tense, an action is repeated or usual. This means that the action can be a hobby, a daily or weekly schedule, or something that often occurs. In contrast, the present progressive denotes action that is happening now, at this very moment. To conjugate the incompleted form of **-in** and **i-** verbs, you need to know the completed form. For **-in** verbs, add the root after the first two syllables of the completed aspect. For the **i-** verbs, add the root after the first three syllables of the completed aspect.

The chart below illustrates how to form the incompleted aspect of the object-focus **-in-** and **i-**verbs.

Infinitive	Completed Aspect	Incompleted	Rules for Forming the Incompleted Aspect
sabihin	*sina*bi	*sinasabi*	Take the first two syllables of the completed aspect + root word.
hanapin	*hina*nap	*hinahanap*	
ibigay	*ibini*gay	*ibinibigay*	Take the first three syllables of the completed aspect + root word.
ilagay	*ilina*gay	*ilinalagay*	

However, when you converse with some native speakers of Tagalog, you might hear them conjugate some **i-** and **-in** verbs somewhat differently. This slight variation occurs in the completed and incompleted verbal conjugations of root words that begin with letters *l, r, w,* and *y.* Look at the chart below to compare the two ways to conjugate. The difference occurs in the completed form. Instead of inserting **-in-** before the first vowel of the base, **ni-** is prefixed.

Conjugation A	Conjugation B	Rules for Forming the Completed Aspect
w*in*alis	*ni*walis	Instead of inserting **-in** before the first vowel of the root, prefix **ni-** to the root.
y*in*aya	*ni*yaya	
(i)l*in*abas	*ni*labas	Instead of inserting **-in** before the first vowel of the infinitive, prefix **ni-** to the root.
(i)r*in*ekomenda	*ni*rekomenda	

Conjugation A	Conjugation B	Rules for Forming the Incompleted Aspect
winawalis	*niwawalis*	For both types of conjugations, take the first two syllables of the completed form followed by the root word.
yinayaya	*niyayaya*	
(i)linalabas	*nilalalabas*	For both types of conjugations, take the first three syllables of the completed form followed by the root word.
ilinalagay	*nirerekomenda*	

Grammar Presentation

1. The chart below shows how to form a question with the interrogative pronoun **ano** and actor-focus verbs.

Ano + Actor-Focus Verbs				
Interrogative	Marker	Verb	Location/ Direction	
			Marker	Noun
Ano	ang	pumapatak / nagpoprotekta	sa	mata niya? / tahanan nila?

2. The chart below shows how to form a question with the interrogative pronoun **ano** and object-focus verbs. The word order for this interrogative sentence is **Ano** + **ang** + OF VERB + **ng** ACTOR. The answer to these types of question is the object, which is replaced by **ano** in the sentence.

Ano + Object-Focus Verbs						
What	Marker	Verb	Actor		Location/ Direction	
			Ng Marker/ Pronoun	Noun	Marker	Noun
Ano	ang	ipinapatak	ng / ng mga / ni / nina	bata / Maria	sa	mata niya?
		dinadala	ko natin / namin / mo ninyo / niya nila			simbahan?

EXAMPLES:

Ano ang ginugulo mo? What are you disarranging/messing up?

Ano ang dinadala mo dito? What are you bringing here?

Ano ang binubunggo niya? What is he hitting?

Grammar Notes

1. **Ano** + actor-focus verbs
   Use an actor-focus verb whenever there is no one or nothing causing the action to occur. This structure indexes the object as the cause of the action.
   Ano ang *pumatak*? What dropped?
   Pumatak *ang tubig*. The water dropped.
   Ano ang *bumuwal*? What fell down?
   Bumuwal *ang puno*. The tree fell down.
   Ano ang *bumukas*? What opened?
   Bumukas *ang pinto*. The door opened.

2. **Ano** + object-focus verbs
   Use an object-focus verb whenever someone or something is causing the action to occur. This structure indexes the actor as the cause of action.
   Ano ang *ipinatak* **mo sa mata ko?** What did you drop in my eye?
   Ipinatak ko *ang tubig* **sa mata ko.** I dropped water in your eye.
   Ano ang *ibinuwal* **mo?** What did you knock down?
   Ibinuwal ko *ang puno*. I knocked down the tree.
   Ano ang *ibinukas* **mo?** What did you open?
   Ibinukas ko *ang pinto*. I opened the door.

II. Saying Dates

In Lesson 4, we learned Tagalog numerals from 1 to 99. In Lesson 7, Spanish numbers were used to tell time. In Lesson 9, we learned to use hundreds and thousands in the context of shopping in the Philippines; and in Lesson 14, we used numbers again to tell exact time. In this lesson, we will study Spanish-derived numbers for saying dates. For expressing a date in Tagalog, most often Spanish-derived numbers are used. The Spaniards introduced the Gregorian calendar to mark the days and years, and now it is simply logical and convenient to employ the Spanish numerals for saying the dates. Aside from that, Tagalog numerals were longer and more difficult to say. For example, 21 would be expressed this way: **may catlong isa** (the first of the group of 30).

	Spanish-derived numbers		Spanish-derived numbers
1	uno, primero	9	nuwebe
2	dos	10	diyes
3	tres	11	nuwebe
4	kuwatro	12	diyes
5	singko	13	nuwebe
6	sais	14	diyes
7	siyete	15	nuwebe
8	otso	16	disisais

17	disisiyete	25	bente singko
18	disiotso	26	bente sais
19	disinuwebe	27	bente siyete
20	bente	28	bente otso
21	bente uno	29	bente nuwebe
22	bente dos	30	trenta
23	bente tres	31	trentay uno
24	bente kuwatro		

To express a date, use the following form: place the letter *a* from Spanish followed by the number and **ng**, which means "of," followed by the month. For example, **a-primero ng Marso** translates as "the first of March."

Petsa		
A-Number	**Ng**	**Petsa**
a-uno	**ng**	**Enero**

Grammar Presentation

The chart below shows how to express the date in a complete sentence. The word order is PREDICATE VERB + SUBJECT + TIME MARKER + DATE. The sentence below translates to: "Independence Day is celebrated every 12th of June."

Dates				
Verb	**Object**		**Time**	
	Marker	**Noun**	**Marker**	**Noun**
Ipinagdiriwang	ang ang mga	**Araw ng Kalayaan**	tuwing	**a-dose ng Hunyo.**

EXAMPLES:
Ipinagdiriwang ang Pasko tuwing a-bente singko ng Disyembre. (conversational)
Ipinagdiriwang ang Pasko tuwing ika dalawampu't lima ng Disyembre. (formal)
Christmas is celebrated every 25th of December.

Ibinibigay ni Mario ang mga bulaklak kay Lisa tuwing a-katorse ng Pebrero. (conversational)
Ibinibigay ni Mario ang mga bulaklak kay Lisa tuwing ikalabing-apat ng Pebrero. (formal)
Mario gives Lisa flowers every February 14th.

Magpupunta ako sa Palawan sa a-primero ng Enero. (conversational)
Magpupunta ako sa Palawan sa ikaisa ng Enero. (formal)
I will go to the Philippines on January 1st.

Grammar Notes

1. There are two ways to express dates in Filipino:
   A- SPANISH NUMBER + **ng** + MONTH
   Ika- TAGALOG NUMBER + **ng** + MONTH

   The former is more conversational, while the latter is more formal.
   A-singko ng Abril.
   Ikalima ng Abril.

Practice

I. Speaking Practice

Work with a partner. Review the following schedule and ask each other when the various events happen. Note that, in real life, the fiestas may happen in a different month than shown here. This calendar is only for purposes of practicing the structure of saying dates.

EXAMPLE:
S1: **Kailan ang Moriones?**
S2: **Sa ikasiyam ng Abril ang Moriones.**
     Sa a-nuwebe ng Abril ang Moriones.

Abril						
Linggo	**Lunes**	**Martes**	**Miyerkules**	**Huwebes**	**Biyernes**	**Sabado**
		1	2	3	4 **Parada ng Kalabaw**	5
6 **Ati-atihan**	7	8	9 **Moriones**	10	11	12
13	14	15 **Pahiyas**	16	17	18	19 **Santa Cruzan**
20 **Pista ng Litson**	21	22	23	24	25	26
27	28	29	30 **Flores de Mayo**			

II. Writing and Speaking Practice

Choose two countries that celebrate the same holiday and compare how they are celebrated. What are some of the similarities and differences? Use the table below to record your responses.

Country: _____	Similarities	Country: _____

III. Writing and Reading Practice

If you could invent your own holiday and/or celebration, what would it be? Draw a picture of this holiday/celebration on a separate sheet of paper. Afterwards, describe this invented holiday/celebration by answering the questions. When you are finished, exchange descriptions with a classmate and read what he or she wrote.

Ano ang pangalan ng pista? _____

Saan ginagawa ang pista? _____

Kailan ginagawa ang pista? _____

Anu-ano ang mga ginagawa sa pista? _____

_____

_____

_____

Bakit ito ginagawa? _____

_____

_____

IV. Listening Practice

 Listen to audio file (20–2) and complete the box below.

> **Word Bank**
>
> **parol** Christmas lantern
> **paligsahan** competition
> **katapangan** bravery
> **pinipintahan** is painting/paints
> **mandirigma** warrior

	Pista	Saan	Kailan	Ginagawa	Dahilan
1.					
2.					
3.					

LESSON 21

Mga Iba't ibang Lugar sa Pilipinas

Places in the Philippines

An Overview of Lesson 21

Objectives
- Give detailed description of events
- Express reaction/feeling about events
- Narrate events in detail

Vocabulary

- Nouns
- Means of Transportation

- Places in the Philippines
- Adjectives

- Verbs (Object- and Actor-Focus)
- Verbs of Direction

Dialogue: Paglalakbay sa Pilipinas *Travel to the Philippines*

Dialogue Comprehension

Activities

Activity 1: Interview
Activity 2: Role-Play
Activity 3: If I Had 100,000 Pesos

Grammar

Examining Form

I.   Contemplated Aspect (**-In**/**I-** Verbs)
     Grammar Presentation: **Sino** + Actor-Focus Verbs/**Sino** + Object-Focus Verbs
     Grammar Notes

Practice
I. Speaking Practice
II. Reading Practice
III. Writing Practice
IV. Listening Practice

Vocabulary 🎧 (21–1)

The vocabulary below will help you describe and express your feelings about events and to participate in the activities in this lesson. Memorize the vocabulary words before proceeding to the dialogue.

Nouns

bayad	fee
labasan	exit
palit	exchange rate
pangarap	dream; goal
pasukan	entrance
payong	umbrella
piloto	pilot
salamin	sunglasses
sekyu	security guard

Means of Transportation

bangka	boat
bapor	ferry
bisikleta	bicycle
bus	bus
dyip	jeepney
eroplano	airplane
FX	taxi van
kalesa	horse-drawn carriage
LRT	Light Rail Transit
motorsiklo	motorcycle
MRT	Manila Railway Transit

padyak	bicycle with sidecar attached
taksi	cab, taxi
traysikel	tricycle, motorcycles with sidecar attached
tren	train

Adjectives

delikado	dangerous
kulang	insufficient
makulay	colorful
sapat	sufficient; enough
sikat	famous

Verbs of Direction

bumaba	to go down
dumiretso	to go straight
kumanan	to turn right
kumaliwa	to turn left
lumiko	to turn
pumarada	to park
sumakay	to ride, get on
umakyat	to go up
umikot	to turn around

Places in the Philippines

Go online and research the following places.

Anilao
Baguio
Banaue
Bicol
Bohol
Boracay
Cebu
Corregidor
Davao
Ilocos Norte
Ilocos Sur
Iloilo
Manila
Palawan
Pangasinan
Puerto Galera
Subic
Tagaytay
Vigan

Verbs

Object-Focus	Actor-Focus	Definition
	-Um- Verbs	
batiin	bumati	to greet
bisitahin	bumisita	to visit
dalawin	dumalaw	to visit
kilalanin	(no actor-focus)	to know someone
kontakin	kumontak	to get in touch with
	Mag- Verbs	
arkilahin	mag-arkila	to rent
bilangin	magbilang	to count
isipin	mag-isip	to think
kanselahin	magkansela	to cancel
kausapin	mag-usap	to talk to someone, to converse
kumbidahin	magkumbida	to invite

-Um- and **Mag-** Verbs		
ibalik	magbalik	to return
ibigin	umibig	to love
iimpake	mag-impake	to pack clothes
ireserba	magreserba	to reserve
itinda	magtinda	to sell
ituro	magturo	to teach
iuwi	mag-uwi	to bring/take home

Dialogue: Paglalakbay sa Pilipinas *Travel to the Philippines*

Hiro has been planning to go to the Philippines. Read his conversation with Jed and answer the Dialogue Comprehension questions.

Hiro: **Oy Jed! Nakabili na ako ng tiket papunta sa Pilipinas.**

Jed: **Talaga, saan-saan ka naman pupunta sa Pilipinas?**

Hiro: **Hindi ko pa masyadong alam. Unang beses kong mamamasyal doon, eh. Ano kaya ang magandang puntahan?**

Jed: **Puwede kang pumunta sa Baguio o Tagaytay. Sikat na sikat ang dalawang lugar na ito dahil sa panahon, sa prutas, at sa mga bulaklak.**

Hiro: **Oo nga. Siguro pupunta ako sa Tagaytay, pagkatapos, tutuloy ako sa Vigan. Marami raw lumang bahay doon at siguro, pupunta na rin ako sa lumang bahay ni dating Pangulong Marcos.**

Jed: **Magandang plano 'yan. Pagkatapos, kung may panahon ka, puwede ka ring pumunta sa Boracay at Palawan. Sikat na sikat ang mga lugar na ito. Nandito raw ang mga pinakamagagandang mga resort sa Pilipinas. Balita ko maganda raw ang mga korales doon at masarap ang mga *seafood*.**

Hiro: **Nako! Tamang-tama, mahilig ako sa mga** *seafood*. **Una kong kakainin ang mga alimango at hipon doon.**

Jed: **O sige, ano pa' ng hinihintay mo? Isulat mo na ang mga plano mo at magtatanong-tanong din ako ng iba pang lugar.**

Dialogue Comprehension

For each of the following statements about the dialogue, place a check mark in the appropriate blank, depending on whether the statement is true, **Tama**, or false, **Mali**.

	TAMA	MALI
1. **Magbabakasyon si Jed sa Pilipinas.**	_____	_____
2. **Pupunta si Hiro sa Baguio, pagkatapos pupunta siya sa Corregidor**	_____	_____
3. **Sikat na sikat ang Corregidor dahil sa mga bulaklak.**	_____	_____
4. **Pagdating ni Hiro sa Boracay, kakain siya ng alimango at hipon.**	_____	_____
5. **Mahilig si Jed sa mga seafood.**	_____	_____

Activities

Activity 1

A. Where in the Philippines would you like to visit in the future and why?

Lugar	Dahilan
Saan: <u>Baguio</u>	**Gusto kong pumunta sa Baguio kasi maganda ang panahon doon at maraming sariwang prutas.**
Saan: _____	
Saan: _____	

B. Interview two of your classmates and ask them about where they would like to visit in the Philippines and why.

Pangalan/Lugar	Dahilan
Hiro **Saan:** <u>Pampanga</u>	**Gustong pumunta ni Hiro sa Pampanga kasi gusto niyang bisitahin ang mga kamag-anak at kaibigan niya doon.**
Saan: _____	
Saan: _____	

Activity 2

Work with a partner. Choose one of the situations below and create a dialogue. After writing the dialogue, act out the situation.

Sitwasyon 1
Nagbabakasyon ka sa Pilipinas nang biglang tumawag ang nanay mo at sinabi niyang kailangan ka na raw umuwi agad. Ang problema wala ka pang tiket. Makipag-usap sa travel agent para mag-book ng lipad mo.

Sitwasyon 2
Nagbabakasyon ka ngayon sa Pilipinas at nawala mo ang mapa mo. Hindi mo ngayon alam kung paano bumalik sa iyong hotel. Kulang ang pamasahe mo para sa taksi kaya gusto mo lang magbus at maglakad. Magtanong ka ng direksyon.

Activity 3

Sumulat ng isang talata tungkol sa sumusunod na pangyayari. Kung mayroon kang isang dang libong piso, saan ka pupunta sa Pilipinas? Bakit mo pinili ang lugar na ito at ano ang mga puwede mong gawin doon? Pagkatapos isulat, basahin ang iyong talata sa klase.

Write a paragraph about the following scenario. If you had PhP100,000.00, where would you go in the Philippines? Why did you choose this place, and what are some of the activities that you would do there? After writing, read your paragraph to the class.

_____

_____

_____

_____

_____

_____

_____

_____

Grammar

Examining Form

The sentences below illustrate the grammar patterns that are presented in this lesson. Review the sentences below and complete the tasks that follow. Discuss your answers with a partner. Consult the following section to check your answers.

1. **Sino ang bumili ng tiket ni Mike papunta sa Pilipinas?**
A1: **Ang Nanay ni Mike.**
A2: **Ang Nanay ni Mike ang bumili ng tiket niya.**
A3: **Bumili ang nanay ni Mike ng tiket niya.**

2. **Sino ang bibisitahin ni Mike sa Vigan**
A1: **Sina Michelle at Linda.**
A2: **Sina Michelle at Linda ang bibisitahin ni Mike sa Vigan.**
A3: **Bibisitahin ni Mike sina Michelle at Linda sa Vigan.**

3. **Sino ang isasama ni Mike sa Pilipinas?**
A1: **Si Katie.**
A2: **Si Katie ang isasama ni Mike sa Pilipinas.**
A3: **Isasama ni Mike si Katie sa Pilipinas.**

4. **Sino ang nagsabi na magandang lugar ang Vigan?**
A1: **Ang Nanay ni Mike.**
A2: **Ang Nanay ni Mike ang nagsabi na magandang lugar ang Vigan.**
A3. **Sinabi ng Nanay ni Mike na magandang lugar ang Vigan.**

1. Look at questions 1, 2, 3, and 4. Underline all the verbs and identify each verb form.
2. Questions 1 and 4 use actor-focus verbs, whereas questions 2 and 3 use object-focus verbs. Discuss your answers to the following questions with your partner:
   a. When do we use actor-focus verbs with the interrogative pronoun **sino**?
   b. When do we use object-focus verbs with the interrogative pronoun **sino**?

3. Look at all the responses and compare A1, A2, and A3. What are the differences in their structure?

I. Contemplated Aspect (**-In/I-** Verbs)

The contemplated aspect is the equivalent of future tense in English grammar. Future tense means that an action has not happened yet but is expected to happen in the future. Remember that when conjugating **-in** verbs for the contemplated form, you reduplicate the first syllable of the infinitive and then follow with the whole infinitive form. However when conjugating **i-** verbs for the contemplated form, you add the root word after the first two syllables of the infinitive.

The chart illustrates how to form the contemplated aspect of –**in**- and **i**- object-focus verbs.

Infinitive	Completed Aspect	Incompleted		Rules for forming the contemplated aspect
sabihin	sinabi	sinasabi	sasabihin	Take the first syllable of the infinitive form, plus infinitive.
hanapin	hinanap	hinahanap	hahanapin	
ibigay	(i)binigay	(i)binibigay	ibibigay	Take the first two syllables of the infinitive, plus root.
ilagay	(i)linagay	(i)linalagay/ inilalagay	ilalagay	

Grammar Presentation

Sino + Actor-Focus Verbs/Sino + Object-Focus Verbs

1. The chart below shows how to form a question with the interrogative pronoun **sino** and **-um-** and **mag-** actor-focus verbs.

Sino + Actor-Focus Verbs					
Interrogative	Marker	Verb		Object	
				Marker	Noun
Sino	ang	bibili magbibigay	ng		tiket? rekomendasyon?

EXAMPLES:
Sino ang babati sa atin? Who will greet us?
Sino ang magkukumbida kay Tobi? Who will invite Tobi?
Sino ang dadalaw sa kaniya? Who will visit him/her?
Sino ang sasama kay Pepe? Who will go with (accompany) Pepe?

2. The chart below shows how to form a question with the interrogative pronoun **sino** and object-focus verbs. In this sentence structure, **sino** translates as *whom* in English.

Sino + Object-Focus Verbs						
What	**Marker**	**Verb**	**Actor**		**Location/Direction**	
			Marker	**Noun/ Pronoun**	**Marker**	**Noun**
Sino	**ang**	isasama	ng ng mga ni nina	<u>bata</u> **Mike** ko natin namin mo ninyo niya nila	sa	<u>Pilipinas?</u>
		bibisitahin				<u>Vigan?</u>

EXAMPLES:

Sino ang babatiin nila? Whom will they greet?
Sino ang kukumbidahin ni Jay? Whom will Jay visit?
Sino ang dadalawin nila? Whom will they visit?
Sino ang isasama ko? Whom will I take with me?

Grammar Notes

1. **Sino** + actor-focus verbs
   Use an actor focus verb whenever the missing information from the **sino** question is the actor of the verb.

   Sino ang bibili ng tiket? Who will buy the ticket?
   Ang nanay ni Mike. (actor) Mike's mother.

   Sino ang magbibigay ng rekomendasyon? Who will give the recommendation?
   Si Patrick. (actor) Patrick.

2. **Sino** + object-focus verbs
   Use an object-focus verb whenever the missing information from the **sino** question is the object of the verb.

   Sino ang isasama ni Mike? Who will Mike bring along?
   Si Katie. (object) Katie.

   Sino ang bibisitahin ni Mike? Who will Mike visit?
   Sina Michelle at Linda. (object) Michelle and Linda.

Practice

I. Speaking Practice

Do some research on the locations listed below and choose two that you would like to visit. Explain why and describe the different activities that one can do there. Use the chart below for your answers.

Anilao	Ilocos Norte
Baguio	**Ilocos Sur**
Banaue	**Palawan**
Bohol	**Pangasinan**
Boracay	**Puerto Galera**
Corregidor	**Subic**
Davao	**Tagaytay**

Lugar	Dahilan	Mga Plano Pagkadating sa Lugar

II. Reading Practice

Panimula

Your group has been assigned to decide who will receive a free package tour to the Philippines. Currently, there are four possible candidates, but only one can be chosen to win the prize of a free roundtrip ticket to the Philippines and PhP 100,000.00.

Carefully consider who should be the winner. You have twenty minutes to read the profile of each candidate and discuss and decide with your group who should win the prize.

Word Bank

kahit even though
makakatulong will be able to help
magsaliksik to research
nakakapagsalita is able to speak
pananaliksik research

Mga Kandidato

Maria Cecilia Santos

Ipinanganak si Maria sa Pilipinas pero pumunta sila ng pamilya niya sa Amerika noong limang taon pa lang siya. *Nakakapagsalita* si Maria ng Tagalog kahit na lumaki siya sa Amerika. Ngayon ay dalawampu't isang taon na siya at pangarap niyang maging isang dyornalista. Sa darating na tag-init, gusto niyang umuwi sa Pilipinas para bisitahin ang kaniyang mga kamag-anak at ang bayan ng kaniyang mga magulang. Iniisip ni Maria na ang biyaheng ito sa Pilipinas ay *makakatulong* sa kaniya para mas maging mabuti siya sa kaniyang trabaho sa hinaharap.

Parehong Pilipino ang mga magulang ni Carlos, pero ipinanganak siya sa Australia. Hindi siya nakakapagsalita ng Tagalog dahil Ingles ang ginamit ng mga magulang niya para kausapin siya noong bata pa siya. Ngayon, nagtatrabaho na si Carlos sa isang bangko at gusto niyang pumunta sa Pilipinas para mas maintindihan nang mabuti ang kultura niya at ng mga magulang niya. Pagdating niya sa Pilipinas, gusto niyang mag-aral ng kultura at wikang Filipino.

Carlos Ramos

William Matthews

Graduate student si Will sa isang unibersidad sa Amerika at ang kaniyang interes sa kaniyang *pananaliksik* ay ang kasaysayan ng Pilipinas noong 1900's. Nag-aral si Will ng Tagalog nang tatlong taon at ngayon ay magaling na siyang magsalita ng Tagalog. Gusto niyang pumunta sa Pilipinas para *magsaliksik* sa mga unibersidad sa Pilipinas at para mag-interbyu ng mga propesor at iba pang mga Pilipino na may kinalaman sa kaniyang pananaliksik. Ito lang ang pagkakataon ni Will na makapunta sa Pilipinas dahil bilang isang estudyante, wala siyang pera.

Isang migrante si Esteban sa Italya. Pumunta siya doon noong nakaraang limang taon. Mahirap ang buhay niya doon at sapat lang ang kinikita niya para makatulong sa pamilya niya sa Pilipinas at mabuhay sa lugar na iyon. Gusto niyang umuwi sa Pilipinas para makita ang kaniyang mga mahal sa buhay kahit sandali lamang.

Esteban Cruz

Ranggo

Based on your group's deliberation, rank the following candidates from highest to lowest with 1 being the highest and most deserving, and 4 the lowest and least deserving of the prize.

_____ Maria Cecilia Santos

_____ Carlos Ramos

_____ William Matthews

_____ Esteban Cruz

Pagpapaliwanag

Explain why you and your group chose this candidate. Use the space provided below to write your groups reasons for choosing this candidate.

_____

_____

_____

_____

_____

_____

_____

_____

III. Writing Practice

Do some quick research into a specific area or location in the Philippines. In a simple paragraph, describe the location you chose by answering the following questions. Use the space provided to write your paragraph.

Anong lugar ito?
Anu-ano ang mga puwedeng gawin sa lugar na ito?
Anu-ano ang mga selebrasyong ipinagdiriwang sa lugar na ito?
Sinu-sino ang mga kilalang taong mula sa lugar na ito?

_____

_____

_____

_____

_____

_____

_____

_____

IV. Listening Practice

Research the Internet and look for the song "Biyahe Tayo" by Rene Nieva. Listen to the song twice and answer the questions in the box below.

Gawain	Pagkain	Pagdiriwang
Base sa kanta, anu-anong mga aktibidad ang puwedeng gawin sa Pagsanjan, Anilao, at Siargao?	Base sa kanta, anu-anong mga pagkain ang puwedeng matikman sa Pampanga, Davao, Dagupan, Bicol, at Balayan?	Base sa kanta, anu-ano ang mga iba't-ibang pagdiriwang na nang-yayari sa Pilipinas?

KULTURANG POPULAR SA PILIPINAS
Popular Culture in the Philippines

When Ferdinand Magellan, the first circumnavigator of the globe, sailed into the islands now known as the Philippine archipelago in 1521, it was reported that the people of the islands sang and chanted sixteen types of songs, various short poems, myths, legends, and epics as they went about their daily living. The native Filipinos "were a singing people." Their myths and legends reflected the people's animistic beliefs, and the Spanish friars who followed Magellan found their way of perceiving and explaining the world laughable. For example, instead of an all-powerful God creating man in his own image and woman from the rib of man, the creation myth they encountered in the Philippines recounts how the first man and woman emerged simultaneously from the nodes of a bamboo. These two myths reflect the clash of the native animistic, matriarchal, egalitarian society with the patriarchal beliefs of Spanish Catholicism. Much of the indigenous oral literature was eradicated, and the native priestesses, called babaylan, were persecuted. What parts of this rich culture were not annihilated were infused by the friars with Christian content to accelerate acceptance of Christianity and conversion. Thus the passion of Christ was chanted in a Southeast Asian way; to this day, it is observed by Filipinos all over the Philippines and even in the diaspora. When the Americans came at the turn of the twentieth century, Hispanized native culture was firmly established.

The American occupation of the Philippines from 1898 to 1946 opened the floodgates for the Americanization of Filipino tastes, values, and culture. The Americans brought vaudeville to Philippine stage and other forms of entertainment. The mass media—radio, television, movies, and American magazines—and the American public educational system, which imposed an American curriculum and English as the medium of instruction from grade school to graduate school, facilitated the wholesale acceptance of American culture and ways of thinking. English became the language of power, government, and education and was an effective tool in the dissemination of American culture. Filipinos followed and imitated the new trends in American arts and cinema, particularly those conveyed by Hollywood. Thus, there are a Fred Astaire, Elvis Presley, and Charlie Chaplin of the Philippines as well as Elizabeth Taylor look-alikes and musical extravaganzas on film patterned after Hollywood. But despite strong American influence, indigenous culture and Spanish Catholicism remained alive and can be discerned in such box office–hit films with folkloric content as *Ang Panday* (*The Blacksmith*), *Pepeng Agimat* (*Jose the Bearer of Talisman*) and *Darna*, the Philippines' wonder woman who existed long before Wonder Woman became a hit in the United States.

Contemporary music and film are two important mediums for popular culture in the Philippines. Through them one is introduced to ideas, perspectives, and influences present in the everyday lives of Filipinos. And just as the people of the Philippines encompass a variety of languages, dialects, religions, political views, and customs, the music of the islands draws on many sources. These varied sources are implicit in the term Original Pinoy or Original Philippine Music—OPM—which refers to music created by Filipinas and Filipinos that draws inspiration from the many traditional Philippine songs and employs indigenous instruments from the different regions. Besides local *kundiman* love songs, the genre is influenced by pop, folk, rock, and ballad songs mainly from the United States and from top Western bands like the Beatles that achieved commercial success during the 1960s and 1970s. Some of the more famous OPM artists in the sixties and seventies include Jose Mari Chan, Pilita Corrales, Nora Aunor, the APO Hiking Society, and Freddie Aguilar. Aguilar in particular received worldwide acclaim for his song "Anak" ("Child") (1977). His rendition of the plaintive, patriotic song "Bayan Ko" ("My Country") (1980) from the pen of popular nationalist poet Jose Corazon de Jesus and set to music in the 1920s by Constancio de Guzman, became the anthem for the People Power Revolution of the 1980s. A popular protest song, "Bayan Ko" has been sung during crucial moments in Philippine history, first against the American occupation of the Philippines in the 1920s and later in the struggle for national democracy in the seventies and eighties. It was also sung during the funeral of the first female president, Corazon C. Aquino, in 2009. Rock 'n' roll was introduced in the 1950s, but the 1990s are notable for the emergence of bands like the Eraserheads (1990s), Rivermaya (1993), Yano, (Simple, 1993), Siakol (Free, Happy and Sometimes Naughty State of Mind, 1994), Parokya ni Edgar (Parish of Edgar, 1993), and Radioactive Sago Project (1999). Two of the most successful Filipino-American musicians are Apl. de Ap of the Black-Eyed Peas and Chad Hugo of Neptunes and N.E.R.D. Today, OPM encompasses all music created by and for Filipinos in the Philippines and in foreign lands—even by foreign composers, but intended for performance by Filipinos.

Other genres of music popular in the Philippines are jazz, Bossa Nova, Latino music, R&B, and reggae. Cebu is known as the Reggae Capital of the Philippines. Hip-hop performed by artists from the Philippines and from the United States is recited in dialects such as Tagalog, Illocano, and Cebuano as well as English. Francis Magalona, who is widely regarded as the King of Pinoy Rap, helped bring the genre into the mainstream with his album *Yo!* This groundbreaking album not only achieved commercial success but was one of the first to articulate complex social messages about drug abuse, political corruption, and poverty in the islands.

Eraserheads (1990s) a new breed of pop/alternative rock band

Philippine cinema is the youngest of all the arts. Film was introduced to the islands in 1897 and, like elsewhere, gradually evolved from silent pictures to talkies and from black-and-white to color. At first, the material was taken from the theater and local literature featuring *zarzuelas*, a kind of musical theater from Spain. In the 1940s, the war brought reality to the movies, but Japanese censorship restricted content. The 1950s saw the golden age of Philippine cinema, which garnered international recognition with such movies as *Genghis Kahn* (1950) by Manuel Conde, shown at the Venice and Cannes Film Festival, and *Anak Dalita* (The Ruins, 1956) by Lamberto Avellana, which won the Golden Harvest Award (Best Picture) at the Asia Pacific Film Festival. The genres that predominated in the 1960s were action, with plenty of Filipino secret agents and cowboys; "bomba," which literally means "bomb," a local term for soft pornographic and B movies; comedy; and drama. However, Philippine cinema also has a history of espousing social messages and exploring social and political themes. During the 1970s, film production was tightly regulated by the Board of Censors for Motion Pictures (BCMP), which was formed to ensure that movies would reflect messages approved by the Marcos dictatorship and promote the governing principles of his so-called New Society. Movies that were deemed to portray the government in a bad light were banned. The social and political environment of the 1970s made it challenging to introduce new themes and approaches to the big screen. Yet, film producers emerged who not only pushed against accepted social and political boundaries but also introduced new styles of directing and editing. Some of the most influential film directors of the 1970s and 1980s include Lino Brocka, Ishmael Bernal, Mike de Leon, Peque Gallaga, and Kidlat Tahimik (Silent Lightning) aka Eric de Guia. Brocka's films often integrated powerful themes pertaining to human rights, national identity, and the LGBTQ (Lesbian, Gay, Bisexual, Transgender, and Queer) community. Tahimik would receive the International Critic's Prize at the Berlin Film Festival for his 1977 experimental film, *Mababangong Bangungot* (*Perfumed Nightmare*).

Since the 1990s, the Philippine movie and music industries have been unable to compete successfully with their American counterparts due to competitive advantages of Hollywood movies, piracy, overtaxation, and a poor economy. However, with digital technologies widely available and no longer affordable only by corporate entities, a new breed of independent film makers has emerged to share their unique stories and visions, bringing home accolades for the country and offering new hope for the ailing industry. Raymond Red, one of the pioneers of independent and alternative cinemas, brought home the prestigious Palme d'Or at the 2000 Cannes Film Festival for his short film *Anino* (*Shadow*). He is one of only two Filipino filmmakers included in the *Oxford History of World Cinema*. In 2009, Brillante Mendoza bested all other entries to the Cannes Film Festival by bringing home the Best Director award for his film *Kinatay* (*Butchered*), about murder and police brutality.

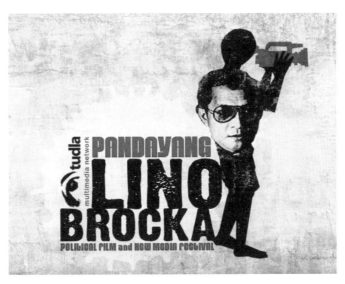

Alternative film festival in honor of director Lino Brocka,
known for relevant and artistic films

LESSON 22

Mga Alamat

Legends

An Overview of Lesson 22

Objectives
• Familiarize yourself with some popular Filipino legends
• Use locative verbs
• Narrate a story

Vocabulary

• Nouns	• **-An/-Han** Verbs	• Adverbs	• Idioms and Expressions
• Adjectives	• Other Verbs	• Suffixes	

Reading Text: Ang Alamat ni Mariang Sinukuan *The Legend of Mary Sinukuan*

Reading Comprehension

Activities

Activity 1: Summary
Activity 2: Skit
Activity 3: Likes and Dislikes

Grammar

Definition of Terms: Indirect Object, Directional-Focus, **-An/-Han** Verbal Suffix, Complement, Actor Complement, Object Complement, Directional Complement

Examining Form

I.   **-An/-Han** Directional-Focus Verbs
     Grammar Presentation
     Grammar Notes
II. Basic Sentence Structure Using Transitive Verbs as Verbal Predicates
     Grammar Presentation
     Grammar Notes

Practice

I.   Speaking Practice
II. Reading Practice
III. Writing Practice
IV. Listening Practice

Vocabulary 🎧 (22–1)

The vocabulary below will help you narrate a story and participate in the activities in this lesson. Memorize the vocabulary words before proceeding to the dialogue.

Nouns

alamat	legend
anting-anting	amulet, invulnerability
bayani	hero
bundok	mountain
bunga	fruit
diwata	fairy, goddess; lovely, beautiful woman
gubat	forest
halaman	plant
pangunahing tauhan	main character; protagonist
puno	tree
puso	heart

Adjectives

mabait	nice
mapagtiis	patient
masipag	hard-working
masungit	short-tempered, irritable
matulungin	helpful
pabaya	careless, negligent
tamad	lazy

Adverbs

samantala	while
sa halip	instead

Suffixes

-an	locative, directional or indirect-object affix
-han	locative, directional or indirect-object affix

Other Verbs

Object-Focus

isumpa	to curse
ipakita	to show
kurutin	to pinch
tuksuhin	to tease
patayin	to kill someone or something

Actor-Focus

gumaling	to feel better, to recover from sickness
magmana	to take after
magpahiram	to lend something to someone
makapasok	to be able to enter
mamatay	to die
mamili	to shop
mag-isa	to be alone
tumabi	to come/go close
tumubo	to grow

-An/-Han Verbs

Infinitive Form	Actor-Focus	Definition
abutan	**mag-abot**	to hand over something to someone
asahan	**umasa**	to rely on
balitaan	**magbalita**	to keep someone posted
basahan	**bumasa**	to read to
bawasan	**magbawas**	to reduce
bayaran	**magbayad**	to pay someone
bigyan	**magbigay**	to give someone something
dalhan	**magdala**	to bring to
halikan	**humalik**	to kiss
hingan	**humingi**	to ask something from someone
hiraman	**humiram**	to borrow something from someone
hulaan	**manghula**	to tell someone one's fortune
kunan	**kumuha**	to take something from someone
kuwentuhan	**magkuwento**	to tell someone a story
lagyan	**maglagay**	to put or place something
lapitan	**lumapit**	to approach someone
ngitian	**ngumiti**	to smile at someone

payagan	pumayag	to allow someone to do something
payuhan	magpayo	to give someone advice
puntahan	pumunta	to go to
sabihan	magsabi	to inform someone
sakyan	sumakay	to ride
sulatan	sumulat	to write someone
samahan	sumama	to go with someone
sundan	sumunod	to follow someone
suutan	magsuot	to dress someone
tawagan	tumawag	to call someone on the phone
tawanan	tumawa	to laugh at someone
tingnan	tumingin	to look at someone/something
turuan	magturo	to teach someone something

Idioms and Expressions

Noong unang panahon . . .   Once upon a time . . . / In the olden days . . .

Reading Text Ang Alamat ni Mariang Sinukuan *The Legend of Mary Sinukuan*

In the olden days, the favorite form of entertainment in the evening was storytelling. Grandmothers or old men used to tell stories in a sing-song manner. Read "Ang Alamat ni Mariang Sinukuan" ("The Legend of Mary, the Undefeated One") and answer the Reading Comprehension questions.

Word Bank

naninirahan living
kalalakihan group of men
gumagalang respecting
nagpasiya decided
pamimitas picking (fruits/vegetables)
sako sack
isinumpa cursed
punuin filled
pinarusahan punished
baboy-ramo wild boar

Noong unang panahon, ayon sa mga tao, may isang matangkad, maganda, at mabait na diwata na *naninirahan* sa Bundok ng Arayat. Madalas siyang bumababa sa bundok para makita ang mga tao. Natutuwa ang diwata sa mga taga-roon sa tuwing nakikita niya ang mga *kalalakihan* na masipag na nagtatrabaho sa bukid, ang mga bata na *gumagalang* sa mga magulang, at ang mga babaeng nagmamahal sa pamilya nila. Dahil dito, tuwing umaga, binibigyan ni Maria ang mga tao ng mga prutas, gulay, at karne.

Ngunit, isang araw, may isang grupo ng kalalakihan ang *nagpasiya* na umakyat sa bundok kahit na alam nilang ipinagbabawal ito ni Maria. "O pare! Talaga pa lang mas madaming mga prutas dito kaysa sa paligid ng bundok. Tara, kainin natin ang mga ito" ang sabi ng isang lalaki habang patuloy ang *pamimitas* sa mga puno. "Oo nga! Pati na mga gulay at mga hayop. O, teka pare! May babaeng papalapit sa atin. Si Maria na yata ito," ang sabi naman ng isa pa.

"Ako si Maria ng Bundok ng Sinukuan," ang pagbati ng diwata sa mga kalalakihan. "Ma… Ma… Maria, kayo po ba ang nagbibigay ng mga pagkain sa amin?" ang sabi ng isang lalaki. Nginitian lamang ni Maria ang mga lalaki at sinabing, "puwede ninyong kainin ang kahit ano'ng gusto ninyo, ngunit huwag ninyo itong ibababa sa bundok," ang sabi ng diwata habang umaakyat papunta sa ituktok ng bundok. Tumango ang mga lalaki habang pinapanood si Maria na papaalis. "O ayan pare, wala na siya, kunin na ninyo ang mga *sako* ninyo at *punuin* na natin ito ng mga prutas, gulay at mga hayop." Nagmadali ang mga lalaki na nagpuno ng mga sako nila pero ang hindi nila alam na habang ginagawa nila ito, pinapanood lang sila ni Maria mula sa ituktok ng bundok.

Habang pababa na ang mga lalaki na dala ang mga sako nila, napansin nila na bumibigat nang bumibigat ang laman nito. "Pare! Sandali lang! Napakabigat nitong dala-dala ko!" ang sabi ng isang lalaki, "Oo nga pare! Tingnan nga natin ang laman nito." Laking gulat ng mga ito nang makita nila na ang laman ng mga sako nila ay naging bato na lamang. "Mga walang utang na loob!" ang malakas na sigaw na narinig ng mga kalalakihan mula sa ituktok ng bundok. Dahil sa sobrang galit ni Maria, *isinumpa* niya ang mga lalaking ito at *pinarusahan* niya sila. Nang, itinuro ni Maria ang kaniyang daliri sa mga ito ay naging *baboy-ramo* ang mga ito. Pagkatapos nito, sinundan pa ito ng iba pang pang-aabuso ng mga tao. Patuloy pa rin ang pagnanakaw nila sa bundok ng mga pagkain. Dahil dito hindi na muling nagpakita si Maria at hindi na rin siya tumulong sa mga tao. Ito ang dahilan kung bakit walang masyadong mga bunga at hayop sa Bundok ng Arayat sa kasalukuyan.

Reading Comprehension

Answer the following questions in Tagalog.

1. **Tungkol saan ang alamat?**

   _____

2. **Ilarawan si Mariang Sinukuan.**

   _____

3. **Saan nakatira si Maria? Ilarawan ito.**

   _____

4. **Anong ginagawa ni Maria tuwing umaga?**

   _____

5. **Ano ang sinabi ni Maria sa mga kalalakihan noong nakita niya sila?**

   _____

6. **Ano ang ginawa ng mga lalaki pagkaalis ni Maria?**

   _____

7. **Ano ang nangyari sa laman ng sako?**

   _____

8. **Ano ang ginawa ni Maria sa mga kalalakihan?**

   _____

9. **Ano ang mensahe ng kwento para sa iyo?**

   _____

10. **Gusto mo ba ang kwento? Bakit?**

   _____

   _____

Activities

Activity 1

Using your own words, write a summary of "**Ang Alamat ni Mariang Sinukuan.**"

_____

_____

_____

_____

_____

_____

_____

_____

Activity 2

In groups of three or four, write a skit based on "**Ang Alamat ni Mariang Sinukuan.**" First, read your script out loud for the teacher to correct, then perform the skit.

_____

_____

_____

_____

_____

_____

_____

_____

_____

_____

In groups of two or three depending on class size, discuss your likes and dislikes about the story you have just read and explain why. Use the table below to record your responses.

Mga Nagustuhan Ko	Mga Hindi Ko Nagustuhan

Grammar

Definition of Terms

Indirect Object	The entity to whom, from whom, and/or for whom the action of the verb is being done. It usually shows the movement of the object toward or away from the actor.
Directional-Focus Verbs	Verbs whose meanings involve some kind of movement toward or in some instances away from the subject of the sentence. It marks the equivalent of the indirect object in an English sentence.
-An/-Han Verbal Suffix	An affix that may indicate location or direction of an action
Complement	A component of a verbal predicate that is a transitive verb. It may be a person, thing, idea, etc. that is not the focus of the action of the verb.
Actor Complement	The doer of the action of a verb that is not actor-focus, expressed as a ng phrase or ng pronoun
Object Complement	The receiver of the action of a verb, expressed as a ng phrase or a sa phrase except with object-focus verbs
Directional Complement	Normally expressed as a sa phrase: **sa** + NOUN, **kay** + PERSONAL NOUN in verbs that are not directional-focus

Examining Form

Review the sentences below and complete the tasks that follow. Discuss your answers with a partner. Consult the following section to check your answers.

Column A	Column B
Nagpunta ang Ita sa palengke.	Pinuntahan ng Ita ang palengke.
Bumibili ng darak si Maria sa mga tao.	Binibilhan ni Maria ng darak ang mga tao.
Nagbigay si Maria ng ginto sa mabuting babae.	Binigyan ni Maria ng ginto ang mabuting babae.
Nagbabayad ng ginto si Maria. sa mga tao.	Binabayaran ng ginto ni Maria ang mga tao.

1. Underline the subjects of the sentences in Column A.
2. Underline the subjects of the sentences in Column B.
3. Circle the actor in each sentence in Column A.
4. Circle the actor in each sentence in Column B.
5. Compare the sentences in column A and B. What differences do you see in sentence structure?

I. **-An/-Han** Directional-Focus Verbs

In the previous seven units, we have learned three different verb focuses and their sets of affixes: actor-focus (**mag-** and **–um-**) in Unit 3 experiencer-focus (**ma-**, **magka-**, and **magkaroon**) in Unit 5; and object-focus (**-in**, **i-**, and **paki-**) in Units 6 and 7. In this lesson, we will devote our attention to understanding directional-focus verbs.

As we've learned, "focus" refers to the semantic relationship a verb has to its subject. Thus, an actor-focus verb selects the doer of the action as its subject, while an object-focus verb selects the direct object or receiver of the action as the subject. A directional-focus verb selects the direction of the action as its subject.

In Unit 7, we pointed out that sentences can be classified according to the focus of the verb used in the predicate. For example, an actor-focus sentence uses actor-focus verbs. An object-focus sentence uses object-focus verbs. Every actor-focus transitive verb has an object-focus or a directional-focus counterpart, and sometimes both. The object-focus or directional-focus counterpart and the sentences formed with that verb have the same meaning as the actor-focus verb or actor-focus sentence but have a different topic or subject than the doer of the action. The topic would be the direct object or the direction of the action.

> EXAMPLES:
> **Nagbigay ako ng singsing kay Ana.** I gave a ring to Ana.
> **Binigyan ko si Ana ng singsing.** I gave Ana a ring.

A directional-focus verb focuses on the equivalent of the English indirect object. An indirect object may be a noun or pronoun that receives the action of the verb indirectly. It answers the question "to whom" or "to what" asked after the verb. In the example above, the indirect object or recipient of the object "ring" is Ana. The first sentence uses the actor-focus verb **nagbigay**, focusing on the subject **ako** that is actor of the verb. The second sentence uses the directional-focus verb binigyan, focusing on "Ana," the subject of the sentence marked by **si**. Notice that the actor is in the **ng** form and not in a focus relationship with the verb.

Indirect objects usually occur with verbs of giving or communicating, like **bigay** (give), **dala** (bring), **sabi** (tell), **kuwento** (tell a story), **kuha** (get), **turo** (teach), etc. They usually name the person or thing to which something is given or for which something is done. The indirect object is the equivalent of "her" in "I gave her a ring."

The affixes used for directional-focus verbs are **-an** and **-han**. The **-an** verbal affix and its variant **-han** mean that the indirect object or the goal or destination of the movement of the verb is the topic or subject of the sentence. In this lesson, the directional-focus verb may indicate that the subject is the equivalent of 1) indirect object in English, the recipient of the object; or 2) the direction of movement or goal of the action.

The **-an/-han** verb indicates the movement of the direct object, marked by **ng**, from the doer of the action, which is also in the **ng** form, to the subject of the sentence, which is in the **ang** form. Hence, the recipient is the topic or subject of the sentence.

EXAMPLES:

Binigyan ko *si Mike* ng bola. I gave *Mike* a ball.

Dinalhan niya *ako* ng pagkain. She/He brought *me* food.

Binayaran ko *si Mike* ng isang daang piso. I paid *Mike* one hundred pesos.

Binasahan ni Maria *ang anak* niya ng libro. Maria read a book *to her child*.

Tinuruan ni Miguel *si Theron* ng Tagalog. Miguel taught *Theron* Tagalog.

Kinuwentuhan niya *ako*. She told *me* a story.

The first three examples indicate that the objects **bola** (ball), **pagkain** (food), and **isang daang piso** (one hundred pesos) are moving from the doer of the action to the subject of the sentence, showing that **-an/-han** verbs have meanings that involve some kind of movement toward or away from the subject of the sentence. For the next two sentences, the direct objects **libro** (book) and **Tagalog** are the information being passed to another individual. The last example employs an intransitive verb, but the kind of information that is being passed on is implicit in the core meaning of the verb base or verb root **kuwento** (story), which is a concrete noun. In all of these examples, the indirect object answers the question, "to whom" concerning the verb and direct object in the English sentence: "To whom did you give a ball," etc.

When we say the source of the direct object, we mean the origin of the direct object. Let us look at the following sentences:

Hiniraman ko *si Maria* ng libro. I borrowed a book *from Maria*.

Binilhan niya *si Patrick* ng kotse. She/He bought a car *from Patrick*.

Ninakawan ng bata *si Kris* ng pera. The kid stole money *from Kris*.

The three sentences above demonstrate that the original source of direct object **libro** (book), **kotse** (car), and **pera** (money) is the subject of the verbs **hiraman** (to borrow from someone), **binilhan** (to buy from someone), or **nakawan** (to steal from someone). In these examples, the question "from whom" in the English sentences helps us identify the subject of the Tagalog sentence.

The verbs in the examples below indicate direction and movement, illustrating that the actor complement is physically moving from one place to another; or the verb shows an idea of some sort of movement exhibited by the actor toward the subject or focus of the verb.

Sinundan ko *siya*. I followed *him/her*.

Linapitan ni Maria *ang bata*. Maria approached *the kid*.

Tiningnan niya *ako*. She/He looked at *me*.

In the first two examples, the actors, **ko** (I), and **Maria** are physically moving from their starting point to their destinations **siya** (she/he), and **bata** (kid). In the third example, though the actor **niya** (she/he) is not really physically moving, the verb **tingnan** still indicates that the actor is coming from one point and what the actor is looking at is the point of its destination and the subject of the sentence.

Now that we have discussed how to use **-an** verbs, let's see how to conjugate them. The chart below gives the conjugation of the verbs **puntahan** (to go to) and **hiraman** (to borrow from someone). The root words that inflect are **punta** (go) and **hiram** (borrow), respectively. To form the infinitive of the verb, attach the suffix **-an** or **-han** to the root word. Use **-an** when the root word ends with a consonant or a glottal stop, and use **-han** when the root word ends with a vowel. Therefore, the root word **punta** takes the suffix **-han**, while hiram takes **-an**. The completed aspect is formed by inserting **-in-** before the first vowel of the infinitive, resulting in **pinuntahan** and **hiniraman**, respectively. The first two syllables of the infinitive followed by the complete infinitive results into incompleted aspect. Lastly, to form contemplated aspect, take the first syllable of the root word and attach the infinitive form of the verb. Notice that the sufix **-an/-han** is always present in all the forms: infinitive, completed, incompleted, and contemplated.

Aspects		-An Verbs	Rules
Infinitive	punta + an	*punta**han***	Attach **-an** or **-han** to end of the root word.
	hiram + an	*hiram**an***	
Completed	p...untahan + in	*p**in**untahan*	From the infinitive, insert **-in** before the first vowel of the infinitive.
	h ... iraman + in	*h**in**iraman*	
Incompleted	pinu + puntahan	*pin**u**puntahan*	Take the first two syllables of the completed aspect, plus the infinitive.
	hini + hiraman	*hin**i**hiraman*	
Contemplated	pu + puntahan	*p**u**puntahan*	Take the first syllable of the root, plus the infinitive
	hi + hiraman	*h**i**hiraman*	

Grammar Presentation

The chart below illustrates how to use directional-focus verbs in a sentence. This is the normal sentence structure for using this kind of verb. The second and third columns give possible **ng** actors or actor complements in a directional-focus sentence. Columns 4 and 5 give some possible subjects or topics of the sentences. The last two columns show the object complement: **ng libro/ ng mga libro**.

Directional-Focus -An Verb						
Verb	Actor		Location/Direction		Direct Object	
-An	Marker	Noun	Marker	Noun	Marker	Noun
Bilhan		mo ninyo		Jamie		
Binilhan [completed]	ni nina	**Patrick** bata	si sina	babae	ng ng mga	libro.
Binibilhan [incompleted]	ng ng mga	ko natin namin mo ninyo niya nila	ang ang mga	ako tayo kami ka kayo siya sila		
Bibilhan [contemplated]						

Below are more examples of directional-focus verbs used in sentences.

EXAMPLES:

Sino'ng dinalhan ng diwata ng prutas noong isang linggo? To whom did the fairy bring the fruit last week?

Dinalhan siya ng diwata ng prutas noong isang linggo. The fairy brought him/her some fruit last week.

Bibigyan ba ni Ben ang matandang babae ng mga pagkain? Will Ben give the old woman some food?

Araw-araw, pinupuntahan niya ang bahay ng kaibigan niya. Every day she/he goes to her/his friend's house.

Grammar Notes

1. You can use –an/-han directional-focus verbs in Tagalog sentences when there is an indirect object in the English sentence. The indirect object in Tagalog becomes the subject of the sentence; thus, **ang** phrases or **ang** pronouns are used. Note that in the first example below "him" in English is in the case of the indirect object, but, since the verb in Tagalog is directional-focus, the pronoun is in the **ang** form, the equivalent of the nominative case.

   A. Pronoun
      Binigyan ko siya ng pagkain. I gave *him* some food.

   B. Proper name
      Binigyan ko *si Maria* ng pagkain. I gave *Maria* some food.

   C. Common noun modified by a possessive pronoun
      Binigyan ko *ang kaibigan ko* ng pagkain. I gave *my friend* some food.

   D. The indirect object in English preceded by the definite article *the*
      Binigyan ko *ang lalaki* ng pagkain. I gave *the man* some food.

2. When there is a prepositional phrase in the English sentence like the one below ("from the library"), it is normally awkward to use an **-an** verb.
      Hiniraman ko *si Mario* ng libro. (correct) I borrowed a book *from Mario*.
      Hiniraman ko *ang aklatan* ng libro. (awkward) I borrowed a book *from the library*.

   The only exception to this rule is when the place has a possessive pronoun.
      Pupuntahan ko ang bahay ng kaibigan ko. (correct) I will go to my friend's house.
      Pupuntahan ko ang bahay. (awkward) I will go to the house.

   Directional-focus verbs are translated into English sentences without direct objects, with the subject of the Tagalog sentence corresponding to the object of the preposition in the English equivalent.
      Pinuntahan ko *ang Cebu.* I went *to Cebu*.

II. Basic Sentence Structure Using Transitive Verbs as Verbal Predicates

In the preceding lessons, we learned about transitive and intransitive verbs. In this section, we will learn about the basic sentence structure when there are transitive verbal predicates that have receivers of action expressed as an object complement, actor complement, or directional complement.

Transitive verbs have one of three focuses: actor, object, or directional. Verbs that don't have complements are intransitive verbs. An actor complement is expressed by a **ng** phrase or **ng** pronoun in sentences that are not actor-focus. The object complement is also expressed by **ng** phrases and pronouns and sometimes by a **sa** phrase. The directional complement is expressed by a **sa** phrase. The complement is not the topic or subject of the sentence but corresponds to the subject of a related major verb formed with the same root word or base. The basic meaning of sentences formed with these different classes of verbs having the same root word but different focus is the same. For example:

a. *Nag*bigay <u>ako</u> ng mga bulaklak kay Sandra. <u>I</u> gave Sandra some flowers.

In this example, the verb uses the prefix **mag-** and is actor-focus Thus, the subject of the sentence is **ako**.

b. *I*binigay ko <u>ang mga bulaklak</u> kay Sandra. I gave Sandra <u>the flowers</u>.

Here, the verb uses the prefix **-i** and is object-focus. The direct object is definite and is marked by **ang**, which makes it the subject of the sentence.

c. **Binigy*an* ko <u>si Sandra</u> ng mga bulaklak.** I gave <u>Sandra</u> some flowers.

In the last example above, the actor is a **ng** pronoun and the object is still **bulaklak**. The focus this time is **Sandra***,* who is the recipient of the direct object.

As you can see, **bulaklak** (flower) is the object complement whatever the focus is. It is preceded by the direct object marker **ng** in both actor-focus and directional-focus sentences. It is still the object complement in object-focus sentence that is a sentence with an object focus verb. Since it is the focus, and focus pertains to the subject of a verb in a sentence, it has to be marked by **ang**.

To summarize, an actor complement corresponds to the subject of an actor-focus verb; an object complement corresponds to the subject of an object-focus verb; and a directional complement corresponds to the subject of a directional-focus verb.

Every major transitive verb belongs to a set of verbs with a common root word. The affixes that form the different verbs using the root word may differ from one another in focus but will have the same meaning, as illustrated above. If the actor-focus verb has an object complement but does not have a directional complement, then the set is included in the object-verb complement kind; if the actor-focus verb has a directional complement but not an object complement, then the set is included in the directional verb complement kind. If the actor-focus verb has both an object complement and a directional complement, then the set is included in the double-object verb complement kind.

All object and directional-focus verbs have corresponding actor-focus verbs. Actor-focus **-um-** verbs would conventionally have **-in-** verb equivalent of the object-focus kind, and **mag-** (AF) would have **i-** verb equivalents in the object-focus set. If a sentence uses an actor-focus verb that has a directional complement, then there will be an **-an** verb counterpart.

EXAMPLE:

AF	**Nagbigay ako sa kanya ng bolpen.**	I gave him/her a ballpen.
DF	**Binigyan ko siya ng bolpen.**	
OF	**Ibinigay ko sa kanya ang bolpen.**	

	Root Word	Affix	Infinitive	Meaning
Actor-Focus	bigay	mag-	*mag*bigay	to give
Object-Focus	bigay	i-	*i*bigay	to give something
Directional-Focus	bigay	-an	bigy*an**	to give to someone

* irregular the "a" in **bigay** is omitted

Now that we have learned all three verbal focuses (actor, object, and directional), let's consider them side-by-side and analyze which focus is more appropriate under certain grammatical circumstances.

The Tagalog word **turo** (to teach) can be conjugated with the **mag-**, **i-**, and **-an** verbal affixes. This means that the focus of a sentence with **turo** can be the actor, the direct object, or the indirect object. Remember that when we talk about focus, we are referring to what is the most important part of the sentence. So, for example, when we say actor focus we mean that in our sentence the actor is the most important piece of information. The same concept applies for the object-focus and directional-focus verbs.

The chart below shows turo with these three affixes in the infinitive and inflected for the three aspects.

	Actor	Object	Directional
Infinitive	magturo	ituro	turuan
Completed	nagturo	itinuro	tinuruan
Incompleted	nagtuturo	itinuturo	tinuturuan
Contemplated	magtuturo	ituturo	tuturuan

The three verb focuses can be used to render the same English sentence—*He teaches me Tagalog*—with three different subjects or focuses.

AF (mag-)	**Nagtuturo** *siya* **ng Tagalog sa akin.**
OF (i-)	**Itinuturo niya sa akin** *ang Tagalog*.
DF (-an)	**Tinuturuan niya** *ako* **ng Tagalog.**

The structure below illustrates an actor-focus sentence.

Actor Focus			
Verb	**Actor**	**Direct Object**	**Indirect Object**
Nagtuturo	siya	ng Tagalog	sa akin.

He teaches me Tagalog.

The structure below illustrates an object-focus sentence.

Object Focus			
Verb	**Actor**	**Direct Object (Subject/Topic)**	**Indirect Object**
Itinuturo	niya	ang Tagalog	sa akin.

He teaches me *Tagalog*.

The structure below illustrates a directional-focus sentence.

Directional Focus			
Verb	**Actor**	**Subject/Topic**	**Direct Object**
Tinuturuan	**niya**	**ako**	**ng Tagalog.**

He teaches *me* Tagalog.

All three sentences are grammatically correct. The preferred focus depends on which element of the sentence the speaker would want to emphasize. To identify which focus to use, it is best to know which has the most priority among the following elements.

Priority of Elements:
1. Direct Object
2. Directional Complement
3. Actor

If the speaker wants to emphasize the performer of the action, then the actor-focus verb would be the recommended verbal predicate for the sentence. If he wants to emphasize or focus on the indirect object, then he should use the directional-focus verb **-an**. However, if he wants to focus on the direct object, then he should use the object-focus verb **i-**. Generally, intransitive verbs use actor-focus verbs. Emphasis on a certain element in the English structure can be expressed by the intonation when speaking or by the use of the passive construction, though this is not the preferred structure in English, where the active voice is usually favored. Here are some sentences in the active voice that emphasize on the different elements of the sentence based on tone and intonation of the voice of the speaker:

I gave *her* the book.
I gave her the book.
I gave her *the book*.
I *gave* her the book.
The book was given to her by me.

In Tagalog, it is the focus system of the verbs that is used to place emphasis on the different elements of the sentence, whether the actor or performer of the action, direct object, or indirect object, or other elements that will be learned in the intermediate and advanced Tagalog courses.

Grammar Presentation

1. Preferred Structure in Tagalog
   When the sentence in English uses a transitive verb, the preferred focus in Tagalog is either the object-focus or directional-focus, depending on whether the object complement or the directional complement is definite or specific. We will explain this concept later.

   Actor-focus verbs are also used in sentences when the topic is being introduced for the first time. The sentence "I will cook chicken tonight" can be translated into three ways, but the preferred structure is actor-focus: "**Magluluto ako ng manok mamayang gabi.**" instead of "**Iluluto ko ang manok mamayang gabi.**" or "**Lulutuin ko ang manok mamayang gabi.**"

   Aside from the above generalization, here are a few guidelines to help you decide which focus to use in a particular sentence construction. These are just general guidelines, and only after a substantial amount of exposure to a lot of material and immersion in the language and culture will you have a feel for what is the best focus and which are the best affixes to use to put across the exact meaning that you want to express.

Actor-focus verbs should be used instead of object-focus verbs in specific instances. The general rule is that if one is talking or asking about the actor or agent of the action or what is being done, then an actor-focus verb is used.

> **Bakit ka nagsusulat?** Why are you writing? (intransitive; talking about the actor)
> **Sino ang sumusulat?** Who is writing? (intransitive; asking for the actor)

> **Maglakad na lang tayo.** Let's just walk. (intransitive)
> **Kumain muna tayo.** Let's eat first. (intransitive) } what would be done?

2. The Direct-Object and Object-Focus Verb

As we have seen, Tagalog sentence structure and parts of speech can be different from what you are familiar with in English. A case in point is what is termed the direct object in a sentence, which is not the same in the two languages. In order to understand this, let us touch first on the concept of definite and indefinite, or specific and non-specific.

In English, the definite article *the* conveys specificity, whereas the indefinite articles *a/an* or *some* convey non-specificity: "the stew" versus "some stew." A definite noun phrase is introduced by **the**, and an indefinite noun phrase is a phrase introduced by an indefinite article *a/an* or **some**. The equivalent of definitie article in Tagalog is the subject marker **ang**.

We first enountered this concept of "definiteness" early on when we introduced the identificational or equational sentence, where both the subject and the predicate are **ang** forms. By **ang** forms we mean the **ang** pronouns (**ako**, **ka**, **siya**, **tayo**, **kami**, **kayo**, **sila**, **ito**, **iyan**, **iyon**) and the constructions **ang** (or its plural form **ang mga**) plus a common noun, or **si** (or its plural form **sina**) plus the name of a person or a pet animal.

> **Si Pat ang sekretarya.** Pat is <u>the</u> secretary. (definite or specific)
> **Ang lalaki ang direktor ng pelikula.** The man is the director of the film. (definite or specific)
> **Sina Jose ang mga estudyante.** Jose and others are <u>the</u> students. (definite or specific)
> **Ang mga bata ang mga bida sa pelikula.** The children are <u>the</u> main characters (protagonists) in the film. (definite or specific)
> **Adobo ito.** This is adobo. (indefinite or non-specific)
> *Ang* **adobo ito.** This is *the* adobo. (definite or specific)

All subjects or topics of a Tagalog sentences are definite. That is, they are all marked by **ang**. The **ang** pronouns are considered definite as well.

3. Object-Focus Verb or Actor-Focus Verb?

Generally, if one is talking about the direct object, that is, the item that receives the action of the verb, the object-focus verb is used. The topic of the following sentences is the direct object:

Siya ang kakausapin mo.	It is her you're going to speak to.
	You're going to speak to her.
Ano ang lulutuin natin?	What are we going to cook?
Sinigang. Lutuin na natin.	Sour soup. Let's cook it now.

Siya in the first sentence is the direct object. The interrogative **ano** in the second sentence above is the direct object. In the last sentence, *it* in English translation stands in for something that both the speaker and listener know already. In Tagalog, *it* isn't stated, which brings us to the second use of object-focus verbs.

When the direct object is already known in the conversation, as in the last example, the object-focus verb is sufficient to express the English *it*. The sentences below have an object-focus verb predicate and no subject or topic. The direct object is not stated, unlike in English, which needs to use *it* for this purpose.

> **Lutuin na natin.** Let's cook it now.
>
> **Kainin mo na.** Eat it now.

We can supply a subject or topic for the sentences above and make the direct object definite. In this case, the subject is marked by **ang**. The English equivalent is marked by *the*. (**Tinola** is a kind of soup in which you first sauté ginger, onion, garlic, and chicken.)

> **Lutuin na natin *ang* tinola.** Let's cook the *tinola* now.

The third use of the object-focus verb is when the direct object in the English sentence is definite, that is, the direct object is introduced by the definite article *the* and not the indefinite article *a/an* or *some*. If the direct object is indefinite, use the actor-focus verb. Referring to the example above, if you wished to say "Let's cook *some* tinola now," you would express this as: **Magluto na tayo ng tinola.** Or, for another example: **Kumain na tayo ng hapunan.** Let's eat dinner now.

> **OF** **Bilhin mo *ang* CD.** Buy *the* CD.
>
> **AF** **Bumili ka *ng* CD.** Buy *a* CD.

When the possessor of the direct object is stated, either with a pronoun or a proper name, this makes the direct object specific and the object-focus verb is used.

> **Hiniram ko ang libro niya.** I borrowed *his* book.
>
> **Hiniram ko ang kotse nila.** I borrowed *their* car.
>
> **Hiniram ko ang libro ni Sandra.** I borrowed Sandra's book.

The object-focus verb is also used when the direct object in English is a pronoun. Because the direct object is the subject or topic in Tagalog structure, the **ang** pronoun is used instead of the equivalent **sa** form, sa kanya: **Sinuntok ko siya.** (I punched *him*.)

> **AF** *****Sumuntok ako sa kanya.** (incorrect)
>
> **OF** *****Sinuntok ko sa kanya.** (incorrect)
>
> **OF** **Sinuntok ako.** (correct: **ako** receives the action.)
>
> I was punched.

4. When to Use Directional-Focus Verbs

When there is an indirect object, use the directional-focus verb if the verb is transitive and the direct object is not specific, that is, not preceded by the definite article *the*.

> **DF** **Binigyan ko siya *ng* libro.** I gave him *a* book.
>
> **DF** **Binigyan ko si Ligaya *ng* bulaklak.** I gave Ligaya *a* flower.

In the above examples, **siya** and **si Ligaya** are definite, being the subjects or topics of the directional sentences, and **libro** and **bulaklak** are indefinite..

> **OF** **Ibinigay ko *ang* kotse sa kanya.** I gave *the* car to him.
>
> **AF** **Ako *ang nagbigay* ng kotse sa kanya.** I was *the one* who gave her the car.

The chart below uses the root word **bili** (buy) to illustrate the three verb focuses (actor, object and directional) in their three aspects as well as the infinitive.

	Actor	Object	Directional
Infinitive	bumili	bilhin	bilhan
Completed	bumili	binili	binilhan
Incompleted	bumibili	binibili	bibilhan
Contemplated	bibili	bibilhin	bibilhan

The uses of three verb focuses are expressed in the following charts for the English sentence *He will buy some food in the cafeteria*. The structure below illustrates an actor-focus sentence.

Actor Focus				
Verb	Actor	D.O.	Indirect Object	Directional Complement/ Prepositional Phrase
Bibili	siya	ng pagkain	para sa akin	sa kapetirya.

The structure below illustrates an object-focus sentence.

Object Focus				
Verb	Actor	D.O.	Indirect Object	Directional Complement/ Prepositional Phrase
Bibilhin	niya	ang pagkain	para sa akin	sa kapetirya.

The structure below illustrates a directional-focus sentence.

Directional Focus				
Verb	Actor	Subject/Topic	D.O.	Indirect Object
Bibilhan	niya	ang kapetirya	ng pagkain	para sa akin.

All three sentences are grammatically correct, but, as was mentioned earlier, it is awkward to use an -**an** verb when the equivalent in the English sentence is a prepositional phrase. Again, the most appropriate focus depends on the speaker's intention: actor-focus if he or she wants to emphasize the performer of the action, or object-focus if he or she wants to emphasize the direct object or receiver of the action. Another sentence that would aslo be correct is: "**Bibilhan niya** *ako* **ng pagkain sa kapetirya.**" This sentence makes the person benefiting from the action of the verb as focus or subject/topic of the sentence. This is called a benefative-focus sentence but will not be studied in this lesson.

Grammar Notes

1. Remember the order of priority of the elements in a sentence when deciding which focus to use.
   a. direct object
   b. directional complement
   c. actor

2. The indirect object in an English sentence is the subject in the Tagalog sentence using an -an directional-focus verb.

    Binigyan ko *siya* ng lbro. I gave *him* the book.

3. Directional-focus verbs can be used when there is no direct object in the English sentence but instead a prepositional object. In this case, the subject or topic of the Tagalog sentence corresponds to the object of the preposition in the English equivalent.

    Pinuntahan niya *ang Boracay*. He went to *Boracay*.

4. All subjects/topics in a Tagalog sentence are definite.

Practice

I. Speaking Practice

A. My Legend

Research the Internet about a legend or folktale that you know. In the table below, list the most important details and events of the plot. Write in complete sentences and employ the different verb focuses that you have learned. Afterwards, based on what you have written, tell the story to the class.

Alamat ng _____
* _____
* _____
* _____
* _____
* _____
* _____
* _____
* _____
* _____

B. Interview

Now interview a classmate about the legend that he or she chose. In the left box below, list all the important details or events of your partner's legend. In the right box, illustrate a scene from the story based on what you understand from your partner's story.

Alamat	Mga Pangyayari

II. Reading Practice

In his novel *Noli Me Tangere* (*Touch Me Not*, 1887), the author Rizal relates the myth of Bernardo Carpio, King of the Tagalogs. Originally, this character came from Spanish-Portuguese history and legend, but he has become a popular hero for Filipinos. In the passage below, read his story and learn about his exploits and why he is important in Philippine consciousness.

Word Bank

makadiyos religious	**pang-aapi** oppression
mandirigma warrior	**mag-alsa** to revolt
nakakatayo can stand	**bihagin** to capture
nakakalakad can walk	**kapangyarihan** power
kagubatan forest	**ipitin** to trap
mangaso to hunt	**patibong** trap
binubunot pulling	**nagpulong** met
sagabal obstacle	**pagsusubok** trying

Si Bernardo Carpio: Ang Hari ng mga Tagalog
Ang Alamat ng Lindol at ang Kuwento ni Bernardo Carpio

Noong unang panahon habang nasa Pilipinas pa ang mga Espanyol, mayroong isang mag-asawang naninirahan sa bayan ng San Mateo, Rizal. Mabait, *makadiyos*, at matulungin ang mag-asawa. Sa bayan nila, lagi nilang tinutulungan ang mga batang mahihirap. Binibigyan nila ang mga ito ng laruan at pagkain. At tuwing hapon naman, laging pumupunta ang mag-asawa sa simbahan para magdasal. Lagi silang nagdarasal na sana isang araw magkaroon sila ng anak.

Dahil sa labis-labis na pagdarasal ng mag-asawa, pinakinggan sila ng Diyos at binigyan sila ng isang lalaking anak. Bukod pa rito, binigyan din ng Diyos ng pambihirang lakas ang anak nila. Ito ang naging dahilan kung bakit pinangalanan nila siyang Bernardo Carpio. Pangalan ito mula sa isang makisig, malakas, at sikat na *mandirigma* mula sa Espanya. Sinasabi na *nakakatayo* at *nakakalakad* na ang sanggol noong isang buwan pa lang ito. At kapag isinasama siya ng tatay niya noong bata pa lang siya sa *kagubatan* para *mangaso*, *binubunot* niya, gamit ang kamay niya, ang mga puno na *sagabal* sa daan nila.

Isang hapon, habang nasa kagubatan si Bernardo, nakarinig siya ng sigaw ng hayop. Tumakbo siya papunta dito at nakita niya ang isang kabayo na may sugat. Ginamot niya agad ito. Nang magaling na ang kabayo, lagi na silang dalawang magkasama kahit saan siya magpunta. Pinangalanan niyang Hagibis ang kabayo niya.

Isang araw, dahil sa pagkapagod ng mga Pilipino sa *pang-aapi* ng mga Kastila, nag-usap-usap ang mga tao na *mag-alsa*. Pinili nila si Bernardo na maging lider ng rebolusyon nila. Narinig ng mga Kastila ang balitang ito at dahil sa takot ng mga Kastila, tinawag nila ang kaibigan nilang engkantado para tulungan sila na *bihagin* si Bernardo. Nagpadala sila ng imbitasyon kay Bernardo na magkita sa isang bundok sa Rizal. Hindi alam ni Bernardo na may inihandang bitag ang mga Kastila. Pagdating ni Bernardo sa ibaba ng bundok, nagulat na lang siya nang may dalawang batong biglang nahulog sa magkabilang gilid niya. Ginamit ng engkatado ang *kapangyarihan* niya para *ipitin* si Bernardo. Sinubukang tumakas ni Bernardo sa mga bato pero magkasinlakas lang silang dalawa ng engkantado. Hindi na makaalis si Bernardo sa *patibong* na ito. Sa tulong ni Hagibis, nakita ng mga rebolusyunaryo kung nasaan si Bernardo. Pero dahil sa kapangyarihan ng engkantado, hindi sila makatulong sa kaniya.

Malaking kawalan ang sinapit ni Bernardo sa mga rebolusyunaryo dahil sa pagkawala ng isang malakas at matapang na lider. Pero lumipas ang ilang taon at nang handa nang lumaban ang mga Pilipino, *nagpulong* ang mga kalalakihan at ginawa nila ang unang sigaw ng giyera sa karangalan ni Bernardo Carpio. Ngayon, sinasabi na sa tuwing lumilindol, ito ang *pagsubok* ni Bernardo na makawala sa dalawang nag-uumpugang mga bato.

Reading Comprehension

Answer the following questions in Tagalog.

1. **Tungkol saan ang alamat?**

   _____

2. **Ilarawan ang mga magulang ni Bernardo Carpio.**

   _____

3. **Ilarawan si Bernardo Carpio.**

   _____

4. **Ano ang nakita ni Bernardo sa gubat isang araw? Ilarawan ito.**

   _____

5. **Ano ang sitwasyon sa Pilipinas sa panahon ni Bernardo Carpio?**

   _____

6. **Ano ang ginawa ng mga Kastila kay Bernardo? Bakit?**

_____

7. **Ilarawan ang engkantado.**

_____

8. **Ano ang dahilan kung bakit lumilindol?**

_____

9. **Ano ang mensahe ng kuwento para sa iyo?**

_____

10. **Gusto mo ba ang kuwento? Bakit?**

_____

_____

III. Writing Practice

Who is your favorite hero? Based on the two legends that you just read, create a similar story describing your hero and his exploits. Your story could be an origin myth like the origin of the name **Bundok Sinukuan** for Mt. Arayat in Pampanga or the origin of earthquakes, similar to the legend of Bernardo Carpio.

Ang Alamat ng _____

_____

_____

_____

_____

_____

_____

IV. Listening Practice

Listen to audio file (22–2).and answer the following questions.

1. **Sinu-sino ang mga pangunahing tauhan sa kuwento?**

_____

2. Ano ang nangyari sa magnanakaw ng kalabaw pagkakain niya ng lansones?

_____

3. Sino ang nakita ng mga tao na nakaputi na pumunta sa lansonesan at kumain nito?

_____

4. May nangyari ba sa babaeng nakaputi pagkakain niya ng lansones?

_____

5. Ano ang tanda na wala nang lason ang lansones?

_____

Sine at Telebisyon
Cinema and Television

An Overview of Lesson 23

Objectives
• Give and understand a summary of a movie
• Express your response to a movie

Vocabulary

• Nouns	• Causative Verbs	• Prefixes
• Adjectives	• Other Verbs	• Idioms and Expressions

Reading Text: Minsa'y Isang Gamu-gamo *Once a Moth (1976)*

Reading Comprehension

Activities
Activity 1: My Favorite Movie
Activity 2: Interview
Activity 3: Muted Dialogue

Grammar
Definition of Terms: Causative Verbs, Direct Actor, Indirect Actor, Main Clause, Subordinate Clause, Time Clause, **Pagka-**, Verbal Root Word

Examining Form
I.   **Pagka-** (Time-clause Verbal Prefix)
     Grammar Presentation
     Grammar Notes
II. The Causative Verb **Magpa-** (Indirect-Actor Focus)
     Grammar Presentation
     Grammar Notes

Practice
I.   Speaking Practice
II.   Reading Practice
III. Writing Practice
IV.   Listening Practice

Vocabulary 🎧 (23–1)

The vocabulary below will help you speak about movies and what you think about them and to participate in the activities in this lesson. Memorize the vocabulary words before proceeding to the dialogue.

Nouns

artista	actor
bakbakan	action
balita	news
banghay	plot
bida	main character
bidang babae	heroine
bidang lalake	hero
drama	drama
eksena	scene
habulan	chase
huli	end
kalakaran	system
kasukdulan	climax
kawalan ng hustisya	injustice
komedya	comedy
kontrabida	villain
kuwento	story
militar	military
nangyari	happen
palabas	show
pamagat	title
pamahalaan	government
pangyayari	event
patalastas	commercial
pagbabalik-tanaw	flashback
pelikulang iyakan	dramatic movie
programa	program
sine	movie
sineng iyakan	tear-jerker

simula	start, opening, beginning
sundalo	soldier
tagpuan	setting
tauhan	character
tunggalian	conflict
trahedya	tragedy

Adjectives

nakakaawa	pitiful
nakakatawa	funny
nakakatakot	scary
nakakaiyak	makes one cry
nakakainis	annoying
nakakagulat	surprising, suspenseful
nakakalito	confusing
nakakalungkot	sad, causing sorrow or distress
nakakabato	boring
pangunahin	main

Causative Verbs

magpaalis	to have someone leave
magpabigay	to have someone give something
magpabili	to have someone buy
magpagawa	to have someone do something

magpahintay	to have someone wait
magpainom	to have someone drink
magpakain	to have someone eat
magpakuha	to have someone get/take
magpalinis	to have someone clean
magpaluto	to have someone cook
magpapunta	to have someone go
magpasama	to have someone go with
magpatulong	to have someone help
magpaturo	to have someone teach
magpatawag	to have someone call

Other Verbs

mangarap	to dream
talakayin	to tackle, to discuss

Prefixes

magpa-	a causative verbal affix
pagka-	after, upon

Idioms and Expressions

bigla na lang . . .	all of a sudden . . .
Sino ang bida sa sine?	Who is the main character?
Saan ginawa ang sine?	Where was the movie made/shot?

Reading Text: Minsa'y Isang Gamu-gamo *Once a Moth*

It's Saturday afternoon, and Grace and Gigette are deciding on what movie to watch for their film class. Read the summary of the movie below and help them by answering the Reading Comprehension questions.

> ### Word Bank
>
> **ngunit** but
> **papeles** documents
> **nabaril** shot (accidental verb)
> **idinedemanda** suing

Ang sineng ito ay tungkol kay Corazon, isang babaeng nakatira malapit sa base militar ng Estados Unidos sa Pilipinas. Kahit na maraming pang-aabusong ginagawa ang mga Amerikano sa mga Pilipino noong panahong iyon, nangarap pa rin siya na pumunta sa Amerika para hanapin ang kaniyang "American dream". **Gusto niyang magtrabaho sa Amerika bilang nars at makakuha ng green card. Pagkakuha niya ng** green card, **gusto niyang kunin ang kaniyang pamilya papunta sa Amerika.**

    Ngunit nang handa na ang mga papeles niya papunta sa Amerika, bigla na lang may trahedyang nangyari. Habang okupado ang buong pamilya ni Corazon sa paghahanda para sa isang salu-salo, nagpaalam ang bata niyang kapatid na pupunta sa bukid. At dahil maraming ginagawa ang lahat, hindi nila siya pinansin. Habang nagpapaturo si Corazon ng mga Pilipinong sayaw sa mga kaibigan niya at nagpapaluto ng pagkain ang nanay ni Corazon, umalis ang kapatid niya at pumunta sa bukid. Doon, may mga sundalong Amerikano na namamaril ng mga hayop. Sa hindi inaasahang pangyayari, nabaril ang kapatid niya at namatay ito. Nagdemanda ang pamilya ni Corazon pero ang naging problema ay nang idinedemanda

na niya ang sundalo, lumabas ang kawalan ng hustisya. Pagkarinig ng sundalo na may subpoena siya, agad siyang nagpakuha ng tiket pabalik sa Amerika. Tinatalakay din ng sineng ito ang relasyon ng Pilipinas at ng Amerika.

Reading Comprehension

1. Ano ang magiging trabaho ng babae pagkadating niya sa Amerika?

_____

2. Ano ang kailangan ng babae para mapetisyon ang kaniyang pamilya papunta sa Amerika?

_____

3. Ano ang trahedyang nangyari?

_____

4. Nasaan ang kapatid niya?

_____

5. Ano ang nangyari sa sundalo na nakabaril sa kapatid ng babae?

_____

Activities

Activity 1

What is your favorite movie? Write the title of the movie in the box on the left and provide a short summary of the movie's plot.

Sine	Buod

Activity 2

Interview two classmates about their favorite movies and fill in the table below.

Sine	Buod
_____	_____
	_____
	_____
	_____
_____	_____
	_____
	_____
	_____

Activity 3

Choose a partner. You and your partner will face each other, but one of you will also face the television or video screen while the other will face in the opposite direction. The teacher will play a short video clip without any sound. The student looking at the screen must describe in detail what she or he sees. At the end of the clip, the teacher will ask all the students who are facing the back to describe what the video clip is about. When they have finished, the teacher will play the clip with the sound on to check how accurate the students' descriptions are.

Grammar

Definition of Terms

Causative Verbs	Verbs that express the idea that someone is causing another person to perform an action.
	EXAMPLE:
	Nagpaluto ako sa kapatid ko ng manok. I had my brother cook chicken.
Direct Actor	Someone who directly performs an action. "My brother" is the direct actor in the following sentence, because "my brother" is the one who cooked the chicken.
	EXAMPLE:
	Nagpaluto ako *sa kapatid ko* **ng manok.** I had *my brother* cook chicken.
Indirect Actor	Someone who causes another person to perform an action. The pronoun "I" is the indirect actor in this sentence. The "I" caused "my brother" to cook the chicken.
	EXAMPLE:
	Nagpaluto *ako* **sa kapatid ko ng manok.** *I* had my brother cook chicken.

Clause	A group of words with a verb, which may or may not form a complete sentence.
Main Clause	A clause that expresses a complete thought. Sometimes called an independent clause, the main clause includes both a subject and a predicate that express a complete thought. EXAMPLE: **Pagkakain ko, <u>umalis sila</u>.** Once/After I finished eating, <u>they left</u>.
Subordinate Clause	A clause that cannot stand alone and is introduced by a subordinating conjunction like **bago** (before), **pagkatapos** (after), **dahil** (because), **bagamat** (although), **kung**, **kapag** (if), **habang** (while), **nang** (when), etc.
Time Clause	A subordinate clause that describes when the action of the verb in the main clause of a sentence occurred. It provides a time frame or frames the action of the verb in the main clause. The subordinating conjunction **nang** (when) is also used in time clauses. This will be taken up in the next lesson. EXAMPLE: <u>**Pagkakain ko, umalis na sila.**</u> <u>Once/After I finished eating</u>, they left.
Pagka-	Time-clause prefix attached to verbal root that conveys the meaning "after performing the action indicated in the core meaning of the root word." It expresses the time after the action of the root.
Verbal Root Word	Sometimes called a verbal stem or verbal base; provides the core meaning of the action of the verb. Usually, a verbal base is a root word.

Examining Form

Review the sentences below and complete the tasks that follow. Discuss your answers with a partner. Consult the following section to check your answers.

1. **Pagkakuha niya ng green card, gusto niyang kunin ang kaniyang pamilya papunta sa Amerika.**
2. **Pagkarinig ng sundalo na may subpoena siya, agad siyang bumalik sa Amerika.**
3. **Pagkadating niya sa Amerika, gusto niyang maging nars.**
4. **Pagkabalik niya sa bahay, nagulat siya sa balita.**
5. **Nagpapaturo si Corazon ng mga Pilipinong sayaw sa mga kaibigan niya.**
6. **Nagpapaluto ng pagkain ang nanay ni Corazon.**
7. **Nagpakuha siya ng tiket pabalik sa Amerika.**

For sentences 1–4,
1. Underline the time clause and box the main clause.
2. Notice the actor used in the time clause: what set of markers and pronouns was used? Is this consistent in all four sentences?

For sentences 5–7
3. Underline the direct actor, circle the indirect actor, and box the direct object.
4. Which part of the sentence takes the **ang** phrase?

I. Pagka- (Time-Clause Verbal Prefix)

Pagka- is a verbal affix that is used to convey an action that frames another action. When attached to a verbal root, it imparts the idea of "after (doing/having done)" or "upon (doing/having done)." It is used to indicate a particular moment. For example, **pagkaalis** combines **pagka-** and **alis** (leave) and means "after leaving, upon leaving." The action denoted by **pagka-** + VERBAL ROOT is a completed action.

Root word	Pagka- + Verbal Root	Rule
alis (leave)	**pagkaalis** (right after someone left)	Affix **pagka-** to the verbal root word.
dating (arrive)	**pagkadating** (right upon arrival)	

Grammar Presentation

1. The chart and examples below illustrate how to use the time-clause prefix **pagka-** in a subordiate clause. **Pagka-** can be termed a prefix that forms adverbs denoting the time after the action indicated by the core meaning of the root word attached to it. Notice that the actor after **pagka-** + VERBAL ROOT is always a **ng** form. This is the same form required when using **pagkatapos** (after), an adverb that we studied in Unit 5.

Time Clause			
Pagka- + Verbal Root Kain	**Actor**	**Direct Object**	**Location**
Pagkakain	ni **Mario** nina **Mario** ng **lalaki** ng mga **lalaki** ko natin/namin mo ninyo niya nila	ng **prutas** ng mga **prutas**	sa **bahay**,...

EXAMPLES:

Pagkarating nila sa bahay ...   After they came home ...
Pagkabili ko ng bahay sa syudad ...   After I bought a house in the city ...
Pagkaalis ni Hiro ...   After Hiro left ...

2. The following chart and examples show how to form a complete sentence with a time clause. Notice that we always start a sentence with the time clause, followed by a main clause. In the examples below, both actions happened in the past, but the action in the time clause happened before the action in the main clause.

Pagka- Sentence Structure	
Time Clause	**Main Clause**
Pagka- + Verbal Root Alis	
Pagkaalis ni Mario sa bahay,	**pumunta siya sa eskwelahan.**

EXAMPLES:

Pagkarating nila sa bahay, nagsimula na kaming kumain. After they came home, we started eating.

Pagkabili ko ng bahay sa syudad, mas malapit na ang biyahe ko sa eskwelahan. Since I bought a house in the city, my commute to school is closer.

Pagkabalik ni Hiro sa Pilipinas, pumunta siya sa bahay ng mga magulang niya. After Hiro returned to the Philippines, he went to his parents' house.

Grammar Notes

1. The actor in the time clause must be a **ng** phrase or a **ng** pronoun.

   EXAMPLE:

   Pagkakain niya, pupunta siya sa parke. After she/he eats, she/he will go to the park.

2. **Pagka-** can be followed by any verbal root or root word used to form a Tagalog verb.

pagka- + **ligo**	→	**pagkaligo**	after/upon taking a shower
pagka- + **sabi**	→	**pagkasabi**	after/upon saying

3. The main clause can be any of the following:

   a. Existential sentence

   Pagkagising ko, mayroong mga bulaklak sa tabi ng kama ko. After I woke up, there were flowers next to my bed.

   b. Identificational sentence

   Pagkaluto ko ng pagkain, siya ang naghugas ng mga plato. After I cooked dinner, she/he was the one who washed the plates.

   c. Actor focus–verb sentence

   Pagkakain niya, mag-aaral siya. After she/he eats, she/he will study.

   d. Direct object focus–verb sentence

   Pagkaluto ni Patrick, lilinisin niya ang kuwarto niya. After Patrick cooks, he will clean his room.

   e. Directional focus–verb sentence

   Pagkakuha ng titser ng award, binigyan siya ng mga estudyante niya ng (mga) bulaklak. After the teacher received the award, his/her students gave him/her flowers.

4. The action in the time clause can be a completed action or a possible action that has not happened yet but may happen, while the action in the main clause can be a completed or contemplated action. The action in the main clause happens after the action in the time clause.

   Pagkaligo ko, kakain ako. After I take a bath, I will eat.

   Pagkaligo ko, kumain ako. After I took a bath, I ate.

5. **Nang** (When): Subordinating Conjunction in a Time Clause
    Nang is a subordinating conjunction used in a time clause to denote a sequence of events relating a time clause to the main clause. Like in the time clause **pagka-** + VERBAL ROOT, the action in the **nang** time clause happens before the action in the main clause. Unlike **pagka-**, the action in the **nang** temporal clause can be in the infinitive form or completed, incompleted, or contemplated aspect.

    > **Nang makuha ng titser ang award, binigyan siya ng mga estudyante ng bulaklak.**
    > **Nang nakuha ng titser ang award, binigyan siya ng mga estudyante ng bulaklak.**

    Both sentences above can be translated as: When the teacher got the award, the students gave her/him a flower. Here are some more examples:

    > **Nang nagluluto ako, dumating ang kartero.** When I was cooking, the postman came.
    > **Nang aalis na ako, biglang umulan.** When I was about to leave, the rain poured/it rained suddenly.

    Other subordinating conjunctions, which we will encounter in the next lesson, are **kapag** and **kung**, both translated as "if" and used to form a subordinate clause that denotes a condition for the action in the main clause.

II. The Causative Verb **Magpa-** (Indirect-Actor Focus)

Magpa- is a causative verbal affix for expressing when a person wants someone to do or make something. When using the **magpa-** affix, two actors are involved, the direct and the indirect actors. The direct actor is the one who directly performs the action, while the indirect actor is the one causing someone to do an action. The indirect actor is the focus, which means the indirect actor takes the **ang** phrase.

Inflection	Aspect	Inflection	Rules
Uwi	Root Word	**Luto**	
magpauwi	Infinitive	*magpaluto*	Prefix **magpa-** to the root word
nagpauwi	Completed	*nagpaluto*	From the infinitive, change **m** to **n**.
nagpapauwi	Incompleted	*nagpapaluto*	From the infinitive, reduplicate **pa**.
magpapauwi	Contemplated	*magpapaluto*	From the incompleted, change **n** to **m**.

Grammar Presentation

The chart and examples below use **magpa-**affixed verbs in a sentence. These are actor-focus verbs. The subject or topic denotes the person or persons causing the action to be enacted. In the typical word order, the verb is followed by the indirect actor, which is marked by an **ang** phrase, and these are followed by the direct actor and then the object. The direct actor is caused to perform the action and is marked by a **sa** marker or replaced by a **sa** pronoun. Sometimes, there may be some confusion in this structure, because the form of the direct actor is the same as the form of a directional complement. In addition, the place or prepositional phrase is also marked by **sa** (in **sa akin**, **sa aklatan**) as the first example sentence shows.

Causative Verb						
Verb	**Indirect Actor** (who causes the action)		**Direct Actor**		**Direct Object**	
Magpa-	**Marker**	**Noun**	**Marker**	**Noun**	**Marker**	**Noun**
<u>Nagpaluto</u> (completed)	ang ang mga	<u>nanay</u>	sa sa mga	<u>bata</u>	ng ng mga	<u>pagkain.</u>
<u>Nagpapaluto</u> (incompleted)	si sina	<u>Luisa</u>	kay kina	<u>Patrick</u>		
<u>Magpapaluto</u> (contemplated)		ako kami tayo ka kayo siya sila		sa akin sa atin sa amin sa iyo sa inyo sa kaniya sa kanila		

EXAMPLES:

Nagpakuha siya sa akin ng mga libro sa aklatan. She/he asked me to get books from the library.

Nagpalinis ako kay Mike ng kuwarto ko. I had Mike clean my room.

Magpapatulong ako kay Mike. I will have Mike help me.

Grammar Notes

1. When using the **magpa-** affix, the direct actor is sometimes omitted.

   EXAMPLE:

   Nagpagupit ako ng buhok. I had a haircut.

2. As in sentences with other verbal affixes, with **magpa-** the indirect actor, direct actor, and direct object can switch places so long as none of them is a pronoun. The following sentences all mean "Martin asked Rene to get a book from the library."

   EXAMPLE:

   Nagpakuha si Martin kay Rene ng mga libro sa aklatan.

   Nagpakuha kay Rene si Martin ng mga libro sa aklatan.

   Nagpakuha ng mga libro si Martin kay Rene sa aklatan.

   Nagpakuha ng mga libro sa aklatan si Martin kay Rene.

3. When there is an indirect object or directional complement, it must be in the **sa** form.

   EXAMPLE:

   Nagpabigay si Will *kay* Mike ng mga bulaklak *kay* Kat. Will asked *Mike* to give flowers *to* Kat.

Practice

I. Speaking Practice

Write the title of your favorite movie on a piece of paper and give it to your teacher. The teacher will stack the favorites of all the students in a pile and then ask each student to take one. The student must describe the movie to his or her classmates using the sentence pattern below. The other students have to guess what movie is being described.

EXAMPLE:

Movie Title: _____ (Keep this a secret)

Clue 1: _____ **ito.** (Genre)

Clue 2: **Nangyari ang sine sa** _____ (Setting)

Clue 3: **Si/Sina** _____ **ang bida sa sine.** (Actor)

Clue 4: **Tungkol sa** _____ **ang sine.** (Plot)

Clue 5: **Ang kasukdulan,** _____ (Climax)

Clue 6: **Sa huli,** _____ (Denouement and End)

II. Writing Practice

Work with a partner. Choose a movie that you have both seen and then create a story map. Using the story map, write a paragraph or two about the movie on a separate sheet of paper.

Movie Title: _____

Setting	Main Characters:	Conflict
Where:		
When:		

Events

III. Writing and Reading Practice

Think of your favorite movie and summarize its plot on a separate sheet of paper. When you're finished, exchange summaries with a partner and read each other's story.

IV. Listening Practice

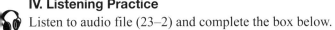 Listen to audio file (23–2) and complete the box below.

Pamagat	Tauhan	Pangyayari	Wakas

Musika at Sayaw

Music and Dance

An Overview of Lesson 24

Objectives
• Understand a Filipino song
• Express your abilities or what you can or cannot do

Vocabulary
• Sayaw at Musika Dance and Music
• **Makapag-** and **Maka-** Verbs (Abilitative Verbs)
• Idioms and Expressions

Reading Text: Turuan Mo Naman Akong Kumanta *Do Teach Me How to Sing*

Reading Comprehension

Activities
Activity 1: Interview: Favorite Type of Music
Activity 2: Favorite Singer and Dancer
Activity 3: Cocktail Party

Grammar
Definition of Terms: Abilitative Verbs

Examining Form
I.   **Maka-** and **Makapag-** Verbs (Abilitative Verbs)
     Grammar Presentation

Practice
I.   Speaking Practice
II.   Reading Practice
III. Writing Practice
IV.   Listening Practice

Vocabulary 🎧 (24–1)

The vocabulary below will help you speak about the music you like and participate in the activities in this lesson. Memorize the vocabulary words before proceeding to the dialogue.

Musika at Sayaw	Music and Dance
awiting-bayan	folk music
awitin tungkol sa pag-ibig	ballad
harana	love song used for serenading a woman
Itik-itik	a type of folk dance in the Philippines. The dance steps imitate the movement of ducks among rice paddies.
kundiman	Filipino traditional love song
makalumang musika	oldies
Maglalatik	a dance that uses coconut shells tied to the breast, back shoulder, knees; literally a person whose occupation is producing "latik," the scum left after cooking and extracting oil from coconut meat
OPM	Original Pilipino Music
Pandanggo sa Ilaw	a type of folk dance that involves balancing oil lamps on one's head and hands
rakistang musika	rock music
Sakuting	a type of folk dance that uses *arnis* or wooden sticks
Sayaw sa Bangko	a type of dance that involves balancing on narrow benches or dance performed on narrow benches
Tinikling	the national dance of the Philippines. Dancers imitate the *tikling* bird's legendary grace and speed by skillfully maneuvering between large bamboo poles.

Makapag- and Maka- Verbs (Abilitative Verbs)

Makapag- Verbs

makapag-aral	to be able to study	**makapag-ipon**	to be able to save money
makapagbakasyon	to be able to take a vacation	**makapag-isip**	to be able to think
makapagbalita	to be able to relay an information or news	**makapaglagay**	to be able to put something
		makapaglinis	to be able to clean
makapagbaon	to be able to take one's provisions, as when going on a trip	**makapagluto**	to be able to cook
		makapagnakaw	to be able to steal
		makapagpatawad	to be able to forgive
makapagbayad	to be able to pay	**makapagreklamo**	to be able to complain
makapagbenta	to be able to sell	**makapagsalita**	to be able to speak
makapagbigay	to be able to give	**makapagsimba**	to be able to go to church
makapagkuwento	to be able to tell a story	**makapagsimula**	to be able to start
makapagdala	to be able to bring/carry	**makapagtanong**	to be able to ask a question
makapaghatid	to be able to send/drop off someone or something	**makapagtiwala**	to be able to trust
		makapagtrabaho	to be able to work
		makapagturo	to be able to teach
makapaghiganti	to be able to take vengeance	**makapag-usap**	to be able to talk
makapaghintay	to be able to wait	**makapag-uwi**	to be able to bring/take something home

<u>Maka- Verbs</u>

makaakyat	to be able to go upstairs/climb	**makapanood**	to be able to watch
makaalis	to be able to leave	**makapasok**	to be able to enter
makababa	to be able to get or go down	**makapasyal**	to be able to go and visit a place
makabalik	to be able to return	**makapili**	to be able to choose
makabangon	to be able to get up from a lying position	**makapunta**	to be able to go
		makarating	to be able to come/arrive
makabasa	to be able to read	**makasakay**	to be able to ride
makabili	to be able to buy	**makasama**	to be able to go with
makakain	to be able to eat	**makasayaw**	to be able to dance
makakuha	to be able to get/take something	**makasigaw**	to be able to shout
makakanta	to be able to sing	**makasulat**	to be able to write
makakita	to be able to see	**makatakbo**	to be able to run
makadaan	to be able to pass through	**makatalon**	to be able to jump
makadalaw	to be able to visit someone	**makatanggap**	to be able to receive
makagamit	to be able to use	**makatanggi**	to be able to refuse/say no
makagawa	to be able to do/make/work	**makatapos**	to be able to finish
makahiram	to be able to borrow/rent	**makatawa**	to be able to laugh
makainom	to be able to drink	**makatawag**	to be able to call
makaiyak	to be able to cry	**makatayo**	to be able to stand up
makalakad	to be able to walk	**makatingin**	to be able to look at someone or something
makalapit	to be able to approach or go near	**makatugtog**	to be able to play a musical intrument
makalangoy	to be able to swim		
makalayo	to be able to get away from	**makatulong**	to be able to help
makaligo	to be able to take a shower	**makaupo**	to be able to sit
makalipat	to be able to transfer or move from one place to another	**makautang**	to be able to borrow money
		makauwi	to be able to go home
makangiti	to be able to smile		

Idioms and Expressions

Buti ka pa	You're better off
Oo naman	Yes, of course
Aba!	an exclamation that expresses surprise, wonder, disgust, depending on how it is used in a sentence. It could also mean "Hey!"
Bilib ako sa iyo	expression usually said in admiration or awe. From the English "believe." Literally "I believe in you."
Sobra ka naman!	You're too much, over the top.

Dialogue: Turuan Mo Naman Akong Kumanta *Do Teach Me How to Sing*

It is a warm Sunday afternoon at Brian's home. Nelson had just arrived to hang out with Brian, who was doing one of the Filipinos' favorite pastimes: karaoke. Read the dialogue below and answer the Dialogue Comprehension questions.

Word Bank

kapag/kung when/if; a subordinating conjunction used to form a conditional clause
that expresses a prerequisite for the action in the main clause to happen
gayuma love potion
patay sa 'yo head over heels about you
taghiyawat pimple
dumudungaw peeping or looking out as in a window

Nelson: **O, ano 'yang kinakanta mo?**

Brian: **Anak.**

Nelson: **Aba! Hindi ko alam na nakakakanta ka pala.**

Brian: **Oo naman. *Kapag* marami akong gawain, gusto kong kumanta.**

Nelson: **Ano naman ang paborito mong kantahin?**

Brian: **Depende sa ginagawa ko. Kapag nagluluto ako, kumakanta ako ng mga lumang kanta at kapag naliligo naman ako, kumakanta ako ng mga kantang tungkol sa pag-ibig.**

Nelson: **Bilib naman ako sa iyo.**

Brian: ***Kung* nag-aaral nga ako, kumakanta ako ng mga kanta sa simbahan.**

Nelson: **Sobra ka naman!**

Brian: **E Ikaw? Ano naman ang ginagawa mo kung marami kang gawain?**

Nelson: ***Kung* nagmamaneho ako, nakikinig ako sa mga rap na kanta at *kung* nasa bahay ako, sinasa-bayan ko ng sayaw.**

Brian: **Aba, hindi ko alam na nakakasayaw ka pala.**

Nelson: **Oo naman. Mananayaw ako noon sa kolehiyo. Nagsasayaw ako dati ng mga tradisyunal na sayaw-Pilipino.**

Brian: **Talaga? Gaya ng ano?**

Nelson: **Nakakapagsayaw ako** *ng maglalatik, tinikling, pandanggo sa ilaw* **at marami pang iba.**

Brian: **Aba. Turuan mo naman ako.**

Nelson: **Sige! Basta turuan mo rin akong kumanta.**

Brian: **Sige. Walang problema! Unahin natin 'tong kanta ng Hotdog noong taong 1970.**

Nelson: **Ano ba 'yang "Hotdog"?**

Brian: **Basta, maganda 'to. Sikat na sikat sila noong mga taong 1970 sa Pilipinas. Magugustuhan mo 'tong "Pers Lab."**

> **Tuwing kita'y nakikita**
> **Ako'y natutunaw**
> **Parang ice cream nabilad**
> **Sa ilalim ng araw**
>
> **Ano ba naman ang sikreto mo**
> **At di ka maalis sa isip ko?**
> **Ano bang gayuma ang gamit mo**
> **At masyado akong patay sa'yo?**
> **Di na makatulog**
> **Di pa makakain**
> **Taghiyawat sa ilong**
> **Pati na sa pisngi**
> **Sa kaiisip sa 'yo**
> **Taghiyawat dumarami**
>
> **Tuwing kita'y nakikita**
> **Ako'y natutunaw**
> **Tuwing daan sa harap mo**
> **Puso ko'y dumudungaw**
>
> **Kelan ba kita makikilala**
> **Sana'y malapit na**
> **Malapit na**

Kakanta sila at susubukan ni Nelson na sumunod kay Brian.

Dialogue Comprehension

1. **Pagkadating ni Nelson, ano ang ginagawa ni Brian?**

   _____

2. **Ano ang kinakanta ni Brian kapag nag-aaral siya?**

   _____

3. Ano naman ang ginagawa ni Nelson kung nagmamaneho siya?

_____

4. Anu-anong klase ng sayaw ang kaya ni Nelson na sayawin?

_____

5. Ano ang kasunduan nilang dalawa?

_____

6. Ano'ng inilalarawan sa kantang "Pers Lab"?

_____

_____

7. Saan ikinukumpara ang isang taong umiibig?

_____

8. Ano pa ang ibang mga nangyayari sa isang nagmamahal?

_____

_____

_____

9. Ano ang ibig sabihin ng "Puso ko'y dumudungaw"?

_____

_____

10. Nasabi ba ang pag-ibig sa minamahal niya sa kantang ito? Ipaliwanag.

_____

_____

_____

Activities

Activity 1

Find a classmate who likes each of the genres of music indicated in the table below and have them explain why. Record your findings below.

EXAMPLE:

Student 1: **Ano'ng klase ng musika ang gusto mong pakinggan at bakit?**

Student 2: **Gusto kong makinig sa OPM kasi nakakarelaks ang tugtog na ito.**

Awitin tungkol sa Pag-ibig	OPM	Rakistang Musika
1. _____ _____ _____	1. **Nelson** **Kasi nakakarelaks makinig sa** **mga tugtog na ganito.**	1. _____ _____ _____
2. _____ _____ _____	2. _____ _____ _____	2. _____ _____ _____
Makalumang Musika	**Rap**	**Awiting-bayan**
1. _____ _____ _____	1. _____ _____ _____	1. _____ _____ _____
2. _____ _____ _____	2. _____ _____ _____	2. _____ _____ _____

Activity 2

Name your favorite singer and dancer in the spaces provided below and explain why they are your favorites.

EXAMPLE:

Si Freddie Aguilar ang paborito kong manganganta kasi gusto ko ang tema ng mga kanta niya.

Iba-iba ang paksa ng kanta niya at kadalasan medyo politikal ang tema ng kaniyang mga kanta.

Manganganta	Dahilan
_____	_____ _____ _____ _____

Mananayaw	Dahilan
_____	_____
	_____
	_____
	_____

Activity 3

Read one of the five biographies of famous Filipinos around the world. After you finish reading, assume the identity of the person you read about and pretend that you are at a cocktail party. Introduce yourself to four other people in the party.

Si *Emmanuel Dapidran Pacquiao* o kilala sa tawag na Manny Pacquiao ay isang Filipino na boksingero, artista, mangnganta, at politiko. Ipinanganak siya noong a-disisiyete ng Disyembre taong 1978. Sa edad na labing-anim, nagsimula na si Manny ng boksing sa propesyonal na antas at sa kasalukuyan, nanalo na siya ng anim na world title sa kompetisyon ng 112, 122, 130, 135, 147, at 154 na libra. Sa tuwing maglalaro si Manny, nakatutok ang buong Pilipinas para magbigay ng suporta sa kaniya.

Si Maria Geraldine Jamora, o kilala sa pangalang Jinkee, ang asawa ni Manny at sila ay may apat na anak at kasalukuyang nakatira sila ngayon sa Sarangani.

Si *Peter Hernandez* o kilala sa tawag na Bruno Mars ay isang mangnganta at musikero na nagmula sa Waikiki, Hawai'i. Ipinanganak siya noong a-otso ng Oktubre taong 1985. Sina Pete at Bernadette Hernandez ang mga magulang ni Peter. Taga-Puerto Rico ang tatay niya, samantalang taga-Pilipinas naman ang nanay niya. Naging popular si Bruno sa kanta niyang "Nothing on You" at "Billionaire". Bata pa lang si Bruno ay nagpakita na siya ng hilig sa pagkanta. Noong apat na taong gulang siya ay pinangalanan na siyang "Little Elvis" ng ilang mga manunulat sa diyaryo. Noong labimpito siya ay lumipat na siya sa Los Angeles para pumirma ng kontrata sa Motown Records noong 2005. Ang pangalang Bruno ay mula sa kaniyang paboritong wrestler na si Bruno Sammartino.

Si *Lea Salonga* ay isang Filipino na mangnganta at artista. Ipinanganak siya noong a-bente dos ng Pebrero taong 1971. Naging kilala siya sa kaniyang pagganap bilang Kim sa musical na pinamagatang Miss Saigon. Sa musical na ito, nanalo siya ng mga award mula sa Olivier, Tony, Drama Desk, Outer Critics, at Theatre World. Si Lea rin ang kauna-unahang Ayano na gumanap bilang Eponine at Fantine sa musical na "Les Miserables" sa Broadway. Bukod pa rito, kumanta rin siya sa mga sine ng Disney tulad ng "Aladdin" noong 1992 at "Mulan" noong 1998 at 2004.

Si *Charmaine Clarice Pempengco* o kilala sa pangalang Charice ay isang mangangangta at artistang Pilipino. Ipinanganak siya noong a-diyes ng Mayo taong 1992. Nakilala si Charice sa Youtube at pinangalanan siya ni Oprah Winfrey na "The Most Talented Girl in the World". Lumabas ang kaniyang unang album noong 2010 at naging pangwalo ito sa Billboard 200. Si Charice ang kauna-unahang Asyanong mangnganta na nakasama sa top 10 ng Billboards 200 album chart.

Ngayon mayroon siyang dalawang sikat na kanta na naging top 40 sa mga ilang bansa. Ang mga kantang ito ay ang "Pyramid" at "Before it Explodes" na isinulat ni Bruno Mars. Bukod sa pagkanta, pinasok din ni Charice ang pag-arte sa Hollywood. Noong 2010, sumali siya sa programa sa telebisyon na pinamagatang "Glee". Dito sa palabas na ito, nakilala siyang si Sunshine Corazon, isang exchange student mula sa Pilipinas.

Si *Allan Pineda Lindo* o kilala sa tawag na api.de.ap ay isang manganganta sa bandang Black-Eyed Peas. Ipinanganak siya noong a-bente otso ng Nobyembre taong 1974 sa Pampanga, Pilipinas. Pilipina ang kaniyang nanay at Aprikano-Amerikano naman ang kaniyang tatay. Sa kasamaang-palad, hindi niya nakilala ang tatay niya. Ang nanay lang niya ang nagpalaki sa kaniya at noong labing-apat siya, inampon siya ng isang Amerikanong pamilya at dinala siya ng mga ito sa Los Angeles. Dito sa Los Angeles, nakilala niya si William Adams o kilala sa tawag na will.i.am. Dito nagsimula ang pagkakaibigan nila na humantong sa pagbuo ng bandang "The Black-Eyed Peas."

Grammar

Definition of Terms

Abilitative verbs	A class of verbs that generally mean to be able to do, make, or perform a specific action. For example: **makakuha** to be able to get
	EXAMPLE:
	Nakapunta ako sa Italya noong isang taon. I was able to go to Italy last year.

Examining Form

Review the sentences below and complete the tasks that follow. Discuss your answers with a partner. Consult the following section to check your answers.

A	B
Nakakapagsayaw siya ng pandanggo sa ilaw.	Nagsasayaw siya ng pandanggo sa ilaw.
Nakakakanta siya ng mga tradisyunal na awiting Pilipino.	Kumakanta siya ng mga tradisyunal na awiting Pilipino.
Makakakain ako ng balut.	Kakain ako ng balut.
Nakapagbiyahe ako sa Italya noong isang taon.	Nagbiyahe ako sa Italya noong isang taon.

1. Compare the sentences in column A and column B. Are there any differences in meaning? If so, identify the differences.
2. Underline all the verbs and identify the verbal affixes. Next identify all the aspects of each verb.
3. When do you think we use **maka-**, and when do we use **makapag-** as a prefix?

I. Maka- and Makapag- Verbs (Abilitative Verbs)

Abilitative verbs are created by adding the prefixes **maka-** and **makapag-** to the root word. **Maka-** is used when the form of the verb is an **-um-** verb. In the example below, the root word is **kain** (eat).

kumain	→	maka- + kain	→	makakain
uminom	→	maka + inom	→	makainom

Makapag- is used when the form of the verb is a **mag**-verb.

magtrabaho	→	makapag- + trabaho	→	makapagtrabaho
maghintay	→	makapag- + hintay	→	makapaghintay

The chart below gives the rule for forming the infinitive form and completed, incompleted, and contemplated aspects of the verbs **makapag-aral** and **makakain**, the abilitative forms of the verbs **mag-aral** and **kumain** respectively. All these verbs belong to the actor-focus type of verbs.

Inflection	Aspect	Inflection	Rules
mag-aral		**kumain**	
makapag-aral	Infinitive	**makakain**	Add the prefix **maka-** or **makapag-** to the root word.
nakapag-aral	Completed	**nakakain**	From the infinitive, change **m** to **n**.
nakakapag-aral	Incompleted	**nakakakain**	Take the first two syllables of the completed, reduplicate "**ka**," plus the root word
makakapag-aral	Contemplated	**makakakain**	From the incompleted, change **n** to **m**.

Grammar Presentation

Abilitative verbs can only be made from words showing action, not emotion or feeling. There are no imperative forms with this class of verbs.

EXAMPLES:

*Makapunta ka sa Italya. (incorrect)

*Makatuwa ka. (incorrect)

1. The chart below shows the structure of a sentence using a **maka-** verb in its three aspects. Notice that the direct object **balut** immediately follows the predicate verb **nakakain**.

Abilitative Verbs Used in Sentences							
Verb	**Object**		**Actor**		**Time**		**Location**
Maka-	**Marker**	**Noun**	**Marker**	**Noun**	**Marker**	**Noun**	**Sa**
Nakakain (completed)	**ng** **ng mga**	**balut**	si sina	**Patrick**	noong	**Lunes**	sa Pilipinas.
Nakakakain (incompleted)			ang ang mga	**bata**			
Makakakain (contemplated)					sa	**Lunes**	

EXAMPLES:

Nakabili ng damit si Edison sa SM noong isang linggo. Edison was able to buy clothes at Shoe Mart last week.

Makakaalis ba siya sa Lunes? Can he leave on Monday?

Nakakapunta ba sina Susana at Greg sa simbahan tuwing Linggo? Are Susana and Greg able to go to church every Sunday?

Hindi makakakanta si Maria ngayong gabi. Maria will not be able to sing tonight.

2. The chart below shows the structure of a sentence using a **makapag-** verb in its three aspects. Notice that the word order is different from the previous **maka-** sentence. The actor, which is also the subject or topic, immediately follows the predicate verb and is followed by the direct object if the verb is transitive.

Abilitative Verbs							
Verb	**Actor**		**Object**		**Time**		**Location**
Makapag-	**Marker**	**Noun**	**Marker**	**Noun**	**Marker**	**Noun**	**Sa**
Nakapagsayaw (completed)	si	ako tayo kami	ng (ng mga)	<u>salsa</u>	noong	<u>Lunes</u>	<u>sa klab.</u>
Nakakapagsayaw (incompleted)		ka kayo siya sila			tuwing		
Makakapagsayaw (contemplated)		Agnes			sa		

EXAMPLES:

Makakapagbiyahe ako sa Italya sa susunod na taon. I will be able to travel to Italy next year.
Nakapaglinis siya ng bahay kagabi. She/He was able to clean the house last night.
Nakakapagtrabaho pa ba siya? Can she/he still work?
Hindi ako makakapagluto ng pagkain mamaya. I will not be able to make (cook) food later.

Practice

I. Speaking Practice

Divide into groups of six. Your teacher will assign each group one of the dances listed below, which you must research on the Internet. Each group must write a report of two to three paragraphs in Tagalog on the dance assigned to them. The report should include the following information: name of the dance, its meaning, the ethnic group that originated it, the purpose of dance, the setting, the costume for male and female dancers, props and accesories, the basic movement, and any background information. Each group will then perform its own version of the dance and present it to the class.

Dances	
Binasuan	Gayong-gayong
Itik-itik	Pangalay
Subli	Kadal Tahaw
Tinikling	Burung Talo

II. Reading Practice

Read the selection below and answer the Reading Comprehension questions.

Word Bank

kaluluwa soul
sinasalamin reflecting
pananalig belief, faith
hinihiling wishing
makiisa to join, unite with
sambayanan nation, crowd
layunin goal
ginagaya copying
kilos movement
banyaga foreigner
pinanggalingan origin

Bakit Tayo Sumasayaw?

Maraming mga sayaw ang mga Pilipino. Ipinapakita nito ang dibersidad ng tradisyon sa sayaw ng mga Pilipino. Nasa isip at *kaluluwa* ng mga Pilipino ang kalikasan ng ating mga sayaw. Ipinakikilala ng uri ng mga sayaw kung sino tayo at *sinasalamin* nito ang kasaysayan, mga kaugalian at *pananalig* ng mga Pilipino. Sa mga sayaw na Pilipino, *hinihiling* ng mga sayaw ang partisipasyon ng mga tao na *makiisa* sa komunidad. Hindi ito katulad ng ballet na para lamang sa mga nag-aral at nagsanay, sa halip, pag-aari ito ng buong *sambayanan*.

Bawat sayaw ay may *layunin*, partikular na konteksto at karanasan ng sambayanan. Pwedeng pagdiriwang, panunuyo, debosyon, sayaw bago sumalakay o sayaw na pandigma mula sa kabundukan ng Cordillera; pang-alay mula sa Mindanao na *ginagaya* ang *kilos* ng isda at ng alon ng tubig sa dagat; o sayaw sa lupa tulad ng kumintang, pandanggo sa ilaw, at subli. Makikita rin sa mga sayaw ang mga elementong katutubo at mga impluwensiyang *banyaga* tulad ng Indian, Tsino, Indo-Tsino, Indonesyo, Malayo, Espanyol, at Amerikano. Ang mga impluwensiyang ito ay makikita sa anyo, layunin, musika, at galaw ng sayaw.

Sa kasalukuyan, tinitingnan ang sayaw bilang libangan, "palabas" na pagkakaaliwan, ehersisyo, at pagpapakita ng galing at husay sa pagkilos. Ginagamit din ito sa diplomasya dahil unibersal ang wika ng *galaw* at indak at hindi kailangan ang wika upang magkaintindihan at makapagbigay ng mabuting pakikipag-ugnayan. Sa mga lugar na pinaglipatan ng mga Pilipino, tumutulong ang sayaw sa pagbubuo ng komunidad at ng pagkatao o Pilipinong identidad. Ang sayaw din ang isang paraan ng pagpapakita ng kung sino ang mga Pilipino—isang paraan at proseso ng balidasyon o apirmasyon ng komunidad, sa Hapon, Amerika, Europa o saan mang lupalop ng mundo na may mga Pilipino na sumasayaw ng sayaw na Pilipino. At sa tuwing sumasayaw sila, binubuhay nila ang kanilang lupang *pinanggalingan*, ang Pilipinas, ang kanilang kasaysayan, tradisyon, at pananalig sa bawat indak at kumpas.

Reading Comprehension

Note in English in the first column the information that you gleaned from each paragraph. Next, work with a partner and ask your partner what he or she understood from each paragraph. Write down your partner's answers in the second column. Lastly, in the third column, work with your partner to come up with a single summary based on the information in the first two boxes.

Unang Talata		
Ang Bersyon ko	**Ang Bersyon ng Kapareha ko**	**Ang Bersyon Namin**

Pangalawang Talata		
Ang Bersyon ko	**Ang Bersyon ng Kapareha ko**	**Ang Bersyon Namin**

Pangatlong Talata		
Ang Bersyon ko	**Ang Bersyon ng Kapareha ko**	**Ang Bersyon Namin**

III. Writing Practice

This activity can be done individually or in groups depending on class size. On a separate sheet of paper, pick a popular song and write your own lyrics to it, then sing the song to the class, substituting your own lyrics.

IV. Listening Practice

Your teacher will play you a song that he or she likes and that suits the level of proficiency and interest of the class. Listen to the song with your eyes closed and feel the emotion that it conveys through its lyrics and melody. Based on this emotion, think of a situation that can fit this feeling and, on a separate sheet of paper, write a dialogue conveying your understanding of the song.

Glossary

Accents used:

Acute accent as in **á, é, í, ó, ú** used in all stressed syllables.

Grave accent as in **à, è, ì, ò, ù** for words with stress on the second to the last syllable and a glottal catch on the last vowel.

Circumflex accent as in **â, ê, î, ô, û** for the last vowel of the word with a glottal catch.

Tagalog-English

A

abogádo/a lawyer
abogasyá/abogasíya law
abreláta can opener
Abríl April
abutín/mag-abót reach
adobo adobo, a typical dish of chicken and pork with garlic, soy sauce, and vinegar
Agósto August
aircon air conditioner
aklátan library
akyát climb, go upstairs
alá úna one o'clock
alágang háyop pet
alalahánin (O.F.) remember
alám (O.F.) know something
alás used in time expressions to mean "o'clock"
albuláryo faith healer, a local healer who uses herbs to cure
ále Miss, Mrs., an address for a woman
Alemán German
alikabók dust
alís departure
alisín/mag-alís remove
alkálde mayor
álon wave
alukín/mag-alók offer something
ambón drizzle
Amérika U.S.A.
amerikána suit, coat
Amerikáno/a American
ámo boss
ampalayá bitter melon
-an object-focus suffix
anák child (son/daughter)
ang singular common noun/proper noun marker
ang mga plural common noun/proper noun marker
ánim six
anó what
Ano ka bá? What's the matter with you?

(A continued)

Anó na? What's up?
Anóng bágo? What's new?
Anú-anó? What are?
aparadór closet, cabinet
ápat four
ápat na líbo four thousand
ápat na raán four hundred
ápatnapû forty
apó grandchild (grandson/granddaughter)
apóy fire
a-priméro first
áraw sun, day
áraw-áraw everyday
Áraw ng Kasarinlán Independence Day
Áraw ng Manggagáwà Labor Day
Áraw ng mga Amá Father's Day
Áraw ng mga Bayáni National Heroes' Day
Áraw ng mga Iná Mothers' Day
Áraw ng mga Patáy All Souls' Day
Áraw ng mga Púsò Valentine's Day
Áraw ng Pasasalámat Thanksgiving Day
arína/harína flour
arkitékto architect
arkitektúra architecture
arnís a Filipino martial arts using two rattan sticks
artísta actor, actress
asáwa spouse, husband, wife
asín salt
asó smoke
áso dog
asúkal sugar
asúl blue
at and
áte elder sister
Ay nako! Oh, my gosh!
áyaw does not like, does not want
áyon sa according to
Ayos lang. Fine.
Ayos na ayos. Great!
ayúsin/mag-áyos repair, organize

B

ba question marker for a yes/no question
babáe female
báboy pork (meat), pig
badminton badminton
bágo new, before
Bágong Taón New Year's Day
bagoóng shrimp paste
bagyó storm
bahaghárì rainbow
báhay house
báhay-bakasyúnan vacation house
báka beef, cow
bakúna vaccine, vaccination
balát skin
bálat birth mark
balatán/magbalát peel
baligtád upside down, inside out
balíkat shoulder
balinguyngóy nosebleed
balkonáhe porch, balcony
banana kyu bananas deep fried and coated in caramelized brown sugar on bamboo skewers
bandá direction, toward/towards (usually followed by **rito**, **riyan**, or **roon**), at about a certain time
bandehádo platter, tray (usually oblong)
bangkâ boat
bangkô bench, stool
bángko bank
baníg mat made of palm leaves or plastic
banílya vanilla
bányo bathroom
báon provision (usually for a trip or vacation)
bapór ferry, ship
baráha playing cards
barberyá barber shop
baryá loose change, coins
baság broken (glass, mirror, etc.)
basáhin/magbasá/bumása read

basaín/magbasâ (v) wet
basketból basketball
basketbolísta basketball player
báso drinking glass
bastós uncouth, rude
basurahán trash can or garbage container
bátà young (boy or girl)
batihín/magbatí beat
batíin/bumátì greet
bató rock, stone
báwal forbidden, prohibited
báwang garlic
bayábas guava
báyad payment, fee
báyan town, country
bénte twenty
bentiladór electric fan
bérde green
béses times (occasion)
bestída/o dress
bétsin monosodium glutamate (MSG), used to make food tasty
béysbol baseball
bibíg mouth
bilángin/magbiláng count
bilhín/bumilí buy
bilóg round, circle
bilyár billiards
binátà bachelor, adult male
bíno wine
bintánà window
bintî leg
binyagán/magbinyág baptize
bisikléta bicycle
bisitáhin/bumisíta visit
bituwín star
biyáhe commute, trip
Biyérnes Friday
Biyérnes Sánto Good Friday
blúsa blouse, top
bóbo stupid, dumb
bodéga storage, warehouse
bóksing boxing
boksingéro boxer
bola ball
bóling bowling
botíka pharmacy
bráso arm
bubúyog bee
Budísta Buddhist
buhángin sand
buhátin/magbuhát lift or carry
buháy alive
búhay life
buhók hair
búkas tomorrow
búkas ng umága/hápon/gabí tomorrow morning/afternoon/night
búkid; palayán field, farm, rice field
búko young coconut, flower bud

búko dyus young coconut juice
bulág blind
bulkán volcano
bulók spoiled, rotten
bulútong-túbig chicken pox
bumabâ go down
bumagyó storm, have a typhoon
bumahâ (v) flood
bumalík go, return, come back
bumilí buy
bundók mountain
bunga fruit
búnggalo bungalow
bungguín/bumunggô hit
bunsô youngest sibling
buról hill
Buti na lang! Thank goodness!
buwán moon, month
buwán-buwán monthly, every month

D

daán hundred unit; road
dágat beach, ocean, sea
dáhil sa because of
dáhon leaf
dáhon ng lawrél bay leaf
dalága single female
dalandán Philippine orange, citrus
dalawá two
dalawampû twenty
dalawáng daán two hundred
dalawáng líbo two thousand
daláwin/dumálaw visit
dalhín/magdalá bring, take
dalírì finger
dápat should
darák rice bran used as hog's feed
datíng/balík arrival/return, going or coming back
daúngan port
daw/raw they say, according to someone
dentísta dentist
diborsyádo/a divorced
diláw yellow
din/rin also, either
dingdíng wall
direksiyón direction
disinuwébe nineteen
disiótso eighteen
disisaís sixteen
disisiyéte seventeen
disiyérto desert
Disyémbre December
diyés ten
doktór doctor
dormitóryo dormitory
dos two
dose twelve
doséna/duséna dozen

dumaán passed by
dumálaw (v) visit; visited
dumatíng to arrive, arrived
dumí dirt, fecal matter
dumirétso go straight
dumúdugô bleeding
duwág coward
dyíp jeepney, jeep
dyús juice

E

Enéro January
eropláno airplane
eskiníta alley
eskwelahán school
Espánya Spain
Estádos Unídos United States
estudyánte student

F

FX taxi van

G

gabí-gabí every night
gadgarín/maggadgád grate
gagambá spider
galón gallon
gamítin/gumámit use
gamót medicine
gamót sa mga pantál medicine for insect bites
gamót sa pagtataé medicine for diarrhea
garáhe garage
gasgás scratch
gatâ coconut milk
gátas milk
gawgáw cornstarch, starch used for clothes
gawín/gumawâ make, fix, do
Gaya pa rin nang dati Still the same
gintô gold
gisántes sweet peas
gitára guitar
gitnâ in between, middle
gobernadór/a governor
góto rice porridge with tripe
grípo faucet
gúbat forest, woods
guláman gelatin, agar-agar
gúlay vegetable
guluhín/gumuló disarrange, become messy
gumaméla hibiscus
gumámit use
gumástos spend
gumísing wake up, woke up
gusálì building
gustó like, want
guwápo/pógi handsome, good-looking

H

habúlin/humábol chase
hagdán stair, staircase, ladder
haláman plant
halámang-gamót medicinal plant
halámang-ugát root crop
Halika! Kain tayo. Come! Let's eat.
halo-hálò shaved ice, milk, and various preserved fruit mixture
hálos almost
halúin/maghálò stir
hamóg dew
hanápin/humánap/maghanáp look for
hanggáng until
Hanggang dito na lang muna ako. Till then.
hángin air, wind
hangúin/maghángò remove from fire
hápon afternoon
Hapón Japanese man, the country Japan
hapúnan supper, dinner
haráp in front
harápàn in front
hayáàn let
Héto buháy pa. Here, still alive.
híkà asthma
hilágà north
hiláw raw, unripe
Hindi po bumubuti. It doesn't seem to be getting better.
Hinding-hindi ko makakalimutan I will never ever forget
hingín/humingî ask for something
hinóg ripe
hintayín/maghintáy wait for
hiramín/humirám borrow
híta thigh
hiwáin/maghíwà slice thinly
hugásan/maghúgas wash
Húlyo July
humánap look for something/someone
humángin blow, as wind
humingî ask for something
humirám borrow, to check out
Húnyo June
huwág don't
Huwébes Thursday
Huwébes Sánto Maundy Thursday

I

i- object-focus prefix
-in object-focus affix
iabót/mag-abót pass, hand over
iadóbo/mag-adóbo make adobo
ibabâ downstairs, below
ibabâ/magbabâ take, bring something down
ibábad/magbábad soak, marinate
ibábaw on top of

ibalík/magbalík return
ibalíta/magbalíta pass the news
ibaón bury
ibáon/magbáon carry or bring provisions; also said of money or food that one takes to work or school
ibigáy/magbigáy give
ibígin/umíbig love
íbon bird
ibúhos/magbúhos pour
idagdág/magdagdág add, include
igisá/maggisá sauté
iháin/magháin serve
iháwin/mag-íhaw grill
ihálò mix
iitsá/mag-itsá throw, toss
ika- ordinal number (when attached to a cardinal number)
ikáw/ka you, second person, singular **ang** pronoun
ikuwénto/magkuwénto tell a story
ilagáy/maglagáy put, place
ilálim under
ilaráwan describe
ílaw light, lamp
ílog river
ilóng nose
ináanak godchild, godson, goddaughter
Inglés English
inhinyéro/a engineer
inítin/mag-ínit heat
inúmin drinks, beverage
inumín/uminóm drink
ipagdíwang/magdíwang celebrate
ipaksíw/magpaksíw cook fish or meat in vinegar
ipaták/magpaták/pumaták drop (as in eyedrop)
ipíli/pumílì choose
ipríto/magpríto fry
isá one
isálin/magsálin pour into another receptacle, translate from one language to another
isáng daán/isandaan one hundred
isáng líbo/isanlibo one thousand
isaúlì/magsaúlì return
isdâ fish
isípin/mag-isíp think
ísla/pulô island
istasyón ng bús bus station
Itálya Italy
itím black
itínda/magtindá sell
itlóg egg
itúrò/magtúrò teach
iuwî/mag-uwî bring home, take home
iyán that (object is near the listener)
iyón that (object is far from speaker/listener)

K

kabáyo horse
kabinet cabinet
kabuté mushroom
káda per, each
kagabí last night
kagát bite
kahápon yesterday
kahéra cashier
kaibígan friend
kailángan need, must
kaínin/kumáin eat
kakaibá unusual
kakláse classmate
kalabása squash, flunk a test or class
kalahátì half
kalamansî citrus, small acidic fruit
kalamansí dyús calamansi juice
kalamidád calamity
kalán stove
kalbó bald
kalderéta goat meat stew
kaldéro pot
kalésa horse-drawn carriage
kaliwâ left
káma bed
kamag-ának relative
kamakalawá two days ago, the day before yesterday
kamakatló three days ago
kamátis tomato
kamáy hand
kamóte sweet potato
kánan right
kanínang umága/tangháli earlier this morning, noon
kaniyá-kaniyá separate checks
kanlúran west
kantahín/kumantá sing
kánto street corner
kánto corner
kapatíd sibling, brother, sister
kapeteryá cafeteria
karéra ng kabáyo horse race
károt carrot
kasaysáyan history
kaseróla casserole, pan
kasí because
kasiyang-kasiya fits well.
Kastílà Spanish
kasundúan agreement
kasuótan wardrobe, outfit
katás juice
katawán body
Katóliko Catholic
katórse fourteen
kaúntì few, little
kausápin/mag-úsap talk to, converse
kawálì frying pan
kay singular proper name (person or animal) marker, to or from, possession

Kay/Ang mahál namán pô! That's too expensive sir/ma'am!

kayó you (plural), second person **ang** pronoun

kayumanggî brown (used to describe skin color)

késo cheese

kidlát lightning

kilalánin know someone

kílay eyebrow

kílo kilogram

kiná plural proper name (person or animal) marker; to or from; possessive

kinábukásan the following day, the next day

kínse fifteen

kíntsay Chinese celery

kíta na láng táyo mámayâ see you later

klínika clinic

ko my, I (**ng** pronoun, first person, singular)

kólera cholera

komedór/kaínan dining room

komportáble comfortable

kóntakin/kumóntak get in touch with

koráles coral

Koreáno/a Korean

koréo mail, post, mail service

kótse car

kubiyértos/kubyértos silverware, tableware

kúbo nipa hut

kubrekáma bed spread, bed cover

kudkúran shredder, grater

kulambô mosquito net

kúlay tsokoláte chocolate-colored, brown

kulóg thunder

kulót curly

kumaliwâ turn left

kumánan turn right

kumbidahín/magkumbidá invite

kumidlát (v) flash, referring to lightning

kúmot blanket

kumúha get

kumulóg (v) thunder

kumunsúlta sa doktór consult a doctor

Kumustá (po/ho) kayó? How are you (sir/madam)?

Kumustá ka? How are you (informal)?

Kumusta na? How's it going?

kuného rabbit

Kung may panahón akó If I have the time

kúnin/kumúha get, take

kurtína curtain

kusínà kitchen

kusinéro/a chef, cook

kutsára spoon

kutsaríta teaspoon

kutsílyo knife

kuwadrádo square

kuwádro frame

kuwárto room, bedroom

kuwátro four

kuwéba cave

kuwintás necklace

kúya elder brother

L

labábo sink

labáhan laundry room

labímpitó seventeen

labíndalawá twelve

labíng- ánim sixteen

labíng- ápat fourteen

labíng-isá eleven

labíngwaló eighteen

labínlimá fifteen

labínsiyám nineteen

labíntatló thirteen

labóg overcooked

lágì always

lagnát fever

lakì size

laláki/laláke male

lalamúnan throat

lambák valley

lamók mosquito

lámpara lamp

lang just, only

lángit sky, heaven

langkâ jackfruit

laruín/maglarô play

lása flavor, taste

láwà lake

leég neck

letsúgas lettuce

libángan hobby

líbra pound

libró book

likód behind, back

lila purple

limá five

limampû fifty

limáng daán/limandaán five hundred

limáng líbo/limanlíbo five thousand

limonáda lemonade

lindól earthquake

Linggó Sunday

linggó week

linggú-linggó every week, each week

linísin/maglínis clean

lipád flight, fly

literatúra literature

litráto picture, photo

lítro liter

liyémpo pork meat, cut from the flank or side

lóla grandmother

lólo grandfather

loób inside

lóro parrot

LRT Light Rail Transit

lúgaw porridge

lúmà ancient, old

lumalâ get worse

lumálahók participating

lumangóy swim

lumápit approached, got closer

lumayô went far away, stayed away

lumikô turned

lumindól quaked

lumípat moved

lumpiyâ Filipino eggroll

lúnas treatment, cure, remedy

lutô cooked

lútong-báhay homemade

lutúin/maglútò cook

lúya ginger

M

maága early

maaksidénte be in an accident

maalála remember

maálat salty

maalikabók dusty

maangháng spicy

maásim sour

mabábà short (height)

mabágal slow

mabaít kind

mabigát strenuous, heavy

mabilís active, fast

mabúti fine, good

mabuti namán good

madalás frequent

madalíng-áraw dawn, sunrise

madapâ fall flat on one's face

madilím dark

madulás slip, slippery

mag- actor-focus verb prefix

magâ swollen

magaán light (weight)

mag-áhit shave

magálang polite

magalíng (sa) good at

mag-almusál eat breakfast

mag-ának family

magandá beautiful

Magandáng tangháli (pô/hô) Good noon (sir/madam)

Magandáng tangháli din namán (pô/hô) Good noon to you too (sir/madam)

magáng-magâ very swollen, really swollen

magbakasyón go on vacation

mag-*bake* bake

magbangkâ take a boat

magbáon take or bring provision (of food, clothes, money, etc.)

magbarkó take a ship

magbásketbol basketball (to play)

magbáyad pay

magbénta sell

magbídyo videogames (to play)

magbigáy give

magbíhis change clothes

magbirô crack a joke

magbisikléta ride a bike

magbuhát lift, raise

magbukás open

magbús ride a bus

magdaán drop by, pass by

magdalá bring

magdasál pray

magdikdík pulverize, pound

magdrám play drums

magdyíp ride a jeep

mag-eropláno ride an airplane

maggitára play the guitar

maghanáp look for

maghapúnan eat dinner

mag-hiking hike

maghilámos wash one's face

maghintáy wait for

maghúgas wash something (dishes, hands, etc.)

mag-ípon save, gather, collect

mag-*jogging* jog

magka- (prefix) have, develop

magkalésa ride a horse-drawn rig

magkapé drink coffee

magkaraóke sing along to the accompaniment of recorded music

magkaroón have, develop

magkasíng- prefix used to denote equal degree of an adjective

magkasipón have a cold

magkíta meet with someone

magkompyúter use the computer

magkótse ride a car

magkuwénto tell a story

maglabá wash clothes

maglagáy put, place, apply

maglakbáy travel

maglampáso mop the floor

maglarô play

maglínis clean

maglútò cook

magmanného drive

magmanného papuntá sa- drive to

magmiryénda/magmeryénda eat a snack

magmotorsíklo ride a motorcycle

magmúmog rinse, wash one's mouth by gargling

magpabakúna get vaccinated

magpabangó wear perfume, cologne

magpahingá take a rest

magpakulô boil

magpasyál stroll

magpiyáno play the piano

magreséta prescribe

magsáing cook rice

magsayáw dance

magsimbá hear mass

magsimulâ start

magsipílyo/magsepílyo brush teeth

magsukláy comb hair

magsulát write

magsuót wear something

magtanghalían eat lunch

magtanóng ask

magtindá sell (store)

magtrabáho work

magtrák ride a truck

magtrén ride a train

magtúrò teach

magúlang parent

maguló messy, disorderly, rowdy, mischievous

magupít cut (with scissors accidentally)

mag-úsap talk with someone

mag-uwî bring/take something home

mahábà long (length)

mahál expensive

Mahál kong My Dear . . . (salutation)

mahángin windy

mahapdî burning feeling, pain

maháwa contaminated or infected

mahínà weak

mahinhín modest, refined

mahírap difficult

mahírap poor

mahíwà cut (with a knife)

mahiyáin shy

mahulí late

mahúli capture

mahúlog fall down

maiklî/maiksî/maigsî short (length)

maíngay loud, noisy

maínit hot, warm

mainitín ang úlo short-tempered

maípit caught by the door or pressed between two objects

maís corn

maís con yélo mixture of shaved ice, milk, and corn

maitím dark-complexioned

makabágo modern

makagát bitten

makalúmà traditional

makapál thick

makasaysáyan historical

makatí itchy

makiníg sa rádyo listen to the radio

makínis smooth

makúnat chewy, ductile

malakás strong

malakí big

malakí-lakí somewhat big

malalâ severe, serious (illness)

malalambót soft (plural)

malambót tender, soft

malamíg cold

malansá fishy

malápad wide

malária malaria

malatâ soggy, soft

maléta luggage

maligamgám lukewarm

maligáw to be lost

maliít small, short

malikót restless, wriggly

malígò take a shower, take a bath

malilimutín absent minded

malínaw na malínaw very clear

malínis clean

maliwánag bright

malungkót sad

malutóng crispy

maluwág/ maluwáng loose

maluwáng spacious

mámà mister

mamantíkà oily

mamasyál promenade, visit a place, walk for pleasure, go around

mámayâ later

mámayáng hápon/gabí later this afternoon/later tonight

mamimíli buyer

manannáyaw dancer

mángangantá singer

manggá mango

manggás sleeve

mánggo dyús mango juice

manghihílot masseuse, midwife

mangkók bowl

mangyári happen

manipís thin, not dense

maniwálà believe

manlaláro ng béysbol baseball player

manlaláro ng pútbol football player

manók chicken

manoód watch (movie, stage play, television show)

manoód ng telebisyón watch television

mansánas apple

mantekílya butter

mantél tablecloth

mantíkà cooking oil

mánunulát writer

maóng jeans, denim

maospitál be hospitalized

mápa map

mapágkumbabâ humble

mapágmahál loving

mapaít bitter
mapayápà peaceful
mapulá red
maputî fair-complexioned
mapútik muddy
marámi many, plenty
Márso March
Martés Tuesday
marumí/madumí dirty
marúyà banana fritters
mas more
masakít painful
masakít ang lalamúnan sore throat
masaráp delicious
masayá happy, cheerful
masikíp cramped
masípag hard working
masírà be destroyed
máskara mask
masúnog burn
masustánsya nutritious
masuwérte lucky
matá eyes
mataás tall
matabâ stout, fat
matabáng bland
matálik na kaibígan best friend
matalíno; marúnong intelligent, wise
matamís sweet
matandâ old
matangkád tall
matángos pointed (referring to nose)
matáo crowded
matápang brave, courageous
matapát honest
matápon be spilled accidentally
matemátika math
matíbay durable
matigás hard, tough
matiyagâ patient
matrápik caught in traffic
matúlog sleep
matulungín helpful
maulán rainy
maúlap cloudy
mawalâ misplaced, lost
Mawaláng-gálang na pô Excuse me, pardon me, sir/ma'am
Mawawala rin itó This (I) will get better
may has, have
may have, there is, there are, there was
mayá't mayâ every now and then
mayábang conceited, boastful
mayáman rich
may-asáwa married
Máyo May
mayroón have, there is, there are, there was
medisína medicine
médyas socks

Méhiko Mexico
mesa table
mgá híkaw earrings
minú-minúto every minute
mísis wife
mistér husband
Miyérkules/Miyérkoles Wednesday
mo your (possessive)
mo you
moderno/a modern
motorsíklo motorcycle
MRT Manila Railway Transit
mukhâ face
mulá sa- from
mulî again
múra cheap, inexpensive
murang-múra ito this is/was really cheap
musikéro/a musician

N

na already
nadapâ stumbled face down or forward while walking
nag-aáral studying
nagsúsuká vomiting
nagtátaé have diarrhea
nagtatrabáho working
nahihílo nauseous, dizzy
naka- wearing the article designated by the root
nakagát bitten
nakakaantók make someone sleepy
nakakadírì awful (taste), feeling of dislike for something dirty
nakakagútom appetizing, make one hungry
nakakahílo nauseating
nakakainís annoying
nakakalibáng entertaining
nakakalúlà make someone anxious due to heights
nakakalungkót make someone sad
nakakamanghâ amazing
nakakapágod tiring
nakakareláks relaxing
nakakatawá funny, comical
nakakatuwâ delightful, likeable
nakatirá residing
nakáwin/nagnákaw steal, stole
Nakú Oh, my gosh
namán on the other hand
namán please
námin our, we (not including the listener)
nánay/iná mother (formal)
nandíto here
nandiyán there (near the listener)
nandoón there (far from the speaker and the listener)
nang time marker

nangyári completed (v past aspect)
naniniwálà believing (incompleted)
naniwálà believed (completed)
nápaka- prefix used for intensified degree of an adjective
napílay sprain (had one)
nársing nursing
nasa- in, at, on
nasaán where (followed by is, are)
nátin our, we (including the listener)
náyon village
náyon town
negosyánte businessman
ng mga plural common noun/proper noun marker
ngâ please
ngayón now
ngípin tooth
ni singular proper name (person or animal) marker, possession
nilá their, they
nina plural proper name marker (person or animal), possession
nínang/nínong godmother, godfather
ninyó your (plural), you (plural)
nitó this (near the speaker), **ng** form, of this, demonstrative pronoun in the genitive or possessive form, used to refer to third person singular when there are two personal pronouns in the third person in a sentence
niyá his, her, he, she
niyán that (near the listener), **ng** form
niyón/noón that (far from the speaker and the listener), **ng** form
Nobyémbre November
noón(g) past time marker
noóng isáng buwán last month
noóng isáng taón last year
noóng nakaraáng dalawáng buwán two months ago
nuwébe nine

O

o sige (pô/hô) all right, see you later (sir/madam), goodbye
o sige na múnà bye for now
o sige na ngâ all right
o sige, kita táyo mámayâ all right, see you later
o sige okay, I see
Okey lang. Fine.
Okey na okey! Great!
Oktúbre October
ónse eleven
opisína office
orasán clock
oras-oras every hour
ospitál hospital
otél hotel
ótso eight

P

pa still
paá foot
paakyát on the way up
paalála notice, reminder
pababâ on the way down
pabalík on the way back
pabilóg circular
padyák bicycle with sidecar attached
pagdálaw visit
pagdiríwang celebration/festival
pagdumí moving one's bowels
pagkagísing namin when (after) we woke up
pagkáin food
pagkatápos/tápos after
pagóng turtle
pagsalúbong welcoming, meeting
pahabâ elongated, long
pakí- please
pakiúlit mo namán ang please repeat
paksíw fish or meat dish cooked in vinegar, salt, ginger, or garlic
pakuluín/magpakuló boil
pakuwadrádo squared
pakwán watermelon
palakaibígan friendly
palambutín/magpalambót (causative) tenderize
palanggána basin
palaspás palm leaves for Palm Sunday
pálda skirt
paléngke market
palipáran airport
pamáhid sa katí anti-itch ointment
pamáhid sa sugát treatment for wounds
pamangkín nephew, niece
pamasáhe fare
pamilíhan wet market; marketplace
pamintá pepper
pamintáng buô peppercorn
pampagána appetizer
pampalása seasoning
pampáng shore
Pampanga province of the Philippines located in the Central Luzon region
pampaták sa matá eye drops
pampawalá ng sakít pain reliever
panaderyá bakery
panahón weather, season
pangánay oldest sibling, eldest child
pángit ugly
pangô flat (nose)
pangunáhing taúhan main character
pansít Filipino noodle dish
pantál welt, slightly swollen part of the skin usually due to insect bites
pantalón pants
papuntá towards

paráda parade
parehong kaliwâ ang paá ko I have two left feet (bad dancer)
páres pair
pasahéro passenger
pasalúbong house gift
pasapórte passport
pasensya ka na I'm sorry
Paskó Christmas
Paskó ng Pagkábúhay Easter
pasyálan tourist destination or any place to spend leisure time
pasyénte patient
patayín/pumatáy to turn off, to kill
patís fish sauce
payát thin
Pebréro February
péra money
permíso permission
péro but
pigsá boil (skin complaint)
Pilipínas Philippines
Pilipíno/a Filipino
pilóta sport similar to racquet ball
pinaka- prefix used to form superlative degree of an adjective
pinaupóng manók roasted chicken (literally, chicken made to sit on salt)
pínsan cousin
pintahán (v) color, paint
pinyá pineapple
pipíno cucumber
pirasúhin/magpiráso cut into pieces
pitákà wallet
pitó seven
pitóng daán seven hundred
pitpitín/magpitpít pound
pitsél pitcher, jug
piyáno piano
platíto saucer, small plate
pláto plate
ploréra flower vase
pólo button-down shirt
pos ópis post office
Pránsya France
presidénte president
présyo price
pridyeder refrigerator
protéktahan/magprotékta protect
Protestánte Protestant
prútas fruit
pukpukín/magpukpók to pound
pulá red
pulbós powder
pulís policeman
pulséras bracelet
pumaráda parked
pumások went to work, school
pumaták dropped
pumáyag agreed
pumuntá went

púnò tree
pupuntahán destination
púro pure
púsà cat
púsò heart
pútbol football
putî white
pútik mud
putúlin/magpútol cut
puwéde can

Q

Quezon City former capital of the Philippines, part of Metro Manila, NCR or National Capital Region, named after Manuel L. Quezon, president of the Commonwealth of the Philippines under the United States

R

rádyo radio
rayúma rheumatism
realisasyón realization
realístiko realistic
rebosádo coated with batter, dish, esp. of shrimps
rekádo seasoning, flavoring for food
reklámo complaint
rékord record
rektánggulo rectangle
rep refrigerator
repólyo cabbage
representá representing another
reséta prescription
restawrán restaurant
retráto picture, photo
rósas pink, rose (flower)
rotónda turn around
Rúso Russian
rúta route

S

sa future time marker
sa singular common noun marker
sa at, from, in, on, to
sa ákin my, mine, to me
sa ámin our, ours, to us, from us (not including the listener)
sa átin our (including the listener)
sa isáng taón (buwán, linggó) next year (month, week)
sa iyó your, yours, to you, from you (**sa** pronoun, singular)
sa íyo your
sa kanilá their, to them, from them
sa kaniyá his, hers, to him, to her, from him, from her
sa mga plural common noun marker
sa súsunód na taón (buwán, linggó) next year (month, week)

saán where (followed by an action word)

Sábado Saturday

sabíhin/magsábi say

sábila aloe vera

sábong cockfighting

ságing banana

sagó at guláman sweet drink with tapioca and agar-agar

saís six

sáker soccer

sakít ailment, illness, disease

sakít ng ngípin toothache

sakít ng úlo headache

sála living room

salaán strainer, colander, sifter

salabát ginger tea

saláin strain, sift

salámat thank you

salamín glasses, mirror

samakalawá next two days

sampálok tamarind

sampû ten

sampúng líbo ten thousand

sána makaratíng ka hope you can make it

sandalî short time, moment, minute

sandali lang just a moment

sandályas sandals

sándo sleeveless undershirt

sandók spoon-like ladle

sangkáp ingredient

sápà small brook, rivulet, stream

sapátos shoes

saríwà fresh

sársa sauce

sawsáwan condiment, sauce, any liquid to dip food

sayáw dance

sayawín (O.F.) dance

Semana Santa Holy Week

senadór senator

serbésa beer

Setyémbre September

si marks the name of a singular person or animal, **ang** form

sibúyas onion

síko elbow

silá they

silángan east

síli pepper

silyá chair

simbáhan church

simulá po noón since then, sir/madam

siná plural proper name (person or animal's name), **ang** marker

sinangág fried rice

sínat slight fever

síne movie

sinehán movie theater

singkít slit-eyed, slanting

síngko five

singsíng ring

sinigáng tamarind-based soup with meat and vegetables or fish or shrimp

sinísipón has/have a cold

síno who

sintóma symptom

sinturón belt

sinungáling liar

sinu-sino who are

sinusúnog being burned

siopao meat bun

sipón cold

sirâ broken, destroyed

sira-sirâ dilapidated

sitsaró snow pea

siyá he, she

siyám nine

siyám na líbo nine thousand

siyám na raán nine hundred

siyangá ba really

siyanga palá by the way

siyansé spatula

siyéte seven

sombréro hat, cap

sopá/supá sofa, couch

sopdrink soda, soft drink

súgat wound

súhà pomelo, grapefruit

súkà vinegar

sukát fit, snug

súkat size, measurement

suklî/baryá change (loose change)

sumakáy rode, got on

sumásakít aching

sumísid dive

sumunód follow

sunduín/sumundô pick someone up, fetch

sunóg burnt

súnog fire

supládo/a snobbish

súrot bed bug

T

tabíng-dágat beach

tábò water dipper

tadtarín/magtadtád chop into small pieces

tagá saán from where

tagá- from

tagaín/magtagâ chop

tagalútò chef, cook

tagapaglútò chef, cook

tag-inít summer

taglagás fall, autumn

taglamíg winter

tagsiból spring

tag-ulán rainy season

tahánan home

tahímik calm, quiet

takípsílim twilight

takpán/magtakíp to cover

táksi cab, taxi

talagá really

talón falls; waterfall; **(v)** jump, dive into the water

talóng eggplant

tamád lazy

tanáwin view, scenery

tandaán (object focus) remember

tandáng rooster

tanggalín/magtanggál remove

tanggapín/tumanggáp receive, accept

tanghálì late

tanungín /magtanóng ask

táo person

tapát across

tapát faithful

tapós the end

tápos and then

tapsilóg dried or cured beef, fried rice and egg

tása cup

tátay/amá (formal) father

tatló three

tatlóng daán three hundred

tatlumpû thirty

taún-taón yearly

tawágin/tumáwag call

táyo we (including the listener)

teka wait up

téla fabric, cloth, textile

telebisyón television

ténga, tainga ear

tigdás measles

tiisín/magtiís endure

tingnán look at

tímog south

Tímog Koréa South Korea

timplahín/magtimplá mix

tindáhan store

tindéro/a storekeeper, seller

tinidór/tenedór fork

títa/tíya/tía aunt

títo/tíyo/tío uncle

títser/gúrò teacher

tiyán stomach

tóge bean sprouts

tokadór dresser

Totoó 'yan. That's true.

tóyo soy sauce

trangkáso flu

tren train

trénta thirty

tréntay úno thirty-one

tres three

trése thirteen

traysikel motorcycle with sidecar attached

tsaá tea

tsamporádo/sampurádo chocolate
rice porridge
Tsína China
tsinélas slippers, slipper
Tsíno Chinese
tsit restaurant bill, check
túbig water
tugtugín/tumugtóg play (musical
instrument)
túhod knee
tumáwag called
tumingín look at
tumúbò grew
tumúlong helped
turísta tourist
tuwíng every
tuyô dry; salted dry fish
tuyuín/magtuyô dry

U
úbas grape
úbe yam
ubó cough
ubúsin/umúbos finish, finished

ulán rain
úlap cloud
úlo head
-um- actor-focus verbal affix
umabánte moved forward
umakyát climbed, went up
umakyát ng bundók climbed a
mountain
umalís left
umambón drizzled
umáraw became sunny
umatrás backed up
umído humid
umíkot turned around
uminóm drank
umulán rained
umútang borrow money, buy
something on credit
umuwî go home
únan pillow
Undás All Saints Day
úno one
up-and-down two-story house
upuán seat

úso trendy, current style

W
walâ not have, (there is/are/was) none
wala namán, waláng bágo nothing
much, nothing new
waláng anumán you're welcome
waláng lamán empty
waláng táo deserted
walís broom
waló eight
walóng daán eight hundred
walóng líbo eight thousand
wéyter waiter
wíkà language

Y
yáya nanny
yayáin/magyayâ invite
yumukó stoop
'yung variant of ang

Abbreviations used:

adj	adjective	O.F.	object focus	s	singular
aux. v	auxiliary verb	pl	plural	s.o.	someone
n	noun	Phil.	Philippine	s.t.	something
geog	geography	pron	pronoun	v	verb

Note: Some English words pertaining to new technology are borrowed directly and have no change in
spelling. Others are spelled using Tagalog orthography.

English-Tagalog

A
able to maka-, makapag-, ma-
(attached to a root verb)
ability may kakayahán
above itaás
absent-minded malilimutín
accept tanggapín/tumanggáp
accident (n) aksidénte, (v) maaksidénte
according to áyon sa
aching sumásakít
across tapát
act (n) pagkilos, (v) kumílos, gawín
active mabilís, aktibo
actor artista, aktór, aktrés
add idagdág/magdagdág
adult may sapát na gúlang, matandâ
afraid takót
after pagkatápos, tápos
afternoon hápon

again mulî
against laban, kontra, salungát
agree sumang-áyon, pumáyag
agree with one (as in climate, food,
etc.) mahiyáng
agreement kasundúan
ailment sakít
air hángin
air conditioner aircon
airplane eropláno
airport palipáran
aisle pasílyo, daánan, pagítan
alive buháy, (lively) masiglá
all lahát
all right o sige na ngâ
All Saints Day Undás
All Souls' Day Áraw ng mga Patáy
alley eskiníta
almost hálos

aloe vera sábila
already na
also din/rin
always lágì
amazing nakakamanghâ
American Amerikáno/a
ancient lúmà
and at
and then tápos
anger gálit
angry gálit
animal hayop
annoyed nainis, nayamót, nabuwísit
annoying nakakainís
answer sagót
anti-itch ointment pamáhid sa katí
anxious balisá, nababagabag, hindi
mapalagáy
anxious (in anticipation) sabík

appetizer pampagána
appetizing nakakagútom, nakakagana
apple mansánas
apply maglagáy, ipáhid/pahíran
approached lumápit, nilapítan
April Abríl
architect arkitékto
architecture arkitektúra
arm bráso
around (at about a certain time, followed by adverb of time) bandáng
arrival datíng
arrive dumatíng
art síning
as katúlad, kapáris, kasíng
as soon as pagka- (attached to a root verb), kaagád
ashamed nahíhiyâ
ask magtanóng/tanungín; ~ **(s.o.) to do something** magpa-/pa-in (attached to a root verb)
ask for something hingín/humingî
asthma híkà
at nása, sa
August Agósto
aunt títa/tíya/tía
aware alám
awesome ang galíng
awful (nasty) nakakadírì

B

baby beybi, sanggól
bachelor binátà, waláng asáwa
back likód, likurán
back up umatrás
backpack bakpak
bad masamâ, salbáhe
badminton bádminton
bag bag
bake mag-bake
bakery panaderyá
balcony balkonáhe
bald kalbó
ball bola
banana ságing
banana fritters marúyà
bank bángko
baptize binyagán/magbinyág
barber shop barberyá
bargain bargeyn, baratilyo
baseball béysbol
baseball player manlaláro ng béysbol
basin palanggána
basketball basketból
basketball player basketbolísta
bath palilígò
bathe malígò
bathe (s.o.) magpalígò/paligúan
bathroom bányo
battery bateryá

bay loók
bay leaf dáhon ng lawrél
be maging (followed by noun or verb; no real verb to be in Tagalog); ~ **afraid of** matakot; ~ **aware of** maláman, mabatíd; ~ **hungry** magútom; ~ **in a hurry** magmadalî; ~ **interested in** maging interesádo; ~ **late** mahulí; ~ **lost** maligáw; ~ **quiet** tumahímik/manahímik; ~ **sick** magkasakít; ~ **sleepy** antukín; ~ **still** huwág gumaláw, pumirmí; ~ **tired** mapágod; ~ **thirsty** maúhaw
beach dágat
beach (shore) tabíng-dágat
bean sprouts tóge
bear (v) (endure) tiisín, batahín, **(carry)** magbatá; madalá/dalhín
beat batihín/magbatí
became sunny umáraw
because kasí
because of dáhil sa
become magíng
bed káma
bedbug súrot
bedroom kuwárto
bedspread kubrekáma
bee bubúyog
beef báka
beer serbésa
before bágo
behind likód
being pagíging
belief pananálig, pananampalatáyà, paniniwálà
believe maniwálà
below ibabâ
belt sinturón
bench bangkô
best friend matálik na kaibígan
bet (n) pustá, **(v)** pumustá
bicycle bisikléta
bicycle with sidecar attached padyák
big malakí
bill (restaurant) tsit
billiards bilyár
bird íbon
birthday bertdey, kaarawan
birthmark bálat
bitten nakagát
bitter mapaít
bitter melon ampalayá
black itím
bland matabáng
blanket kúmot
bleeding dumúdugô
blind bulág
blog blog
blouse blúsa
blow (wind) humángin
blow-dry blow-dry

blue asúl
boat bangkâ
body katawán
boil magpakulô, pakuluín (causative)
boil pigsá (skin complaint)
book libró
borrow hiramín/humirám
borrow money umútang
boss ámo
bottle bóte, botélya
bottom ilálim
bowl mangkók
bowling bóling
boxer boksingéro
boy (young) bátang laláke
boyfriend boypren, nobyo
bracelet pulséras
brave matápang
break (rest) pahingá
break (v) balíin
bright maliwánag
bring magdalá/dalhín; ~ **home** iuwî/mag-uwî
broken (glass, mirror, etc.) baság
broken (destroyed) sirâ
broom walís
brown (skin color) kayumanggî
brush hair mag-brush ng buhok
brush teeth magsipílyo/sepílyuhin
Buddhist Budísta
bug súrot
building gusálì/bilding
bungalow búnggalo
burn (skin) pásò
burned nasúnog
burning (feeling pain) mahapdî
burnt sunóg
bury ibaón
bus bus
bus station istasyón ng bús
business bísnes, negósyo
businessman negosyánte, bisnesman
but péro, ngúnit
butter mantekílya
button-down shirt pólo
buy bilhín/bumilí; ~ **(s.t.) on credit** umútang/utángin
buyer mamimílí
by the way siyangá palá
bye for now o sige na muna

C

cabbage repólyo
calamansi juice kalamansí dyús
calamity kalamidád
call (n) táwag. **(v)** tawágin/tumáwag
calm tahímik
can (n) láta
can (pseudo-v) puwéde, maaari
can opener abreláta
capture mahúli/hulíhin

car kótse

carry (provisions, money, or food one takes to work or school) ibáon/magbáon

cashier kahéra

casserole kaseróla

cat púsà

catch (fish) (n) húli

Catholic Katóliko

caught (by the door or pressed between two objects) naípit; ~ in traffic matrápik/natrapik

cave kuwéba

celebrate ipagdíwang/magdíwang

celebration pagdiríwang

chair silyá/silya

change (v) magpalít/palitán

change (loose change) suklî/baryá

change clothes magbíhis

charge (cellphone) mag-charge

charger charger

chase habúlin/humábol

chat chat, mag-usap

chat online mag-chat online

cheap (inexpensive) múra

check (bill in restaurant) tsit

cheese késo

chewy makúnat

chicken manók

chicken pox bulútong-túbig

child (son/daughter) anák

child (not an offspring) bátà

China Tsína

Chinese (male/female) Tsíno/Tsína

Chinese celery kintsáy

chocolate-colored, brown kúlay tsokoláte

choice mapagpipilían/mapapagpilían

cholera kólera

choose ipílì/pumílì

chop tagaín/magtagâ

chop into small pieces tadtarín/magtadtád

Christmas Paskó

church simbáhan

circle bilóg

circular pabilóg

citrus (small variety) kalamansî

citrus (Phil. orange) dalandán

class úrì, kláse

classmate kakláse

clean (v) linísin/maglínis

clean (root) línis

clean (adj) malínis

clear maliwánag, malínaw

climb akyát

clinic klínika

clock orasán

close (v) isará/magsará

closed (adj) saródo

close (distance) malapit

closet aparadór

cloth téla

clothes mga damít

cloud úlap

cloudy maúlap

coast baybáy, baybáyin, apláya

coat (formal suit) amerikána

coated with batter, dish, esp. of shrimps rebosádo

cockfighting sábong

coconut niyóg

coconut milk gatâ

coffee kapé

cold (sickness) sipón

cold (temp., weather) malamíg

collect mag-ipón

color (n) kúlay, (v) pintahán

colorful makúlay

comb hair magsukláy

come (call someone) halika

come (approach) lumápit

come (arrive) dumatíng

come back bumalík

comfortable komportáble

commute (n) biyáhe

complain magreklámo

complaint reklámo

complete kumpléto

completed natápos

conceited makaakó

condiment sawsáwan

confident may tiwálà, nagtitiwálà

conserve (save) típírin

conserve (gather) tipúnin

conserve (as in forest) alagáan

consult kumunsúlta/kunsultahín

contaminate (infect) maháwa

conversation pag-uusap, usapan

cook (n) kusinéro/a/tagalútò, (v) lutúin/maglúto

cook rice magsáing

cooked (adj) lutô

cooking oil mantíkà

cool (temp.) malamíg-lamíg, présko (breeze)

coral koráles

corn maís

corner kánto

cornstarch (for clothes) gawgáw

cost halagá

cough ubó

count bilángin/magbiláng

country báyan

cousin pínsan

cover (n) takíp, (v) takpán/magtakíp

cow báka

coward duwág

crack básag, lámat

crack a joke magbirô

craft kasanáyan, kagalíngan

cramped masikíp

cream kréma

creamy makrema

create gumawâ, lumikhâ

crime krímen

criminal kriminál

crispy malutóng

crooked baluktót

cry (n) iyák, (v) umiyák

crowd mga táo, karamihan ng táo

crowded matáo, masikíp

cucumber pipíno

cup tása

curly kulót

curtain kurtína

cut (v) putúlin/magpútol

cut (with a knife; may be accidentally) mahíwà

cut (with scissors, may be accidentally) magupít

cut into pieces pirasúhin/magpiraso

D

dance (n) sayáw, (v) magsayáw, sayawín

dancer mananáyaw

dark madilím

dark-complexioned maitím

date pétsa

daughter anák na babáe

dawn madalíng-áraw

day áraw

day before yesterday kamakalawá

death kamatáyan

December Disyémbre

delete alisín, burahín, delete

delicious masaráp

deny ipagkailâ, tumanggí

department store pamilíhan, department store

departure alís, pag-alís

describe iláráwan

deserted waláng táo

desk mésa, eskritóryo

dessert panghimagas, póstre

destination pupuntahán, lugár

destiny kapaláran, tadhánà

destroyed nasírà

development debelopment, pag-unlad

dew hamóg

die mamatáy

different ibá

difficult mahírap

dilapidated sira-sirâ

dining room komedór, kaínan

direction direksiyón; ~ toward (usually followed by rito, riyan, or roon) bandá

dirty marumí/madumí

disagree hindi sumang-áyon, sumalungát

disarrange guluhín/gumuló

discount táwad, diskuwénto
discussion diskusyón, tálakayan
disease sakít
dive (n) talón, sísid, **(v)** tumalón, sumísid
divorce dibórsyo
divorced diborsyádo/a
do gawín/gumawâ
doctor doktór
does not like/want áyaw
dog áso
don't huwág, 'wag
door pintô
dormitory dormitóryo
downstairs ibabâ
doze umidlíp
dozen doséna/duséna
draw magdrowing
dream (n) panagínip, **(v)** managínip
dress (n) bestída/o, **(v)** magbestída/o
dresser tokadór
drink (n) inumín, **(v)** inumín/uminóm
drink coffee magkapé
drinking glass báso
drive magmaného
drive to magmaného papuntá sa
drizzle ambón
drizzled umambón
drop (eyedrop) ipaták/magpaták/ pumaták
drop by magdaán
drunk lasíng
dry (adj) tuyô
dry off tuyuín/magtuyô
durable matíbay
dust alikabók
dusty maalikabók
each káda
ear ténga/tainga
earlier this morning kanínang umága

E

early maága
earrings mgá híkaw
earthquake lindól
east silángan
Easter Paskó ng Pagkabúhay
easy madalî
eat kaínin/kumáin
eat a snack magmiryénda/ magmeryénda
eat breakfast mag-almusál/mag- agahan
eat dinner maghapúnan
eat lunch magtanghalían
egg itlóg
eggplant talóng
eight ótso, waló
eight hundred walóng daán
eighteen disiótso, labíngwaló
elbow síko

elder brother kúya
elder sister áte
electric fan bentiladór
eleven labíng-isá, ónse
elongated pahabâ
email (n) email, **(v)** mag-email
empty waláng lamán, basyó
encourage palakasín ang loób
endure tiisín/ magtiís
engineer inhinyéro/a
English Inglés
enter pások
entertaining nakakalibáng
entrance entráda, pasukán
erase burahín
even (adj) pantáy
every tuwíng
every hour oras-oras; ~ **minute** minú- minúto; ~ **night** gabí-gabí; ~ **week** linggú-linggó
every now and then mayá't-mayâ
everyday áraw-áraw
example halimbáwà
excited excited; sabík
exclaim ipinaháyag, iginiít, sinábi
Excuse me, pardon me, sir/ ma'am Ekskyus pô, Makikiraán pô Pasintábi pô, Paumanhín pô; Mawaláng-gálang na pô
exit (n) labásan, **(v)** lumabás
expensive mahál
export (n) export, **(v)** mag-export
expose maglantád
extra extra, ekstra
eye matá
eyebrow kílay
eyedrops pampaták sa matá

F

fabric téla
face mukhâ
fact katunáyan
fail a class bumagsák sa klase
fair (just) makatarúngan
fair (medium) katamtáman
fair-complexioned maputî
faith paniniwálà, relihiyón
faith healer albuláryo
faithful tapát, matapát
fall (root) húlog
fall down (v) mahúlog
fall flat on one's face madapâ
fall (autumn) taglagás
fame katanyagán
family mag-ának, pamilya
famous sikát
far maláyò
fare pamasáhe
farm búkid; palayán
farmer magsasaká
fast mabilís

fat matabâ
fate kapaláran
father tátay, amá (formal)
Father's Day Áraw ng mga Amá
faucet grípo
favor pabór, pakíusap
fear (n) tákot, **(v)** matákot
fearful (adj) takót
February Pebréro
fee báyad
feed pakaínin
feel (with fingers) salatín
feel bad masama ang pakiramdám; ~ **good** maganda/mabuti ang pakiramdám; ~ **ill** may-sakít; ~ **sick** may-sakit; ~ **well** mabuti ang pakiramdám
fell down with the face forward nadapâ, narapâ, maparapâ
female babáe
ferry bapór
fever lagnát
few kauntî
fewer mas konti/kauntî
field búkid
fifteen kínse, labínlimá
fifty limámpû
Filipino Pilipíno/a
fill punuín
final (last) hulí
fine mabúti
finger dalírì
finish (consume) ubúsin/ umúbos, **(end, complete)** tapúsin
fire (n) apóy, súnog, **(v)** mag-apóy
first a-priméro
fish (n) isdâ, **(v)** mangisdâ
fish sauce patís
fishy malansá
fit sukát, lapat
fits well kasiyang-kasiya
five limá, síngko
five hundred limáng daán/limandaán
fix (v) ayúsin/mag-áyos gawín/ gumawâ
flash (lightning) kumidlát
flat (nose) pangô
flavor lása
flight lipád
flood (n) bahâ, **(v)** bumahâ
flour arína/harína
flow dáloy
flower bulaklák
flower bud búko
flower vase ploréra
flu trangkáso
flunk a test or class kalabása, bumagsák sa kláse
fly (n) (insect) lángaw
fly (v) lumipád
follow sumunód

food pagkáin
foot paá
football pútbol
for para
for example halimbáwà
forbidden báwal
forest gúbat
fork tinidór/tenedór
forty ápatnapû
forward (direction) pasulóng
forward (in front) sa harapán
four ápat, kuwátro
four hundred ápat na raán
fourteen katórse, labíng- ápat
frame kuwádro
France Pránsya
frequent madalás
fresh saríwà
Friday Biyérnes
fried rice sinangág
friend kaibígan
friendly palákaibígan, magíliw
from mulá sa-, sa, tagá-
from where tagá saán
front haráp
frown simángot, (v) sumimángot
fruit bunga, prútas
fry ipríto/magpríto/ipritos
frying pan kawálì
full (container, room, etc.) punô, (stomach) busóg
fun masayá
funny nakakatawá
future hinaharáp, kinabukásan

G

gallon galón
garage garáhe
garbage basúra
garlic báwang
gather mag-ípon, ipúnin
gelatin guláman
German Alemán
get kumúha, kúnin; ~ **better** gumalíng/ magpagalíng: ~ **worse** lumalâ
get in touch with kóntakin/kumóntak
get up tumayô, bumángon
ginger lúya
ginger tea salabát
girl bátang babáe
girlfriend gérlpren/nóbya
give ibigáy/magbigáy
glass (drinking) báso
glass (window) salamín
glasses (eyes) salamín
go síge; ~ **back** bumalík; ~ **down** bumabâ; ~ **fast** magmabilís, bilisán; ~ **outside** lumabás; ~ **slow** bagálan, magdahan-dáhan; ~ **straight** dumirétso; ~ **up** umakyát; ~ **upstairs** umakyát

go away (leave) láyas, umalís; ~ away (move away) lumayô
go for a walk maglakád; (stroll) mamasyál
go home umuwî
go on vacation magbakasyón
go online mag-online
go out (with s.o.) lumabás (kasáma)
go shopping magsyáping, mamilí
go to bed/sleep matúlog
go to school pumások sa eskwéla
go to the market mamaléngke
God Diyos, Bathalâ
godchild (godson, goddaughter) ináanák
godfather nínong
godmother nínang
gold gintô
good (taste, quality, ethical) mabúti; ~ (response to greeting) mabuti namán
good at magalíng (sa)
Good Friday Biyérnes Sánto
Good morning (sir/madam) Magandáng umága (hô/pô)
Good noon (sir/madam) Magandáng tanghálì (pô/hô)
gossip tsísmis
governor gobernadór/a
grandchild (grandson, granddaughter) apó
grandfather lólo
grandmother lóla
grape úbas
grapefruit súhà
grate gadgarín/maggadgád
grater kudkúran
Great! Magalíng!
great (high in rank) dakilà
green bérde
greet batíin/bumátì
grew tumúbò
grill iháwin/mag-íhaw
grow (v) lumakí
guava bayábas
guitar gitára

H

hair buhók
half kalahátì
hand kamáy
handbag handbag
handsome guwápo/pogì
happen mangyári
happy masayá
hard matigás
hard-working masípag
has/have/had may, mayroón, nagkaroón
has/have (develop) nagka- (attached to a noun)

has/have/had a cold sinisipón, nagkasipón
has/have diarrhea nagtátaé
has/have fun nagsayá
has/have oneself vaccinated nagpabakúna
hat sombréro
head úlo
headache sakít ng úlo
health kalusúgan
healthy malusóg
hear maríníg
hear mass magsimbá
heart púsò
heat (n) ínit, (v) inítin/mag-ínit
heavy mabigát
height taás
helped tumúlong/tinulúngan
helpful matulungín
her sa kaniyá/siyá
her (ng pron) niyá, (sa pron) kaniyá
here (said of an object or person) nandíto
Here, still alive. Héto buháy pa.
hi hi, kamustá/kumustá
hibiscus gumaméla
high mataás
hike mag-hiking
hill buról
him (sa pron) sa kaniyá
his/her (ng pron) niyá, (sa pron) sa kaniyá
historical makasaysáyan
history kasaysáyan
hit bungguín/bumunggô
hobby libángan
Holy Week Semána Sánta
home tahánan
homemade lútong-báhay
honest matapát
hope pag-ása
Hope you can make it. Sána makaratíng ka.
horse kabáyo
horse-drawn carriage kalésa
horse race karéra ng kabáyo
hospital ospitál
hot (temp.) maínit
hot (spicy) maangháng
hotel otél/hotél
house báhay
how paáno
How's it going? Kumustá na?
how many Ilán
how much magkáno
how old (person or animal) ilang taón
hug yákap
human táo
humble mapágkumbabâ
humid umído

hundred unit daán
hurry dalî
hurt (v) sumakít
husband mister/asáwa
hut kúbo

I

I have two left feet. Parehong kaliwa ang paá ko.
I will never ever forget. Hindíng-hindi ko makakalimútan.
I'm sorry pasensya ka na-/ ikinalulungkot ko
if kung
ignorant ignoránte, mangmáng, waláng alám
ignore balewalaín
ill maysakít
illness sakít
immediately agád
import import, angkát
important importánte, mahalagá
in sa
in (followed by a noun) nasa
in between sa gitnâ
in front haráp, harapán
include isama, **(add)** idagdág/ magdagdág
incompleted (said of action) nangyayári
incredible di kapani-paniwálà
Independence Day Áraw ng Kasarinlán
indoors sa loób
infected naháwa
inform sabíhan
information impormasyón
infrequent madálang
ingredient sangkáp
inside loób
insider taga loób
intelligent matalíno; marúnong
intend iukol
intent layon
intention intensyón
introduce ipakilála
invest mag-invest
invitation imbitasyón
invite kumbidahín/magkumbidá, yayáin/magyayâ
island ísla, pulô
Italy Itálya
itch katí
itchy makatí

J

jackfruit langkâ
January Enéro
Japan Hapón
Japanese (person) Hapón
jeans maóng

jeep/jeepney dyíp
joke (n) bírò, dyok, **(v)** magbirô
jog mag-jógging
juice dyús, katás
July Húlyo
June Húnyo
just lang
just a moment sandali lang/saglít lang/teka
justice katarúngan

K

keep itágò
key (lock) súsì
key in i-key in
kid bátà
kill patayín/pumatáy
kilogram kílo
kind mabaít
kiss halík
kitchen kusínà
knee túhod
kneel lumuhód
knife kutsílyo
know (s.o.) kilalánin, **(s.t.)** alám (O.F.)
Korean Koreáno/a

L

Labor Day Áraw ng Manggagáwà
lack kawalán, kúlang
ladle sandók
lake láwà
lamp lámpara, ílaw
language wíkà
last hulí; ~ **month** noóng isáng buwán; ~ **night** kagabí; ~ **year** noóng isáng taón
late mahulí, tanghálì
later mámayâ; ~ **this afternoon** mámayáng hápon; ~ **tonight** mámayáng gabí
laugh (v) tumáwa/tawánan
laundry room labáhan
law abogasyá/abogasíya
lawyer abogádo/a
lazy tamád
leaf dáhon
leave (s.t., s.o.) alís, íwan
left (direction) kaliwâ
leg bintî
lemonade limonáda
less kulang
let hayáan
lettuce letsúgas
liar sinungáling
library aklátan, laybrari
lie (untruth) kasinungalíngan
lie (v) higâ
life búhay
lift buhátin/magbuhát

light (n) ílaw, **(v)** iláwan
light (adj, color) mapusyáw
light (adj, weight) magaán
lighten gaanán
Light Rail Transit LRT
lightning kidlát
like gustó
list (n) listáhan, **(v)** ilistá/maglistá
listen makiníg/pakinggán
listen to the radio makiníg sa rádyo
liter lítro
literature literatúra, pánitikan
live (show) layb
live (v) mabúhay
live (in a house, place) tumirá
living room sála
lock kandádo
long (length) mahábà
look tingín/tingnán
look at tingnán/tumingín
look for hanápin/humánap/maghanáp
loose maluwág/maluwáng
loose change baryá
lose pagkawalâ
lose (game) pagkatálo
loud maíngay
lousy (book, show, etc) pángit, waláng kuwénta
love ibígin/umíbig
loving mapágmahál
low mabábà
lower mas mabábà
luck suwérte
lucky masuwérte
luggage maléta
lukewarm maligamgám

M

mad (very angry at s.o.) galít na galít
mad (crazy) lukú-lukó, lóko/a, balíw
madly lókong-lóko
mail koréo, sulat
main protagonist pangunáhing taúhan
mainly sa kalakhán
major medyor, pangunáhin
make gawín/gumawâ
make a reservation magresérba
make adobo iadóbo/mag-adóbo
make fun of pagtawanán, biruin, i-good time
make (s.o.) do something magpagawâ; ~ **(s.o.) happy** pasayahín; ~ **(s.o.) laugh** patawánin; ~ **(s.o.) sad** palungkútin
malaria malárya
male laláki
man laláki; mamà
mango manggá
mango juice mánggo dyús

many marámi

map mápa

March Márso

market paléngke, pamilíhan

married may-asáwa

marry (a couple) magkasál/ikasál

marry (s.o.) pakasalán

mask máskara

mass mísa

massage (n) masáhe, **(v)** hilútin

masseuse manghihílot

mat baníg

math matemátika

Maundy Thursday Huwébes Sánto

may (aux. v) puwéde, maaárì

May Máyo

maybe sigúro

mayor alkálde/meyor

meal pagkáin; almusál, tanghalían, hapúnan

mean (adj) matáray

mean (v) ibig sabíhin

measles tigdás

measure sukatín

measurement súkat

meat (food) karné, lamán

meat bun siopáo

medicine gamót, medisína; ~ **for diarrhea** gamót sa pagtatáe; ~ **for insect bites** gamót sa mga pantál

meet (s.o.) makilála

meet with someone magkíta, makipagkita

meeting pagsalúbong, miting, púlong

merchant tindéro/a

mess guló; kálat

messy maguló

Mexico Méhiko

middle gitnâ

midwife manghihílot

mild (drink) hindi matápang; ~ **(disposition)** mahináhon

milk gátas

mirror salamín

mischievous maguló, malikót, pílyo

misplaced nawalâ

miss (misunderstand) hindi maintindihán

miss (target) hindi tamáan

Miss ále, Binibini (Bb.), Miss

mister mámà, mistér

mix (v) ihálò, timplahín/magtimplá

modern makabágo, moderno/a

modest mahinhín

Monday Lúnes

money péra

monosodium glutamate (MSG) bétsin

month buwán

monthly buwán-buwán

moon buwán

mop the floor maglampáso ng sahíg

more mas

mosquito lamók

mosquito net kulambô

mother (formal) nánay, iná, **(informal)** nay

Mothers' Day Áraw ng mga Iná

motorcycle motorsíklo

motorcycle with sidecar traysikel

mountain bundók

mouth bibíg; bungángà

move ùrong, ~ **forward** umabánte

moved lumípat

moved one's bowels dumumí

movie síne, pelikulá

movie theater sinehán

Mrs. Ginang (Gng.), Mísis, ále

mud pútik

muddy mapútik

mushroom kabuté

music mùsika

musician musikéro/a

must kailángan

My Dear (letter salutation) Mahál Kong

N

nanny yáya

nap idlíp

National Heroes' Day Áraw ng mga Bayáni

nauseating nakakahílo

nauseous nahihílo

near malápit

neat malínis at maáyos

neck leég

necklace kuwintás

need kailángan

nephew pamangkín

net (fishing) lambát

nervous ninenérbiyós

new bágo

New Year's Day Bágong Taón

news balítà

newspaper diyáryo, peryódikó

next sunód, súsunód; ~ **day** kinábukásan; ~ **month** buwán; ~ **two days** samakalawá; ~ **week** linggó; ~ **year** sa isáng taón

nice (thing) magandá, **(trait)** mabaít

niece pamangkín

night gabi

nine nuwébe, siyám

nine hundred siyám na raán

nineteen disinuwébe, labínsiyám

no hindî

nod (n) tangô, **(v)** tumangô

noise ingay

noisy maíngay

none walâ

north hilágà

nose ilóng

nosebleed balinguyngóy

not hindî

not have walâ

note talâ

note (music) nota

nothing walâ; ~ **much** wala namán

nothing new waláng bago

notice (n) paalála, **(v)** napansín

November Nobyémbre

now ngayón

nurse nars

nursing nársing

nutritious masustánsya

O

occasion okasyón

occasionally paminsan-mínsan

occur nangyári, **(thought)** maísip

ocean dágat

October Oktúbre

of ng

off (radio, light, stove, etc) patáy

offer alók, handóg

offer something alukín/mag-alók

office opisína

often madalás

oh ow

Oh, my gosh Nakú; Ay nakó!

oil langis, mantikà

oily mamantíkà

okay ókey, áyos, o sige

old (person or animal) matandâ, **(object)** lúmà

oldest sibling pangánay

on nasa-, sa

on the other hand sa kabiláng dako, namán

on the way back pabalík; ~ **down** pababâ; ~ **up** paakyát

on top of ibábaw

one isá, úno

one hundred isáng daán/isandaán

one way one way

onion sibúyas

online online

only lang

open (adj) bukás

open (v) magbukás/ibukás

ordinal number iká- (when attached to a cardinal number)

organize ayúsin/mag-áyos

ought dapat

out labás

out of tune sintunádo

outdoors sa labás

outside labás

outsider tagá labás

own may, mayroón

own (adj) saríli

owner may árì

P

pain sakít
pain reliever pampawalá ng sakít
painful masakít
paint (v) pintahán
pair páres
palm leaves (used for Palm Sunday) palaspás
pan kaseróla
pants pantalón
parade paráda
parent magúlang
park park, párke
park (car) (v) magpark
parrot lóro
participate sumáli; lumahók
partner partner; kapares
pass (s.t.) iabót/mag-abót
pass the news (give) ibalítà/magbalítà
passed by dumaán
passenger pasahéro
passport pasapórte
password password
patient (adj) matiyagâ; may pasénsiya
patient (n) pasyénte
pay magbáyad/ibáyad
payment báyad
peace kapayapáan
peaceful mapayápà
peel balatán/magbalát
people táo, taumbáyan
pepper pamintá, síli
peppercorn pamintáng buô
per (each) káda, báwat
permission permíso
person táo
pet alágang háyop
pharmacy botíka/parmásya
Philippine orange dalandán
Philippines Pilipínas
photo litráto, retráto
piano piyáno
pick pulútin, damputín, pilíin
pick someone up sunduín/sumundô, daánan
pick up pulútin, damputín
picture litráto, retráto
pig báboy
pill tabléta, píldoras
pillow únan
pineapple pinyá
pink rósas
pitcher pitsél
place ilagáy/maglagáy
plain (adj) símple
plain (n) kapatágan
plan pláno; balak
plane eropláno
plant haláman
plate pláto

platter bandeháado
play maglarô, larô, laruín; ~ **basketball** magbásketbol; ~ **drums** magdrám; ~ **musical instrument** tugtugín/tumugtóg; ~ **the guitar** maggitára; ~ **the piano** magpiyáno; ~ **videogames** mag-video game
playing cards (n) baráha
please namán, ngâ, pakí- (attached to a root verb)
please repeat pakiúlit mo namán ang
plug in mag-plug in
point (n) túlis
pointed (referring to nose) matángos, matúlis
policeman pulís
polite magálang
pomelo súhà
poor mahírap
porch balkonáhe
pork báboy
porridge lúgaw
port daúngan
post poste; koréo
post office pos ópis
poster poster; paskíl
pot kaldéro
pound (n) líbra
pound (v) pukpukín/magpukpók; (crush) pitpitín/magpitpít,
pour ibúhos/magbúhos
pour into another container isálin/ magsálin
powder pulbós
power kapangyaríhan
powerful makapangyaríhan
prescribe (v) magreséta
prescription reséta
present (n) (gift) regálo, (souvenir from travels) pasalúbong; (v) iharáp, magkaloób
press (v) umípit/ipítin
press (clothes) plántsahin/ mamalántsa
president presidénte
pretty magandá
price présyo
pride pagpapahalagá sa sarili
protect protéktahán/magprotékta
Protestant Protestánte
proud mayábang
prove patunáyan
provide magbigáy/bigyán
provision (usually for a trip or vacation) báon
pull hiláhin/humíla
pulverize magdikdík
pure púro
purple lila
purse pitákà, bag

push túlak
put ilagáy/maglagáy
put down ibabâ; ilapág

Q

quaked (v) lumindól
question (n) tanóng, (v) magtanóng/ tanungín
quiet tahímik
quite médyo, (very) totoó, lubós

R

rabbit kuného
radio rádyo
rain ulán
rainbow bahaghárì
rained umulán
rainy maulán
rainy season tag-ulán
raise (v) magtaás, (child, livestock) magpalakí (grow) magtaním
raw hiláw
reach abutín/mag-abót
read basáhin/magbasá/bumása
real túnay
realistic realístiko
realization realisasyón
realize mapagtantô, maláman
really siyánga ba, talagá
receive tanggapín/tumanggáp
record (n) rékord, (v) irékord, italâ
rectangle rektángguló
red mapulá, pulá
refrigerator rep, pridyedér
refuse tumanggí/tanggihán
relative kamág-ának
relax reláks
relaxed nagreláks
relaxing nakakareláks
remember alalahánin/maalála; tandaán
remove alisín/mag-alís, tanggalín/ magtanggál; ~ **from fire** hangúin
repair ayúsin/mag-áyos
represent representá
representing another magrepresentá/ irepresentá
request hilíng, makiúsap, pakiúsap
resident residénte, naniníráhan
rest (n) (repose) pahingá, (residue) ang natirá; (v) magpahingá
restaurant restawrán
restless malikót, hindi mápalagáy
return (n) pagbalík, (v) ibalík/ magbalík, isaúlì/magsaúlì
rheumatism rayúma
rice (boiled) sináing, kanin, (fried) sinangág, (grain) bigás; ~ **with tocino and egg** tósilog; ~ **with tapa (smoked beef) and egg** tapsilog
rice field búkid, palayán

rich mayáman

ride a bike magbisikléta; **~ a bus**
magbús; **~ a car** magkótse; **~ a**
horse-drawn rig magkalésa; **~**
a jeep magdyíp; **~ a motorcycle**
magmotórsíklo; **~ a train** magtrén;
~ a truck magtrák; **~ an airplane**
mag-eropláno

ridicule pagtawanán, libakín, tuyaín

ridiculous kalokóhan, katawá-tawá

right kánan

right away kaagád-agád

ring singsíng

rinse magmúmog

ripe hinóg

river ílog

road daán

rock bató

room kuwárto

rooster tandáng

rot mabulók

rotary (traffic circle) rotónda

rotten bulók

round bilóg

round trip rawntrip, balíkan

route rúta

rude bastós

run takbó

run errands mag-errands, maglakád

Russian Rúso

S

sad malungkót

sale sale, baratílyo

salt asín

salty maálat

same parého

sand buhángin

sandals sandályas

Saturday Sábado

sauce sársa

saucer platíto

sauté igisá/maggisá

save (money) mag-ípon

say sabíhin/magsábi

school eskwelahán

scratch gasgás

screen iskrín; tábing

sea dágat

search maghanáp/hanápin

season panahón

seasoning pampalása, rekádo

seat upuán

see tingnán, makíta

see you later kita na lang táyo
mámayâ

sell itíndá/magtindá; **(as a car, land,**
house, clothes) magbénta; **(s.t. such**
as small items in store) magtindá

senator senadór

send ipadalá/magpadalá

separate (adj) hiwaláy; **~ checks**
kaniyá-kaniyá

September Setyémbre/September

serious seryóso, **(sick)** malalâ, grábe

serve iháin/magháin

service serbísyo

seven pitó, siyéte

seven hundred pitóng daán

seventeen disisiyéte, labímpitó

shame hiyâ

shampoo siyámpu, gúgò

shave mag-áhit

ship **(n)** barkó, bapór, **(v)** ipadalá,
isakáy sa bapór

shirt shert, pantaas, kamisadentro

shoes sapátos

shop **(n)** tindáhan, pagawáan, shop,
(v) mamilí

shore pampáng

short **(height)** mabábà, **(length)**
maiklî/maiksî/maigsî

short time **(moment)** sandalî

short-tempered mainitín ang úlo

shorts kórto, shorts

should dápat

shoulder balíkat

shout sumigáw

shower **(n, rain)** ambón, **(v)**
umambón

shut sarádo

shrimp hípon

shy mahiyáin

sibling **(brother or sister)** kapatíd (na
lalake o babae)

sick may sakít

sickness sakít, karamdáman

silence katahimíkan

silent matahímik

silly sira-úlo, tangá, lokó-lokó

since **(because)** dáhil; **(time)** mulá

sing kantahín/kumantá

sing along to the accompaniment of
recorded music magkaraóke

singer mangangantá/mang-aáwit

single isá

single **(marital status)** waláng asáwa

single female dalága; **~ male** binátà

sink labábo

sit upô

sit down maupô/umupô

six ánim, saís

sixteen disisaís, labíng- ánim

size lakí, súkat

skin balát

skirt pálda

sky lángit

sleep matúlog

sleeve manggás

sleeveless undershirt sándo

slice híwà; **~ thinly** hiwáin/maghíwà

slip **(v)** madulás/dumulás

slipper tsinélas

slow mabágal

small maliít

smart magalíng, ismárte

smart phone smart phone

smile ngitî

smoke asó

smooth makínis

snobbish supládo/a

snug sukát

so kayâ

soak ibábad/magbábad

soap sabón

soccer sáker

socks médyas

soda sopdrink

sofa sopá/supá

soft malalambót, **(overcooked)** labóg

soggy malatâ

some ilán

someday bálang áraw

something isáng bágay

somewhat médyo

somewhere bandá diyán/riyán

son anák na laláke

soon malápit na

sore masakít

sore throat masakít ang lalamúnan

sorry ikinalulungkot, sori, paumanhín

sour maásim

south tímog

South Korea Tímog Koréa

soy sauce tóyo

space espásyo

spacious maluwáng

Spain Espánya

Spanish Kastílà

spatula siyansé

speak magsalitâ

spend **(money)** gumástos

spicy maánghang

spider gagambá

spill matápon

spoil **(food)** mapánis

spoiled **(child)** lakí sa láyaw

spoon kutsára

spouse asáwa

sprain **(has one)** napílay, may pílay

spring **(season)** tagsiból

square kuwadrádo

stair hagdán

stand up tumayô

star bituwín/bituín

start magsimulâ

stay **(behind)** maíwan, manatílì,
(reside) mamalágì

steal nakáwin/nagnákaw/ninakaw

still pa

stir halúin/maghálò

stomach tiyán

stone bató

stool bangkô
stool (feces) dumí, táe
stoop yumukô
store tindáhan
storekeeper tindéro/a
storm (n) bagyó, **(v)** bumagyó
stout matabâ
stove kalán
straight tuwíd, derétso
straighten up ayúsin
strain saláin/magsálà
strainer salaán
street kalsáda, daán, kálye
street corner kánto
strenuous work mabigát na gawáin
stroll magpasyál
strong malakás
student estudyánte
study mag-áral
stupid bóbo
subtract bawásan
succeed magtagumpáy
success tagumpáy
sugar asúkal
suit amerikána
summer tag-inít
sun áraw
sunburn sunburn, sunóg ang balát
Sunday Linggó
sunglasses sunglasses
sunscreen sunscreen
super súper
supper hapúnan
support supórta, alalay
support (livelihood) susténto
surf the Web mag-surf sa Web
sweet matamís
sweet peas gisántes
sweet potato kamóte
swell magalíng
swim lumangóy
swollen magâ
symptom sintóma

T
T-shirt t-sert/t-shert
table mesa
tablecloth mantél
take (bring) magdalá, **(get)** kunín; ~ **a bath** malígò; ~ **a boat** magbangkâ; ~ **a rest** magpahingá; ~ **a ship** magbarkó; ~ **a shower** malígò
take away alisín
take provision of (food, clothes, money, etc.) magbáon
take something down ibabâ/ magbabâ, tanggalín
talk magsalitâ; ~ **with someone** makipag-úsap
talk to kausápin/mag-úsap
tall mataás, matangkád

tamarind sampálok
taxi táksi; ~ **van** FX
tea tsaá
teach itúrò /magtúrò
teacher títser/gúrò
tear (eye) (n) lúhà
tear (n) púnit, **(v)** punítin
tease tuksuhin, birúin
television telebisyón
tell sabíhin
tell a story ikuwénto/magkuwénto
ten diyés, sampû
tender malambót
tenderize palambutín/magpalambót (causative)
terrible teríble, nakakatakot, **(service)** teríble, pangit
terror malaking tákot, kilábot
text (cell phone) (v) magteks
Thank goodness! Buti na lang!
thank you salámat (sa iyo)
thanks salámat
Thanksgiving Day Áraw ng Pasasalámat
their (ng pron) nilá; **(sa pron)** sa kanilá
there is/are may, mayroón; ~ **was/ were** may, mayroón
they (ng pron) nilá, **(ang pron)** silá
they say daw/raw
thick makapál
thief magnanákaw
thigh hítà
thin (adj) manipís, **(person)** payát
thing bágay
think isípin/mag-isíp
thirteen labíntatló, tríse
thirty tatlumpû, trénta
this (ng, near the speaker) nitó
though káhit
thousand unit líbo
three tatló, tres
three days ago kamakatló
three hundred tatlóng daán
throat lalamúnan
throw iitsá/mag-itsá
thunder (n) kulóg, **(v)** kumulóg
Thursday Huwébes
ticket tiket; bilyete
till hanggáng
Till then Hanggáng dito na lang múnà
time (era, epoch) panahón, **(hour)** óras
times (occasions) béses
tire (car, bicycle) góma
tire (v) mapágod; mahápò
tiring nakakapágod
to sa
toe daliri ng paá
together magkasama
tomato kamátis

tomorrow búkas; ~ **afternoon** búkas ng hápon; ~ **morning** búkas ng umága; ~ **night** búkas ng gabí
too (including) patí, **(likewise)** din/ rin, namán, man
tool gámit, kagamitán
tooth ngípin
toothache sakít ng ngípin
toothbrsuh sepílyo sa ngipin
top ibábaw
tour maglakbáy/lakbayín, tour
tourist turísta
toward papuntá
towel tuwálya
town náyon
tradition tradisyón, kaugalián
traditional makalúmà, tradisyunál
train tren
translate isálin/magsálin
trash basúra
trash can basurahán
travel maglakbáy
tray (usually oblong) bandeháHo
treat (illness) gamutín
treatment lúnas
tree púnò
trendy úso
Tuesday Martés
turn (direction) lumikô; ~ **left** kumaliwâ; ~ **off (as in light, stove, or radio)** patayín; ~ **on (as in light, stove, or radio)** buksán, paandarín; ~ **right** kumánan
turned around umíkot
turtle pagóng
twelve dóse, labíndalawá
twenty bénte, dalawampû
twilight takípsílim
two dalawá, dos; ~ **days ago** kamakalawá; ~ **months ago** noóng nakaraáng dalawáng buwán
two hundred dalawáng daán/dos siyéntos
two-story house up-and-down

U
ugly pángit
unaware waláng alám
uncle títo/tíyo/tío
under ilálim
unfair hindi makatarúngan
unfortunate sawimpálad, málas
unimportant hindi mahalagá, hindi importánte
United States, USA Amérika/Estádos Unídos
unlock buksán/ibukás/magbukás
unlucky málas
unripe hiláw
until hanggáng
unusual kakaibá, di karaniwan

up pataás
upper itaás, dákong itaás
upside down baligtád
upstairs itaás
urgent madalían, apuráhan
urgent (important) importánte
use (n) gámit, **(v)** gamítin/gumámit
use the computer magkompyúter
user (computer) user
user name user name
usual karaníwan
usually kadalásan

V

vacation bakasyón
vacation house báhay-bakasyúnan
vaccination bakúna
vague malábò
Valentine's Day Áraw ng mga Púsò
valley lambák
vanilla banílya
vegetable gúlay
very napaka- (attached to a root adj),
  (exactly) mísmo, **(extremely)**
  masyádong (followed by an adj)
very clear malínaw na malínaw
very swollen magáng-magâ
view tanáwin
village náyon
vinegar súkà
visit (n) bisitáhin/bumisíta, daláwin/
  dumálaw, pagdálaw, **(v)** bumisita,
  bisitahin
volcano bulkán
vomit súka

W

wait hintáy; sandalî
wait for hintayín/maghintáy
wait up téka, sandalî
waiter wéyter
wake (s.o.) gisíngin

wake up gumísing
walk lákad
wall dingdíng
wallet pitákà
want gustó
wardrobe kasuótan
warehouse bodéga
wash hugásan/maghúgas, **(s.t.**
  dishes, hands, etc.) maghúgas/
  hugásan; ~ **clothes** maglabá; ~
  one's face maghilámos; ~ **one's**
  hands hugásan/maghúgas ng
  kamáy; ~ **one's mouth by gargling**
  magmúmog
watch (n) panonoód, **(v)** manoód,
  (movie, stage play, television show)
  manoód
water túbig
water dipper tábò
watermelon pakwán
wave (n) álon
wave (v) umálon; ~ **hand** kumawáy
weak mahínà
wear (s.t.) magsuót. **(perfume,**
  cologne) magpabangó
wear out (become tired) mapágod,
  (break) masírà, **(thing)** malúmà
weather panahón
weave hábi
Wednesday Miyérkules/Miyérkoles
week linggó
weight bigát, timbáng
Welcome! Mabúhay!
welcome (n) pagsalúbong, **(v)**
  sumalúbong
welt pantál
west kanlúran
wet (oneself, s.t.) basaín/magbasâ
What are? Anú-anó?
What's new? Anóng bágo?
What's the matter with you? Anó
  ka ba?

What's up? Anó na?
while hábang, samantálang
whisper (v) bumulóng/ibulóng/
  bulungán
white putî
wide malápad
wife mísis, asáwa, maybáhay
will (desire) hangád, **(testament)**
  testaménto, hulíng habílin
will (future time) (rendered by future
  aspect of verb (contemplated) e.g.
  will go) púpuntá
win (v) manálo
wind hángin
window bintánà
windy mahángin
wine bíno, álak
winter taglamíg
wish (n) hangád, **wish (v)** maghangád
woman babáe
wonderful magalíng, napakagalíng
working nagtatrabáho
worry (n) nakakapag-alalá, **(v)** nag-
  aalalá, mabalisá
wound súgat
write magsulát/sumúlat
writer mánunulát
wrong malî

Y

yam úbe
year taón
yearly taún-taón
yell sumigáw
yellow diláw
yesterday kahápon
You're welcome. Waláng anumán.
young (boy or girl) bátà
youngest sibling bunsô
your (to you) sa íyó; **(pl) (to your)**
  sainyó

Index